STANDING AT THE CROSSROADS
STORIES OF DOUBT IN RENAISSANCE ITALY

LEGENDA

LEGENDA is the Modern Humanities Research Association's book imprint for new research in the Humanities. Founded in 1995 by Malcolm Bowie and others within the University of Oxford, Legenda has always been a collaborative publishing enterprise, directly governed by scholars. The Modern Humanities Research Association (MHRA) joined this collaboration in 1998, became half-owner in 2004, in partnership with Maney Publishing and then Routledge, and has since 2016 been sole owner. Titles range from medieval texts to contemporary cinema and form a widely comparative view of the modern humanities, including works on Arabic, Catalan, English, French, German, Greek, Italian, Portuguese, Russian, Spanish, and Yiddish literature. Editorial boards and committees of more than 60 leading academic specialists work in collaboration with bodies such as the Society for French Studies, the British Comparative Literature Association and the Association of Hispanists of Great Britain & Ireland.

The MHRA encourages and promotes advanced study and research in the field of the modern humanities, especially modern European languages and literature, including English, and also cinema. It aims to break down the barriers between scholars working in different disciplines and to maintain the unity of humanistic scholarship. The Association fulfils this purpose through the publication of journals, bibliographies, monographs, critical editions, and the MHRA Style Guide, and by making grants in support of research. Membership is open to all who work in the Humanities, whether independent or in a University post, and the participation of younger colleagues entering the field is especially welcomed.

ALSO PUBLISHED BY THE ASSOCIATION

Critical Texts
Tudor and Stuart Translations • *New Translations* • *European Translations*
MHRA Library of Medieval Welsh Literature

MHRA Bibliographies
Publications of the Modern Humanities Research Association

The Annual Bibliography of English Language & Literature
Austrian Studies
Modern Language Review
Portuguese Studies
The Slavonic and East European Review
Working Papers in the Humanities
The Yearbook of English Studies

www.mhra.org.uk
www.legendabooks.com

ITALIAN PERSPECTIVES

Editorial Committee
Professor Simon Gilson, University of Oxford (General Editor)
Professor Francesca Billiani, University of Manchester
Professor Manuele Gragnolati, Université Paris-Sorbonne
Professor Catherine Keen, University College London
Professor Martin McLaughlin, Magdalen College, Oxford

Founding Editors
Professor Zygmunt Barański and Professor Anna Laura Lepschy

In the light of growing academic interest in Italy and the reorganization of many university courses in Italian along interdisciplinary lines, this book series, founded by Maney Publishing under the imprint of the Northern Universities Press and now continuing under the Legenda imprint, aims to bring together different scholarly perspectives on Italy and its culture. *Italian Perspectives* publishes books and collections of essays on any period of Italian literature, language, history, culture, politics, art, and media, as well as studies which take an interdisciplinary approach and are methodologically innovative.

Managing Editor
Dr Graham Nelson, 41 Wellington Square, Oxford OX1 2JF, UK
www.legendabooks.com

Standing at the Crossroads

Stories of Doubt in Renaissance Italy

❖

Marco Faini

LEGENDA

Italian Perspectives 58
Modern Humanities Research Association
2023

Published by Legenda
an imprint of the Modern Humanities Research Association
Salisbury House, Station Road, Cambridge CB1 2LA

ISBN 978-1-83954-163-6 (HB)
ISBN 978-1-83954-164-3 (PB)

First published 2023

Copy-Editor: Maureen Epp

CONTENTS

Drifting, drowning in a purple sea of doubt

— Sixto Rodriguez, *Jane S. Piddy*, 1970

ACKNOWLEDGEMENTS

The project of this book was initially supported by an Andrew W. Mellon Fellowship at Villa I Tatti, the Harvard University Center for Italian Renaissance Studies. It was subsequently funded by a three-year Marie Skłodowska Curie Global Fellowship granted by the European Research Council under Grant Agreement No. 792225 and carried out at the Universities of Toronto and Venice. I wish to express my gratitude to these institutions for their generous funding.

I am especially grateful to Villa I Tatti, the University of Toronto, and Ca' Foscari University of Venice for providing me with exceptional resources; their amazing library collections as well as their vibrant communities have proved crucial in the writing process of this book.

The supervisors of my Marie Curie Fellowship, Marco Sgarbi and Nicholas Terpstra, have given me invaluable insights as well as material support. In 2015 Nick Terpstra encouraged me over a beer to pursue my then-shapeless project on doubt; I am grateful for his suggestions. I was fortunate enough to have the chance to present my work at some outstanding institutions: the Group for Early Modern Studies (GEMS) at the University of Ghent; the Department of French and Italian and the Renaissance Studies Program at Indiana University, Bloomington; the Centre for Reformation and Renaissance Studies in Toronto (thanks to Natalie Oeltjen for helping me on many occasions); the Toronto Renaissance and Reformation Colloquium and the Emilio Goggio Chair in Italian Studies at the University of Toronto; the Dipartimento di Studi Umanistici of the University of Udine; and the Centre d'Études Supérieures de la Renaissance, Tours. Élise Boillet has been, as always, a wonderful and knowledgeable colleague. Together we organized a conference on *Le doute dans l'Europe moderne* and co-edited its proceedings. This was a valuable step in my research, and I am grateful to all the colleagues who took part in the conference and in the volume. Many friends and colleagues provided me with suggestions or generously shared with me their work: Damiano Acciarino, Simonetta Adorni Braccesi, Guido Arbizzoni Artusi, Elisa Brilli, Giuseppina Brunelli, Paolo Cherchi, Giuseppe Crimi, Francine Daenens, Constance Furey, Maria Antonietta Garullo, Chriscinda Henry, Michele Lodone, Guerrino Lovato, Franco Pierno, Paolo Procaccioli, and Eugenio Refini.

Bringing our research to a broad public of non-specialists is a major challenge and a pleasant commitment. In September 2020, I had the privilege of collaborating with the Science Gallery Venice Foundation on *The Art of Doubt*, an event that allowed me to work with virtual reality artists in the beautiful context of the Venice Film Festival. My admiration and heartfelt thanks go to those whose contributions made that special event possible: Neal Hartman, Francesco Lonardi, Matteo Lonardi, Michel Reilhac, and Erica Villa.

The administrative staff in the Department of History at the University of Toronto and in the Department of Philosophy and Cultural Heritage at Ca' Foscari University have promptly taken care of countless issues. In particular, I wish to thank Carlo Bertato, Laura Burighel, Silvia Cadamuro, Eugenia Delaney, and Fiorella Giacometti.

Maureen Epp has painstakingly revised this manuscript through its many stages, improving the style, spotting mistakes and inconsistencies, and alerting me to problematic passages. I am thankful for her unwavering commitment.

Finally, my mother has watched over me from afar over the years. For all that she never said and for all that she did, I thank her. This book is dedicated with love to Paola Ugolini for always believing in me, for making me a new and better person, for always showing me the way, and for sharing it with me.

M.F., Buffalo, January 2023

LIST OF FIGURES

INTRODUCTION

Wise Donkeys and Wicked Friars

Spain, circa 1522: A man dressed in rags is riding his mule towards the city of Montserrat. Suddenly, a Moor ('saracenus quidem'), also on muleback, approaches.[1] As they continue together, the two begin to chat. When the discussion turns to the Virgin Mary, however, some disagreements arise. The Moor concedes that she may have conceived without the help of a man — but that after giving birth she was still a virgin, he will not believe. To support his position, he suggests a series of natural causes. The other man does his best to make him change his mind, but in vain. The two part ways, and the Moor quickly disappears from sight.

The first man remains troubled, feeling he has not done enough to persuade the Moor; he has failed to accomplish his duty and not defended the Virgin's honour to the best of his abilities. He wonders if he should have stabbed the Moor; perhaps he can still catch up to him and do so. Yet he doubts ('tandem dubius remansit') this will be possible, since the Moor was heading towards a village off the main road. The man does not know what to do. Unable to make a decision, he can at least decide to let his mule decide for him. If, when they come to the crossroads ('bivium') between the main road to Montserrat and the road leading to the small village, the mule heads towards the village, he will search out the Moor and kill him.[2] Otherwise, he will proceed to the town of Montserrat.

The mule takes the main road, away from the village, and the Moor will never know that his life has been in danger. Before reaching Montserrat, the man stops in another village and buys himself a piece of rough fabric in order to make himself a humble pilgrim's robe. After all, he is headed to Jerusalem. His name is Ignatius of Loyola.

This episode comes from Loyola's autobiographical account, which does not have a proper title. Published as *Acta Patris Ignatii*, it is also known in French as *Le récit du pèlerin* and in Italian as *Il racconto del Pellegrino*. It is a remarkable story of doubt on multiple levels. The Moor voices his doubts concerning the virginity of Mary. Ignatius has doubts as to what to do with the Moor. The mule has no doubts, but in solving those of Ignatius, it implicitly reverses a famous medieval episode involving a donkey and doubt — the tale known as the 'Paradox of Buridan's Ass'.[3] Finally, Ignatius's reaching a crossroads is a *mise-en-abyme* of the whole tale: in Renaissance iconography, doubt is represented as a man standing at a crossroads. As John M. McManamon has suggested, 'Ignatius presents himself as an odd Hercules at the moral crossroads':[4] Ignatius thus embodies a variation of the myth of Hercules torn between the opposite paths of vice (*voluptas*) and virtue (*virtus*), a tale that was revived at the end of the fifteenth century, first in Germany and then in Italy, and enjoyed lasting success in Italian art.[5]

Ignatius describes himself as torn between opposite desires, unable to make a decision. The struggle between his impulses leaves him paralysed and weary of examining the two conflicting possibilities. This story comes very early in Ignatius's conversion process. The conflict between his opposite desires does not merely concern the choice between going straight to Montserrat and from there to Jerusalem, or instead making a detour to kill the Moor. It is the choice between a former knightly ethos — resurfacing in the regret at having been unable to defend the Virgin's honour and the desire to obtain his vendetta by killing the Moor — and a newly emerging saintly vocation.[6]

Doubt appears as a condition affecting both body and mind. Unable to make up his mind, Ignatius lets his irrational animal decide in his place.[7] His human reason stalls, and the body follows suit. He feels discontent and a certain sadness deep in his mind ('moveri moestitia quadam animum sensit').[8] While located internally, doubt was perceptible through visible signs. In Book II of Pietro Aretino's hagiography *La vita di santa Caterina* (The life of Saint Catherine, 1540), the saint is summoned to the presence of Emperor Massenzio. A persecutor of the Christians, Massenzio is inclined to kill Catherine, who has converted the majority of his people. Yet he is also ready to be merciful towards a young woman of royal descent. Because of these conflicting feelings, when he sees the saint standing in his tribunal, 'he lets out of his chest one of those heavy sighs produced by a doubtful heart'.[9] A doubter is 'similar to the waves of the sea, moved by the wind, that is, he has not any firmness in him'.[10]

The lack of calm is distinctive of doubters; an excess of bodily agitation reflects inner unrest. The prologue to the fifth book of the *Revelations* of St Birgitta of Sweden (*c.* 1303–1373), titled *Book of Questions*, opens with the description of a doubter. In one of her visions, Birgitta sees Christ sitting on his throne, with the Virgin Mary at his feet along with a multitude of saints and angels. A ladder unites the earth and the heavens; sitting 'midway up the ladder' Birgitta sees 'a man whom she recognized and who was still alive, a learned scholar in the science of theology but full of guile and devilish wickedness'. This man will address his 'questions' or 'doubts' (we will come back to the distinction between the two in Chapter 1) to Christ, as if to tempt him. His behaviour is telling:

> *With his most impatient and agitated bearing* he seemed more like a devil than a humble monk. For the lady [i.e., Birgitta] could see all the inner thoughts and feelings of the monk's heart and how he disclosed them to Christ the Judge seated on the throne *through his uncontrolled and agitated way of questioning* [...]. Lady Birgitta then saw and heard in spirit how Christ the Judge, *with a meek and gentle bearing*, responded to those questions briefly one by one with utmost wisdom.[11]

The doubter's agitation is connected to his 'devilish' and wicked soul, as opposed to Christ's calm and gentle bearing resulting from his infinite wisdom. In the opening lines of the first interrogation ('Interrogacio prima'), this characterization is further stressed: '[With] an impatient and agitated bearing, as though full of wickedness and guile, he put questions to the Judge.' Doubt was made tangible and visible by a series of bodily effects, connected to a recognizable psychological condition. One could say there existed a bodily rhetoric of doubt and that Renaissance readers and viewers were able to recognize and decipher the signs announcing such a condition. Stillness, melancholy, sighs, inability to make up one's mind, a tiredness of the mind and of the soul were all signs that a person was having doubts. Doubters were imagined as walking in the night, standing at a crossroads, sitting with their faces resting on the palms of their hands (signalling the connection between doubt and melancholy). What was this condition of doubt that seems also to have affected the founder of the powerful Company of Jesus? Were people of the early sixteenth century particularly prone to falling into doubt?

Why Doubt?

This book documents the ways in which Renaissance Italy produced a rich and multifaceted vernacular 'culture of doubt', eventually turning it into an object of discourse and building around it multiple forms of sociability. In some respects, this book may be seen as a social and cultural history of doubt, reconstructing the partially lost richness of a cultural category instrumental in shaping European identity. Montaigne's *Essays* (1580, 1582, 1588) and Descartes's *Meditations on First Philosophy* (1641) describe doubt as a quintessentially solipsistic experience, a sort of mental experiment carried out in the secret of one's chamber. As such, early modern doubt is often perceived as a distressing experience. The opening gesture of the *Meditations* is in fact one of retirement: 'I have withdrawn into seclusion.' From within the boundaries of his self-inflicted seclusion, Descartes will accomplish his purpose, to 'attack the very principles that form the basis of all my former beliefs' so that the 'whole structure' of knowledge can be 'utterly demolished'.[12] Descartes's exercise leads him to his famous and uncanny hypothesis that 'some evil spirit, supremely powerful and cunning, has devoted all his efforts to deceiving me'.[13] Because of this evil spirit, 'there is nothing [...] of which it is not legitimate to doubt'.[14] Descartes takes us into a hallucinatory world in which there are no boundaries between reality and imagination or between waking and dreaming; in fact, he writes, 'I see so clearly that waking can never be distinguished from sleep by any conclusive indications that I am stupefied; and this very stupor comes close to persuading me that I am asleep after all.'[15]

Alec Ryrie suggests that doubt in seventeenth-century England was intertwined with incredulity and triggered by emotions such as anger and fear.[16] This book contends that doubt should not be entirely identified with such emotions or the distressing experiences described by Montaigne and Descartes, nor should it be thought of only in relation to the tradition of scepticism or to religious incredulity. Instead, doubt was a nuanced condition connected with a wide range of emotions; the following chapters will explore the many varieties of doubt, its different cultural functions, and (some of) the discourses in which these functions were articulated.

In exploring the many varieties and functions of doubt, this book touches on four possible views of doubt: the first view, a sort of 'degree zero', considers doubt as a mere question, a curiosity, devoid of any potentially disruptive consequences; the second considers doubt as an individual condition, either intellectual or psychological (spiritual, emotional); the third considers doubt as a condition of uncertainty about (or disbelief in) a specific fact (for example, the immortality of the soul); the last view considers doubt as an object in itself, something that can be discussed, described, even painted. I am especially interested in how early modern Italian texts dealt with doubt as a cultural object, with the caveat that there is no hierarchy between these competing conceptions of doubt and that two or more of them can be present at the same time in the same work, embedded within each other.

Late fifteenth- and early sixteenth-century Italy saw an increasing interest in doubt: tales of doubt, descriptions of doubts and doubters, allegories and images of doubt appear in a large and varied corpus of texts from this time. Poems, *novelle*, religious pamphlets, dialogues, books of 'problems', and games are only some of the sources that this book explores. The majority of these sources are in the vernacular, thus potentially having been read by and circulated across a broad readership. These texts did not target a specialized readership such as humanists trained in philosophy or theology. Because they avoided the technicalities of philosophy, instead presenting doubt in entertaining ways, these works were palatable to individuals from different walks of life. I reconstruct these discourses on doubt and, where possible, their underlying cultural strategies. I am not, therefore, presenting an account of individual conditions of doubt, nor of how doubt was experienced by individuals belonging to different social classes. However interesting such an account would be, it would be severely curbed by the lack of sources pertaining to the large number of individuals with limited or no access to literacy.[17] Certainly, it is sometimes hard to distinguish between accounts of individual conditions and more general reflections on doubt, as they sometimes grow out of each other. Whenever possible, I try to connect individual psychological and emotional experiences to broader cultural contexts.

It is certainly not unusual to find individuals voicing doubts; more significant is the accumulation of discourses on and descriptions of doubt. These discourses appear to have special relevance in the early sixteenth century and therefore call for scholarly attention. My primary focus is on how Italian discourses on doubt help us cast an archaeological glance over this crucial early modern category, accounting for its richness and distinction from formal scepticism and other philosophical strands. The choice to shift attention away from those authors — such as Pietro Pomponazzi or Giovanfrancesco Pico della Mirandola — who are traditionally featured in histories of Renaissance scepticism and turn to authors and works not generally recognized as part of this canon is deliberate. Accordingly, I have retrieved and put in dialogue with each other a number of references to doubt generally overlooked by scholars of early modern uncertainty. This allows us to look at doubt with a fresh perspective and from unusual angles, moving away from the historiographic categories traditionally associated with doubt such as atheism, scepticism, libertinism, and so on.

Doubt, I would argue, is an emotionally and intellectually ambiguous, if not ambivalent, notion, a fluid rubric covering a series of different phenomena as well as a psychological, intellectual, and physical state affecting both individuals and social groups. As such, it potentially extends to every aspect of life, not limiting itself to religious matters or to the definition of the limits of knowledge. In other words, doubt cannot and should not be employed as a synonym for scepticism (or in religious matters, for unbelief). Rather, in this book I aim to capture a peculiar mode of Italian culture that cannot entirely be identified with individual conditions of doubt on the one hand or with philosophical theories or schools on the other, and suggest that this mode represents a distinctive feature of the Italian Renaissance. Italy presents a fascinating case study: the richness of its culture of doubt closely follows its cultural development and the presence of a printing industry, the likes of which can hardly be found elsewhere in Europe for some time. At the same time, Italy was affected — before and perhaps more directly than other European countries — by the momentous political and religious events that took place at the end of the fifteenth century and in the first decades of the sixteenth century. I am not in a position to judge whether Renaissance Italians were more or less doubtful, more or less existentially troubled than their ancestors or their descendants. We can say, however, that they were very much inclined to talk about doubt. Did the extraordinary events they experienced somehow contribute to eliciting reflections on doubt? Some of the sources analysed in this book seem to suggest that this was indeed the case. While existential uncertainty and intellectual unrest in general were certainly not unique to Renaissance Italy, the unprecedented and concurrent changes in the political, religious, and cultural order taking place from the late fifteenth century onwards may have produced a specific response, possibly accelerating already ongoing processes. And while war, famine, political revolution, and religious struggle had long been part of Western history, new technological developments such as the printing press made them widely and swiftly known across the Italian peninsula for the first time. If historical factors prompted uncertainty in local realities, their propagation through new media amplified and spread such feelings.

In his *Social History of Skepticism*, Brendan Dooley suggests that 'the modern history of skepticism is more than the history of a few disembodied minds engaging with the texts of Sextus Empiricus or Diogenes Laertius'. Dooley explores the rise of a sceptical attitude with special regard to historiography, early modern journalism, and politics during the seventeenth and early eighteenth centuries. This book covers a different time span and different subjects, and yet I subscribe to Dooley's opinion that when investigating doubt, we deal with 'a variety of skepticism closely related to but not included among the purely intellectual trends' traditionally investigated by scholars.[18] There is a tendency to an increasingly conscious sceptical attitude over the sixteenth and early seventeenth centuries, gaining ground among both those who did and those who did not have a proper humanistic background. In referring to the early sixteenth century, we can replace the word 'scepticism' with 'perplexity' or 'doubt'. We may see in the widespread presence of doubt the cradle of the more conscious sceptical or libertine positions of the late Renaissance. Yet we should be cautious and avoid tracing a sort of evolution from an early sixteenth-century 'before', marked by a blurry notion of doubt, to a more intellectually equipped sceptical 'after'.

We must, in other words, resist the temptation to read teleologically the late fifteenth- and early sixteenth-century reflections on doubt and try instead to capture its essence. If we are able to do so, we will realize that this condition of doubt is rarely a purely intellectual phenomenon; more often than not, it is the result of and response to precise external conditions. Richard Popkin, in his *History of Scepticism*, concentrates 'principally on the ideas of the person independent of circumstances', stressing that 'striking an appropriate balance between intellectual history and cultural history is extremely difficult'.[19] This focus on the individual over circumstances has led to the creation of a restricted canon of male-authored works setting the tone of early modern uncertainty.[20] This process risks losing the voices of those people from all walks of life who expressed their doubts and who reflected on doubt, the use they could make of it, and its possible consequences. Thus instead of singling out specific authors and works — a 'canon' or 'gallery' of significant and outstanding sources — I have woven together multiple threads, combining different voices, and whenever possible put them in dialogue with the circumstances, the historical and cultural setting of Italy in the first half of the sixteenth century, exploring how and why doubt became the object of literary and visual representations within specific contexts. In doing so, I have had to take into account the fuzzy and polysemic nature of the word 'doubt', which could refer to simple questions as well as to the explicit and deliberate denial of philosophical or theological beliefs. There is a striking contrast between the accuracy with which doubt is defined, including subtle distinctions between different 'qualities' of doubt, and a certain sloppiness in the actual use of the word. My interest lies less in the content of individual doubts than in the ways of articulating them. In other words, I study the very act of doubting, its forms and its social consequences. If scepticism is a more or less recognizable intellectual current, doubt is an elusive notion, surfacing in different forms, testifying to both the intellectual curiosity and the spiritual unrest of early modern Italians.

This approach may indeed turn out to be the only way to verify the actual existence of a culture of doubt in Renaissance Italy. In a stimulating book, Paolo Cherchi suggests that an attitude of doubt was a missed opportunity in Italian culture. Already at the end of the fifteenth century, Italian intellectuals had begun to explore the topic of ignorance, producing a number of paradoxical praises of ignorance over learning. This was a sceptical trend that voiced a dissatisfaction with traditional, sterile culture and instead identified with ignorance. Its voices were numerous and diverse, and by the first decades of the sixteenth century the trend had become recognizable and productive. This critical attitude, matched with an early though restricted circulation of sceptical philosophy, might have had revolutionary consequences. However, it was in France, not in Italy, that doubt became the fulcrum of a cultural and intellectual revolution. This revolution not only led to Montaigne and Descartes, thus 'opening the doors to modernity',[21] it also cleared the path to rejuvenating those disciplines that could help overcome the ubiquitous presence of doubt: historiography, philology, chronology, archaeology, and so on. According to Cherchi, doubt failed to achieve similar results in Italy. Despite the discourses on and praises of ignorance that could have planted the seeds of a new culture, it was outside Italy that such seeds bore fruit.

Italy had its own culture of doubt: Cherchi finds its traces in the tradition of 'books of questions' that explored doubt in matters of love or natural philosophy, in the rationalist tradition of Italian, especially Paduan, Aristotelianism, and finally in the blossoming field of 'casuistry', or the study of cases of conscience. What these typologies of doubt had in common was that 'they were doubts of judgement or assessment and they never concerned the instruments or even the parameters of knowledge itself'.[22] In other words, Italian doubt concerned 'the solution, not the intellect that pose[d] it'.[23] If Cherchi is right, is there any point in studying the Italian mode of doubt? My answer is affirmative, provided that we do not look for major works analogous to those produced by French culture, and that we look at the Italian culture of doubt from a different angle. We will then discover that discourses on doubt were produced in a variety of contexts, by a number of social agents, and in different forms, literary and not. Even if these numerous but scattered discourses did not succeed in establishing an innovative tradition, their sheer number testifies to a culture that challenged dogmatism and was fully conscious of the prehensile and polymorphous nature of doubt — and is therefore worth exploring.

Leaving aside the classics of early modern scepticism and learned works engaging with the peaks of the philosophical tradition meant sailing uncharted waters when it came to selecting sources. I have chosen to explore a wide variety of works, among which, in a confessional age, religious texts inevitably make up the lion's share. After all, the original sin, according to some, was an act of doubt: 'Satan pushed Eve to doubt, and from doubt to consent, and from consent to sin.'[24] Nevertheless, religion is only a part of a larger picture. Many of my sources are purposely lesser-known works that openly engage with doubt and do so outside and beyond the spaces traditionally associated with philosophical speculation. Some readers will be taken aback by the absence of certain pre-eminent authors such as Niccolò Machiavelli, Francesco Guicciardini, and Ludovico Ariosto. Certainly, for example, the *Orlando furioso* could have exposed its countless readers from all social groups to the ambiguous glance that Ariosto casts over some crucial contemporary issues, such as truth or the role of women in contemporary society. The whole structure of the poem could be read as a 'doubt machine', with its display of alternative paths and contradictions, although one might wonder how many of Ariosto's sixteenth-century readers would have been able to read between the lines of his refined and paradoxical irony or perceive the existential meaning of his narratological system. I thought it intriguing to leave for once in the background the great masterpieces of the cinquecento that have been magnificently explored by a wealth of scholarship, and instead turn my attention to a galaxy of other texts in search of a broader culture of doubt. My preference was for works explicitly dealing with doubt, works that, so to speak, put their readers in direct contact with descriptions and definitions of doubt rather than obliquely suggesting the topic. Why did so many authors feel the need to tell stories of doubt, expand on doubt, and expose their readers to such a complex (and at some point, dangerous) category? Were they responding to their readers' needs? Can these sources put us in contact — maybe even more than their more celebrated counterparts — with the mental landscape of early sixteenth-century Italians and help us understand how and to what extent doubt was part of it?

I am not implying here any kind of dichotomy between 'high' and 'low' or 'popular' and 'elite' culture. It is true, though, that the diversity of my sources allows me to intercept a wide range of approaches and reactions to doubt, some of which may indeed bring us in closer contact with the feelings and expectations of ordinary people. I refer to 'ordinary people' to point to large chunks of population exposed to vernacular culture through a variety of media — printed, oral, visual — without distinguishing between urban and rural folk or between different social groups. My notion of 'ordinary people' may appear blurred, and this is inevitably so, since the ideas and feelings of ordinary folk are lost to us unless they are mediated by writing. Nonetheless, the filter of the written word, either in the form of literary texts or judicial records, however distorting, is not necessarily a form of effacement. Moving away from the technicalities of theology or philosophy and turning to vernacular texts that even persons of medium to low literacy could potentially understand allows us to glimpse how doubt became a familiar experience across a large portion of the social spectrum. We may not be able to assess whether rural folk were more inclined to doubt than urban folk, or whether bourgeois groups reflected on doubt more systematically than the nobility, or to what extent doubt was gendered. All the same, stretching the gamut of sources as broadly as possible can point us to the circulation of ideas and feelings and to the reciprocal exchange and interaction between different levels of society.[25]

Many of the authors I investigate in this book were accomplished humanists or theologians (after all, humanists too are entitled to their doubts) in whose works one detects the need to address an audience larger and more diverse than that of those who were trained in humanistic culture. Because of this, one often finds in them glimpses of the perplexities and anxieties of ordinary folk and of the ways people addressed them. As I have mentioned, these perplexities, anxieties, and doubts were not necessarily of an intellectual nature — philosophical doubts, so to speak. More generally, and probably even more intriguingly, doubt signalled the acute, if intuitive, perception of the increasing complexity of reality and of the role of external events therein. Hence the difficulty of discerning between right and wrong, real or illusory, and the related embarrassment over deliberation.

Circumstances

I must therefore turn to the issue of circumstances. What were the conditions that brought on this 'crisis of doubt' (adapting the expression 'Phyrronian crisis' that scholars apply to the second half of the century) in the early sixteenth century? Why not choose to start my analysis earlier? After all, the fifteenth century was a century of anxiety, and this anxiety was often rooted in late medieval culture.[26] Medieval culture had known doubt and perplexity, too: John Arnold speaks of the existence in the Middle Ages of 'a dissent of plurality, doubt, and relativism', leading in some cases to 'what we might call comparative religion'.[27] This book could have started with the year 1362, when the fifty-eight-year-old Petrarch wrote a letter to the Florentine Francesco Bruni (1315?– after 1385), sketching his intellectual self-portrait. Countering the exceedingly high opinion in which his interlocutor held him, Petrarch wrote (*Seniles*, 1. 6):

> I am indifferent to sects, greedy for the truth. Since the search for it is arduous, I, a lowly and feeble seeker without self-confidence, often embrace doubt itself in place of truth to avoid becoming entangled in error. Thus, slowly I have become a squatter in the academy, one of many, and the latest in the humble throng, granting myself nothing, affirming nothing, doubting all but what I consider a sacrilege to doubt. Here, then, is your Hippias who once dared to profess all things in philosophical circles; with you he professes nothing beyond the anxious search for truth, nothing beyond doubt and ignorance.[28]

Petrarch embraces doubt and the sceptical philosophy of the academy, which he knew through Cicero's *Academica*, as his intellectual habit.[29] However, since this is not meant to be purely a history of intellectuals embracing doubt but a survey of how and why doubt became a social concern and the object of a field of discourses and representations, I have chosen to narrow my focus to a more restricted time span, stretching approximately from the 1490s to the 1560s, on the assumption that the generation born between 1480 and 1510 faced unprecedented challenges.

Peter Burke describes the 1490s to the 1520s as 'terrible years for the Italians'.[30] The period covered by this book is marked by momentous and sometimes calamitous events: the dates of 1492 (Columbus's voyage to America and the year of the death of Lorenzo the Magnificent) and 1494 (Charles VIII's invasion of Italy) have a predictable symbolic importance. Nevertheless, they can function as the starting point for the analysis of a crisis that was certainly rooted in previous years and unfolded in the first decades of the following century. Early sixteenth-century Italians faced unprecedented circumstances and a series of shocks. The voyages of exploration and their impact on both learning and the European mental landscape, the constant pressure of the Turks, the Reformation, the Italian Wars with their ever-changing allegiances, the 1527 sack of the (no longer) Eternal City: all this fostered a sense of fear and, one may safely surmise, uncertainty.[31] This picture is well known and is effectively summarized by Theodore K. Rabb, who speaks of a 'world that seemed to be crumbling'.[32] The Italian Wars brought with them economic stagnation and were often connected with outbursts of plague and famine;[33] the plague could prompt spikes in violence and the rate of homicides, which in turn could foster a general sense of fear, instability, and anxiety.[34] Traumatic events determined variations in the structure of society, even at the micro level, with the balance of power shifting in unforeseen ways, causing a reorganization of societal structures and ties.[35] To these alterations of the social texture were added other factors of uncertainty that contributed to the sense of instability experienced by early modern Italians.[36] Here is how the chronicler and notary Francesco Muralto from Como reported the extraordinary turn of events that accompanied the summer of 1494:

> In a certain church in the Vigezzo valley, near the lake Maggiore or Verbano, there appeared an image of the Holy Mary Mother of Jesus Christ whose face spilled blood in great quantity and for several days in a row; and it was odoriferous so that people gathered from all parts.
> That year, in the whole countryside of Como there was such a great flood due to hailstorms that all the fruits were devastated; besides, the violence of the winds eradicated the majority of the chestnut and walnut trees to an unheard-of extent, so that the countryside of Como was completely devastated, and this was the penultimate day of July 1494. King Charles, most powerful king of the French, the son of Louis, in this year 1494 on the 15th of September, came to Lombardy (and this was the work of Ludovico Sforza, uncle of Gian Galeazzo the sixth duke of Milan) with a mighty army, directed against Alfonso king of Naples, for he [i.e., Charles] claimed that his reign rightfully belonged to him [...]. But there are many things that should not be said to everybody because everyone is doubtful, and so will remain, many people say many things, but no one knows what they are saying; therefore, in these times one must remain silent, although it is true that people everywhere are burdened by princes with taxes so that they can hardly survive.[37]

Several layers of uncertainty are folded into this climatic description: enigmatic incidents pertaining the natural and supernatural order seem to announce an extraordinary military and political event, the causes of which remain unfathomable despite — or because of — the intense circulation of unreliable information; and on top of this, a bitter attack on a political order perceived as corrupt. That not only Italy but the whole of Europe was on the brink of destruction was the message of a 1480 astrological prediction by Antonio Arquato. Addressed to the King Mattias Corvinus of Hungary, this prognostication announced the devastation of Europe in the year 1507 as a result of a threatening conjunction of planets that was to happen in 1504. Originally written in Latin and circulated in both manuscript and print all over Europe, it also survives in a vernacular version whose opening lines announced 'horrendous and miraculous things' befalling the world, which soon 'will all be crying' ('tutto il mondo serà in pianti').[38] The text foresaw the fall of Constantinople, wars and plague in Africa and in Europe, a pestilence in Venice, the coming of a king from the north who would wage terrible wars, floods, and, strikingly, the appearance of a heresiarch from northern Europe who would turn the people against the Holy See ('uno grande heresiarcha venerà da septentrione suvertendo populi contra el voto de la sedia apostolica').[39]

The awareness of living in unprecedented times that we perceive in Muralto's and Arquato's words was by no means an exception. To contemporary observers, the first decades of the sixteenth century were an extraordinary period to live in, with few antecedents in history. A letter from Anton Francesco Doni (1513–1574) to Paolo Giovio (1483/86–1552) vividly captures the sense of astonishment caused by the whirling events of the early cinquecento:

> If I recall well, it is only a few years ago that I came into this world [...], and I have witnessed such amazing things. I remember as if it were yesterday evening the remarkable negligence in helping Rhodes and its loss, I have seen the wounds suffered by Christianity in the defeat and death of so many Christians under the walls of Pavia, when the king of France was made prisoner; was not the sack of Rome so horrible, when the pontiff remained captive for so long: don't you think that these two events were extraordinary? And the ensuing plague and famine; haven't I seen the siege of Florence and the ruin of such a large army and state; then, which seldom happens, the crowning of the emperor in Bologna with such majesty, at the hands of such a great pontiff? But let us return to the disgraces. The deluge that came in Rome because of the Tevere, wasn't it another sack? Sure enough, if we are to trust Holy Scripture, we are close to the end of this world machine, which will be wars, plague, famine, earthquakes, and mighty signs.[40]

Doni then lists all the astounding political events that shook Italy, Europe, and the Mediterranean, interspersing his list with references to catastrophic natural phenomena (the 'mighty earthquakes in the Mugello and Scarperia, and the fires [volcanic eruptions] in Pozzuoli and in Sicily')[41] and the troubles and divisions of the Roman Catholic Church (not only 'sects and seditions against the Church' but also 'the son of the pope made duke' of two cities, Parma and Piacenza, turned by Paul III into a family feud and entrusted to his son Pier Luigi).[42] The last section of the letter is a detailed description of the flood that inundated Florence and the Mugello, causing incalculable damage to crops, houses, and mills and destroying all goods as well as books of accounts, leading peasants and merchants to their ruin. It is a beautiful though bitter excerpt, and one is tempted to compare it to Leonardo da Vinci's drawings of deluges now in the Royal Collection at Windsor, those visions of 'homicidal forces meant to perpetually erase the very concept of life'.[43] A short and revelatory aside interrupts for a moment Doni's graphic description of the flood as he pauses to observe that 'in this way, little by little, we receive blows from heaven without even realizing it'.[44] It is an almost blasphemous statement that seems to convey the inability to make sense of a reality too complex to handle, affecting one with unforeseen disgraces and blows.

Reality(?)

Francesco Guicciardini had voiced a similar anxiety in an August 1525 letter to Machiavelli, in which he wrote, possibly referring to the political context, that he had nothing of importance to report. He added, however: 'I believe that we are all wandering in the darkness, but with our hands tied behind our backs, so that we are not able to avoid the blows.'[45] This sense of being sleepwalkers in an unpredictable reality and the perception of looming danger could be perhaps taken as an emblem of widespread feelings extending beyond the political sphere to which Guicciardini was alluding. Frequently expressed in a variety of texts, the sense of being sleepwalkers or people wandering in the darkness was probably more than a metaphor to early modern Italians.[46] This leads to one last point concerning the idea of early modern reality. Without venturing into complex speculations, we can suggest that 'reality' was a rather loose and grainy category. The level of overlap and confusion between dreaming and being awake, illusion and actual events that early modern people could experience is for us nowadays partially lost — hence, I suggest, the sense of walking around in darkness without being able to predict events or impending dangers, or even the approaching end of time.

Uncertainty spread to visual culture as well. Diletta Gamberini has written beautifully about the interest in *amphibolia* (a form of ambiguity) in the first quarter of the sixteenth century. This peculiar artistic technique shows viewers a moment in a story in such a way that it is impossible to determine whether the moment preceded or followed a certain action. It was a point in which 'action was suspended or ambiguous' and open to multiple solutions.[47] Chriscinda Henry, analysing some Leonardo's drawings from the 1480s and 1490s, highlights the role of 'visual trickery' and the 'deceptive nature of appearances' that seem to pervade late fifteenth- and early sixteenth-century art.[48] While apparently distant phenomena, these cultural features can be considered part of a broader culture of doubt, resulting less in a sceptical crisis than in an exploration of the margins and ambiguities of knowledge and of perception, as well as the delights of uncertainty. Similarly, the endless variety of nature becomes a source of pleasure and challenges, raising doubts and interrogations. Girolamo Cardano devoted a hefty Latin treatise, *De rerum varietate* (1557), to the variety of nature. The same sense of amazement is conveyed by other, less ambitious works whose paratexts often voice the authors' sense of amazement when confronted with the variousness of things and their possible explanations. Doubt is at the same time the consequence of the observation of such richness and a tool to navigate it. Let us consider the work by Cesare Crivellati on the thermal baths of Viterbo, the *Trattato de i bagni di Viterbo* [...]. *Si mostra il modo di usarli, e si adducono molti dubbij intorno a tal materia* (A Treatise on the baths of Viterbo [...]. In which it is shown the way to use them, and many doubts are advanced concerning this matter).[49] In his *Proemio* (foreword), Crivellati pays a dithyrambic tribute to the wonders of nature:

> Numerous, nay, infinite are the wonderful things created by the almighty hand of God in this world for [the benefit of] men's health and preservation. Among them, although I could speak of many which surpass for their marvel and amazement several others (albeit all are wondrous), it seems to me, nevertheless, that waters are, no less than the others, most worthy of awe and admiration.[50]

Thermal baths are, in a way, a synecdoche of nature, because no one will be able to penetrate all their infinite secrets. The 'variety of opinions' of those who have dealt with this topic in the past leaves Crivellati 'marvelled and stupefied'.[51] A sort of gnoseological impasse seems to be the almost inevitable result of the too many secrets that we face; as a consequence, Crivellati apparently gives up the ambition to discover the truth, since 'the matter [is] exceedingly difficult and obscure'.[52] For him, knowledge is more an operation of reordering pre-existing opinions, possibly adding something new, than a process of authentic discovery.[53] The scholar relinquishes here his ambition to venture into the labyrinths of nature and, along with it, his ambition to attain the truth.

Literary texts, too, convey the sense that already in the second half of the fifteenth century, decoding reality was problematic and reality was less 'real' and transparent — and therefore more doubtful — than one may have expected. A *canzone*, previously attributed to Petrarch himself but in fact written by an anonymous fifteenth-century *petrarchista*, reflects for example on the puzzling connection between sleep and wakefulness. 'Sopra la riva ove 'l sol ha in costume' (On the shore where the Sun is used to) is remarkable in many respects, and especially because of its description of the House of Sleep and of sleep itself, here represented as an old man. The last stanza fully conveys the sense of the 'illusory instability of existence [...] an irreconcilable fracture of reality', or in other words, the sense of the deceitful nature of what we call reality.[54] In the *canzone*, the boundaries between wakefulness and sleeping, truth and illusion are shadowy to the point that we can barely tell whether we are asleep and dreaming or fully awake. This acute sense of the delusional nature of our perceptions and the fragile barrier between wakefulness and dreaming seems to predate, according to Emilio Pasquini, the treatment that these themes will receive in the baroque era and, most notably, in Calderón de la Barca's masterpiece *La vida es sueño* (1635). The concluding stanza of the anonymous *canzone* reads:

> So, moving from his home, this old man,
> Now raising, now bending down his eyes,
> Hitting his breast with his beard,
> Here sleeps in every season
> Without intermission; and after he came
> Among us, everyone is full of sleep,
> All our acts have been restrained:
> To sleep, to snore, to sweat are the art
> Of which we have long been the masters.
> Sleeping, maybe we will go to heaven
> Since we have already filled our pages with dreams.
> I myself, while I speak, I can hardly resist
> Sleep, hardly can I write,
> Half asleep, half alive.[55]

Sleep — like doubt — appears here an obstacle to human activities, to the point that it also seems to hinder faith. The line 'sleeping, maybe we will go to heaven' is in fact problematic; it could be interpreted either ironically (as Pasquini suggests), in the sense that we will sleepwalk to heaven (but how?), or more seriously, that in our condition of sleep we *might* go to heaven, casting a shadow over the possibility of an afterlife (or for us to reach it because of our spiritual torpor, as the reference to the vanity of 'pages filled with dreams' could suggest). The poet himself is half asleep and half alive, as if life and death, wakefulness and sleep were interchangeable states. Thus, we cannot be sure that what he is writing is a dream or reality, and to what extent we can trust him.

Dreams and sleep are the subject of countless works in the Renaissance; the topos of the invocation of sleep has been thoroughly explored.[56] Sleep is often compared to death, and yet, rarely does sleep act like a force able to hinder our very perception of reality as in this *canzone*, in which Pasquini detects a 'shadowy fullness of life', an almost unconscious drive to death.[57] In the last stanza the anonymous poet seems to detach himself from his classical and contemporary sources, as if trying to convey a feeling for which the tradition has no models to offer. Thus, the *canzone* appears to be voicing a new condition, pointing to both intellectual vacuity (the pages filled with dreams, the reference to the 'art' of sleeping and snoring) and to a moral lassitude, sharpened by the doubtful nature of our existence (*if* we exist at all).

The porous nature of the boundary between being awake and dreaming points to the weak status of reality in early modern times. 'Reality' was besieged and undermined by a variety of phenomena and forces, making visual evidence highly fluid and unstable to early modern Europeans. Dreams, visions, apparitions, ecstasies, raptures, and miracles were common experiences in medieval and early modern Europe.[58] The discernment of spirits (i.e., the distinction between divine or demonic spirits) was a crucial question that required prudence and vigilance on the part of devotees and churchmen.[59] Phenomena such as the witches's sabbath threatened the boundary between dream and reality; in it, imagination and fact were virtually indiscernible, leading theologians to write many a book on the subject.[60] Not by chance, Popkin has suggested that Descartes may have been prompted to write his first *Meditation* by the 1634 trial of 'witches' in Loudun, France.[61] On a more ordinary level, magic and the wonders of perspective produced astonishing effects, once again challenging people's ability to establish clear-cut distinctions between what was inside their minds and what existed in the outside world. We will see much of these challenges that extraordinary events posed to the interpretation of visual evidence and to the very perception of something like 'reality'.

A famous episode, unusual but not isolated in early modern European history, nicely demonstrates how layered reality could be to the early modern eye. In 1517 the Brescian Bartolomeo Martinengo, Count of Villagana and Villachiara (1487–1558), wrote a letter to Onofrio Bon, Veronese *nunzio* in Venice. Bearing the date 23 December 1517, the very short text described a most extraordinary event and was printed, translated into several languages, and published all over Europe. In the text, Martinengo recounts how in the small town of Verdello near Bergamo, over the previous eight days, two armies led by kings were seen coming out of a wood three or four times a day. After preliminary speeches among the kings and the ambassadors, the two armies clashed with a violence so terrible that it could be compared only to one's own death. After the end of each battle, those brave enough to approach the battlefield had been able to see only some pigs, which quickly disappeared into the wood. Bartolomeo claims to have witnessed the event with some companions: once the pigs were gone, he could make out on the ground the signs of carriages, horses' hooves, and soldiers' footprints; trees were turned to shreds. This had caused 'huge amazement' ('grandissimo stupor'), and Martinengo thought authorities in Venice should be informed of such puzzling events. Such was the power of this apparition that two of Martinengo's servants or companions were so scared that they fell ill ('un paro di nostri sono amalati da paura').[62]

This is not a story of doubt: Bartolomeo seems sure that those he saw were demons unleashed from hell, and a long tradition rooted in folkloric culture could confirm him in this belief. However, the story shows how seemingly imaginary events could be so real as to affect one's physical health, not to mention one's mental sanity. It was important therefore to ascertain, in each case, the true nature of the phenomenon, whether it was real (and by real, I suggest, actually taking place outside one's imagination) or purely a delusion, and whether it came from God or the devil. Early modern people believed in a broader range of phenomena than we do: they were ready to admit the reality of what we would label as 'prodigious' or 'wondrous' events. And yet, even these events were ruled by laws that could be counterfeited, be it by the skills of artists or magicians, by the devil, or by fraudulent impostors. Early moderns were fully aware of these possibilities, and we may thus assume that their attitude to reality was complex. Reality was layered, the result of a negotiation between subjectivity and a complex set of experiences. The world was not, in other words, a *Gegenstand*, an object that stood in front of and against a subject that perceived it and measured it. It was precisely in the cracks of a fragile continuum between sensory experience, illusions, delusions, and wonders, and in the tension between what was imaginary, the projection of one's mind, and what was factual that doubt blossomed. Nonetheless, doubt was not merely the result of 'amazement', to use Martinengo's words: it could also be a privileged tool to move across the many levels of reality, to cautiously assess experience. If this was true for all of Europe over several centuries, the peculiar conditions of Italy during the period considered in this book brought doubt to a new dimension.

Information

When depicting the landscape of sixteenth-century Italian uncertainty, several factors should be taken into account. One is the availability of information, something that has already been referred to. In a time when the printing press was expanding and news circulation was accelerating, especially in the city of Venice, manipulation of information was becoming a pressing issue. Between the piazza and the palace there lay a space packed with false information either stemming from or directed against the prince or the government. Scholars such as Sandro Landi and Filippo de Vivo have reconstructed the intricacies of the circulation of early modern information, especially in the second half of the sixteenth century and the seventeenth century.[63] This was a time of transition in which forms of more or less shared power give way to absolutist control, with the prince exerting a stronger grip on the public sphere. That the information coming from the palace was not trustworthy — and that newsletters and newspapers were not reliable — was part of the rise of the sceptical crisis of the late sixteenth and seventeenth centuries, as

Dooley argues in his *Social History of Skepticism*. Yet already in the mid-sixteenth century, one finds the signs of a rising awareness of manipulated information and fake news, something that must have contributed to increased suspicion and doubt. Aretino lambasted the 'folk who, [...] being naturally credulous and talkative, claim the certainty of which not only is doubtful but even impossible, and of this I am a witness myself'.[64] Matteo Francesi, in a satiric poem titled 'Capitolo sopra le nuove' (Capitolo on the news), lampooned those in the piazza who 'talk of Turks, Italies and Spains and Frances | Armies, freedom, wars, and coalitions' and make fun of 'the news unknown to those who tell it', noting that 'things are never told as they are'.[65] These inventors of news, Francesi adds, never mention 'those who brought the news, those who wrote it, or its author'; not only do they circulate it orally but also set it down in writing.[66] News, Francesi concludes, 'is a thing for Ambassadors' and for those who occupy prominent places in the government, not for commoners.[67]

Again at the beginning of the 1550s, Doni mused on false information in *I marmi*. In this work, Doni stages conversations between private citizens, including historical characters, on a number of topics. In one of these dialogues, he has his characters reflect on the political use of distorted information. After recalling recent extraordinary events such as the appearance of a new island and a monster in Germany, the characters talk about the truthfulness of newsletters, which are often counterfeited. One individual claims that if he were a ruler and his people were in dire straits for some reason, he would circulate newsletters that gave hope to the people. These lies should not come directly from him, however, but from unnamed 'other people'. In the case of a famine, for example, the ruler should distribute newsletters saying that somewhere it is raining corn. Another of Doni's characters remarks that 'newsletters from faraway lands are the delight of commoners'.[68] In these early texts we see the dawning consciousness of the possibility of manipulating information, as well as a reflection on the political use of distorted news. We may assume that such consciousness was not confined to restricted circles of humanists but originated in widespread assumptions. Certainly, voicing such concerns in literary works in the vernacular contributed, in a somewhat circular manner, to reinforcing them. Therefore, when considering the landscape of doubt in early modern Italy, we should keep in mind that doubt could play a defensive role. If people, commoners in particular, took delight in newsletters, predictions, and letters carrying stories from remote lands, they could also be aware that rulers could and often did tamper with them.

I will stop here, trusting that this sketch of late fifteenth- and early sixteenth-century Italian society offers enough justification to explore the rise of a 'culture of doubt' in this book.

Towards a New Season

I have chosen to conclude this account at the threshold of the 1560s, a decade that is, much like the 1490s, a symbolic watershed. The end of the Council of Trent (1563) ushered in a new era in which spaces of doubt were restricted or silenced. At the same time, the second half of the century was also marked by the spread of sceptical ideas on a large scale. Henri Estienne's translation of the *Outlines of Pyrrhonism* (1562), Sebastian Castellion's *De arte dubitandi et confidendi ignorandi et sciendi* (1563, although unpublished until 1937), Michel de Montaigne's *Essays* (1580, 1582, 1588), Francisco Sanches's *That Nothing Is Known* (*Quod nihil scitur*, 1581) are the landmark texts of a new season of European scepticism, wherein doubt becomes a recognizable if not codified trend. In the same period, theologians grew increasingly interested in moral uncertainty. Recent scholarship has begun to systematically investigate the development of casuistry and probabilism and their complex philosophical implications.[69] One may be inclined to think that the Counter-Reformation silenced doubts and imposed an ironclad prohibition on dissenting voices. This may be true in some respects; it is also true, however, that post-Tridentine theologians promptly understood the growing complexity of an entangled world. If doctrinal doubts could not be tolerated, moral doubts of unprecedented subtlety (and consequences) required some degree of flexibility and new theological tools. Missionaries, for example, had to face all sorts of doubts concerning the sacraments, the ways they were administered, their validity, and the possibility of adapting them to new contexts. Missionaries turned to Roman institutions to be enlightened, and the dossiers containing their doubts and questions are known as *dubia circa sacramenta*. These documents are not only crucial in reconstructing an institutional history of the Roman Church but also in showing how 'missionary spaces are the reign of exception, of deviation from norms, of particular cases' — or in other words, of doubt.[70]

To assess how these tools and the new criteria for moral choice impacted people's lives would be fruitful but lies beyond the scope of this study. Although I do not argue in favour of a radical distinction between a pre- and post-Tridentine world, other scholars have already produced excellent studies on uncertainty in the post-Trent period, assessing changes and continuities. In taking on the challenge of exploring an earlier portion of the long-lasting 'age of anxiety' so wonderfully analysed by William J. Bouwsma, I have assumed that such a portion presents a character of its own, different from what preceded and from what will follow.[71] By engaging with doubt and uncertainty at a time when this aspect of Italian culture is less ossified, less codified, I aim to shed new light some on some of the *longue durée* processes of early modern European culture.

The five chapters of this book proceed as follows. Chapter 1 opens with a short survey of the sixteenth-century printed book market, taking stock of the countless works on various topics that advertise doubt on their title pages. The semantic overlapping between 'doubt' and 'question' suggests that these works testify more to the intellectual curiosity of early modern Italians than to their incredulity. It is important, then, to map the meaning(s) of doubt by exploring dictionaries and reference works. From the Middle Ages onward, and especially in late fifteenth- and early sixteenth-century dictionaries, doubt was carefully described and connected — via a pseudo-etymology — to the idea of standing at a crossroads, of being unable to choose between two paths. After surveying the allegories of doubt in Cesare Ripa's *Iconologia*, the chapter delves into fifteenth- and sixteenth-century manuals for confessors. In these works, authors draw on Scholastic philosophy to pitch doubt against other similar but distinct categories ('scruple', 'opinion', 'suspicion', etc.), carefully describing its characteristics, noting its psychological, physical, and moral consequences, and suggesting apt remedies against it.

The second chapter investigates how, starting in the final decades of the fifteenth century, vernacular literary texts such as poems and *novelle* appropriated the subject of doubt. Following a preliminary exploration of texts that talk of doubt as an existential condition, the discussion moves to quattrocento Florence and a local habit of expressing religious doubts through sonnets. Figures such as Luigi Pulci and Feo Belcari used the vernacular to convey religious doubts to a large audience. The interest in doubt in non-technical texts can also be seen in the evolution from the Middle Ages of two popular stories: that of 'Doubting Thomas' and that of the 'Doubt of Joseph'. A consideration of literary and visual sources demonstrates how these stories of doubt intersect with issues of justice and with historical events such as the Italian Wars. The final section of the chapter explores tales of doubt in literary works produced in the courts and cities of the Po Valley. In the works of Antonio Urceo Codro, Giovanni Sabadino degli Arienti, and Panfilo Sasso (among others), vernacular poetry and prose (along with Latin) are effectively used to stage fascinating tales of doubts and doubters for a wide readership, thus suggesting that doubt was becoming an appealing topic even outside the circles of the learned.

Chapter 3 examines doubt in connection with women and their role in early sixteenth-century spiritual life, a time and place marked by the presence of women imbued with special charisma. 'Holy mothers' and 'living saints' became the catalysts of circles in which their spiritual gifts of prophecy, miracles, and visions went hand in hand with their political influence. The gifts of charismatic women, however, were often puzzling and ambiguous: visions, prophecies, miracles, and ecstasies all required proper interpretation. The nature of these gifts was itself problematic, as they could be either signs of divine inspiration or tricks of the devil. Doubt became a privileged instrument with which to navigate a world of enigmatic signs. On the one hand, authors of devotional treatises encourage the practice of doubt as a paradoxical form of higher faith. Yet on the other hand, they also make distinctions between different qualities of doubt: for example, a doubt of incredulity as opposed to that of amazement. At the heart of this heated spirituality one detects the broader problem of women's relationship with God, in which doubt played an important role. In particular, two tales of doubt that circulated in the visual arts and in literary texts from the Middle Ages onward reveal how doubt was crucial in assessing, defining, and understanding the relationship between God and women. These two tales — that of the 'Doubting Midwife' and of the *Noli me tangere* (the moment when Mary Magdalene meets the resurrected Christ) — serve as an introduction to this chapter, which continues with an analysis of some significant spiritual works in the vernacular (poems and religious pamphlets) by such authors as Gabriele Biondo, Antonio Pagani, and Serafino da Fermo.

The fourth chapter further explores the role of doubt in the religious crisis of the sixteenth century. The letters exchanged between Gasparo Contarini, Paolo Giustinian, and Vincenzo Querini document the doubts, anxieties, and psychological distress connected with the aspiration to a life of spiritual seclusion. As the Reformation spread in Italy, several authors came to reflect on doubt and on its uses and consequences. One of the most notable was Juan de Valdés, whose teachings assign to doubt a complex and at times positive role. Among his followers, however, figures such as Vittoria Colonna and Giulia Gonzaga openly voiced another, more troubling side to doubt in the light of the new ideas on *sola fide* salvation. Michelangelo Buonarroti's poetical allegory of doubt and Camillo Renato's musing on the spaces of doubt in his *Apologia* point to the growing desire to define and make sense of an increasingly intricate notion. Finally, the stories of some of Valdés's followers provide an opportunity to reflect on issues of social and personal identity, and on how in the central decades of the century, radical doubt turned from an exhilarating experience of intellectual freedom into an experience of severance and loss of one's self.

Early modern doubt is often perceived as a solitary and distressing experience, one carried out in the secret of one's chamber. In Renaissance Italy, however, there existed a sociability of doubt. Chapter 5 explores some fascinating forms of this sociability, beginning with Francesco Marcolini's *Sorti* (1540, 1550), a game of chance in which doubt is a recurrent presence. The *Sorti* can be connected to the works of Daniele Barbaro, who penned, among others, five sonnets on doubt (1542), a seemingly unique short treatise on doubt in poetical form. These sonnets mark a radical shift, for we can see here how doubt became an object of discourse in its own right. While discussing doubts through the medium of poetry was not unusual, here is a discussion of doubt itself, the equivalent of a philosophical treatise, only through vernacular poetry. Barbaro's reflection is situated against the cultural backdrop of the Veneto and its academies, in particular the Academy of the Infiammati and the Academy of the Dubbiosi (founded by Fortunato Martinengo), which were central to the cultural milieu of the Veneto in the 1540s and 1550s. In the *Lettere di molte valorose donne* (1548) and the *Quattro libri di dubbi* (1552), Ortensio Lando (a good friend of Martinengo's) intimates a kind of virtual academy through the casting of several characters, historically connected with the Academy of the Dubbiosi or with Martinengo's circles, who discuss their doubts. Reading literary texts could also foster dangerous doubts with tragic outcomes, as shown in the story of Francesco Calcagno, a priest who was tried in 1550 and executed because of his heretical opinions and doubts, formed after having read, among others, Antonio Vignali's *La Cazzaría*. Calcagno's story works as an apt conclusion, as the 1550s mark the point at which the story of doubt takes on a new shape.

Notes to the Introduction

1. *Acta Patris Ignatii scripta a P. Lud. Gonzalez de Camara*, in *Fontes narrativi de S. Ignatio de Loyola et de Societatis Iesu initiis*, I: *Narrationes scriptae ante annum 1557*, ed. by Dionysius Fernandez Zapico S.I. and Candidus de Dalmases S.I. (Rome: Monumenta Historica Societatis Iesu, 1943), pp. 323–507 (p. 383). The autobiography (for the period 1521–38) was narrated by Ignatius himself to Ludovico González between 1553 and 1555 and originally written in Spanish. I quote the Latin version (1559–61) by Hannibal Coudret (1525–1599). Starting from paragraph 79, the text is in Italian because González, who was in Genoa by the time he was writing that section, had no Spanish amanuensis available ('Hoc tempore Ludovicus noster extendit italice, deficient amanuense hispano, partem Actorum quam Romae extendere non potuerat', p. 342).

2. Ibid., p. 385.

3. Nicholas Rescher, 'Choice without Preference: A Study of the History and of the Logic of the Problem of "Buridan's Ass"', *Kant-Studien*, 51 (1960), 142–75.

4. John M. McManamon S.J., *The Text and Context of Ignatius of Loyola's 'Autobiography'* (New York: Fordham University Press, 2013), p. 24.

5. Erwin Panofsky, *Ercole al bivio e altri materiali iconografici dell'Antichità tornati in vita nell'età moderna*, ed. by Monica Ferrando (Macerata: Quodlibet, 2010; 1st edn: *Hercules am Scheidewege und anderen antike Bildstoffe in der neueren Kunst* (Leipzig: B.G. Teubner, 1930)).

6. 'The discussion indicates that the two had a language in common — the Moor did not use Arabic — and perhaps they shared a basic knowledge of Christian catechism. The topic of discussion mirrors the broader social and theological issues of the encounter: honor in Spanish chivalric culture and purity of blood in Spanish religious culture. [...] At that point in his life, Ignatius was a zealot. He has a hyperchivalric reaction to the Moor's suggestion that Mary lost her virginity when Jesus was born. [...] But Ignatius has made sufficient progress in the spiritual life that he questions his first instincts and the broader imperatives of *hidalgo* culture.' Ibid., p. 23.

7. Although the mule is an instrument of God: 'accidit ut Dei clementia [...] mula tamen [...] regium iter sequeretur'. *Acta Patris Ignatii*, p. 385.

8. Ibid., p. 383.

9. 'Si lasciò uscir dal petto un di quei sospiri grevi che forma il cor dubbioso.' Pietro Aretino, *Vita di santa Caterina*, in *Opere religiose*, II: *Vita di Maria Vergine; Vita di santa Caterina; Vita di san Tommaso*, ed. by Paolo Marini (Rome: Salerno Editrice, 2011), pp. 303–456 (p. 390).

10. 'Colui che dubita è simile all'onda del mare mossa dal vento, cioè non ha in sé fermezza alcuna.' Serafino da Fermo, *Alcuni dubi circa l'oratione, per modo di problemi, numero cento, non meno utili che succinti*, in *Opere del R. P. Serafino del Firmo* (Venice: Comin da Trino di Monferrato, 1569), fols 56^v–94^v (80^r). As a consequence, the doubter's prayers won't be satisfied because of their lack of faith. The metaphor comes from the Epistle of James (1, 6–7). It is also present in the *Beneficio di Cristo* (1543): 'Colui che dubita è simile all'onda del mare, la quale è sbattuta e agitata da' venti, per la qual cosa non pensi quell'uomo di dover ricevere cosa alcuna da Dio'. Benedetto da Mantova, *Il beneficio di Cristo: Con le versioni del secolo XVI documenti e testimonianze*, ed. by Salvatore Caponetto (Florence: Sansoni; Dekalb: Northern Illinois University Press; Chicago: Newberry Library, 1972), p. 79.

11. *The Revelations of St. Birgitta of Sweden*, II: *Liber caelestis, Books IV–V*, trans. by Denis Searby, introduction and notes by Bridget Morris (Oxford: Oxford University Press, 2008), pp. 271–72; my italics. The Latin texts reads as follows: 'Et in medio eiusdem scale videbat predicta domina religiosum quondam sibi notum adhuc corpore tunc viventem magne literature in sciencia theologie, plenum quoque dolo et malicia dyabolica. Qui videbatur in gestu suo impacientissimo et inquieto magis dyabolus quam humilis religiosus. Videbat namque tunc dicta domina cogitationes et omnes affecciones internas cordis eiusdem religiosi et quomodo ipse illas propalabat Christo iudici in throno sedenti cum gestu inordinato et inquietissimo per modum questionum. Videbat eciam et audiebat domina Birgitta, qualiter Christus iudex ad illas questiones cum gesto mansuetissimo et honesto sigillatim et compendiose sapientissime respondebat'; 'impacientissimos et inquietos habens gestos quasi dolo et malicia plenus interrogando dixit'. *Revelationes sanctae Birgittae, Revelaciones lib. v: Liber questionum*, ed. by Birger Bergh (Uppsala: Almqvist & Wiksells Boktrickery AB, 1971), pp. 97–99.

12. René Descartes, *Meditations on First Philosophy: With Selections from the Objections and Replies*, ed. by Michael Moriarty (Oxford: Oxford University Press, 2008), p. 12.

13. Ibid., p. 16.

14. Ibid.

15. Ibid., p. 14.

16. Alec Ryrie, *Unbelievers: An Emotional History of Doubt* (Cambridge, MA: Harvard University Press, 2019).

17. Such research would be fascinating and more feasible for the late sixteenth and early seventeenth centuries, thanks to the greater availability of judiciary records and ego-documents for this period.

18. Brendan Dooley, *The Social History of Skepticism: Experience and Doubt in Early Modern Culture* (Baltimore: Johns Hopkins University Press, 1999), p. 1.

19. Richard H. Popkin, *The History of Scepticism: From Savonarola to Bayle* (Oxford: Oxford University Press, 2003), p. xxiii.

20. See for example the recent work by Marco Sgattoni, *La rinascita dello scetticismo tra eresia e riforma* (Urbino: Quattroventi, 2018).

21. 'Parlare di "centralità del dubbio" nel mondo francese non è un'iperbole; e non lo è neppure ricordare che il dubbio partorì il *cogito* cartesiano, una vera e propria epifania che dischiuse le porte della modernità.' Paolo Cherchi, *Ignoranza ed erudizione: L'Italia dei dogmi di fronte all'Europa scettica e critica (1500–1750)* (Padua: Libreria universitaria, 2020), p. 110.

22. 'Erano dubbi di giudizio o di valutazione e non riguardavano mai gli strumenti o anche i parametri della conoscenza stessa.' Ibid., p. 114.

23. 'Ma il dubbio "all'italiana" [...] riguarda la soluzione e non l'intelletto che lo pone.' Ibid., p. 113.

24. 'Satan tirò Eva al dubbio e dal dubbio al consenso e dal consenso al fallo.' Pietro Aretino, *Vita di Maria Vergine*, in *Opere religiose*, II: *Vita di Maria Vergine; Vita di santa Caterina; Vita di san Tommaso*, ed. by Paolo Marini, pp. 91–302 (p. 168).

25. This section is indebted to the lively Italian discussion on 'popular' culture that has been revived by Francesco Benigno in his *Words in Time: A Plea for Historical Re-Thinking* (London: Routledge, 2017; 1st Italian edn, Rome: Viella, 2013); see the review essay by Ottavia Niccoli, 'Cultura popolare: Un relitto abbandonato?', *Studi storici*, 56 (2015), 997–1010. See also *Un mondo perduto? Religione e cultura popolare*, ed. by Lucia Felici and Pierroberto Scaramella (Rome: Aracne, 2020).

26. Remo L. Guidi, *L'inquietudine del Quattrocento* (Rome: Tielle Media, 2007).

27. *Belief and Unbelief in Medieval Europe* (London: Bloomsbury, 2011 (2005)), p. 229. See also Guglielmo Russino, 'Un medioevo incredulo: A proposito di scetticismo e imposture', *Mediaeval Sophia: Studi e ricerche sui saperi medievali*, 3 (2008), 162–68; Thomas Lienhard, 'Athéisme, scepticisme et doute religieux au Moyen Âge: Notes de lecture à propos de trois publications récentes', *Revue de l'Institut français d'histoire en Allemagne*, 3 (2011) <https://journals.openedition.org/ifha/194> [accessed 23 July 2021].

28. Francis Petrarch, *Letters of Old Age: Rerum Senilium libri I–XVIII*, vol. I: *Books I–IX*, trans. by Aldo S. Bernardo, Saul Levin, and Reta A. Bernardo (Baltimore: Johns Hopkins University Press, 1992), p. 28. Here is the Latin text: 'Sectarum negligens, veri appetens, quod quoniam quesitu arduum, ego, quesitor infimus atque infirmus, sepe diffidens mei, ne erroribus implicer dubitationem ipsam pro veritate complector. Ita sensim achademicus advena, unus ex plurimis inque humili plebe novissimus, evasi, nil michi tribuens, nil affirmans dubitansque de singulis, nisi de quibus dubitare sacrilegum reor. En tuus ille Hippias in conventu olim philosophico cunta profiteri ausus: tecum nichil preter inquisitionem veri anxiam preterque dubietatem atque inscitiam profitetur.' Francesco Petrarca, *Le senili: Libri I–VI*, ed. by Ugo Dotti and Felicita Audisio (Turin: Nino Aragno, 2004), pp. 106–08.

29. Petrarch devoted a whole work to his and others' ignorance (*De sui ipsius et multorum ignorantia*, first drafted in 1367 and revised until 1370). Conceived as a polemical reply to four Aristotelian friends who had accused him of ignorance (probably in matters of natural philosophy), the work aims to show the inevitable imperfection of every form of knowledge. Petrarch is aware of his own ignorance and claims to place faith over knowledge, aiming to be rather a good man than a learned one. He shows that all philosophers, including Aristotle, have erred on many subjects. In doing so, he of course displays his immense erudition. The work is, broadly speaking, sceptical in that it acknowledges the limited and imperfect nature of knowledge.

30. Peter Burke, *Tradition and Innovation in Renaissance Italy: A Sociological Approach* (London: Fontana-Collins, 1974), p. 329.
31. On fear in early sixteenth century Italy, see Micaela Valente, '*Fuggire la burrasca*: Inquietudini e paure nell'Europa della prima età moderna', in *Per un lessico della paura in Europa: Spunti per una riflessione*, ed. by Fabiana Ambrosi, Carolina Antonucci, Ida Xoxa (Rome: Sapienza Università Editrice, 2018), pp. 11–21. On the geographical explorations and the rise of scepticism, see Danilo Marcondes, 'The Anthropological Argument: The Rediscovery of Ancient Skepticism in Modern Thought', in *Skepticism in the Modern Age: Building on the Work of Richard Popkin*, ed. by José R. Maia Nieto, Gianni Paganini, John Christian Laursen (Leiden: Brill, 2009), pp. 37–53; Anthony Grafton, with April Shelford and Nancy Siraisi, *New Worlds, Ancient Texts: The Power of Tradition and the Shock of Discovery* (Cambridge, MA: Belknap Press of Harvard University Press, 1992). On the fear of the Turk, see also for further bibliography, Maria Chiara Cantelmo, 'La paura del turco in Europa tra la caduta di Costantinopoli e la battaglia di Lepanto (1453–1571)', in *Per un lessico della paura*, ed. by Ambrosi, Antonucci, and Xoxa, pp. 47–55.
32. 'In religion, politics, economics, and society, cherished authorities by the score were under attack, and centuries-old values no longer commanded unquestioned adherence. [...] Catholics, Lutherans, and Calvinists — not to mention the radical sects — clung to irreconcilable world views; overseas discoveries revealed the falsity of ancient geographic assumptions, and brought to light human beings, such as cannibals, whose principles were unthinkable to a European; departures in social, political, and economic affairs changed traditional relationships and institutions beyond recognition: the autonomy of the locality, the supremacy of the aristocracy, and the subservience of the merchant no longer seemed unchallengeable [...] and then Copernicus and Vesalius announced that the descriptions of nature associated with Ptolemy and Galen, which had been revered for over a thousand years, were wrong. No succession of events so disruptive of safe and comfortable suppositions had occurred for hundreds of years. As expectations lost their cogency, an atmosphere of groping and unease descended. Europe's leaders, philosophers, and artists grappled with a world that seemed to be crumbling around them. The sense that all solid landmarks had disappeared pervades the writing of the age.' Theodore K. Rabb, *The Struggle for Stability in Early Modern Europe* (New York: Oxford University Press, 1975), 37.
33. Guido Alfani, *Calamities and the Economy in Renaissance Italy: The Grand Tour of the Horsemen of the Apocalypse*, trans. by Christine Calvert (Basingstoke: PalgraveMacMillan, 2013).
34. Colin Rose, 'Plague and Violence in Early Modern Italy', *Renaissance Quarterly*, 71 (2018), 1000–35.
35. Giuseppe Levi, *L'eredità immateriale: Carriera di un esorcista nel Piemonte del Seicento* (Milan: Il Saggiatore, 2020 (1985)).
36. I am consciously using words such as 'uncertainty', 'anxiety', and 'fear' as synonyms to identify a generic condition of lack of certainty from which doubt originates. As we shall see, doubt includes, or is closely related to, all these meanings.
37. 'Apparuit in quadam ecclesia existente in valle Vigezii lacus majoris seu Verbani figura santae Mariae genitricis Jesu Christi quae in facie producebat sanguis in magna quantitate et per multos dies: et erat fragrantis adeo quod populus undique confluebat. Hoc anno fere in toto agro Cumano fuit tanta inundatio grandinum quod fructus fuerunt omnes devastati, sed conflatio ventorum evertit majorem partem arborum castaneorum et nucum, adeo quod nunquam fuit tale ante auditum; adeo quod ager Cumanus remansit in totum devastatus et fuit die penultima Iulii 1494. Rex Charolus Francorum rex potentissimus, filius Ludovici, hoc anno 1494 die XV Septembris, auctore Ludovico Sfortia patruo Io. Galeaz. Ducis VI Mediolani venit in Lombardiam cum maximo apparatu belli peragens contra Alfonsum regem Neapoli quim [*sic*] asserebat regnum ad se spectare [...]. Sed multa sunt quae non sunt apud omnes dicenda propter quod, et quod erit, dubius est cunctus, multi multa dicunt, sed nullus est quod sciat quod dicat: ideo tacendum est ist temporibus, verum est quod populi ubique sunt oppressi oneribus principum adeo quod vix possunt vivere.' Francesco Muralto, *Annalia*, ed. by Pierluigi Donini (Milan: cura et impensis Aloisii Daelli, 1861), pp. xxv–xxvi. Muralto's Latin is often incorrect, as the editor of text acknowledges in his introduction. In particular, the concluding sentence suffers from a very approximate syntactic construction; my translation tries to convey what seems to me its intended meaning.

38. Germana Ernst, 'Aspetti celesti e profezia politica: Sul "Prognosticon" di Arquato', *Bruniana & Campanelliana*, 11 (2005), 635–46 (p. 643). I quote the vernacular version of a judgement on Arquato's text by three other astrologers: Carlo Drusiano, Odoardo Farmiense, and Americo Polono. Their commentary encapsulates large chunks of the original text.

39. Ibid., p. 645.

40. 'S'io mi ricordo bene, e' son pure assai pochi anni che venni in questo mondo [...], e ho veduto cose così stupende! Io ho memoria come se fosse stato ier sera, tanta negligenza in soccorrere Rodi che si perdé, veduto le ferite che ha ricevute la cristianità nella rotta e morte di tanti cristiani sotto Pavia, con l'esser prigione un sì fatto re di Francia; non fu ancora un sacco di Roma sì orribile, e si stette tanto rinchiuso il pontefice: parvi che queste due fussero onorate? La peste che seguì poi e la fame; non ho io veduto l'assedio d'una Fiorenza e un essercito sì grosso e un dominio sì rovinato; poi (che aviene di rado) una incoronazione dell'imperatore a Bologna, con tanta maestà per mano d'un sì gran Papa? Ma torniamo a' danni: il diluvio che venne a Roma per il Tebro, non fu egli un altro sacco? Certo se noi diamo fede alle Scritture Sante, noi siamo vicini alla fine di questa macchina, che saran guerre, pestilenze, fame, terremuoti e gran segni.' Anton Francesco Doni, *Le novelle*, II/1: *La zucca*, ed. by Elena Pierazzo (Rome: Salerno, 2003), pp. 501–02.

41. 'Sì gran terremoti alla Scarperia e tutto il Mugello, e i fuochi di Pozzuolo e di Sicilia?' Ibid., p. 503.

42. 'Delle sette contro la Chiesa e delle sedizioni, vorreste voi meglio?'; 'La Chiesa non diede due città e fece il figliuol del papa duca di quelle?' Ibid., p. 505.

43. 'Forze omicide rivolte a cancellare per sempre il concetto stesso della vita.' Guidi, *L'inquietudine*, p. 414.

44. 'Così noi di mano in mano n'abbiamo delle bastonate dal cielo e non ce n'accorgiamo.' Doni, *Le novelle*, II/1: *La zucca*, p. 506.

45. 'Di nuovo non intendo niente che habbia nervo, et credo che ambuliamo tutti in tenebris, ma con le mani legate di dietro per non potere schifare le percosse.' Niccolò Machiavelli, *Lettere a Francesco Vettori e a Francesco Guicciardini*, ed. by Giorgio Inglese (Milan: Rizzoli, 1989), p. 318.

46. Guidi, *L'inquietudine*, pp. 440–44.

47. 'L'azione risulta come sospesa e ancora ambigua.' Diletta Gamberini, 'Rappresentare le lacerazioni dell'animo: Archetipi letterari dell'*amphibolía* di Pomponio Gaurico', *I Tatti Studies in the Italian Renaissance*, 23 (2020), 213–40 (p. 235).

48. Chriscinda Henry, 'Leonardo da Vinci, Parody, and Pictorial Magic', in *Playthings in Early Modernity: Party Games, Word Games, Mind Games*, ed. by Allison Levy (Kalamazoo: Western Michigan University, 2017), pp. 73–96 (p. 77).

49. First printed in Viterbo by Agostino Colaldi, 1596; reprinted in Rome by Bartholomeo Bonfadino, 1599. I use the edition printed in Viterbo by Girolamo Discepolo, 1604.

50. 'Molte, anzi infinite, sono le cose maravigliose che ha creato l'onnipotente mano d'Iddio nel mondo per la salute e conservatione dell'huomo, tra le quali, come che molte se ne potessero raccontare, che avanzano di maraviglia e di stupore molte altre (quantunque tutte maravigliose) pare a me nondimeno che le acque [...] siano a par di tutte le altre dignissime di stupore e di maraviglia.' Crivellati, *Trattato de i bagni*, p. 5.

51. 'E in vero, chi potrà con l'intelletto suo penetrar tutti quei secreti che nelle acque de' bagni in diverse parti del mondo si ritrovano? Io quanto a me [...] resto talmente stupito e meravigliato della tanta varietà d'opinioni di quelli che di tal materia hanno trattato che non so concluder altro se non che per ancora non se ne sia ritrovato il vero.' Ibid., pp. 5–6.

52. 'Essendo [...] la cosa troppo difficile, e troppo oscura.' Ibid., p. 8.

53. 'Intendo ciò fare secondo il giuditio di quelli che di tal materia hanno trattato; e se cosa alcuna vi aggiungerò, sappi, o Lettore, che sarà più tosto per dirne ancor io quel che mi detta il mio debole intelletto, e spesso per concordare qualche varietà d'oppinioni che per intender di trattar cose nuove, o per mostrare d'haver ritrovato il vero intorno a questo.' Ibid. In 1617 Mariano Ghezzi, a doctor and philosopher from Sinalunga, near Siena, published his work *De i bagni di San Casciano [...] con le cautele destinate da osservarsi nell'uso dell'acqua, e con espositione de i dubbij più curiosi, e delle questioni più gravi* [...] (Ronciglione: appresso gli heredi di Domenico Domenici).

54. 'Illusoria instabilità dell'esistenza [...] un'insanabile frattura del reale.' Emilio Pasquini, 'Il mito

della casa del sonno', in *Le botteghe della poesia: Studi sul Tre-Quattrocento italiano* (Bologna: il Mulino, 1991), pp. 115–98 (p. 132).

55. 'Così mosso dal nido esto vecchione, | Or alzando or chinando gli occhi soi | E con la barba percotendo il seno, | Però se dorme qui d'ogni stagione | Senza alcun mezzo; e poscia che 'n fra noi | Giunse costui, di sonno è ciascun pieno, | A tutti gli atti nostri è posto un freno: | Dormir, russar, sudar, sognar son l'arte | Di che maestri lungo tempo semo. | Dormendo, forsi in paradiso andremo, | Ché già de' sogni avem piene le carte. | Io medesmo dal sonno a pena, parte | Ch'io parlo, mi difendo, a pena scrivo, | Adormentato mezzo e mezzo vivo.' Ibid., p. 125.

56. Stefano Carrai, *Ad somnum: L'invocazione al sonno nella lirica italiana* (Padua: Antenore, 1990).

57. 'Un'ombrosa sazietà di vita'. Pasquini, 'Il mito', p. 132.

58. Stuart Clark, *Vanities of the Eye: Vision in Early Modern European Culture* (Oxford: Oxford University Press, 2007).

59. Nancy Caciola, *Discerning Spirits: Divine and Demonic Possession in the Middle Ages* (Ithaca, NY: Cornell University Press, 2006).

60. Clark, *Vanities of the Eye*, Chap. 4.

61. Popkin, *The History of Scepticism*, pp. 149–50.

62. There exist several versions of the letter. I am quoting from the one printed on a single sheet and kept in the Biblioteca Marciana of Venice, available at <https://edit16.iccu.sbn.it/new-home1>. On the episode, see Ottavia Niccoli, *Prophecy and People in Renaissance Italy*, trans. by Lydia G. Cochrane (Princeton: Princeton University Press, 1990), pp. 65–82.

63. Sergio Landi, *Naissance de l'opinion publique dans l'Italie moderne: Sagesse du people et savoir de gouvernement de Machiavel aux Lumières* (Rennes: Presses universitaires de Rennes, 2006); Filippo de Vivo, *Information and Communication in Venice: Rethinking Early Modern Politics* (Oxford: Oxford University Press, 2007); see also the enlarged Italian version of de Vivo's book: *Patrizi, informatori, barbieri: Politica e comunicazione a Venezia* (Milan: Feltrinelli, 2012).

64. 'Il quale [i.e., il vulgo], per essere naturalmente credulo e parlante, afferma per certo non pure il dubbio, ma l'impossibile ancora e di ciò rendo testimonianza io.' Aretino, *Vita di Maria Vergine*, in *Opere religiose*, II, ed. by Marini, p. 265.

65. 'Discorron Turchi, Italie, e Spagne e Francie, | Armate, libertà, guerre, unione'; 'Nuove che non le sa chi le racconta'; 'Perché la cosa mai non si ridice | Com'ella sta.' Mattio Francesi, 'Capitolo sopra le nuove', in *Il secondo libro dell'opere burlesche di M. Francesco Berni, del Molza [...] et di diversi autori [...]* (Florence: Heredi di Bernardo Giunti, 1555), fols 58^r–59^v (fol. 58^{r-v}). See Mario Infelise, *Prima dei giornali: Alle origini della pubblica informazione (secoli XVI e XVII)* (Rome: Laterza, 2005), p. x and Chap. 1.

66. 'Né pensar che t'alleghino altrimenti | Chi portò, chi lo scrisse, o l'Autore.' Francesi, 'Capitolo', fol. 58^v.

67. 'Le nuove cosa son da Imbasciadore, | Da huomin grandi di stato e governo | Et non da quei che van per la minore'. Ibid., fol. 59^r.

68. 'I pronostici e le novelle, i trovati, le lettere de' paesi strani, son la confezzion de la plebe.' Anton Francesco Doni, *I marmi*, ed. by Carlo Alberto Girotto and Giovanna Rizzarelli (Florence: Olschki, 2017), p. 301.

69. Stefania Tutino, *Shadows of Doubt: Language and Truth in Post-Reformation Catholic Culture* (Oxford: Oxford University Press, 2014); Stefania Tutino, *Uncertainty in Post-Reformation Catholicism: A History of Probabilism* (Oxford: Oxford University Press, 2018); Carlo Ginzburg, *Nondimanco: Machiavelli, Pascal* (Milan: Adelphi, 2018); *A Historical Approach to Casuistry: Norms and Exceptions in a Comparative Perspective*, ed. by Carlo Ginzburg with Lucio Biasiori (London: Bloomsbury, 2018); Rudolf Schuessler, *The Debate on Probable Opinions in the Scholastic Tradition* (Leiden: Brill, 2019).

70. 'En ce sens les espaces missionaires sont le règne de l'exception, de la déviation de la norme, des cas particuliers.' Paolo Broggio, Charlotte de Castelnau-L'estoile, and Giovanni Pizzorusso, 'Le temps des doutes: Les sacrements et l'Église romaine aux dimensions du monde', in *Administrer les sacrements en Europe et au Nouveau Monde: La curie romaine et les dubia circa sacramenta*, ed. by Paolo Broggio, Charlotte de Castelnau-L'estoile, and Giovanni Pizzorusso (= *Mélanges de l'École française de Rome: Italie et Méditerranée*, 121 (2009)), pp. 5–22 (p. 19).

71. William J. Bouwsma, 'Anxiety and the Formation of Early Modern Culture', in *A Usable Past: Essays in European Cultural History* (Berkeley: University of California Press, 1990), pp. 157–89.

CHAPTER 1

A Young Man in the Dark

Imagine it is the year 1600, and you are a Venetian perusing the bookstalls near the Rialto. You are merely passing the time, with no intention of buying a particular book. Leafing through loose quires or parchment-bound volumes, your eyes soon catch a recurring word — 'doubt' — although spelled in countless ways: *dubii, dubij, dubbii, dubbij, dubbi, dubitationi*. No matter your profession or your interests, you will certainly find something to suit your tastes and your pocketbook, from cheap prints to hefty volumes, from worn-out editions printed almost a century before to brand-new volumes. You can find books on dietary regimes, recipes, plague, or anatomy.[1] If you have an interest in music, Pietro Aaron and Angelo da Pizzighettone will help resolve your doubts in that area.[2] If you happen to be curious about thermal baths, Cesare Crivellati will have all the answers to your questions.[3] If, more seriously, you are concerned with the well-being of the dead (in the afterlife, that is), treatises on indulgences and jubilees may help relieve some of your anxieties.[4] If you are a Benedictine nun, you will find a vernacular translation of the section of Benedict's Rule regarding nuns, with the explanation of some doubts.[5] Or you might be concerned about other religious groups in your city: in places like Venice and Rome there exist large Jewish communities, and from the point of view of Christian doctrine, Jews pose a threat because they voice doubts about its truth. In Counter-Reformation times, knowing how to address these doubts is important, and therefore you might find helpful a book by Fabiano Fioghi, lecturer of Hebrew at the College of Neophytes (founded in 1577 and intended for the conversion of young Jews and Muslims), dedicated to this topic.[6] If instead you are in search of some light entertainment, why not consider a work containing the resolutions to the three greatest doubts concerning donkeys, dogs, cats, and mice?[7] If, on the contrary, your taste inclines more towards lofty humanistic works, you might consider buying the *Discourses* by the Ferrarese Annibale Romei. There you will find seven dialogues, on beauty, human love, honour, duels, nobility, wealth, and the question of whether Arms are superior to Letters, along with 'the answers to all doubts that are usually raised concerning these subjects'.[8]

Such a broad-ranging selection of books devoted to doubt prompts the question of what early modern Italians meant when referring to doubt. In particular, we see here how blurred the distinction between 'doubt' and 'question' could be. Did early modern Italians use the term 'doubt' in a rather loose sense to denote every type of intellectual curiosity? Or were they careful to define doubt as distinct from other competing notions? As we shall see, both attitudes to doubt existed. Doubt could be understood as curiosity, as question, even as a fear of something; nonetheless, dictionaries gave quite unequivocal definitions of what doubt was and the condition to which it applied. In the realm of philosophy or theology, scholars were even more careful in pitting doubt against the large and varied galaxy of uncertainty.

Doubts or Questions?

Early modern Italians were not hopelessly sceptical, though. Certainly they enjoyed a reputation for atheism, and if Englishmen 'were tempted by doubt, they were liable to be called Italianate'.[9] And humanists lamented 'thick and ignorant men, used to reprehending what they do not understand, do not believe in, and [who] make fun of all the sayings and deeds that appear to them more noble than their uncouth intellect deems possible to achieve'; hence 'they believe that all the good and approved maxims of virtuous men, all their notable examples, and all their glorious deeds are not true, but [have been] found, just like fables and tales of old women, and invented to provide fun for idlers during vigils'.[10] Most of all, though, the above-mentioned and other similar works testify to a widespread curiosity, and to an inclination to investigate the reasons behind natural or social phenomena. Diligent writers satisfied the interests of their readers by asking the questions they had or may have had in mind. I use the word 'question' (*questione*) because 'doubt' and 'question' were largely interchangeable terms. Despite certain undertones that 'doubt' could have, authors and printers did not shy away from printing the word, even on the frontispieces of religious works.

While 'doubts' were mostly an addition or an appendix to the main topic of a given work, there existed also an ancient and medieval tradition of books of 'problems' and 'questions'. As we will see in Chapter 5, these books, which can be traced back to the pseudo-Aristotelian *Problemata*, discussed issues pertaining to moral or natural philosophy as well as other subjects such as love.[11] It was probably the polygraph Ortensio Lando who first used the term 'doubt' to designate a collection of questions or problems (*Quattro libri de dubbi*, 1552 and 1556).[12] More often, however, the discussion of doubts represented an effective didactic tool, which especially in religious works could take the form of a dialogue between a master and a student. Of course, there were illustrious medieval antecedents for this pattern.

One of them was Honorius of Autun's *Elucidarium* (early twelfth century). Honorius (*c.* 1080–1154?) intended his work as a guide, cast in the form of a dialogue between master and disciple, to the fundamental tenets of Christian doctrine, or, as Gabriella Zarri puts it, to the 'most elementary questions of a Christian'.[13] The work went through thirty-two editions in Italy between 1481 and 1584, generally under the title *Libro del maestro e discepolo*. The title was usually followed by a subtitle specifying that the work addressed questions of faith. Only in the Venetian edition printed in 1537 by Pietro Nicolini da Sabbio does the word 'doubt' appear on the frontispiece: *Libro del maestro e discepolo, chiamato Lucidario ne [sic] quale si dichiara molte belle sentenze, e gran dubii della sacra scrittura* (Book of the master and the disciple called

Lucidario, in which many beautiful passages and doubts from Holy Scripture are explained).

Another best-seller of the genre was the *Specchio de la santa madre Chiesa* (A mirror of the holy mother Church; the title slightly differs from edition to edition) by the French theologian Hugh of St Victor (1096–1141). This work shares the didactic nature of the *Elucidarium* but addresses specifically the formation of the parish clergy. Because of this focus, it was often printed along with another popular work, the *Manipulus curatorum* (Handbook for curates; early 1330s) by the Spaniard Guido de Monte Rochen (1300–1333).[14] The *Specchio* was usually published (with minor differences) under the title of *Opera utilissima a qualunche fidel christiano intitulata specchio de la santa madre ecclesia* (A most useful work for every faithful Christian called mirror of the holy mother church). However, in at least three editions the word 'doubt' appears on the frontispiece.[15] It is possible that some of the topics discussed in these works, which were perfectly orthodox in themselves, resonated with contemporary discussions.[16] Certainly, the pattern of a dialogue between master and disciple continued well into the sixteenth century, as the *Dottrina del ben morire* [...] *con molte utile resolutioni di alcuni belli dubii theologici* (A doctrine on dying well [...] with many useful solutions to some beautiful theological doubts) by the Bolognese regular canon Pietro da Lucca (d. 1522) shows.[17] The work, printed at least twelve times from 1515 on, is in fact a sermon, as Pietro declares in the foreword.[18] In order to help his listeners better understand, he resorts to 'a fictional narration' ('imaginata narratione').[19] The work thus establishes a narrative frame that tells the story of a young merchant who gets lost in a wood and meets a centenarian hermit. The hermit persuades the young man of the importance of being prepared to die; the sermon is interspersed with short dialogues between the two characters. At the end, the young man asks the hermit to answer to his 'beautiful doubts' ('belli dubii') — he has twelve of them, and, interestingly, in the running titles at the top of the pages they are designated as 'questions' ('quesiti'), which highlights how doubt and question could be, and in fact often were, synonyms (as we have seen with St Birgitta's *Book of Questions*, described in the Introduction).[20] The strong didactic features of the work are emphasized (at least in the edition I consulted) by the numerous woodcuts that although very simple in style are nevertheless placed in dialogue with the text, accurately illustrating the correspondent passages.

The template of the *Elucidarium* was successful and continued well into the Counter-Reformation, as the *Specchio spirituale* by the Milanese *minore osservante* Angelo Elli shows. Elli (1557?–1617) wrote his work in 1595, as he himself declares in its last lines. It was printed in Brescia in 1596 and again in 1598 and 1599; in total, it went through eleven editions up until 1755. The complete title reads *Specchio spirituale del principio, e fine della vita humana; diviso e distinto in quindici ragionamenti et in cento cinquanta dubbi principali fatti tra 'l maestro e il suo discepolo in dialogo* (Spiritual mirror of the beginning and end of human life; divided and distinguished in fifteen dialogues and in one hundred and fifty principal doubts discussed in a dialogue between a master and his disciple).[21] The dialogue between student and master is meant to elucidate doubts concerning past or future events (death, the Last

Judgement, etc.). In the foreword (*Proemio*) to the work the number of doubts is increased to two hundred, which reflects their actual number. These doubts should prove useful for every 'spiritual person' possessed of 'holy and sincere curiosity', particularly because, Elli argues, they have actually been asked of him in the past and are thus connected with his pastoral practice. Yet an edition of the work features in the Index of Prohibited Books in 1714 for a series of passages dealing with evil spirits, their apparitions, and their influence.[22] Stirring up doubts could lead, even unintentionally, down a slippery path.

Examples like these could be easily multiplied. They show a certain degree of overlap between the practice of asking questions and the habit of doubting, suggesting that in the rapidly expanding world of the printing press, knowledge was growing equally rapidly. In virtually all fields new opinions, different explanations, and possible views were made available. In a highly vocal society one should also take into account the interplay between orality and print culture: the practice of common reading, discussions, and listening to popular preachers fostered the overlapping of diverse and at times discordant voices.[23] This again does not point to any kind of scepticism but rather testifies to the need to master the intricacies of a new culture. So, for example, in a city like Ferrara, where Calvinist ideas circulated, the doctor Antonio Musa Brasavola embarked on writing a long 'Life of Christ'. The work, begun in 1540/41, was cast in the form of a dialogue with Eleonora d'Este, daughter of Alfonso I, Duke of Ferrara, and Lucrezia Borgia, and recorded a real encounter.[24] In the dialogue, Eleonora, a nun in the Franciscan monastery of the Corpus Domini, voices her need to learn more about the life of Christ, since she has heard different preachers express different versions of it. When she turned to the Gospels, she found that they disagree on many points. She has therefore summoned Brasavola, asking six fellow nuns to join them sitting in a circle, and begins to interrogate him. As Adriano Prosperi suggests, '[W]e see in Eleonora a determination not to be a passive listener, which [...] finds its expression in the form of doubt.'[25] The conversation begins, in Brasavola's words, from a place 'most serious and more intricate than the labyrinth', with questions that human reason can hardly solve.[26] These doubts concern, among other matters, reasons for the creation of the world and human beings, the original sin, why God became a man, and why God created the world at the precise moment he did. And yet, the first question that Eleonora asks is whether God exists. The work, despite its Savonarolian inspiration and its attacks on the corruption of the church, does not stray from orthodoxy. At the same time the many doubts voiced by Eleonora in this long dialogue spell out the need to understand, to make sense of problems, contradictions, and uncertain aspects of Catholic devotion. While the resolution of doubts is instrumental to the didactic format of the master-disciple dialogue, in this work one perceives a real desire to venture into the encyclopedic and, in Brasavola's words, labyrinthine world of Catholic belief.

So much for the ambiguity between 'doubt' and 'question': it is time to turn to vocabularies and see what the standard definitions of doubt were and what their implications could be.

Definitions and Etymologies

Perusing medieval and early modern vocabularies can be a taxing exercise for historians, who have to make their way through definitions at times exceedingly laconic, at times impossibly verbose. In the case of doubt, the exercise is worth the effort, for the vocabularies (I am using this term in a rather loose sense) yield some interesting definitions. These definitions have two elements in common, which we may respectively term visual and emotional. The visual element of doubt is mostly connected, through a questionable etymology, to the idea of a crossroads, the point from which two or more paths depart. As for the emotional element, doubt is often connected with fear. 'To doubt' means in several languages 'to be uncertain of something', but also 'to be afraid of something'. What are we afraid of when we doubt? Most of the time we fear that the path we have not taken, the choice we have not made was the correct and safe one.

Already in the seventh century CE, Isidore of Seville, in Book x of his *Etymologies*, defined 'doubtful' as 'uncertain, as if in two directions' ('Dubius, incertus; quasi duarum viarum').[27] A few centuries later, Uguccione da Pisa, scholar and Bishop of Ferrara (from 1190 to his death in 1210), elaborated on the image of the crossroads in his *Derivationes*. He suggested, in a somewhat tortuous way, that the verb *dubitare* (to doubt) could be a contraction of an earlier expression along the lines of *duabus viis bitare*. The expression, based on a slightly grammatically incorrect use of the verb *bito* (to proceed, but also to arrive at), could be approximately translated as 'to proceed until a crossroads'. The second option Uguccione offers for the etymology of *dubitare* is more straightforward: the verb could be explained as *duivitare*, hesitating between two directions.[28] In any case, the idea of a crossroads, the point where two (or more) ways converge, seems to be inscribed in the very word *dubium*. Doubt as the condition of someone faced by two equivalent options also surfaces in Dante's *Divine Comedy*:

> Between two foods, equally at hand and tempting
> Left free to choose, a man would die of hunger
> Before he could bring either to his teeth —
> So would stand still, caught between the cravings
> Of two ferocious wolves, in equal fear of both,
> So would a hound, stock-still between two does:
> Just so, if I kept silent, urged in equal measure,
> By my doubts, I merit neither praise nor blame,
> Since my silence was forced, not freely chosen.[29]

Finding the correct origin of the term 'doubt' must have been an appealing challenge for scholars, who show some degree of creativity in their efforts. This is the case, for example, for Nicolò Perotti (1430–1480), a celebrated humanist and man of the church. His work *Cornucopiae*, which he dedicated to Federico da Montefeltro, Duke of Urbino, originated as a commentary on Martial but soon turned into a *summa* of humanistic knowledge, replete with philological and linguistic discussions.[30] According to Perotti, *dubius* was a constructed word coming from the preposition *de* (from) and the verb *habeo* (to have). The resulting word points to the lack of something, which Perotti identifies as comprehension. Being doubtful therefore means to be lacking in understanding.[31] Later in the text, Perotti reverts to a more traditional explanation of 'doubt': 'And so *dubium* includes two ways, so that "doubtful" is said as if someone had two ways and chose one without knowing.'[32] Perotti somehow adds a step to the traditional etymology: the person who arrives at the crossroads now takes one of the two ways, but does so without knowing why.

Perotti's *Cornucopiae* served as a model for the so-called *Calepinus*, possibly the most successful Renaissance vocabulary, published by the humanist Ambrogio Calepio (1435–1511) in 1502. Calepio, who quotes Perotti almost verbatim, offers the following definition of 'doubtful' (curiously, he does not have one for 'doubt'): 'He is said to be doubtful who has two possible ways and chooses one without knowing.'[33] In the following year, 1503, another reference work came out that was destined to enjoy a widespread and steady success until 1681. Titled *Polyanthea*, the text was the work of a doctor and man of the church from Savona, Domenico Nani Mirabelli.[34] His definition of doubt sums up all the previous ones and is therefore particularly rich. In fact, Mirabelli claims not to be a *sapiens* and therefore unable to provide the definition of words. What he does instead is list all the available definitions. He also distinguishes between *dubitatio* and *dubium* (although the two words are overlapping), since both words are available to designate the same process:

> *Dubitatio* means the acknowledgement of both parties because of the lack of discernment, accompanied with fear, and inability to accept either of them.

> *Dubium*. According to Isidore in his Book of Etymologies, doubt is an undifferentiated movement between the two parts of a contradiction.

> Doubt is the equivalence of two opposite reasons according to the Philosopher [Aristotle].

> Doubt is composed of *de* and *habeo* as, as if *dehabens*, that is, deprived of comprehension [...].[35]

In the mid-cinquecento, the Ferrarese humanist Francesco Alunno connects doubt with fortune in *Della fabbrica del mundo* (The machinery of the world, 1546).[36] In this work, Alunno tries to combine a vocabulary based largely — but not only — on the 'Three Crowns' (Dante, Petrarch, and Boccaccio) with a sort of encyclopedia centred on a cosmological structure. The work is organized according to different cosmological entities (God, Sky, World, Elements, etc.), and to each of them Alunno assigns certain words, based on their affinity to that particular entity. Each section is then organized into subdivisions. We find 'doubt' in the section on 'Sky', under the subdivision 'Fortune'. The sky is connected with destiny and the eternal appearing and disappearing of things, which are ruled by fortune; it is only natural that doubt, the quintessence of instability, finds its place in such company. Alunno distinguishes between 'doubt' as a noun ('dubitatione') and as an adjective ('dubbio'). In the earlier editions of *Della fabbrica*, doubt is not defined; rather, the author provides its Latin equivalent ('dubium') and a series of examples of its use.[37] In later editions, doubt as a noun is connected with other nouns (which Alunno gives in their Latin form) such as 'ambiguity' ('ambiguitas'), 'hesitation' ('haesitatio'), and 'scruple' ('scruple'). As an adjective, 'doubt' is connected with words such as 'ancipital' ('anceps'), 'uncertain' ('incertus'), 'ambiguous' ('ambiguus'), 'suspicious' ('suspiciosus'), and 'varied' (varius). This showcases the richness of the early modern vocabulary of uncertainty: doubt is connected with ideas such as instability, ambiguity, variety, duplicity.[38]

In Aldo Manuzio the Younger's *Eleganze*, doubt is described under the entry 'dubio' and under that of 'animo dubioso' (doubtful soul) as the condition of being torn between two options or thoughts.[39] In Girolamo Garimberti's *Concetti divinissimi* (Most divine concepts, printed twenty-two times from 1550 to 1596), doubt or 'dubitare' is defined as 'a certain suspension of the soul' ('una certa sospensione d'animo') concerning our trust in others, the soul, our strength, our judgement.[40] Garimberti's is a rhetorical work aiming to instruct readers on how, under which terms, and in which of the three rhetorical genres certain conditions of the soul can be employed to persuade with 'probable or apparent reasons'.[41] The *concetti* that apply to the act of doubting apply also to that of 'temere' (to fear, to be afraid of).[42] In addition, doubting is compared to distrusting ('diffidare'), with the difference that doubt 'is accompanied by an ambiguity of the soul', whereas those who distrust seem to show a certain degree of firmness (having already made up their mind as to the unreliable nature of something).[43]

The aforementioned books, along with several others, were proper intellectual 'utensils'.[44] They provided writers and poets with the building blocks for their works: not only words and definitions but also quotations, making readily available the rhetorical and lexical richness of antiquity. As Renaissance literature was largely based on reuse, rewriting, plagiarism, and imitation, the importance of these works can hardly be underestimated.[45]

Standing at the Crossroads

Doubt is thus associated with fear and mistrust, but also with the condition of being stuck between two options, as with a person standing at the crossroads. This definition is at the basis of the allegorical descriptions of doubt codified later in the century, if not in the early seventeenth century when Cesare Ripa included doubt among the allegories of his *Iconologia*. It appears that doubt had not received a proper iconography until that moment. For example, it is not included in the *Dictionary of Iconography*, a manuscript produced in the last quarter of the sixteenth century and now housed in the Getty Institute in Los Angeles. The manuscript lists some four hundred allegorical personifications, many taken from descriptions and accounts of masquerades and ceremonies held in Florence on diverse occasions; other personifications are from Giorgio Vasari's *Ragionamenti*. However, doubt is not included among these.[46] Nor have I found references to doubt in works such as Pierio Valeriano's *Hieroglyphica* or in other common repertories of images. Even its representation in emblems seems to have been quite scarce. This suggests that it took some time for doubt to enter the mental landscape of early modern Italians as a recognizable object of discourse.

FIG. 1.1. 'Dubbio', in *Iconologie ou la science des emblemes, devises, etc.* [...] *par J.[ean] B.[audoin]*, 1 (Amsterdam: Adrian Baakman, 1698), p. 66.

It is to Ripa's *Iconologia* that we must turn, then, if we want to understand how early modern people imagined doubt. The work was first published in 1593 without images, which were added with subsequent printings; it was reprinted several times, becoming a handbook for whoever wanted to paint or fresco allegorical images. Ripa provides three possible allegorical representations of doubt. The first, and the most detailed (Figure 1.1), describes doubt as

> [a] young man beardless, in darkness, dressed in clothing of changing colours, he shall hold a lantern in one hand and stick in the other; he will extend his left foot to show that he is walking. Doubt is an ambiguity of the mind, concerning knowledge and, as a consequence, [an ambiguity] also of the body, concerning action. It is painted as a young man because people of this age, not being well trained in pure and simple truth, easily call everything into doubt and equally easily give their assent to different things. The stick and the lantern mean experience and reason, with which help doubt easily walks or stops. The darkness symbolizes the variety of human discourses, because of which it [doubt] is unable to rest, always walking new ways, and therefore it is depicted extending its left foot.[47]

As Sonia Maffei notes in her commentary to the text, the personification of doubt recalls the iconology of the pilgrim, or wanderers such as St Christopher or the philosopher Diogenes. Some of the elements that accompany Doubt — the walking stick, the symbolism of the wandering man, the dialectic between light and darkness — allow a comparison of Ripa's allegory of Doubt to that of Error (Figure 1.2):

FIG. 1.2. 'Errore', in Cesare Ripa, *Nova iconologia* (Padua: Tozzi, 1618), p. 165.

A man almost dressed like a rover, blindfolded, groping around with his stick, as if trying his way to find assurance, and it always goes with Ignorance. According to the Stoics, error means losing your way and deviating from your path, in the same way as not erring means walking a straight line without faltering in this way or the other, so that we can say that all our workings, both of the body and the mind, are always part of our travel or pilgrimage, at the end of which, if we do not err, we hope to reach happiness. [...] Being blindfolded means that when the light of the intellect is darkened by the veil of worldly interests, one easily incurs error. The stick with which he [Error] is trying his way represents the senses — in the same way the eyes represent the intellect — because, just as they are more corporeal, so its [the intellect's] acts are less connected with the senses and more spiritual [...].[48]

In both cases, Ripa emphasizes the metaphors of wandering (or pilgrimage) and blindness, and in both cases, he stresses how Doubt and Error affect the workings of the body as well as those of the mind. These allegories can be compared to those of Habit ('Consuetudine') and Knowledge ('Dottrina'). Knowledge (Figure 1.3) is represented as a mature woman dressed in a scarlet robe, symbolizing gravitas; she is sitting, holding a sceptre crowned by a radiant sun and holding an open book with her other hand. From the sky dew rains down, symbolizing knowledge. In turn, the sceptre with the sun represents 'doctrine's supremacy over the horrors of the night of ignorance'.[49] Habit is represented as a wandering man, like Error and Doubt. But in this case, it is a white-bearded old man whom experience has made expert; therefore, he is not blindfolded. He also holds a stick and a scroll with the motto 'We gather strength as we go'.[50]

FIG. 1.3. 'Dottrina', in Cesare Ripa, *Nova iconologia* (Padua: Tozzi, 1618), p. 152.

Ripa provides two further allegories of Doubt. The first represents a man holding a wolf by its ears; according to an ancient proverb, this meant being uncertain about a decision, because deciding to let the wolf loose would be to risk one's life, while perpetually holding on to the wolf would be absurd and impossible.[51] The final allegory shows a naked man uncertain about which of three possible ways to take:

> A naked man, pensive, who is at the crossroads of two or three ways: he will look confused for not being able do decide which path to take. And this kind of doubt has a hopeful outcome while the other [the person holding the wolf] entails the fear of a negative outcome, and he is naked for being irresolute.[52]

The subject of a man standing at a crossroads recalls the iconography of Hercules at the crossroads between vice and virtue. However, Ripa was also familiar with the sceptical tradition, as the reference to the three ways suggests. In the entry for 'Investigazione' (Investigation, or Research), included in the *Iconologia* starting from 1613 edition (Figure 1.4),[53] Ripa characterizes it as

> [a] woman with wings on her head, whose dress is sprinkled with ants. She raises her right arm and the index finger of the same hand, pointing to a crane flying in the air and with the pointing finger of her left hand a dog who holds his head to the ground, looking for the quarry. [...] As to the meaning of the dog, the philosopher Sextus Empiricus writes, first book, chap. 14, that the dog in the described position means Investigation, because when it is after its quarry and it reaches a crossroads of three ways, without seeing which way the quarry took, after smelling the first path, it smells the second; and if it does not

INVESTIGATIONE.

FIG. 1.4. 'Investigazione', in Cesare Ripa, *Nova iconologia* (Padua: Tozzi, 1618), p. 267.

smell that the quarry has taken either of them, it does not smell the third, but it is resolute in running, reasoning that the quarry must necessarily have taken the third [path].[54]

The exemplum of the dog comes from Sextus Empiricus's *Outlines of Pyrrhonism*, where one reads the following passage:

> And, according to Chrysippus, who shows special interest in irrational animals, the dog even shares in the far-famed Dialectic. This person, at any rate, declares that the dog makes use of the fifth complex indemonstrable syllogism when, on arriving at a spot where three ways meet, after smelling at the two roads by which the quarry did not pass, it rushes off at once by the third without stopping to smell. For, says the old writer, the dog implicitly reasons thus: 'The creature went either by this road, or by that, or by the other; but it did not go by this road or by that; therefore, it went by the other.'[55]

Sextus Empiricus aims to demonstrate that

> [a]nimals having disparate perceptual experience, none of them enjoys a better grasp of the nature of things in themselves, and thus all we can do is to state how things appear to be to us in each case, advancing no claim on the real nature of what is in question.[56]

What is relevant in Ripa's *Iconologia* is that the iconographies of Doubt and Investigation show a different take on the crossroads. While in the first case the choice between alternatives seems to paralyse the young man standing naked in front of them, in the second the dog is able to reason correctly, leading it to the desired conclusion. Doubt, however, is also able to set knowledge in motion or rejuvenate it, dismantling old opinions and replacing them with more correct ones.

FIG. 1.5. 'Qua Dii vocant, eundum', in Andrea Alciato,
Emblemata cum commentarijs amplissimis
(Padua: apud Petrum Paulum Tozzium, 1621), p. 52.

The image of the crossroads was not invented by Ripa; it had enjoyed ample circulation in the sixteenth century. It features, for example, in Erasmus's *Adagia* and particularly in I. ii. 48, 'In trivio sum':

> Ἐν τριόδῳ εἰμὶ λογισμῶν I am at the crossroads of decision. This is applied to those who are in doubt and of uncertain mind, hesitating as to which alternative to choose, like travellers who come to a place where three roads meet, and are doubtful about which way to take. 'Way' or 'path' is often used by Greek authors to mean a choice of plan.[57]

Erasmus compares doubt to the situation of a traveller reaching a crossroads where three roads meet. The image of a three-way crossroads also appears in some editions of Andrea Alciato's *Emblemata*, one of the most successful European collections of emblems. Originally printed in Augsburg in 1531, the *Emblemata* circulated all over Europe in Latin as well as in French, Italian, Spanish, and German translations. Among the emblems, one titled 'One must go where the Gods call him' ('Qua Dii vocant, eundum') uses the idea of three roads crossing. In it, a statue of Mercury, god of travellers, presides over the crossroads. Travellers are called to hang wreaths on the statue of the god, who points them in the right direction. Alciato provides a philosophical reading of his emblem centred around the idea that all humans are travellers standing at the crossroads, and all would take the wrong way unless God shows them the right path:

> At a parting of the ways, there is a hillock of stones. Rising above it is a half-statue of a god, fashioned as far down as the chest. So the hill is Mercury's. Travellers, hang wreaths in honour of the god who points out the road to you. We are all at the crossroads, and on this track of life we go wrong unless God himself shows us the way.[58]

There are several images for this particular emblem in the different editions of Alciato's work, but the crossroads is especially evident in the one printed in 1621 in Padua (Figure 1.5).[59] However, it would appear that no codified iconography of doubt existed before the end of the century. The emergence of this iconography thus points to the growing relevance of doubt as a cultural object in contemporary culture. While there were attempts at creating personifications of doubt, it was not until Ripa's authoritative manual that one such personification came fully to existence.

Learning to Distinguish

As we have seen, doubt could be connected with words like 'suspicion' and 'scruple', which pointed to the Scholastic philosophical and theological vocabulary. In the fifteenth and sixteenth centuries these words enjoyed a renewed circulation in manuals for confessors. Turning to this particular kind of text is useful for understanding the constellation of words of uncertainty and the experiences they designated. Behind the subtle theological distinctions there lay in fact real people with feelings whose causes, much like early modern confessors, we must learn to discern. Crucial definitions of doubt were elaborated in the field of moral theology by confessors who, building on the Scholastic tradition, felt the need to make accurate distinctions between competing forms of uncertainty. In manuals (or *summae*) for confessors we find insightful reflections on doubt as opposed to apparently similar forms of uncertainty, as in this explanation: 'Doubt, according to St Isidore in the book of Etymologies, is an undifferentiated movement between the two parts of a contradiction. Or, one could say, doubt is the equality of opposite reasons, according to the Philosopher.'[60]

Isidore and Aristotle provided the Franciscan Angelo da Chivasso (*c.* 1410–1495) with the two definitions of doubt that, with few variations, we encounter in almost all manuals for confessors. The highly influential *Summa Angelica* — a collection of cases of conscience that took its name from its author — was printed at least twenty-four times between 1486 and 1628. Organized, as is often the case with these texts, in encyclopedic form with the entries in alphabetical order, the *Summa* was easy to consult. Under 'Openione', Friar Angelo, building on Thomas Aquinas, ventures into a series of distinctions between 'doubt', 'opinion', 'faith', 'science', and 'scruple'. These distinctions may appear to us of an entirely intellectual nature, but early modern Europeans would have thought otherwise. Nurturing doubt was deeply different from having scruples. Both conditions could be considered an illness of the soul (and of the body as well), yet doubt entailed the danger of committing capital sin, whereas scruples were usually regarded as leading to petty sins. These definitions were fundamental for confessors, who were called to ascertain the degree of uncertainty of their penitents and soothe their remorseful souls. Friar Angelo therefore writes:

> Opinion is the intellect's consent to something not because it is sufficiently moved by its proper object but because of a certain reasonable choice that leads it to incline voluntarily towards one part more than towards the other, yet being doubtful and being afraid of the other part [...]. But faith comes with certainty and without this fear. Science is instead the consent of the intellect, which is moved by an object known in itself, as is the case with the first principles. [...] Doubt is an undifferentiated movement between the two parts of a contradiction [...]. Scruple is when the intellect inclines towards one part because of weak conjectures [...]. And this is called also suspicion and pusillanimity of the soul, which we must dispel.[61]

We find the same distinctions in another best-seller of the genre, the *Manuale de' confessori* (A manual for confessors) by the Spaniard Martín de Azpilcueta (1492–1586), better known as Dr Navarrus. A theologian and an economist, Azpilcueta spent the final years of his life in Rome. His work was first published in Portuguese in 1552 and between 1564 and 1629 was printed in Italy ninety times; to these editions one should add those of his *Opera omnia* and the editions published outside Italy.[62] According to Navarrus, too, who is in turn relying on Thomas Aquinas, science and faith represent a form of true knowledge, although science is more certain since it is a judgement on what we see, whereas faith is a judgement concerning what we cannot see.[63] By contrast, opinion, doubt, and scruple represent uncertain forms of understanding and knowledge; science and doubt represent respectively the maximum and the minimum of certainty on this scale.[64]

I shall pause briefly to draw attention here the immense early modern output of manuals for confessors: more than three hundred titles appeared in the period between the 1470s and the mid-1600s (amounting to some thirteen hundred editions).[65] These texts found their way not only to ecclesiastical libraries but also to the private libraries of lay devotees, both noble and bourgeois.[66] They contained collections of cases of conscience, that is, moral problems that often challenged traditional doctrine. Moral dilemmas plagued the souls of both confessors and devotees; particularly in the rapidly evolving post-Trent world, scruples and doubts multiplied as the economy grew more complicated than ever, science posed new challenges, and the increasingly connected world offered Europeans novelties that affected their everyday lives.[67] Moral theologians built collections of hundreds, if not thousands, of such cases to offer confessors reliable guidance, alleviating at once believers' and confessors' anxieties regarding what was and what was not permitted. For example, Marco Scarsella, a theologian from Tolentino in the Marche but active in Venice, gathered seven thousand cases in the first edition of his *Giardino di sommisti* (1589), and by the time he published the second edition in 1592 he had twelve thousand.

The cases of conscience covered all aspects of human activity, from sexual practices to economics, and therefore represent an invaluable source for understanding a large portion of early modern life. Cases of conscience entailed a degree of uncertainty and the necessity to apply general principles to specific cases; traditional doctrine could not account for all possible events, which could often be addressed only on the basis of probable opinions.[68] Confessors had to understand whether an opinion concerning a given action was truly probable, and whether and why a different opinion was more probable, and therefore morally safer (according to 'tutiorism', one should always stick to the more probable and safer opinion).[69] 'Probable' meant that something — in this case an opinion — could be proved (*probabilis*) on the basis of authorities and tradition, and 'opinion' did not have the highly subjective meaning we nowadays assign to this word.[70] A probable opinion was, in other words, a considered judgement, an arguable position on something which, despite not having the full certainty of a scientific judgement, was nevertheless true or true enough to provide safe ground for a moral choice. In the case of real doubt, no opinion could be found to support a decision and therefore the individual should refrain from acting; in all other cases, uncertainty could be overcome with the help of carefully selected opinions.

Starting in the fifteenth century, some theologians suggested that a certain degree of freedom could be allowed in moral choices. This was likely connected to the growing complexity of society and to the rise of new types of cases of conscience (*casus conscientiae*) that had been unknown to medieval society.[71] Theologians proposed that it was not always necessary to accept the safest option as long as the chosen one was safe. This new position opened the path to the doctrine later known as probabilism, elaborated in the mid-sixteenth century at the School of Granada and subsequently adopted by Jesuits.[72] Daniel Schwartz suggests that probabilism must be considered as a doctrine not addressed to a 'moral agent in doubt' but rather to 'moral experts, principally confessors and moral theologians'. Probabilism acknowledges that multiple possible opinions exist; from the point of view of the 'moral expert' it means 'taking into account one's fallibility' and acknowledging 'the advisee's epistemic position' (that of being unable to distinguish between the many opinions of the learned theologians).[73] Certainly, agents were under no circumstance permitted to make moral decisions light-heartedly, without a thorough examination of the different options.[74] Yet individual conscience came to have a more sizeable role in comparison to the law when it came to moral decisions. The effect was that

> [f]or late scholastic writers, [...] probabilistic reasoning could soothe an agent's anxiety in a difficult situation of moral choice by diffusing the psychological burden imposed by an over scrupulous conscience. The aim of the probabilistic method was always to show that we need not be paralysed by hesitation in a case of conscience just because our moral judgments can not make a claim to demonstrative certainty.[75]

At the same time, the notion of scruple came to occupy an increasing space in theological reflection.[76] Jean Delumeau has argued that scruple became a veritable disease in the period between the fifteenth and the eighteenth centuries. This was a new development, since Aquinas, as Delumeau points out, did not address scruple. It was only in the later Middle Ages, by the end of the fifteenth century, that a 'scrupulous religious anxiety had [...] become a phenomenon of European civilization'.[77] Scruples typically concerned sexual temptations and imaginings as well as blasphemy, since an excessive fear of God's punishment could lead to anger against Him. The inability to distinguish between venial and deadly sins pushed devotees to an excess of self-examination and an abuse of confession. Although women and simple folk were especially inclined to fall prey to scruples, this was by no means an experience peculiar to the lower classes. Theologians began to explore the world of doubt, distinguishing between doubt and scruple or between 'speculative' and 'practical' doubts, building on refined philosophical notions such as that of 'probable certainty', thus extending further the boundaries of uncertainty.[78] The Dominican and Maestro di Sacro Palazzo Silvestro Mazzolini (1456/57–1527), in his *Summa summarum*, also known as the *Summa Silvestrina*, argued that doubt has a double nature ('dubium est duplex'). He distinguished between a 'probable' doubt (proper doubt) and 'dubium scrupulosum'. Doubt is 'scrupulosum' when someone is uncertain because of a weak suspicion of having committed a sin. This kind of doubt can and must be swiftly resolved by resorting to the advice of a 'good man' ('ad consilium boni viri').[79] It is by contrast a grave and possibly mortal sin to expose oneself to proper doubt, on the assumption that 'risking to commit a capital sin was already a capital sin'.[80] The definition of doubt provided by Mazzolini differs slightly from those we have so far considered: he states that doubt is probable when 'the probable reasons towards the two sides are almost equal'.[81] It has been suggested that this could possibly be the first mention of equal probability 'in a systematic discussion of the choice of opinions. [...] The main point is that Mazzolini does not only refer to equally strong reasons but to (roughly) probable reasons that are equal'.[82] Moreover, scholars have noted that both Scholastic and humanistic traditions 'increasingly began to use the notion of equi-probability in the decades following 1500 [...]. The earliest uses in the sixteenth century [...] were in commentaries or works on moral theology'.[83] For our present purposes, this is a striking observation that helps place the rise of notions such as equi-probability and undecidability in the early decades of the sixteenth century. At a time of the revival of ancient scepticism, moral theology too, elaborating on the concept of doubt, stressed the impasse arising from 'an equal balance of reasons or evidence'.[84] We may well consider the appearance of such notions as the sign of an increased weight of doubt in Renaissance culture. That it was moral theologians who elaborated on such notion should not surprise us. In fact, doubt affects our capability of making a rational choice and exposes us to mortal sin:

> Believing or doubting whether a given action is a deadly sin [...] comes from having reasons for each part. Because of this, in such a condition of doubt ['dubitanza'], man, in order not to sin, must choose the best part, because if he chooses that which seems bad to him and not supported by reasons, he will always sin.[85]

This crystal-clear rule was not always easy to follow in real life. In fact, one was required to obey to one's conscience, even if this meant committing a wrongful action, for acting against one's conscience was a graver sin. If a person thought that a given act, in a given time (here and now, so to speak) was right, then they were required to perform it, even if they did not know whether this act was permitted in general (this amounts to the distinction between epistemic and practical doubt). In this way, early modern theologians came to build a taxonomy of conscience distinguishing, as for example Azpilcueta (Navarrus) does in his *Manuale*, between a certain, doubtful, and scrupulous conscience:

> Conscience too is divided into sure, doubtful, and scrupulous. Certain conscience is the one that judges something to be true. Doubtful conscience is the one that judges equally true something and its contrary. Scrupulous conscience is the one that judges something to be true but acknowledges an argument or some appearance against such judgement.[86]

As Azpilcueta puts it, 'sure conscience' can be based on science, faith, or opinion, and can be either true or false — moral certainty having nothing to do with intellectual knowledge. What really matters is that if one feels that an act is absolutely morally sure, one must perform it: 'the man to whom she [i.e., con-science] dictates that he must kill, must commit this act, for he would sin if he did not kill'.[87] Distinguishing between these different kinds of conscience became an imperative task for confessors.[88]

If scruple is, in a certain way, less dangerous than doubt, it is potentially more destructive, an insidious illness rising from the 'pusillanimity of the soul' ('pusill-animitas spiritus').[89] Unlike doubt, and because of its ambiguous nature, halfway between the bodily and the spiritual realm, scruple can and must be cured. This is because pusillanimity (lack of determination, timidity) causes spiritual turmoil, turmoil produces desperation, and desperation eventually kills (the body and the soul).⁹⁰ Mazzolini furnishes some causes for the excess of scruple. First, this particular weakness of the soul can be caused by a cold or melancholic complexion, naturally inclined to fear. A severe illness affecting the anterior section of the brain, impacting on the faculty of imagination, can produce scrupulosity. The illness of melancholy, affecting the middle section of the brain and impairing the faculty of reason, can produce the same effect. Also among the causes of pusillanimity are the physical weakness produced by an excess of fasting or a protracted wake, the company of other 'scrupulosi', or the devil's temptations.⁹¹ Surprisingly, the first and foremost cure against scrupulosity is not spiritual: it consists in 'medicines and moderate recreations' ('per medecinas et moderatas recreationes') that take away the cause of scruple, that is, the physical condition of illness.⁹² Other remedies of a spiritual nature follow closely the list provided by Antonino da Firenze (Antonino Pierozzi, 1389–1459), Mazzolini's source for this section.⁹³

Mazzolini in fact relies heavily on the *Summa sacrae theologiae* (1440–59) by Antonino da Firenze, the Archbishop of Florence. In the chapter on conscience, one of the subsections is dedicated to 'scrupulous conscience'. According to Antonino, 'pusillanimitas' is a 'disordered fear' ('inordinatum timorem').⁹⁴ He follows Albertus Magnus's distinctions between science, faith, opinion, doubt, and scruple, whereas other theologians draw on Thomas Aquinas, as we have seen.⁹⁵ Again, these seemingly abstract distinctions are in fact necessary to ascertain a specific bodily, spiritual, and psychological condition. It is only thanks to the correct application of these categories that the confessor, like a good doctor (Antonino stresses the importance of turning to 'moral doctors', 'morales medicos'), can identify the symptoms of a specific moral disease and cure it. In the particular case of scruple — also called 'wrongful conscience, or fear of the conscience, or pusillanimity' — confessors face an insidious condition of uncertainty.⁹⁶ Later on, apparently, scruple came to coincide with moral uncertainty at large; according to the seventeenth-century theologian Raffaele Grillenzoni, scruple is also called 'trepidation, fear, pusillanimity, melancholy, madness, anguish, sadness, and doubt, for scruple is always accompanied by doubt'.⁹⁷ As another theologian put it, 'arrogance and self-esteem' are scruple's real mother, and 'folly, weakness of judgment, a sick fantasy' are its 'wet nurse'.⁹⁸

Antonino da Firenze describes scruple (or suspicion, 'suspicio') as a sort of sadness that 'burdens the soul' ('aggravantem animam') and 'consumes the strength' ('consumit vigorem').⁹⁹ This sadness is often prompted by a cold complexion, characteristic of, for example, 'old and melancholic women'.¹⁰⁰ It sometimes originates from madness or melancholy, diseases that, as we have seen, damage the imagination or reason.¹⁰¹ Negligence of one's bodily regime can also lead to scruple: not only a lack of sleep or an excess of fasting but also the 'continuous recitation of Psalms or of offices'.¹⁰² Typically, the scrupulous person recites their devotions but gets distracted or is under the impression that they were not paying enough attention. They thus begin anew, fearing they may have offended God. Sometimes it is the devil who provokes scruples by moving, with God's permission, the 'melancholic humours', thus altering the faculty of imagination and raising disordered fears.¹⁰³ The companionship of fearful people can also foster scruples: 'unus scrupulosus facit alium scrupulosum'.[104] Scruple is thus placed at the intersection of the bodily, mental, and social realm. Besides, uncertainty and doubt cannot be disconnected from the backdrop of late medieval spirituality, suggesting the ambiguity of what will later be labelled ceremonies, or exterior signs of devotion. Paradoxically, the same practices that were meant to assure future salvation could instead lead not only to mental disorder but also to spiritual desperation and therefore to one's spiritual death.

The person assailed by excessive scruples could, however, resort to suitable medicines. First of all, this individual should turn to 'moral doctors, prelates and confessors and apt consultants'.[105] Antonino suggests seven useful practices to adhere to in order to overcome one's scruples: (1) preparation for receiving God's grace (by acknowledging and confessing one's sins); (2) the 'careful study of Holy Scripture'; (3) 'continuous prayer'; (4) following the 'safe choice of someone's opinion'; (5) the 'imitation of humble obedience'; (6) the 'brave demolition of scruples'; and (7) the 'right interpretation of precepts'.[106] The fourth point is the most complicated and requires a long discussion of probable opinions, something Antonino touches upon also in addressing the sixth point, where he articulates the distinction between doubt and scruple. In cases of scruple, in fact, one can always lean towards an interpretation of or opinion on one's condition. Probable reasons and the justifying opinion of 'some doctors [of the church]' ('alicuius doctoris') grant that one does not commit sin, even if this opinion should prove less safe than others, or even wrongful. 'Just as', Antonino writes, 'many ways lead to a city, although one may be safer than the other', so 'some reach the heavenly city by one way, some by another', and all do it 'in a safe way, although some in a safer way.'[107] In this passage, scruples and probable opinions are thus conflated. By contrast, when no opinion makes us lean towards one option or the other, we are in a condition of doubt. Under such a condition, Antonino argues, 'he who performs a doubtful action' is sinful, and 'regardless of whether [this sin] is deadly or not, he commits a mortal sin because he exposes himself to deadly sin'.[108]

The bodily nature of scruple receives constant attention from theologians, who stress how it may result from alterations of the brain, unhealthy lifestyles, and excessive devotional practices. Fear, visions of unreal things, or a generally pathological condition can arise in those who have a special predisposition. Some theologians even list among the consequences of scruple 'madness, syncope, fever, pain'.[109] Specific signs accompany the condition, signs that help understand its origin. For example, if a scruple is caused by 'mania' or 'melancholy', the person subject to it will faint, be suspicious, and inclined to madness, and must be cured by doctors.[110] If instead a scruple comes from natural causes, as it would from a cold and fearful but otherwise healthy disposition, then the person affected by scruple will be suspicious, skittish, hard to satisfy, anxious.[111] Physical and spiritual doctors were called to cooperate in mitigating the effects of moral uncertainty on early modern individual.

This excursion into early modern moral theology shows some of the intricacies of doubt, a multilayered notion that philosophers and theologians carefully distinguished from similar but distinct conditions. The attention paid to doubt, scruple, and their consequences suggests the relevance that moral uncertainty had in the early modern world. We should not assume, however, that the 'anatomy of doubt' we have explored belonged only to the world of theologians. Literature could also help acquaint people with these apparently intricate notions. As a means of concluding this chapter, I will recount one example that shows very well how scruples and doubts could turn into literary characters.

In the official biographies of Filippo Neri we read of two cases in which he delivered individuals from a serious condition of scruple.[112] Neri (1515–1595) preached a spirituality focused on joy and was known in Counter-Reformation Rome as 'the saint of joy'. It is not surprising, then, that he was believed to be particularly effective in curing scruples. The two episodes recorded in his biographies also had a scenic afterlife in a *rappresentazione*, a theatrical piece in five acts on the life of Filippo authored by the Neapolitan Francesco Gizzio (1626–1698), himself a member of Neri's oratory, and published in his *L'echo armoniosa delle sfere celesti* (The harmonious echo of celestial spheres).[113] This work collects discourses on various theological matters as well as Gizzio's seventeen pieces of religious theatre. The text on Filippo Neri bears the clunky title *La conca fatta canale delle grazie* (The basin of graces turned into a channel). In the third scene of the third act, some interesting characters make their appearance on stage: Melancholy and her sons Scrupolo, Scrupoletto, Scrupoluccio, Scrupolino. The names of the children of Lady Melancholy showcase the different levels of intensity of scruple. Each of them boasts about his effectiveness, and in particular Scrupolino prides himself on being able to enter 'cloisters, monasteries, convents, congregations; I take my lodgings in the heart of priests and laypeople; in the conscience of married women and widows, of nuns and *pinzochere*'.[114] Scrupolino specializes in tormenting religious people, but neither does he overlook 'old people, young people, and infants'.[115] Scrupolo and his brothers breathe doubts into the brains of their victims, each one whispering his questions, insinuating possibilities, suggesting possible mistakes, as we see happen in the sixth scene, where each of the scruples asks questions of his victim in rapid succession. The scenic effect must have been entertaining, especially because all the actors were 'young boys and kids' ('garzonetti e figliuoli'), as we read in a prefatory letter to the reader by the printer, Giuseppe De Bonis.[116]

Such works must be set in the context of the Oratorian devotion, in which 'music, little sermons by the children and the Fathers, sometimes some sacred dialogues', as well as mystery plays had a central catechetic role.[117] These representations were performed throughout the year in different parts of town and, as De Bonis recalls, were by no means limited to the internal attendance of the Oratorians. Rather, they took place 'with the attendance, sometimes, [...] of more than five thousand souls of all conditions and profession, of prelates, officials, knights and, in particular, of innumerable religious people of all orders, especially reformed and observant'. The plays were meant to foster a devotion based on emotions, *affetti*, and apparently they reached their goal:

> [S]o great was the pious attention of the spectators who came to these representations that not only common and ordinary people (seeing their own

children who, while acting, shed most tender tears), but even noble, learned, and distinguished people were moved to tears in seeing them and listening to them.[118]

Thus, we can add theatre and literature to the list of cures for scruple recommended by Antonino and his followers. That doubt could leave the realms of philosophy and theology and become a pleasant and entertaining literary object — even a character — should not be taken for granted. The following chapters will reconstruct the history of how and when this became possible.

Notes to Chapter 1

1. See, for example, Michele Savonarola, *Libreto* [...] *de tute le cose che se manzano comunamente e piu che comune, e di quelle se bevono per Italia, e de sei cose non naturale, et le regule per conservare la sanita delli corpi humani con dubij notabilissimi* (Venice: Simone de Luere, 1508; repr. Venice, 1515); Luis Lobera de Avila, *Fabrica del'huomo* [...]. *Aggiuntovi alcune dotte, e curiose dubitationi* [...] (Alessandria: Ercole Quinciano, 1597); *Tesoro di varii secreti naturali. Tratta da diversi auttori famosissimi, & più volte sprementati in molte persone, opera molto giovevole alla sanità de' corpi humani, con la dichiaratione di molti dubij. Et il modo di far e conservar il vino* (Venice: Gio. Battista Bonfadino, 1600).
2. Pietro Aron, *Compendiolo di molti dubbi, segreti, et sentenze intorno al canto fermo et figurato* [...] (Milan: Io. Antonio da Castelliono, c. 1550); Angelo da Pizzighettone, *Fior angelico di musica* [...] *nel qual si contengono alcune bellissime dispute contra quelli che dicono, la musica non esser scienza. Con altre molte questioni, & solutioni di varii dubii* (Venice: Agostino Bindoni, 1547).
3. *Trattato de bagni di Viterbo* [...]. *Nel quale si trattano le qualità, & il valore di essi. Il modo di usarli, la regola del vivere, & alcuni dubbij, curiosi intorno a tal materia* (Viterbo: Agostino Colaldi, 1596).
4. A selection could include Sebastiano Fabrini, *Dichiaratione del giubileo dell'Anno santo. Nel quale si tratta ancora il modo di conseguirlo, & di fare il peregrinaggio di Roma; con la risolutione di molti dubij bellissimi sopra questa materia* (Venice: Fioravante Prati, 1599; repr. twice in Rome, 1600); Niccolò Malnipote, *Il tesoro celeste dell'indulgenza per li vivi, et per li morti.* [...] *Con le resolutioni de molti dubbii* (Naples: Horatio Salviani, 1580; repr. twice in Venice, 1589); Cesare Bottoni, *Osservationi sopra i giubilei* [...]. *Opera utile et necessaria, non solo a semplici, ma anco a persone ecclesiastice per saper rispondere alli dubbij che vengono mossi sopra gli giubilei* (Piacenza: Giovanni Bazachi, 1587; repr. 1589).
5. *Regula del sanctissimo Benedetto patre nostro: Tradutta in quelle parte che conuengono a noi monache; con le declarationi sopra quella, fatte per satisfactione della conscientia delle religiose che viuano sotto la regula del sancto Benedetto della osseruanza regulare composta per commissione & authoritade del nostro reuerendissimo monsignor episcopo circa le dubitationi che possino occorrere in obseruatione de ditta regula* (Venice: a Santo Moyse nelle case noue Iustiniane, appresso il Bastione, per Francesco di Alessandro Bindoni & Mapheo Pasini compagni, 1529). The work was reprinted in Venice, 1532, 1547, 1594; and Palermo, 1589.
6. *Dialogo fra il cathecumino e il padre cathechizante composto per Fabiano Fioghi* [...] *lettore della lingua hebrea nel collegio de neophiti. Nel qual si risolvono molti dubij, li quali sogliono far li hebrei, contro la verità della santa fede christiana* (Rome: heredi d'Antonio Blado, 1582); on the 'doubts' of the Jews, see Martina Mampieri, '"The Jews and Their Doubts": Anti-Jewish Polemics in the *Fascicolo della vanità giudaiche* (1583) by Antonino Stabili', *Yearbook of the Maimonides Centre for Advanced Studies*, 1 (2016), 59–75.
7. *Opera nuovamente composta in la solutione di tre grandissimi dubbi sopra de gli asini, cani, gatti e topi* (Florence: Domenico Celamaio, 1571/72).
8. *Discorsi* [...]. *Con le risposte a tutti i dubbii che in simili materie proponer si sogliono* (Venice: Ziletti, 1585). The work was reprinted in Ferrara, 1586; Verona, 1586; Pavia, 1591; and Venice, 1594.
9. Ryrie, *Unbelievers*, p. 41.
10. 'Huomini ignoranti et grossi, i quali, usati a riprehendere ciò che none intendono, non credono et fannosi beffe di tutti i detti et facti che paiono loro più degni che il loro rozo ingegno non

dimostra potersi fare'; 'tutte le buone et approvate sententie, tutti i notabili exempli et tutti i gloriosi facti degl'huomini virtuosi credono essere non veri, ma come favole et novelli di vechierelle trovati et fincti per dare a veghia agli otiosi dilecto'. Matteo Palmieri, *Vita civile*, ed. by Gino Belloni (Florence: Sansoni, 1982), p. 150.

11. Iolanda Ventura, '*Per modum quaestionis compilatum*: The Collections of Natural Questions and Their Development from the 13th to the 16th Century', in *Allgemeinwissen und Gesellschaft*, ed. by Paul Michel, Madeleine Herren, and Martin Rüesch (Düren: Shaker, 2007), pp. 275–317.

12. Paolo Procaccioli, 'Un cultore del dubbio dell'Italia del Rinascimento: Ortensio Lando', in *Le doute dans l'Europe moderne*, ed. by Élise Boillet and Marco Faini (Turnhout: Brepols, 2022), pp. 189–206.

13. Gabriella Zarri, *Libri di spirito: Editoria religiosa in volgare nei secoli XV–XVII* (Turin: Rosenberg & Sellier, 2009), p. 70.

14. The work enjoyed a wide European circulation: we know of 180 manuscripts and at least 119 editions, twenty-one of which were printed in Italy between 1473 and 1500.

15. This is the case with the Venetian edition of 1523 (Guglielmo da Fontaneto), the 1535 Brescia edition (Damiano & Iacomo Philippo fratelli), and the 1536 Bolognese edition (V. Bonardo da Parma and Marcantonio da Carpo). The title of the work reads in this case *Opera volgare intitolata Specchio de la santa madre Chiesa, ne la quale si dechiarano molte bellissime espositioni e dubii circa la fede nostra* (A vernacular work called mirror of the holy mother church, in which several beautiful declarations and doubts are explained that concern our faith). We learn from the colophon that the Bolognese inquisitor Leandro Alberti had reviewed the work. According to the online catalogue Edit16 <https://edit16.iccu.sbn.it/new-home1>, there is only one extant copy of this work in Italy, in the Biblioteca Comunale Lorenzo Leoni of Todi. A manuscript note declares that it was bought for ten denari in July 1540, probably by one Rev. Argenti de Cesina (?). A later note says that the book belonged to Monte Santo of Forlì (?), probably the Benedictine abbey of Santa Maria del Monte near Cesena.

16. For example, Gabriella Zarri has highlighted how the several passages concerning purgatory in the *Elucidarium* could still be appealing to sixteenth-century readers, particularly at a time when belief in purgatory was under fire; see Zarri, *Libri di spirito*, pp. 30–31.

17. See also the *Dyalogo del maestro e del discepolo* by Antonio da Pinerolo, printed three times between 1539 and 1549; Zarri, *Libri di spirito*, p. 118.

18. Gabriella Zarri, *Le sante vive: Profezie di corte e devozione femminile nella prima età moderna* (Turin: Rosenberg & Sellier, 1990), Chap. 4; Elena Bonora, *I conflitti della Controriforma: Santità e obbedienza nell'esperienza religiosa dei primi barnabiti* (Florence: Le Lettere, 1998), pp. 160–64.

19. *Dottrina del ben morire composta per el reverendo padre Petro da Lucha [...] con molte utile resolutione de alcuni belli dubii theologici* (Venice: per Comino de Luere, 1529), fol. 1^v.

20. Ibid., fol. 24^v. Examples of the young man's doubts include whether we are obliged to desire death, whether we should think badly of those who die of a sudden or violent death, and whether it is licit to pray to a dying person that they appear after their death to reveal their condition, etc. Since some of the questions regarded the state of the soul and its destination immediately after death, as well as when the final judgement takes place, they touched upon potentially critical issues (as we shall see).

21. Brescia: Policreto Turlini, 1598.

22. Pierre Pirri, 'Elli (Ange)', in *Dictionnaire de spiritualité ascétique et mystique*, IV/1 (Paris: Beauchesne, 1960), cols. 599–600; Costanzo Cargnoni et al., *Storia della spiritualità italiana*, ed. by Pietro Zovatto (Rome: Città Nuova, 2002), p. 426. According to Massimo Petrocchi, the work is an early example of the Quietist ideas that were condemned later in the seventeenth century. Petrocchi, *Storia della spiritualità italiana*, II, *Il Cinquecento e il Seicento* (Rome: Edizioni di Storia e Letteratura, 1978), pp. 216–17.

23. On oral culture and its interactions with the printing press, see *Oral Culture in Early Modern Italy: Performance, Language, Religion*, ed. by Stefano Dall'Aglio, Luca Degl'Innocenti, Brian Richardson, Massimo Rospocher, and Chiara Sbordoni (= *The Italianist*, 34 (2014)). On early modern reading practice, see Marina Roggero, *Le vie dei libri: Letture, lingua e pubblico nell'Italia moderna* (Bologna: il Mulino, 2021).

24. The work was probably completed around 1547; see Antonio Musa Brasavola, *La vita di Iesu Cristo*, ed. by Adriano and Anna Prosperi (Turin: Nino Aragno, 2020).

25. 'C'è una determinazione di Elonora nel non voler essere una ascoltatrice passiva che [...] si esprime nella forma del dubbio.' Adriano Prosperi, 'Antonio Musa Brasavola e la sua *Vita di Cristo*: Introduzione', in Brasavola, *La vita di Iesu Cristo*, pp. ix–lxxx (p. liv).

26. 'Perché me occorrono gravissimi dubbi e più intricati del labirinto.' Ibid., 8.

27. Isidoro di Siviglia, *Etimologie o origini*, ed. by Angelo Valastro Canale (Turin: Utet, 2004), I, 810. The English translation is from *The Etymologies of Isidore of Seville*, trans. with introduction and notes by Stephen A. Barney et al. (Cambridge: Cambridge University Press, 2006), p. 217.

28. 'Dubito-as; et est dubitare quasi duabus viis bitare, quod est esse incertum; vel dubitare quasi duivitare, idest duarum viarum esse incertum. Unde dubius, quasi duvius, idest incertus quasi duarum viarum, et comparatur dubius magis dubius, dubiissimus, unde dubie.' Uguccione da Pisa, *Derivationes*, ed. by Enzo Cecchini et al. (Florence: Sismel-Edizioni del Galluzzo, 2004), II, 348. I thank Guido Arbizzoni Artusi for helping me with this passage.

29. Dante Alighieri, *Paradiso*, transl. by Robert Hollander and Jean Hollander (New York: Anchor Books, 2007), pp. 90–91. 'Intra due cibi, distanti e moventi | D'un modo, prima si morria di fame, | Che liber'omo l'un recasse ai denti; | Sì si starebbe un agno intra due brame | Di fieri lupi, igualmente temendo; | Sì si starebbe un cane intra due dame: | Per che, s'i' mi tacea, me non riprendo, | Da li miei dubbi d'un modo sospinto, | Poi ch'era necessario, né commendo.' Dante Alighieri, *Paradiso*, ed. by Anna Maria Chiavacci Leonardi (Milan: Mondadori, 1994), pp. 107–08.

30. It was Federico's son Guidubaldo who sponsored the first printed edition of 1489 (thirty-eight were to follow until 1536); Paolo D'Alessandro, 'Perotti, Niccolò', in *Dizionario biografico degli italiana*, LXXXII (Rome: Istituto dell'Enciclopedia italiana, 2015) <http://www.treccani.it/enciclopedia/niccolo-perotti_(Dizionario-Biografico)/> [accessed 21 May 2020].

31. 'Item ex *de* et *habeo* componitur dubius quasi dehabens, hoc est, non intelligens.' Nicolò Perotti, *Cornucopiae sive commentarii linguae latinae* [...] (Milan: Giovanni Maria De Ferrariis, 1506), col. 579; my italics.

32. 'Ita dubium quod duas vias habeat unde dubius dictus quasi duas vias habens et utram eligat nesciens.' Ibid., col. 1107.

33. 'Dubius dicit qui duas vias habeat et utram eligat nesciens; sicut ambiguum quod in ambas agi partes possit.' Ambrogio da Calepio, *F. Ambrosii Calepini Bergomatis* [...] *Dictionarium* [...] (Paris: Josse Bade, 1510), fol. D2ᵛ. The connection between doubt and ambiguity also comes from Perotti; see *Cornucopiae*, col. 743.

34. Amedeo Quondam, 'Strumenti dell'officina classicistica: *Polyanthea* & Co.', *Modern Philology*, 101 (2003), pp. 316–35.

35. 'Dubitatio [...]. Est autem dubitatio iudicio deficiente acceptio utriusque partis cum formidine et ad neutram partem determinatio. Dubium [...]. Est autem dubium motus indifferens in utranque partem contradictionis secundum Isyd[ori] Li[ber] Ethimologiar[um]. Dubium est aequalitas rationum contrariarum secundum Philosophum. Dubius a *de* et *habeo* componitur, quasi *dehabens*, hoc est non intelligens [...].' Domenico Nani Mirabelli, *Polyanthea. Opus suavissimis floribus exornatum* [...] (Savona: Francesco Selva, 1503), fol. 105ᵛ; my italics.

36. Francesco Alunno, *Della fabbrica del mundo libri dieci ne quali si contengono le voci di Dante, del Petrarca, del Boccaccio, del Bembo e d'altri buoni autori, mediante le quali scrivendo si possono esprimere con facilità e eloquenza tutti i concetti dell'huomo e di qualunque cosa creata* [...] (Venice: N. de Bascarini, 1546). On Alunno (born Francesco Del Bailo, 1485–1556), see Angela Piscini, 'Del Bailo, Francesco', in *Dizionario biografico degli Italiani*, XXXVI (Rome: Istituto dell'Enciclopedia italiana, 1988) <http://www.treccani.it/enciclopedia/francesco-del-bailo_(Dizionario-Biografico)/> [accessed 27 April 2020]; Ivano Paccagnella, 'La grammatica nei primi vocabolari: Le *Regolette particolari della volgar lingua* di Francesco Alunno', in *La nascita del vocabolario*, ed. by Antonio Daniele, Ivano Paccagnella, and Riccardo Drusi (Padua: Esedra, 2014), pp. 11–31, esp. 20–25.

37. I was not able to check the 1546 edition of *Della fabbrica*; I have used instead the 1548 (?) reprint by the same printer, fol. 22ᵛ.

38. Francesco Alunno, *Della fabbrica del mondo* [...] (Venice: appresso Gio. Battista Uscio, 1588), fol. 24ʳ.

39. Aldo Manuzio, *Eleganze insieme con la copia della lingua toscana e latina* (Venice: Paolo Manuzio, 1556). Edit16 lists forty-eight editions up until 1600.

40. Girolamo Garimberto, *Concetti divinissimi* [...] *per iscrivere, e ragionar familiarmente* (Venice: Comin da Trino, 1562), fol. 57^r.

41. 'Hanno pur per lor fine il persuadere, il qual si acquista hora con ragioni o probabili o apparenti.' Ibid., fol. 1^v.

42. Ibid., fol. EE3^r.

43. 'Diffidare che vuol dire non fidarsi [...] è [...] come il dubitare ma differentemente imperoché il dubitare è accompagnato da ambiguità d'animo e 'l diffidare dalla risolutione.' Ibid., fol. 59^v.

44. 'Libri-utensile', according to Amedeo Quondam's definition. Quondam, 'Strumenti dell'officina classicistica', p. 318.

45. See Paolo Cherchi, *Polimatia di riuso: Mezzo secolo di plagio (1539–1589)* (Rome: Bulzoni, 1998); *Renaissance Rewritings*, ed. by Helmut Pfeiffer, Irene Fantappiè, and Tobias Roth (Berlin: De Gruyter, 2017).

46. Stefano Pierguidi, 'Un anonimo repertorio di personificazioni della fine del Cinquecento', *Studi romani,* 53 (2005), pp. 51–93.

47. 'Giovanetto senza barba, in mezzo alle tenebre, vestito di cangiante, in una mano tenga un bastone, nell'altra una lanterna, e stia col piè sinistro in fuora, per segno di caminare. Dubbio è un'ambiguità dell'animo intorno al sapere, e per conseguenza ancora del corpo intorno all'operare. Si dipinge giovane, perché l'uomo in quest'età, per non esser abituato ancora bene nella pura e semplice verità, ogni cosa facilmente rivoca in dubbio, e facilmente dà fede egualmente a diverse cose. Per lo bastone e la lanterna si notano l'esperienza e la ragione, con lo aiuto delle quali due cose il dubbio facilmente o camina o si ferma. Le tenebre sono i campi d'i discorsi umani, ond'egli, che non sa stare in ozio, sempre con nuovi modi camina, e però si dipinge col piè sinistro in fuora.' Cesare Ripa, *Iconologia*, ed. by Sonia Maffei and Paolo Procaccioli (Turin: Einaudi, 2012), p. 146.

48. 'Uomo quasi in abito di viandante, ch'abbia bendati gl'occhi, e vada con un bastone tentone, in atto di cercare il viaggio per andare assicurandosi, e questo va quasi sempre con l'ignoranza. L'errore (secondo gli Stoici) è un uscire di strada e deviare dalla linea, come il non errare è un caminare per la via dritta senza inciampare dall'una o dall'altra banda, talché tutte l'opere o del corpo o dell'intelletto nostro si potrà dire che siano in viaggio o in pellegrinaggio, dopo il quale, non storcendo, speriamo arrivare alla felicità. [...] Gl'occhi bendati significano che quando è oscurato il lume dell'intelletto con il velo de gl'interessi mondani, facilmente s'incorre ne gli errori. Il bastone con il quale va cercando la strada, si pone per il senso, come l'occhio per l'intelletto, perché come quello è più corporeo, così l'atto di questo è meno sensibile e più spirituale [...].' Ibid., p. 165.

49. 'Il dominio che ha la dottrina sopra li orrori della notte dell'ignoranza.' Ibid., p. 146.

50. 'Uomo vecchio in atto di andare, con barba canuta, et appoggiato ad un bastone con una mano, nella quale terrà ancora una carta, con motto che dica "Vires acquirit eundo." Porterà in spalla un fascio d'istromenti, co' quali s'esercitano l'arti, e vicino avrà una ruota d'arrotare coltelli. L'uso imprime nella mente nostra gl'abiti di tutte le cose, li conserva a' posteri, li fa decenti, et a sua voglia si fabrica molte cose nel vivere e nella conversazione. Et si dipinge vecchio perché nella lunga esperienza consiste la sua auttorità [...].' Ibid., pp. 114–15.

51. The source for this proverb is Terence's *Phormio*, and the direct source for the image could have been, as Maffei glosses, Piero Valeriano's *Hieroglyphica* (1567).

52. 'Uomo ignudo, tutto pensoso, incontratosi in due overo tre strade, mostri esser confuso per non saper risolvere qual di dette vie debbia pigliare. E questo è dubbio con speranza di bene, come l'altro con timore di cattivo successo, e si fa ignudo per essere irresoluto.' Ripa, *Iconologia*, p. 147.

53. See Maffei, commentary to Ripa, *Iconologia*, p. 675.

54. 'Donna colle ali alla testa, il cui vestimento sia tutto sparso di formiche. Tenga il braccio destro e il dito indice della medesima mano alto, mostrando con esso una grue che voli per aria e col dito indice della sinistra un cane il quale stia colla testa bassa per terra, in atto di cercare la fiera. [...] Del significato del cane, Sesto Pironese filosofo, nel primo libro cap. 14, dice che il cane nella guisa che dicemmo denota Investigazione perciocché quando seguita una fiera, e arrivato

ad un luogo dove sono tre strade, e non avendo veduto per qual via sia andata, esso, odorata che abbia la prima strada, odora la seconda e se in nessuna di esse sente che sia andata, non odora la terza, ma risoluto corre, argomentando che necessariamente sia andata per essa.' Cesare Ripa, *Iconologia [...] notabilmente accresciuta d'immagini, di annotazioni, e di fatti dall'abate Cesare Orlandi [...]* (Perugia: Piergiovanni Costantini, 1765), pp. 321–22.

55. Sextus Empiricus, *Outlines of Pyrrhonism*, ed. by R. G. Bury (Cambridge, MA: Harvard University Press, 1933), pp. 41–43.

56. Luciano Floridi, 'Scepticism and Animal Rationality: The Fortune of Chrysippus' Dog in the History of Western Thought', *Archiv für Geschichte der Philosophie*, 79 (1997), pp. 27–57 (p. 30).

57. *Collected Works of Erasmus*, xxxi: *Adages I i 1 to I v 100*, trans. by Margaret Mann Phillips, annotated by R. A. B. Mynors (Toronto: University of Toronto Press, 1982), p. 190; cf. *Opera omnia Desiderii Erasmi Roterodami*, ii/1: *Adagiorum Chilias prima*, ed. by M. L. van Poll-van de Lisdonk, M. Mann Phillips, and Chr. Robinson (Amsterdam: North Holland, 1992), p. 264: Ἐν τριόδῳ εἰμὶ λογισμῶν id est In trivio sum consilii. In eos, qui dubitant quique incerti sunt animi haesitantes quid potissimum elegant. Translatum ab iis, qui faciunt iter et, si quando trivium occurrerit, addubitant quam viam oportet ingredi. Nam via pro ratione consilii frequenter apud Graecos autores reperies.'

58. 'In trivio mons est lapidum. Supereminet illi | Trunca dei effigies pectore facta tenus. | Mercurii est igitur tumulus: suspende, viator, | Serta deo, rectum qui tibi monstrat iter. | Omnes in trivio sumus, atque hoc tramite vitae | Fallimur, ostendat ni deus ipse viam.' Andrea Alciato, *Emblematum liber* (Augsburg: Heinrich Steyner, 1531), fol. D8^v. The original text and English translation are available at <https://www.emblems.arts.gla.ac.uk/alciato/books.php?id=A31a≥ [accessed 31 May 2020].

59. Padua: apud Petrum Paulum Tozzium, 1621, p. 52.

60. 'Dubio secondo S. Isidoro nel libro delle Ethimologie è uno moto indifferente nell'una e l'altra parte della contraddittione. Overo dirai che il dubio è una equalità di ragioni contrarie secondo il filosofo.' Angelo da Chivasso, *Della somma angelica [...] nuovamente di Latino in lingua italiana tradotta dal reverendo frate Girolamo Menghi [...] parte prima [...]* (Venice: alla Libraria della Speranza, 1594), fol. 156^v.

61. 'Openione è uno consenso dell'intelletto ad alcuna cosa non perché sufficientemente sia mosso dall'oggetto proprio ma per una certa ragionevole elettione, volontariamente declinando in una parte più presto che nell'altra, nondimeno con la dubitatione nel timore dell'altra parte [...]. Ma la fede è con la certezza senza tale timore. La scienza poi è un consenso dell'intelletto mosso dall'oggetto per se stesso conosciuto, sì come è nei primi principi. [...] Ma il dubbio è un moto indifferente dell'una e l'altra parte della contraditione [...]. Il scropulo poi è quando l'intelletto per leggieri congetture [...] si muove ad una parte. Et questo anco è detto sospicione e pusillanimità di spirito, la quali si deve scacciare.' Ibid., parte seconda, fol. 115^v.

62. See the catalogue of editions in Miriam Turrini, *La coscienza e le leggi: Morale e diritto nei testi per la confessione della prima età moderna* (Bologna: il Mulino, 1991), pp. 365–78; Vincenzo Lavenia, *L'infamia e il perdono: Tributi, pene e confessione nella teologia morale della prima età moderna* (Bologna: il Mulino, 2004), pp. 219–64 (p. 219); see also Perez Zagorin, *Ways of Lying: Dissimulation, Persecution, and Conformity in Early Modern Europe* (Cambridge, MA: Harvard University Press, 1990), pp. 153–85; Wim Decock, 'Martín de Azpilcueta (Dr Navarrus)', in *Great Christian Jurists in Spanish History*, ed. by Rafael Domingo and Javier Martínez Torrón (Cambridge: Cambridge University Press, 2018), pp. 115–32.

63. Science is 'conoscimento con che si giudica quel che si vede'; faith is instead a 'conoscimento con che fermamente giudichiamo esser così quello che non vediamo'. See Martín de Azpilcueta, *Manuale de' confessori, et penitenti [...]* (Venice: Gabriel Giolito de' Ferrari, 1569), p. 893.

64. Opinion is 'conoscimento con che giudichiamo alcuna cosa che non vediamo esser così, però non fermamente, con timore che il contrario sia vero'; doubt, 'conoscimento di due cose contrarie senza giudicare che alcuna di quelle sia verità'; scruple, 'conoscimento di alcuna cosa che rappresenta alcuna apparentia contro quello che si sa, crede, pensa, o dubbita senza saper giudicare il contrario'. Ibid., p. 893. See Schuessler, *The Debate on Probable Opinions*, pp. 30–36.

65. Turrini, *La coscienza*, 66.

66. Ruggero Rusconi, *L'ordine dei peccati: La confessione tra Medioevo ed età moderna* (Bologna: il Mulino, 2002), pp. 225–26.

67. Tutino, *Uncertainty in Post-Reformation Catholicism*.

68. See Adriano Prosperi, 'Casistica', in *Dizionario storico dell'Inquisizione*, ed. by Adriano Prosperi, Vincenzo Lavenia, and John Tedeschi (Pisa: Edizioni della Normale, 2010), I, 291–92; Margherita Palumbo, 'Conscientia, casus conscientiae', in *Coscienza nella filosofia della prima modernità*, ed. by Roberto Palaia (Florence: Olschki, 2013), pp. 203–33.

69. 'The epistemic uncertainty involved in opining need not be resolved in order to attain a moral safety or certainty for actions that engendered blamelessness and precluded sinning. [...] Accordingly, "safety" (*securitas* or *tutitas*) or "certainty" (*certitudo*) in conscience was ascribed when an agent followed the right rules for action under moral uncertainty, the objective risk of violating a divine precept notwithstanding. [...] Agents who properly managed moral risks, including a reasonable search for information, forestalled sin regardless of the (epistemically uncertain) objective rightness or wrongness of their actions. [...] The certainty arising in this respect from proper proceedings was called "probable certainty" (*certitudo probabilis*) or "moral certainty" (*certitudo moralis*) from the fifteenth century onward.' Schuessler, *The Debate on Probable Opinions*, pp. 47–48.

70. '*Probabilis* was a qualitative predicate accruing to propositions and opinions, claiming that the propositions in question were fit for adoption and sufficiently, although not optimally, backed by reasons for truth [...]. *Opinio probabilis* can therefore be translated as approved or approvable opinion.' Ibid., pp. 37–38.

71. 'A general feature of fifteenth century moral thought was a heightened awareness of the need for casuistry. An interest in the problems of daily life was shared by philosophers, confessors, canon-lawyers and theologians alike.' M. W. F. Stone, 'The Origins of Probabilism in Late Scholastic Moral Thought: A Prolegomenon to Further Study', *Recherches de théologie et philosophie médiévales*, 67 (2000), pp. 114–57 (p. 144).

72. The bibliography on this issue is huge; as a sample, see the publications by Schüssler, Schwartz, Maryks, and Tutino mentioned in this chapter.

73. Daniel Schwartz, 'Probabilism Reconsidered: Deference to Experts, Types of Uncertainty, and Medicines', *Journal of the History of Ideas*, 75 (2014), pp. 373–93 (p. 380).

74. Choices 'had to be made with attentive, prayerful deliberation in order to arrive at absolute certainty of conscience, which these and all other authors, regardless of the ethical school they belonged to, always required'. Robert A. Maryks, *Saint Cicero and the Jesuits: The Influence of the Liberal Arts on the Adoption of Moral Probabilism* (London: Routledge, 2016), p. 68.

75. Stone, 'The Origins of Probabilism', p. 156. See also Rudolf Schüssler, 'Jean Gerson, Moral Certainty, and the Renaissance of Ancient Scepticism', *Renaissance Studies*, 23 (2009), pp. 445–62.

76. Scholars generally indicate three main protagonists in this theological turn: Jean Gerson, Antoninus of Florence, and the German Johannes Nider (*c.* 1380–1438); see Thomas Brogl, ' "Ÿegliches näch sín vermugen": Johannes Nider's Idea of Conscience', in *Between Creativity and Norm-Making: Tensions in the Early Modern Era*, ed. by Sigrid Müller and Cornelia Schweiger (Leiden: Brill, 2013), pp. 61–76.

77. Jean Delumeau, *Sin and Fear: The Emergence of a Western Guilt Culture, 13th–18th Centuries*, trans. by Eric Nicholson (New York: St Martin's Press, 1990), p. 315.

78. Ambroise Gardeil, 'La "certitude probable"', *Revue des sciences philosophiques et théologiques*, 5 (1911), 237–66 and 441–85; Thomas Deman, 'Probabilis', *Revue des sciences philosophiques et théologiques*, 22 (1933), 60–90. See also Edmund F. Byrne, *Probability and Opinion: A Study in the Medieval Presuppositions of Post-Medieval Theories of Probability* (The Hague: Martinus Nijhoff, 1968).

79. *Sylvestrinae Summae, quae Summa Summarum merito nuncupatur pars prima* [...] (Lyon: apud Ioannem Frellonium, 1554), pp. 293–94. The *Summa* was first published in 1506 and published over forty times during the sixteenth century (it had also a manuscript circulation prior to its print publication). According to Miriam Turrini, the *Silvestrina* was one of the last late medieval *summae* and did not disrupt the medieval casuistic tradition established in the thirteenth century; Turrini, *La coscienza*, p. 151. On Mazzolini, see Simona Feci, 'Mazzolini, Silvestro', in

Dizionario biografico degli Italiani, LXXII (Rome: Istituto dell'Enciclopedia italiana, 2008) <https://www.treccani.it/enciclopedia/silvestro-mazzolini_%28Dizionario-Biografico%29/> [accessed 14 November 2022].

80. Schuessler, *The Debate on Probable Opinions*, p. 47.

81. 'Cum scilicet rationes probabiles ad utramque partem sunt quasi aequales', *Sylvestrinae Summae*, pp. 293–94.

82. Rudolf Schüssler, 'Equi-Probability prior to 1650', *Early Science and Medicine*, 21 (2016), 54–74 (p. 67). The author also notes that '[d]istinctions between different kinds of doubt were common in the Middle Ages, often recalling Aquinas' distinction between truly balanced doubt that excludes assent and doubt that merely motivates a fear of error without precluding assent. The notion of probable doubt also appeared in Aquinas and other medieval scholastics, but it merely indicated a well-motivated doubt. It is noteworthy that Mazzolini invests the concept of probable doubt with a different meaning, one that refers to a balance of probable reasons. He thus builds on a tradition that characterized doubt through an equilibrium of reasons, but additionally emphasizes the role of probability on both sides. This, as documented, leads him to an explicit ascription of equal probability.' Ibid., pp. 67–68.

83. Ibid., pp. 70–71.

84. Ibid., 72. See also Schüssler, 'Jean Gerson'.

85. 'Credere, o dubitare d'alcuna cosa se sia peccato mortale [...] è da sapere che all'hora questa credenza o dubitanza nasce, quando si ha alcuna ragione all'una parte et all'altra. Per la qual cosa in questa dubitanza sempre l'huomo deve (per non peccare) accostarsi alla parte migliore, perché accostandosi a quella che li par cattiva e senza ragione sempre peccarà.' Marco Scarsella, *Giardino di sommisti* [...] *parte prima* [...] (Venice: Giacomo Antonio Somasco, 1600), fol. 192^v.

86. 'Anco si parte la conscienza in certa, dubbiosa, e scrupulosa. La certa è quella che giudica per vero alcuna cosa. La dubbiosa è quella che non giudica più vero l'uno che il suo contrario. La scrupulosa è quella che giudica alcuna cosa per vera contra la quale se gli offerisce alcuno argomento o apparenza.' Azpilcueta, *Manuale*, p. 894.

87. 'La conscienza certa o sia scienza, o fede, o opinione, o sia erronea, o vera, obliga chi ha a fare quello che gli detta sotto pena di peccato mortale se sotto quella pena gli detta, e se sotto veniale, veniale. [...] A colui che detta che deve uccidere è obligato a compirla in questo senso che pecca se non uccide.' Ibid.

88. It has been argued that the introduction of these different typologies of conscience characterizes the sixteenth-century theory of conscience and of moral deliberation in conditions of uncertainty, as opposed to medieval views (in particular to the category of erring conscience, *irrendes Gewissen*); cf. Rudolf Schüßler, *Moral im Zweifel*, I: *Die Scholastische Theorie des Entscheidens unter moralischer Unsicherheit* (Paderborn: Mentis, 2003), pp. 93–94, who speaks of a 'new system of conscience analysis' ('eine neue Systematik der Gewissensanalyse', p. 93).

89. Silvestro Mazzolini, *Sylvestrinae summae* [...] *pars secunda* [...] (Lyon: apud Ioannem Frellonium, 1554), p. 399.

90. 'Pusillanimitas parat perturbationem, perturbatio desperationem, desperatio vero interimit.' Ibid.

91. Ibid.

92. Ibid.

93. Ibid., pp. 399–400.

94. *B. Antonini Archiepiscopi Florentini* [...] *Summa Sacrae Theologiae* [...] *pars prima* [...] (Venice: apud Bernardum Iuntam & socios, 1571), fol. 68^r.

95. See, for example, *Beati Alberti Magni* [...] *Summa de creaturis divisa in duas partes quarum prima est de quatuor coaevis, secunda de homine* [...]. *Operum tomus decimus-nonus* (Lyon: sumptibus Claudii Prost., Petri et Claudii Rigaud, Hieronymi Delagarde, Ioan. Ant. Huguetam, 1651), p. 242 (De homine, tractatus I, q. 51).

96. 'Scrupulus a quibusdam vocatur erronea conscientia, timor conscientiae, pusillanimitas.' *B. Antonini Archiepiscopi Florentini* [...] *Summa Sacrae Theologiae*, fol. 68^r.

97. 'Trepidatione, timore, pusillanimità, tristezza, pazzia, angoscia, mestitia e dubbio, essendo sempre lo scrupolo dal dubbio accompagnato.' Raffaele Grillenzoni, *Affanni dell'anima timorata,*

co' suoi conforti e rimedii. Aggiuntovi il metodo per risanare un'anima inferma di scrupoli (Venice: Francesco Salerni, 1676), pp. 309–10. The work was first printed in 1644 and put on the Index in 1688 on the charge of quietism.

98. 'Nasce all'hora da superbia e riputation propria come da vera madre, e ha per sua nutrice la pazzia e debolezza di giuditio, infirmità di fantasia [...].' Agostino da Montalcino, *Lucerna dell'anima. Somma de' casi di conscientia* [...] (Venice: Damian Zenaro, 1590), pp. 67–68.

99. *B. Antonini Archiepiscopi Florentini* [...] *Summa Sacrae Theologiae*, fol. 68^r.

100. 'In foeminis vetulis et melancolicis.' Ibid.

101. 'Quandoque causatur pusillanimitas seu scrupulus ex egretudine manica vel melancholica quae est infirmitas capitis per quam leditur imaginatio et quandoque ratio.' Ibid.

102. 'Indiscretam psalmorum vel officiorum decantationem.' Ibid.

103. 'Causatur et aliquando scrupulos ex tentatione diabolica. Potest enim diabolus, Deo permittente, movere melancolicos humores in homine, per quos imaginatio vel errare potest, aut turbari ad timorem inordinatum.' Ibid.

104. Ibid., fol. 68^v.

105. 'Morales medicos, praelatus et confessores, consultores idoneos.' Ibid.

106. 'Ad gratiam Dei preparatio [...] sollicita sacrae Scripturae indagatio [...] orationis devotae continuatio [...] opinionis alicuius tuta electio [...] obedientiae humilis imitatio [...] scrupulorum animosa abiectio [...] praeceptorum discreta epicaizatio, i.e. interpretatio.' Ibid.

107. 'Sicut enim diversae viae tendunt ad unam civitatem, licet una tutior alia sit. Sic ad civitatem coelestem alius sic, alius sic vadit et tute, licet aliquis tutiori modo.' Ibid.

108. 'Ille qui agit id de quo est dubium, utrum est mortale vel non, peccat mortaliter quia periculo se exponit mortali.' Ibid.

109. 'Induce alla pazzia, cagiona sincope, febri, dolori.' Grillenzoni, *Affanni dell'anima*, p. 311.

110. 'Quando lo scrupolo viene da melanconia o dalla mania [...] fa che il tale scrupoloso patischi svenimenti, sii sospettoso e, per dirlo in una parola, dij nel pazzo, onde bisogna darlo in mano de' medici corporali.' Ibid., p. 330.

111. 'Quando lo scrupolo viene da causa naturale, come dalla complessione sana ma timorosa, ma fredda, è facile a conoscere imperciocché lo scrupoloso di questo modo è sospetoso, ombroso, difficile da contentare, da sodisfare, sta ansioso.' Ibid.

112. Giacomo Pietro Bacci, *Vita di S. Filippo Neri* [...] (Bologna: Eredi di Domenico Maria Barbieri, 1666), pp. 149–50 (the first edition of this work appeared in 1622). See Mario De Gregorio, 'Un *long-seller* agiografico: *La Vita di San Filippo Neri* di Giacomo Pietro Bacci', in *Le fusa del gatto: Libri, librai e molto altro* (Torrita di Siena: Società Bibliografica Toscana, 2015), pp. 115–30.

113. Naples: per il De Bonis Stampatore Arcivescovile, 1693. See Teresa Megale, 'Gizzio, Francesco', in *Dizionario biografico degli italiani*, LVII (Rome: Istituto dell'Enciclopedia italiana, 2001) <http://www.treccani.it/enciclopedia/francesco-gizzio_(Dizionario-Biografico)/> [accessed 23 August 2020].

114. 'Scrupolino entra per tutto, ne' chiostri, ne' monasteri, ne' conventi, nelle congregationi; io alloggio nel petto de' preti e de' secolari, nella coscienza di femine maritate e vedove, di Monache e di pinzoccare.' Gizzio, *L'echo armoniosa*, p. 40.

115. 'Porto scrupolini a Camaldoli et a Giesuini, a Zoccolanti e a Cappuccini; a colli torti e a Teatini; a vecchi, a giovanetti et a fanciullini.' Ibid.

116. Ibid., fol. a3^v.

117. 'Per distogliere quanto sia possibile l'anime da così insidiose facende [i.e., dishonest comedies and plays], il glorioso patriarca e amabilissimo padre di tutti san Filippo Neri nella città capo del mondo [...] trattenendo con dilettevole pascolo così la gioventù come ogni età, tanto secolari quanto religiosi, introdusse in Roma gli oratorii vespertini con musica, sermoncini de' fanciulli e de' Padri e alle volte con qualche sacro dialogo [...] onde sì come di tutte l'altre regole, così di questi oratorii con musica e con sacre rappresentationi sono immitatrici l'altre Congregationi in diverse parti fondate, tra le quali questa di Napoli [...].' Ibid., fol. a3^r.

118. 'Rappresentandosi nell'inverno dentro l'Oratorio della loro chiesa e casa. Nella primavera sopra l'amena collina della Montagnola. E nell'està et autunno nel chiostro di Sant'Agnello con la frequenza alle volte [...] di più di cinque mila anime d'ogni stato e conditione, de Prelati,

officiali, cavalieri e in particolare d'innumerabili religiosi di tutte le religioni, anco più riformati et osservanti. Era sì grande la compuntione de gli uditori che convenivano a queste sacre rappresentationi che non solo persone plebee et idiote nel vederle e udirle (scorgendo i medesimi figliuoli recitanti versare tenerissime lagrime) commoveansi a pianto, ma anco personaggi nobili, dotti e qualificati.' Ibid., fol. a3$^{\text{r-v}}$.

CHAPTER 2

Tales of Doubt

On the evening of the first anniversary of his first son's death at age ten, Giovanni di Pagolo Morelli (1371–1444) retires for bed, only to be assaulted by the devil most fiercely ('assalendomi durissimamente').[1] He starts by suggesting that the prayers Giovanni has just recited are in vain and that the soul — his soul — is 'nothing, or just a little breath'.[2] This most classic of doubts opens the way to a series of temptations and attacks on the part of the devil in an attempt to lead Giovanni to a point of desperation. When, after turning to the crucifix, Giovanni finally manages to fall asleep, he begins to dream a complex allegorical dream. At some point during the dream, his son Alberto, whom he had mistreated while alive, appears to him. Giovanni begs him to answer to his doubts ('mi risponda [...] alla mia domanda e a' miei dubbi').[3] Giovanni desires to know whether Alberto died because of his (Giovanni's) sins; if he will have other children; if he will gain a better place in the world; and, finally, whether he will die young or in his old age. Alberto's answers are somewhat evasive and sound more like *ricordi*, pieces of practical wisdom, than revelations from a blessed soul or otherworldly creature. Nevertheless, Giovanni wakes up the following morning partially retaining his fear but also feeling a new sense of happiness ('mi destai tutto ispaventato e 'n parte allegro').[4]

Morelli's readers would easily relate to his sense of spiritual solace. A benign entity, his son's spirit, has given him all the answers he needed; the spiritual battle staged by Giovanni in his dream between Christ and his patron saints (John the Baptist, Anthony, Benedict, Francis, Catherine of Alexandria) on the one side and the devil on the other has been successful. Even when fearful allegorical creatures threatened Giovanni, his saints were ready to intervene; for example, when a dangerous sow (an allegory of carnal sin) was hunting him, St Catherine readily appeared and dismembered the animal with her wheel.[5] The language of emotions mixes fear and joy; doubts and their answers are projected onto external entities, evil or benign spirits. Giovanni's mundane doubts are — to some extent — resolved, and the lurking fear of eternal damnation neutralized by the powerful intervention of his patron saints. Giovanni's devotions have not been in vain; sticking to them — worshipping his sacred images, praying, invoking his patron saints — will assist him in his path to salvation.

In his spiritual battle, Giovanni has the privilege of experiencing what others go through on their deathbeds. In fact, we might say that we see here the pattern of the dramatic end-of-life scene, that moment of supreme doubt when God and the devil compete for the dying one's soul. It is then that the devil enters with his doubts. '[I]n order not to leave him at rest in any way,' writes Girolamo Savonarola in 1496,

> the devil begins tempting him in his faith, saying: 'If I cannot have you in one way, I will have you in another.' So he puts in his fantasy that the truth is not true, and says: 'What do you think faith is? Once the body is dead, the soul is dead too.'[6]

For this reason, friars used to recite the Credo when one of their brethren lay dying, but the soul induced to desperation only need 'return to the crucifix' and 'look to its goodness, for He wanted to be crucified and killed to save you'.[7] According to Domenico Capranica (1452), dying people have to go through five temptations, the first of which concerns faith, as the devil 'involves the dying person in several mistakes and many superstitions and heresies'.[8] These are just 'illusions' of the devil, who is 'a liar and the father of lies'.[9] The dying one is not alone in this battle; in fact, being 'subject and obedient to the Holy Roman Church' is a weapon that can be relied on in this time of temptation.[10] Catholicism could create multiple concerns among its devotees, related to possible misdeeds and shortcomings in their everyday practices, devotional or not. In this way it fostered doubts, scruples, and a general sense of anxiety. It also provided, nonetheless, a wealth of reassuring guarantees. Saints could intercede and protect, and those very ceremonies, if correctly performed, were sufficient to grant salvation.

This chapter explores the shift that turned the expression of doubts from an individual act, an inner dialogue carried out in the secret of one's chamber, into a social act, described in literary texts. Discussions on issues such as the immortality of the soul, the possibility of miracles exceeding natural laws, and free will found their natural place in theological and philosophical treatises in Latin. That they increasingly became the subject of literary works in the vernacular testifies not only to the spread of anxieties and forms of unbelief but also to a shared interest on the part of lay readers. Most of the texts that I will explore do not hint at the anti-Christian strand of quattrocento thought that was mostly shared among humanists; rather, these texts suggest the need to verify and ascertain certain truths that could be — or were — challenged.[11]

Poetical Voices

Poetry is traditionally the place where the lovesick poet voices his (or her) tormented interiority. The condition of doubt, of being torn between two equally destructive forces, is specific to the Petrarchan poet. One example will suffice: in Petrarch's sonnet 'Questa humil fera, un cor di tigre, o d'orsa' ('This kind, wild beast, this tiger's heart, or bear's'), the poet laments that his beloved 'in tears, in laughter, amid fear and hope, | Spins me around and makes me uncertain'.[12] The English version, however accurate, cannot fully convey the significance of *inforsare* that magnificently expresses the woman's power to turn all the poet's emotions and feelings into a doubtful condition. Interestingly, as pointed out by Marco Santagata, Petrarch is borrowing the verb *inforsare*, created by Dante and used in *Paradise*, XXIV; here for the first time, the verb is used in the active form.[13] Dante uses the verb *inforsare* in the context of a philosophical discussion on the nature of faith between St Peter and himself, presented as an academic disputation between master and novice. The fulcrum of the discussion is certainty and how faith is connected with certainty of what we do not see. It is from this highly speculative context that Petrarch borrows *inforsare* and applies it to the lover's condition.

Sometimes, poets voice a broader anxiety, as if the condition of doubt were not unique to lovers but a more general feature of human life. Pandolfo Collenuccio from Pesaro (1444–1504), nowadays best known for his *Compendio de le historie del Regno di Napoli* (A summary of the histories of the Kingdom of Naples, posthumously published in 1539), was a writer in Latin and the vernacular besides holding several public offices in Pesaro, Firenze, and Ferrara. Collenuccio had a strained (to say the least) relationship with the *signore* of Pesaro, Giovanni Sforza, who had had him imprisoned for sixteen months. Collenuccio was eventually released, thanks also to the intervention of Ercole d'Este, and spent some fifteen years at the Ferrara court. He then begged Sforza permission to return to Pesaro. Sforza first granted him consent to return to his hometown, then had him arrested and eventually strangled. Among Collenuccio's poems in the vernacular is a 'Canzone alla morte', a long invocation to death in which, as scholars have pointed out, one finds scarce reference to a Christian afterlife and future reward for virtue.[14] However, in Collenuccio's poems we do not find doubts levelled against orthodoxy. Instead, doubt seems to concern only one's interiority, possibly as a result of Collenuccio's tormented existence. In this vein, in a sonnet to the Virgin he claims that 'the desire for either freedom or death is doubtful', this condition being the result of his imprisonment which led to the loss of everything he holds dear in life.[15] Even more interestingly, doubt as a sign of existential unrest emerges from a poem dedicated to the planting of oranges ('Regola da piantare et conservare melaranci'). After providing detailed instructions on how to prepare a suitable garden for the plants and how to plant them, Collenuccio suddenly remarks that the ceaseless labour of the peasant resembles our own restless condition:

> One tries hard to avoid preoccupations, and yet is wrapped in them.
> Truth is always hidden from our eyes
> Until at the end comes the one
> Who makes our life so doubtful.[16]

'Doubtful' refers here to death and could mean 'uncertain' as well as 'dreadful'. However, whatever Collenuccio's views in matters of religion were, we find here nothing more than the reflection of his misfortunes and a moralistic consideration of the troubles of human condition. Life is full of *affanni*, and it is so precisely because truth is hidden from us and we live in constant fear of death: the combination of these factors makes life doubtful, that is, both dreadful and uncertain (or dreadful because uncertain).

In 1490, Collenuccio served for six months as *podestà* of Florence. He was a personal friend of Lorenzo de' Medici and of several Florentine intellectuals; around 1479 he also took part in a poetical *tenzone* — along with Poliziano and Girolamo Benivieni — on the relationship between love and fortune, sparked by a sonnet by Lorenzo ('S'entr'agli altri sospir ch'escon di fore').[17] He may thus have been acquainted with the role doubt played within Florentine culture and with at least one polemic that shook the Laurentian circle in the early 1470s. The episode involved three sonnets attributed to Luigi Pulci, although they may have been conceived by or in collaboration with his fellow intellectual Benedetto Dei, who enjoyed a reputation as an atheist. The sonnets completely denied the immortality of the soul, miracles, and the existence of an afterlife. Putting in writing expressions of incredulity or atheism was not unprecedented in Florentine culture. Alessandro Ciachi had done so in his sonnet 'Dal tetto in su è nugolo e sereno' (From the roof up it is either cloudy or clear).[18] The sonnet seems to deny the existence of God: above the roof there is only sky. Ciachi makes fun of hypocrites, of those who 'wait for the dove' (the Holy Spirit), and in the last lines seems to imply that heaven is a condition that wealthy people enjoy on earth, while hell is the condition assigned to the poor.

In the case of Pulci, however, the sonnets involved a more radical attack on religion that also contained dangerous political connotations. As scholarship has shown, Pulci's attacks targeted Marsilio Ficino and his growing influence within the Laurentian circle. More than being an atheist himself, Pulci advocated a return to more traditional forms of devotion, labelling Ficino and his followers as hypocrites. At stake was also Pulci's personal position and his declining fortune among Florentine intellectuals. Benedetto Dei had more radical views than Pulci and may have been the mind behind the poems. One sonnet in particular, 'Costoro che fan sì gran disputazione' (Those who make such a great dispute), sparked outrage among the Florentines. Dei transcribes in his manuscript chronicle five responses to this sonnet that denies the immortality of the soul. The fourth of these responding sonnets reproaches Pulci not only for having written against the immortality of the soul but also for divulging such ideas in a sonnet ('Però, tu che scrivesti in ciò 'l contrario | E divulgasti per un tuo sonetto').[19] Paolo Orvieto has attributed the sonnets to Feo Belcari, recognized as a sort of official authority in matters of religious doubts.[20] Lorenzo de' Medici himself had addressed a sonnet to Belcari ('Lo spirito talora a sé redutto'), asking him to clarify a doubt concerning grace. Pulci composed two more parodical sonnets: 'In principio era buio, e buio fia' (In the beginning there was darkness, and darkness will be), in which he attacks the hypocrisy of religious practices (and this was perhaps the first of the three poems to be written); and 'Poich'io partii da voi, Bartolomeo' (After I left you, Bartolomeo), in which, apparently, he makes fun of miracles.[21] These sonnets caused a stir in Florence, as Pulci recalled in his *Morgante* and in another sonnet from 1473–74, 'Sempre la pulcia muor, signore, a torto' (My Lord, the flea always dies wrongfully), where he claimed,

> There is so much fuss because of a sonnet
> That it seems that I killed with my sword
> Those who shout, just for the sake of it.[22]

Whether those who made a fuss about Pulci's and Dei's sonnets (especially the one denying the immortality of the soul) belonged to the Laurentian circle, or whether rumours spread beyond the ruling elite, we should notice the social dimension of these doubts and the choice to circulate them through literary texts.

That the five responses to 'Costoro che fan sì gran disputazione' were penned by Florentine Feo Belcari (1410–1484) is also interesting. A number of Belcari's forty-two sonnets are responses to 'doubts' expressed by several correspondents (one of them, Giovanni de' Pigli, or de' Pilli, asks Feo about two doubts). Francesco del Maestro Andrea Sargiaio's doubt, for example, revolves around salvation: 'I move to question your glorious | Intelligence, on mortals' salvation | Whether anybody can be saved thanks to others' works.'[23] Belcari was recognized by his contemporaries as a resolver of doubts, as Giovanni de' Pigli acknowledges in one of the afore-mentioned sonnets he addresses to Feo: 'Ingegno esperto a solver dubii e passi' (Skilled mind in solving doubts and passages).[24] These several examples demonstrate how religious doubts became the object of discourse in the vernacular, and in the form of poems. Doubts did not necessarily imply incredulity or scepticism; they did imply the need to make sense of complex problems, suggesting that religious dogma was not accepted passively, even when it concerned the main tenets of Catholic orthodoxy. The expression of doubts shows the need of a bourgeois milieu in the central decades of the fifteenth century to understand theological issues that originated in the late Middle Ages. As has been suggested, the tight metrical scheme of the sonnet helped to address rigorously such questions, as in the tradition of philosophical disputations (the quatrain usually destined to express doubt and the tercet, its solution).[25] It is worth noting the relevance of these 'doubts', which points to the social dimension of the discussions involving the poet and his correspondents, some of whom were members of the Florentine artisanal groups.

Intellectuals acted within a society that was very vocal in expressing its doubts, as the Florentine historian and chronicler Bartolomeo Cerretani (1474–1524) reports in his *Dialogo della mutatione di Firenze* (A dialogue on the mutation of Florence, 1520), in a fascinating segment on his fellow citizens' doubts in matters of faith. The dialogue revolves around events following the year 1512, when the Medici returned to Florence. The interlocutors are Girolamo and Lorenzo, followers of Savonarola who are travelling to Germany, attracted by the fame of a 'venerable churchman', Martin Luther; Giovanni di Bernardo Rucellai, supporter of the Medici; and Francesco Guicciardini, then *governatore* of Modena, where the dialogue takes place.[26] Girolamo shares the Savonarolian idea of an imminent renovation of the church; religion has 'grown old in the mind of men and women',

> [s]o that almost everyone, these days, visits temples out of shame and fear and prelates celebrate the Mass in them, apart from a few places, not to lose their benefits; but neither kind of people believe that God exists, that the Son became flesh, etc., but [they believe that] the world has always been, is, and will be with the same corruption and generation of all forms, such as immobile, vegetative, sensitive, and rational beings, and that man, for being nobler than the other beings, should take advantage of them all and that, once men are dead, everything is over for them.[27]

Cerretani recounts doubts that seem to verge on outright atheism. While doubts on the existence of God (or plain denial thereof) were not uncommon, other subtler and creepier doubts could make their way into the mind of Renaissance Italians. What if God in fact existed and were a fool, a delirious entity? What could be the consequences? If the idea that a universe working like a well-tuned though godless machinery was after all acceptable, that of a universe ruled by a demented ruler could have uncanny consequences. A line from a poem by Savonarola (titled 'On the ruin of the world', 1472) suggests that such opinion was not uncommon: 'Some deny you, some say that you are delirious' ('Chi te nega, chi dice che tu sogni').[28] Such expression of anti-Christian feelings could open the door to disquieting thoughts.

The extension of religious doubts worried the Catholic Church, and rightly so. In fifteenth- and early sixteenth-century Florence, humanists and intellectually curious merchants discussed the materialistic ideas of Lucretius at large. Doubts on the immortality of the soul were surely not peculiar to Renaissance Florence, as they had surfaced throughout the Middle Ages.[29] Yet Florence was the place where Lucretius had been first rediscovered. His rediscovery and the fortune of *De rerum natura*, especially after 1494, fostered these ideas, and it is not unlikely that 'in this highly vocal society [Florence] that exchanged ideas in piazzas, in shops and on street corners, non-Latinists and even the illiterate could have picked up their gist and understood their relevance to the present situation'.[30] At the other end of the scale, Pietro Pomponazzi's treatise *De immortalitate animae* (On the immortality of soul, 1516) was perhaps the most famous among the treatises questioning this matter.[31] In 1513, the Fifth Lateran Council issued a decree that professors of philosophy, when lecturing on the soul, should remind their listeners of the truth of the Christian religion. In 1517, the synod of Florence prohibited the reading of Lucretius in schools.[32] Doubts concerning the Resurrection, the immortality of the soul, and the Eucharist (and transubstantiation) are well attested in the previous centuries as well. Preachers had been vocal about the many doubters of these articles of faith since at least the thirteenth century, and complaining about the corruption of present times was certainly commonplace.[33] We may thus infer that traditionally, doubt in matters of faith had to do with the divine nature of Christ, the Creation, the existence and the immortality of the soul, and the existence of otherworldly realms or predestination. Later on, in the seventeenth and eighteenth centuries, these doubts became matters of everyday discussion across all social strata.[34]

Doubt and Justice

Florence is an interesting case study in light of a more comprehensive definition of doubt, one that does not identify it exclusively with incredulity. If on the one hand Florentine poets did not shy away from voicing their atheism or at least their doubts in matters of religion, on the other hand doubt served other purposes in Florentine civic life, as shown by the Florentine fortune of the story of 'Doubting Thomas'.

The doubt (or incredulity) of Thomas is perhaps the most famous story of doubt in Western culture. The story refers to an episode, told in the Gospel of John, that takes place after the Resurrection of Jesus Christ. Thomas was not present when the risen Christ appeared to the disciples; he therefore refuses to believe in the

Resurrection unless he can put his finger into Christ's wounds. When, after eight days, Christ returns to the house where the apostles meet, he invites Thomas to touch his body. At this point, Thomas recognizes Christ and calls him 'My Lord and my God'.[35] Nowhere in his Gospel does John say explicitly that Thomas actually touched the resurrected body. Rather, the action is suspended at the very moment when Thomas is about to perform his gesture of incredulity, which never fully takes place. Nevertheless, the moment of touch became a staple of subsequent literary and visual representations of the episode. Possibly its most astounding depiction is that by Caravaggio in his *Doubting Thomas*, painted in 1601/02 for the private collection of Marquis Vincenzo Giustiniani (now in Potsdam).

Thomas was by no means perceived as a negative figure; on the contrary, especially in the post-Trent period he came to be 'a useful model for modern believers: good Catholic Christians could waver and return to the fold stronger in their convictions'.[36] The story of Thomas has been the object of countless theological interpretations, an account of which lies well beyond the scope and limits of this study. I shall only stress that the episode involves a series of distinctions between 'faith', 'belief', and 'doubt'. Scholars have suggested that Thomas did not lack faith, as his subsequent evangelizing activity eloquently demonstrates. He rather lacked faith during one precise moment of his life, despite being a fervent believer. Thus, doubt prompts a distinction between 'faith' and 'belief': 'doubt is not the opposite of faith, and [...] belief is distinct from faith'.[37] Glenn Most, who has authored one of the most thorough surveys of the subject, has identified Thomas's desire to put his finger into Christ's wound as a moment of 'hyperbolic doubt'.[38] Nevertheless, he demonstrates that Thomas never actually touched Christ, as subsequent readings and pictorial versions of the episode tend to assume, leading to a misunderstanding of 'not just some detail of John's account, but its deepest and most fundamental message'.[39] It was the subsequent exegetical tradition that deemed it necessary to stress the moment of touch, to cast away possible doubts concerning the materiality of Christ's body and the veracity of his resurrection.

To further complicate the picture is Thomas's peculiar relation to Christ. First of all, as John stresses twice, Thomas means 'twin', as does the Greek translation of his name (Didymos). In many cultures, Most observes, 'Thomas is burdened by the negative associations [...] linked with the phenomenon of a twin birth', for twins 'are thought to be produced either by the mother's adultery or by divine intervention (or both).'[40] As Most insightfully points out, there is an etymological connection between Thomas the doubter and Thomas the twin:

> For in the narrative John has devised, Thomas plays above all the role of a doubter, and in many languages [...] the words for 'doubt' and for 'two' are etymologically related. [...] This widespread usage suggests that doubt is being conceived above all as the response to a situation in which there are two alternatives, of which it is not certain which is the right one. As the twin, the second son who cannot easily be distinguished from the first one, Thomas is the perfect embodiment of doubt in general and of doubt about identity in particular.[41]

Such issues of identity were further complicated in the tradition of the Gnostic apocryphal Gospels, in which Thomas came to be identified as the twin of Jesus Christ, his mortal brother, the 'dark twin'.[42] In general, according to Most, John provides a narrative frame in which doubt shifts from a moment of sceptical crisis to a positive phase of discovery and confirmation of faith. It is thanks to Thomas's doubt that analogous doubts of future readers and believers are once and for all dispelled.[43]

We may not expect all Renaissance people to have been familiar with the theological intricacies of the 'Doubting Thomas' episode. Nonetheless, most of them were certainly well acquainted with the visual representations — paintings, frescoes, statues, reliefs, and so on — depicting this scene, which especially during the Middle Ages was often connected with the meeting between the resurrected Christ and Mary Magdalene (the so-called *Noli me tangere* episode, see Chapter 3).[44] Both iconographies were common enough in the early modern period, and both revolve around the problematic issue of touching the body of the resurrected divinity and the epistemological problem of the knowledge of the divine.[45] Erin Benay and Lisa Rafanelli stress the gendered nature of the two episodes and their different destinations. While the *Noli me tangere* was mainly directed towards women for their exercises of private devotion, the 'Doubting Thomas' story generally had public and male connotations.

In late fourteenth-century Tuscany and in the following decades, Thomas's 'inquisitorial touch' came to be perceived as a positive, male virtue.[46] As such, it was often depicted 'near the entrances of Tuscan courthouses', reminding 'jurors of the necessity for evidence'.[47] Franco Sacchetti (1332/34–1400) wrote in 1377 a series of tercets for a lost fresco of *Doubting Thomas* in the Sala dell'Udienza (where public hearings were held) in the Palazzo Vecchio in Florence. The text reads:

> Touch the Truth as I do, and you will believe
> In the absolute Justice of the Trinity
> Which always exalts each person who sits in judgement.
> Direct your hand to the Truth and your eyes to heaven,
> And all your speech and your every deed
> To the common good without exception.
> Search for Truth, Justice will result;
> Direct your whole and free mind to the Common good,
> Because without this, a government is deficient.[48]

As has been observed, these three stanzas of three lines represent a precise commentary on the now-lost image of doubting Thomas; in doing so, they turn the original religious meaning of the episode into an entirely civic one. Sacchetti's penchant for the 'new', 'strange', and 'unpredictable' could have been the basis for this iconographic turn, forcing a new reading upon a well-known image.[49] In this context, the experience of doubt is a crucial moment in civic life, the moment that must precede judgement and assent to truth. In addition, one should recall that the Tribunal of the Mercanzia had commissioned from Andrea del Verrocchio a bronze version of the *Incredulity of Thomas*, to be placed on an external niche of Orsanmichele in Florence. As Most suggests, Thomas 'functioned as the patron saint of the mercantile courts, justifying the importance of the principle that one must test carefully before pronouncing judgement'.[50] Besides this, Thomas was a favourite saint of the Medici family, while 'the holy girdle of Mary given to Thomas was preserved in Prato as a religious relic [...] of central importance to the city's cultural identity'.[51] Thomas was thus a central figure in Florentine civic and public devotion; his incredulity was less a moment of scepticism than a reminder of the importance of fair decisions in justice and trade.

Contemporary poetry extolled Thomas as a model of faith, as we can see in a sonnet in honour of St Thomas by the Bolognese poet Girolamo Pandolfi, also known as Girolamo Casio or Girolamo Casio de' Medici (1467–1533).[52] The sonnet is included in the *Vite dei santi* (Lives of the saints) dedicated to Pope Clemens VII in 1524.[53] The work had been conceived under Leo X, who suggested to Casio in a somewhat unflattering way to avoid love poetry, for he would have been outdone by many other poets. Instead, he could try his hand at spiritual poetry. Casio then decided to compose a series of hagiographies in the form of sonnets.[54] The sonnet devoted to Thomas lists the moments that followed the Resurrection, including the apparition to Mary Magdalene and to Thomas. The apostle is the only one to whom Christ 'offered his holy wounds', whereas he gave only 'joy and shame' to Mary Magdalene. Interestingly, Casio suggests that Thomas's doubt is more useful to us than Peter's 'pure faith'. Peter seems to represent an unattainable model, whereas believers could identify more readily with Thomas's unsure faith and with his doubts.[55] A similar, positive view of Thomas appears in a *lauda* by the Florentine Francesco degli Albizzi and featured in a collection of *laudi* first published in Florence in 1485.[56] The author opens his short poem with the doubt of Thomas:

> Those who want to have God's great mercy
> Should turn to St Thomas with great faith.
> O disciple of Christ, St Thomas
> Witness of faith to the whole world
> You did not want to believe in truth with no reason
> Unless you could touch the joyful body
> Of Jesus. But touching it, you believed.[57]

The text goes on to recall Thomas's evangelizing and proselytizing mission, his being the recipient of the Virgin's girdle, and his martyrdom.

Doubting Joseph

The 'Doubting Thomas' episode shows how stories of doubt could be designed to reinforce faith while also touching issues of social justice and social relations. Stories of doubt were complex and evolved over the decades, sometimes losing — at least partially — their disruptive potential. One such instance is the episode known as the 'Doubt of Joseph', 'Dream of Joseph' or 'Sleeping Joseph'. The story intersects with developments in Italian society, and at the turn of the fifteenth century the disquieting aspects of Joseph's doubt appear to be neutralized in favour of a more orthodox reading of this evangelical episode. The episode is told in the Gospel of Matthew:

> After His mother Mary was betrothed to Joseph, before they came together,
> she was found with child of the Holy Spirit. Then Joseph her husband, being

a just man, and not wanting to make her a public example, was minded to put her away secretly. But while he thought about these things, behold an angel of the Lord appeared to him in a dream, saying: 'Joseph, son of David, do not be afraid to take to you Mary your wife, for that which is conceived in her is of the Holy Spirit.' (Matthew 1. 18–20)

Joseph's moment of uncertainty and fear is resolved by the prodigious intervention of the angel: 'Then Joseph, being aroused from sleep, did as the angel of the Lord commanded him and took to him his wife' (Matthew 1. 24).

Matthew only alludes to Joseph's doubt, whereas the author of the Protogospel of James expands on the moral dilemma of Joseph and his emotional distress:

> When she was in her sixth month, behold, Joseph came home from his building, and entered his house, and found Mary pregnant. He struck himself in the face and threw himself to the ground in sackcloth, and wailed bitterly saying: 'How can I face the Lord God? What kind of prayer can I make about her since I received her a virgin from the temple of the Lord God, and I did not protect her. Who has conspired against me? Who has done this evil deed in my house? Who took the virgin away from me and defiled her?[58]

Joseph then confronts Mary, spelling out his suspicions:

> Then Joseph stood up from the sackcloth and called Mary and said to her: 'You have been cared for by God — why have you done this? Have you forgotten the Lord your God?' [...] But she wailed bitterly and said, 'I am pure and have not known a man.' And Joseph said to her 'How then are you pregnant?' And she answered, 'As the Lord my God lives, I do not know from where it came to me.'[59]

These passages are far more emotionally charged than those in the Gospel of Matthew: for example, both Mary and Joseph are represented as weeping bitterly. In addition, Joseph is afraid, finding himself caught in a moral conundrum: his doubts do not merely concern the origin of Mary's pregnancy but the course of action he is to take and his inability to make a morally sound decision:

> Then Joseph was very frightened and kept quiet from her, considering carefully what to do about her. And Joseph said to himself: 'If I keep her sin a secret, I will be found in opposition to the law of the Lord; but if I expose her condition to the children of Israel, I fear that perhaps the child inside her is angelic and I will be found handing over innocent blood to a death sentence. What then should I do with her? I will secretly divorce her.'[60]

It is only after exploring his moral dilemma that Joseph falls asleep and receives the angel's visitation:

> And night laid hold of him, and behold, an angel of the Lord appeared to him and said: 'Do not be afraid of this child, for that which is inside her is from the Holy Spirit. She will have a Son and you will name him Jesus; for he will save his people from their sins.' And Joseph arose from his sleep and glorified the God of Israel for showing him favor. And he guarded the child.[61]

In the Gospel of Pseudo-Matthew, Joseph even claims that he wants to take his life, and he accuses the Five Virgins who had followed Mary into his house of purposefully misleading him by pretending that she was pregnant by an angel of the

Lord.[62] This puzzling episode has been the object of countless exegetical efforts. In particular, the nature of Joseph's doubt seems to be controversial. Is he afraid that Mary committed adultery? If so, his doubt concerns the course of action he should take, faced as he is by two apparently non-viable options: either he takes Mary with him, hiding her sin; or he exposes her to shame, and possibly death, as an adulteress. It has also been suggested that Joseph 'begins to shrink from taking the final step of taking into his house one so close intimate with God. This would be a natural reaction in Joseph, given that he had the Old Testament outlook of fear of God'.[63] In other words, Joseph knows that Mary is with child from the Holy Spirit, and yet he is afraid and thinks to put her away in secret. It is at this point that the angel intervenes, showing Joseph the path he should take; in doing so, he does not reveal anything new, for Joseph already knows the divine nature of Mary's pregnancy. Rather, the angel gives Joseph an order, thus solving his moral dilemma.[64]

From the Middle Ages onwards, the moment of Joseph's doubt lent itself to different interpretations, among which the view that Joseph believed Mary to have committed adultery was possibly the most widespread. As such, it was explored in a variety of literary sources ranging from Latin poems to vernacular ones to mystery plays. During the Middle Ages, Joseph was a somewhat shadowy figure, mostly represented as an old and at times foolish character. His influence began to grow in the early fifteenth century, as for example shown by the works of the theologian Jean Gerson. In 1413 Gerson wrote a vernacular tract on Joseph titled *Considérations sur Saint Joseph*, and the following year he began a Latin poem titled *Josephina*, which he completed in 1415 during his attendance at the Council of Constance. Gerson meditates at length on the episodes of Jesus's infancy and on the everyday familial life he conducted with Joseph and Mary. It has been suggested that 'the entrance of a virile, hardworking and loving man into the drama of salvation' might have had a social explanation:

> The coming of Joseph asserts the new vitality of town culture, where physical labour, guilds and production had become an integral part of everyday life. St Joseph the carpenter was a model for the kind of hardworking people to whom Gerson preached on Sundays.[65]

In addition, Joseph's increasing relevance pointed to a new model of male affectivity and parenthood, as well as defining a new pattern of sanctity:

> Here was a saint who was not a martyr, a strong and capable man who chose to live celibately within marriage. [...] For Gerson Joseph's life was peaceful and harmonious [...] Gerson [...] provided a model of masculine affective spirituality where masochism and martyrdom were absent.[66]

A number of texts belonging to different genres expanded instead on the moment of Joseph's doubt and its comic effect.[67] In a *novella* by Franco Sacchetti, the painter Giotto is strolling around Florence with a group of friends when he comes across a *dipintura* (possibly a fresco) of the Virgin and St Joseph. One of his friends asks him why Joseph is always painted 'so melancholic' ('così sempre malinconoso'), to which Giotto wittily replies: 'Isn't he right, for he sees his wife pregnant and he does not know of whom?'[68] In a fifteenth-century *sacra rappresentazione*, the so-called *Passione di Revello* (a locality in modern Piedmont, where the drama was staged in 1481), Joseph's doubt is explicitly seen as the work of the devil, Sathanas.[69] It is Sathanas who appears to Joseph in his dreams, suggesting to him that Mary is with child:

> Mary your wife, I tell you,
> She is big, big as someone who is about to give birth.
> Her eyes are blank, her face is dark
> Her breasts are heavy beyond measure,
> She is bashful because she is afraid
> That you realize her fault.
> You know as well as me, you man of God,
> That you have never slept with her:
> Someone else, I tell you, has impregnated her.
> What will you do now, Joseph,
> You, who have always been just,
> And, as you know, have always loved justice?[70]

Once awakened, Joseph is tormented by doubts and he makes up his mind to go visit his spouse. Meanwhile, Mary begs the Lord to help her, as she realizes that her condition will trouble Joseph; God therefore decides to send Gabriel to reassure her. When she meets Joseph, the two have a short conversation during which Joseph does not show his inner turmoil. His doubts do not leave him, however, and he speaks to himself:

> Alas Joseph, poor old man,
> What will you do, you poor wretch?
> You were right to say: 'I do not want a wife,
> I do not want to suffer so many bitter pains.'[71]

Joseph then ponders the course of action he should take; at this point, the text follows quite closely that of Matthew's Gospel. Unlike in the Gospel, however, in the *Passione di Revello* Joseph falls asleep again. While he is fast asleep the Archangel Michael flies to Sathanas and orders him to stop tempting Joseph and return to hell. Meanwhile, Gabriel appears to Joseph in his sleep and reassures him that Mary is with child from the Holy Spirit. Eventually, Joseph begs Mary for forgiveness and the episode concludes. The *Passione* plays clearly with caricatural features, easily recognizable in Joseph's jealousy and in the description of the Virgin, which lacks any form of decorum.

Joseph's doubt is given a similar treatment in a poem by Antonio Cornazzano (c. 1430–1483/84), who was active for a long time at the Sforza court of Milan. His poem *Vita della gloriosa vergine Maria* (Life of the glorious Virgin Mary), dedicated to Ippolita Maria Sforza (wife of the future king of Naples Alfonso d'Aragona), originally drafted around 1457/58 and revised in light of the first printed edition (1471), had more than twenty editions by 1591.[72] Cornazzano doubles the moments of doubt in his narration of the Annunciation, giving ample space to Mary's doubts, too. At the same time, the description of Joseph is even more of a caricature than that in the Revello *Passione*, despite the courtly environment for which the work was meant. At the moment of the Gabriel's salutation, Mary suspects that something in his words may be less than appropriate. The angel understands Mary's doubt and reassures her, announcing that she will give birth to Jesus.[73] A second moment of doubt occurs when Mary wonders how this could be, since she knows no man. Gabriel promptly understands this second doubt and reassures her, announcing to Mary her miraculous pregnancy.[74]

By contrast, the description of Joseph's doubts seems intended to prompt readers' laughter. According to the Gospel of Pseudo-Matthew, the High Priest gathered in the temple the descendants of David in order to choose Mary's groom from among them. Each was to carry a rod, and he whose branch blossomed would become Mary's husband. In Cornazzano's account, when flowers sprout on Joseph's branch he is disappointed, for he realizes he is too old for such a beautiful young woman: 'Then began the acute pain | Of jealousy, and he perhaps often cursed | The rod for bearing flowers and leaves.'[75] When he discovers Mary's pregnancy, Joseph's jealousy seems to get the best of him. The portrait of Joseph as a poor, jealous old man, far from perfection, is certainly undignified:

> Joseph, who was never so good
> That he did not see a thorn under a rose
> Gazes at these deeds that are not hers
> [...] And so, the poor old man
> Began to rage with jealousy.[76]

The word used to describe Joseph's reaction (*imbestiare*) — and the reaction itself — goes beyond all rules of decorum, and Cornazzano expands amply on Joseph's puzzlement. On the other hand, Joseph also knows Mary's modesty and simplicity, and he is aware of how all the young men who look at her turn their carnal appetite to the contemplation of God. Cornazzano then mentions Joseph's decision to leave Mary, which gives him the opportunity to insert a theological digression to reflect on why Joseph could be called 'just' in the Gospel if he nurtured such thoughts.[77] We could say that the digression adds a third layer of doubt to the episode, introducing, after the doubts of Mary and Joseph, those of Cornazzano (and his readers). We grasp in the theological content of these lines the subtly disquieting nature that this episode must have had for fifteenth-century devotees; Cornazzano chose to resort to the *Glossa ordinaria* (the exegetical apparatus to the Bible accrued over the centuries) to make sense of this seeming conundrum:

> And in explaining his leaving
> The glossa to the Gospel comments
> On his thought of abandoning her.
> He who said that Joseph was just
> How could he call him just if he knew that,
> And that he would depart from his wife?
> But then he absolves him aptly and readily in two ways:
> Either he left her for being unworthy
> Of coming close to her and committing a dishonest act,
> Or because it was the custom of that kingdom
> To stone a woman guilty of fornication.
> It was better to leave,
> So that he calls him rightly 'just'.
> [...]

> And so, full of love frenzy,
> The chaste old man left wavering;
> He was jealous of him, whom he later raised.[78]

The concluding sequence of the passage builds on the episode of Joseph's dream. Joseph sighs and cries, while the angel asks him how he dared to leave such an exquisite creature as Mary. While Joseph cries, the angel reproaches him for his scant faith: 'You show yourself as a man of little faith | For you place little trust in God's valour.'[79]

In Cornazzano's tale we see a stratification of doubts: those of Mary highlight her perfectly chaste and exemplary nature; those of Joseph point to a momentary lack of faith, their caricatural treatment possibly serving to stress their absurd nature and steer readers away from nurturing similar perplexities. Finally, the readers' and writer's own doubts as to the baffling theological import of the tale require from the author a proper discussion referring to the commonly accepted exegetical apparatus of the *Glossa ordinaria*.

The first edition of Cornazzano's poem comes at the beginning the 1470s, a decade that saw a marked increase in the cult of St Joseph. The following decades, and particularly the first quarter of the sixteenth century, witnessed an upsurge in the foundation of churches, chapels, altars, and confraternities dedicated to Joseph. Contemporary works of art 'bespeak an aggrandizement of Joseph's pictorial role'; at the same time, one must acknowledge the 'surge in popularity of certain iconographies that signify and emphasize his standing in grace and status as intercessor', which include the 'Nativity with Shepherds', the 'Flight into Egypt', and the 'Rest on the Flight'.[80] Joseph is now seen as the protector of the Virgin and Child, the so-called *nutritor Domini*, the one who nourished the living God, while also being the first witness, aside from Mary, to his incarnation.[81] His role of protector of the Virgin made him a particularly prominent figure in Venice, whose symbolical identification with Mary was part of its civic identity. In a time of constant trouble because of fights with the Turks, the Italian Wars, and the perceived threats of the Jews, Joseph became the ideal intercessor to which Italians and Venetians in particular turned for protection. As Carolyn Wilson points out, '[C]ertain dedications to St Joseph in Lombardy, Emilia, and the Veneto are definitely linked to specific episodes of social crisis: outbreaks of plague and violent anti-Semitism and military events at the time of the Italian and Cambrai Wars.'[82]

Beginning in the 1480s, St Joseph's Day became a civic festivity across Italy. In Venice, Joseph was the protector of the guild of carpenters, of ship builders of the Arsenale (*marangoni de nave*), of 'vendors of milk and dairy products (*pestrineri*)', and of the guild of 'makers and vendors of lasagna and pasta (*lasagneri*)'.[83] As the 'first convert', Joseph was seen as a facilitator of conversion of Jews and Turks, a figure who fit into the proselytizing mission of the Catholic Church. The figure of Ottoman warrior kneeling in front of the Virgin and Child in Vincenzo Catena's *Warrior Adoring the Infant Christ and the Virgin* (1521–31, London, National Gallery) may reflect this connotation. In this particular case the role of Joseph is not clear;[84] yet in general one can assume that 'the various interpretations of Joseph's iconography

[...] suggest that the basic theology of Joseph articulated in ecclesiastic writings must have been widely understood by believers during the late Quattrocento and early Cinquecento'.[85] The 'Sleeping Joseph' or the 'Doubt of Joseph' was part of this process of popularization of Joseph's cult; the episode progressively lost its 'popular, humorous element' and acquired its 'primary function [...] to denote Joseph as the recipient of God's word in dreams, that is, the recipient of divine revelation'.[86] There exist several examples of this iconography, which is 'traditional for Nativities throughout the Trecento and Quattrocento'.[87] One may recall here Giotto's version in the Scrovegni Chapel in Padua, or Gentile da Fabriano's *Nativity* in the predella of his *Adoration of the Magi* (1423, Florence, Santa Trinita), Giovanni Bellini's *Nativity* (early 1470s, Pesaro, Museo civico), or again, Jacopo Bassano's *Nativity with Shepherds and Sts Victor and Corona* (1568, Bassano del Grappa, San Giuseppe).[88] There are no humorous elements in these depictions of Joseph.

Certainly, representations of a sleeping Joseph may establish a connection with his moment of doubt, reinforced by the almost overlapping iconographies of the gestures of sleep and those of melancholy or sorrow.[89] This evolution is reflected in written sources. Again, Carolyn Wilson has called attention to the vernacular 'Life of Joseph' added by Nicolas Jenson to his 1475 edition of the *Golden Legend* by Jacopo da Varazze (Voragine); in 1481, a 'Life of Joseph' was added to the edition of the vernacular Bible printed by Giovanni Ragazzo for Lucantonio Giunta.[90] The author of this text feels compelled to specify that Joseph decided to leave Mary, but he never 'thought her pregnancy proceeded by a man', and while Joseph was reflecting on this the angel Gabriel appeared to him in a dream.[91]

This progression towards a dignified image of Joseph, along which popular aspects are abandoned, is evident from the treatment accorded by Erasmus to the doubt of Joseph in his *Paraphrasis* on the Gospel of Matthew (1522). Italian readers had access to the translation by Bernardino Tomitano (1547), dedicated to Caterina Sauli and made at the behest of her husband, Giovanni Gioacchino da Passano.[92] Tomitano's translation was put on the Index in 1554, and in 1556 he published a sort of self-apology in which he lamented that he had been fooled by Erasmus, who had masterfully disguised his mistakes under the veil of his 'doubtful metaphors', 'doubtful speeches', and 'doubtful way of reasoning'.[93]

In Erasmus's narrative, Joseph realizes the change in Mary after the Annunciation, as she grows radiant with divine light. Everything around her appears to be more than human, and yet he recognizes 'the fragility of her age and of her sex', having seen it in ordinary girls. Any other husband would raise a scandal, but not Joseph, who was chosen to silence all gossip. His goodness of heart and his wisdom are so well known that nobody could think that he would accept being 'his wife's pimp' ('il ruffian di sua moglie') or sheepishly accept someone else's son under his roof. The 'most innocent' ('innocentissimo', an adjective repeated more than once) Joseph cannot bring his desire for revenge to even voicing his concern, in order not to upset Mary (that is to say, he has no desire for revenge at all). Yet his inner turmoil does not subside; Erasmus emphasizes throughout his paraphrasis Joseph's distress, melancholy, and disquiet:

So, he suffers in his soul from hidden thoughts which silently torment him; instead [of pursuing some revenge] he tries to find a way to divorce her without shame and danger for the maid. Because of this, up to that moment it was God's will that the most innocent husband should suffer in his soul those excruciating sufferings, and that he should be troubled by such bitter suffering, for this was necessary to the certainty of faith.[94]

Joseph's doubts are thus set in the context of a providential plan, 'the certitude of faith' being possibly Joseph's own faith and that of the believers who meditate on his doubts. Erasmus elaborates on Joseph's inner turmoil in his version of Gabriel's speech. Gabriel first asks him: 'Joseph, son of David, what is this suspicion of yours, which scourges your soul and torments you with such bitter passion? What are these sighs of yours? What is this turmoil of yours?'[95] Joseph wakes up happy and ready to fulfil God's desire, 'shaking off all his melancholy' ('lasciando in disparte ogni maninconia').[96]

Erasmus's text allows us to gauge the change in the perception of Joseph. Not only does his character now lack all humorous innuendos, he has become — at least for the moment — mostly a melancholic doubter. Pietro Aretino, in his narration of the life of Mary (*Vita di Maria Vergine*, 1539), also stresses the moment of Joseph's melancholy, describing how Sleep, while Joseph is 'confused by the lies of suspicion', makes him place his left arm on a table, letting his head fall on his elbow.[97] Aretino's Joseph, too, is torn between his suspicion, for which he begs mercy to the Lord, and his certainty that 'there is no stain in the immaculate woman'.[98]

To conclude this survey, I shall quote the eighteenth-century edition of Cesare Ripa's *Iconologia*, 'augmented with images, notes, and facts' by Cesare Orlandi. Orlandi reprints Ripa's text, adding to the allegories examples (facts) taken from sacred history, secular history, and literary sources, these being 'imaginary (or wondrous) facts'. To explain the entry 'Doubt' (see the previous chapter) he chooses as a *fatto storico sagro* the story of 'Doubtful St Joseph' as told in a sonnet by the Sienese playwright Girolamo Gigli (1660–1722). Gigli's Joseph '[d]oubtful remained, and then he feels remorse of his doubt | And between Faith and the senses his heart duels. | In the end, his faith surrenders, and quietly he wants | To walk far away'.[99] It is the angel's intervention then that leads Joseph to acknowledge the mystery taking place in Mary's womb and to believe in her mystical purity. One may surmise that in addition to all the reasons that determined Joseph's fortune, his being a doubter may have made him popular with believers who themselves lived in an age of doubt.

Along the Po Valley

We have described so far works that point to what we may call a 'social life of doubt'. Other texts seem to reinforce this view — texts, this time, that come from the northern courts and cities of the Po Valley.

I will begin with an anecdote that takes us to Forlì, the court of Pino Ordelaffi, some time between 1477 and 1480. During a banquet, a guest presents Ordelaffi (1436–1480) with a huge crossbow whose bow is made of wood and iron. A discussion arises as to the reason for this particular feature of the weapon. A young doctor from Verona tries to provide an explanation, drawing on Aristotle's works, which he quotes in Latin. Also sitting among Ordelaffi's guests is the Bolognese humanist Antonio Urceo Codro (1446–1500), then preceptor of Pino's son, Sinibaldo II (1467–1480). Codro was a pleasant man and a popular figure in Bologna (he has a wonderful tale about a young fruit seller at the Bologna market addressing him as *barba*, 'old uncle', despite his being not even fifty). Codro praises the young doctor's speech but suggests that Aristotle may have been wrong.[100] The doctor is slightly offended and rebukes Codro for casting a shadow on Aristotle's authority; to which Codro replies that, if needed, he is ready to confute the first principles and very axioms of philosophy. A staunch Aristotelian, the Veronese doctor maintains that it is not possible to deny or doubt the 'first principles'. For example, the proposition 'Whatever one says either is or is not' ('Quodcumque dicitur aut est aut non est') must be true. Codro's reply consists of just two words: 'I doubt' ('Ego dubito'). The doctor triumphantly argues that if Codro is doubtful of a proposition, at least he must be sure of being doubtful. Codro fights back, affirming that in fact he is even doubtful of being doubtful ('Ego dubito an dubitem hanc propositionem'). The Veronese then subtly suggests that if he doubts being doubtful, Codro doubts at least something (and is therefore sure of something). Codro, predictably, replies that he is doubtful whether he doubts of being doubtful ('Ego dubito an dubitem, dubitemne').

The discussion must have gone on for awhile; with supreme irony, Codro cuts it short by saying that he has limited himself to adding only one 'I doubt' to each of the doctor's sentences. When the doctor has inserted 'to doubt' twice in his sentence, Codro has merely repeated it thrice ('Et si ille bis 'dubitare' dicebat, ego ter repetebam'), replying to the doctor's 'you doubt to doubt' with 'I doubt to doubt to doubt'. Finally, the doctor resorts to the Scholastic principle that 'one should not dispute with those who deny first principles' ('contra negantes principia non est disputandum'). For his part, Codro was probably ignoring the maxim that during banquets 'it is not convenient to talk about subtle, doubtful, or difficult things', as Matteo Palmieri had warned in his *Vita civile*.[101] Yet we readers cannot but share the sense of amusement that Codro feels in telling his story of doubt.

We read this delightful anecdote in Antonio Urceo Codro's *Sermo VI* (c. 1497), the prelude to his academic course on Aristotle and Homer at the University of Bologna. This introductory lesson of sorts is devoted to the topic of how human life is full of errors ('de mendaci mortalium vita').[102] The Bolognese *magister* delivered his introduction in front of a packed classroom that barely contained the crowd that had flocked to hear him. Pronounced in a lively Latin, full of references to daily life and funny, if not salacious, stories, Codro's *sermo* deals with truth and falsehood and how to tell a true proposition from a false one (starting from Aristotle's *On Interpretation*). It would seem that if something certain and true can be found in human knowledge, it should be found in the works of Aristotle, the 'philosopher of truth'. Yet David has written in his Psalms (116) that 'every man is a liar' ('omnis homo mendax'). How can we escape this impasse?

In fact, we must admit that nothing can be known with certainty, as all arts and disciplines seem to rely on doubtful principles ('constant rebus dubiis') and on opinions devoid of proof ('opinionibus nulla prorsus apparente demonstratione').[103] Codro, who seems to predate here Agrippa's work *De incertitudine et vanitate scientiarum* (On the uncertainty and vanity of the arts and sciences, 1530; first translated into Italian by Lodovico Domenichi in 1548), provides a short overview of the weaknesses of all sciences and their practitioners. Scholars of grammar, dialectic, natural sciences, ethics, law, medicine, poets and historians: all have conflicting views and opinions. Nothing can be derived with absolute certainty, even from the principles of the most rigorous sciences such as mathematics. At the same time, the senses offer us false images and impressions, so we cannot trust them either. The boundaries between true and false are weak and porous; in addition, what Codro argues with regard to the intellectual level holds true also on the ethical plane. Codro easily shows how poets, astrologers, common people, even popes, cardinals, and members of the clergy all lie, and so do kings, emperors, princes, and notaries, down to merchants and craftsmen. The conclusion of Codro's speech is somewhat bitter: truth is wonderful and worth of praise, but 'among men it is rare and hard to find, and many people lie out of ignorance, or because of their corrupted senses, or because they want to, or maybe out of interest'.[104]

Codro had already expounded some of these themes in his long *Sermo I*, written around 1494–95 and certainly after the French invasion of Italy in September 1494. The text, an introduction to a course on Homer, Terence, and Euripides, revolves around the idea of *fabula*. Everything human is a *fabula*, a vain tale destined to disappear soon; everything changes shape (the *sermo* deals extensively with metamorphosis), everything is unstable and eventually dissolves into death. If, Codro writes, 'fable is what has neither truth nor verisimilitude, what truth, what certainty has this life of ours? What darkness has it, rather, what uncertainty?'[105] The category of *fabula* is at the same time comic and carnivalesque and tragic, and aptly describes the human condition, or at least Codro's perception of it. Nothing is certain, mutability is everywhere, what we hold true and even sacred is exposed to the laws of time.[106] Codro's sceptical attitude (he knew Pyrrho of Elis, whom he quotes in his *Sermo VI*) is interesting in that it concerns all forms of knowledge and human activity. Besides, it is not merely an intellectual posture; rather, it moves from the overlap in the meaning of 'true' and 'false' in both the ethical and intellectual sense. Codro's scepticism thus turns into a grotesque perception of human life as radically marked by hyperbolic uncertainty. Codro sketches a radical condition of doubt that transcends the purely epistemological dimension. One is tempted to connect his view to the crisis precipitated by the French invasion led by Charles VIII. Although one should not presume a causal connection between that event and Codro's thought, it is safe to assume that the condition of political and cultural uncertainty of the mid-1490s must have somehow affected his views.

Doubt, uncertainty, the sense of the vanity of human life could thus become the object of entertaining discussions held during a banquet or a university lecture. If we tend to think that these were somewhat elitist spaces, we ought to remember, as Codro himself points out, that inaugural lectures were attended by scholars of all disciplines, by senators and knights, as well as by 'schooled commoners' ('plebeios [...] litteratos').[107] In the ensuing decades, as we will see in Chapter 5, doubt will become the fulcrum of other forms of sociability, often outside the spaces of the university. Salons, academies, and domestic interiors will replace (or be juxtaposed with) courts and universities as the spaces of doubt; letters, dialogues, games, and discussions will take the place of lectures and prolusions.

In a university town such as Bologna, the likes of Codro and, later on, Pomponazzi, could teach their lessons on doubt and uncertainty and plant the seeds of incredulity. Vernacular texts coming from northern Italian courts seem to confirm the circulation of doubts outside classrooms. One should avoid a top-down conception: ideas discussed by university *magistri* could have overlapped with popular beliefs or with ideas spread, for example, by preachers. It is, however, undeniable that some contemporary poems and *novelle* show an interest in stories of doubt and doubters. Because *novelle* often represent the microcosm of a city (Florence, Naples, Bologna, etc.) and purport to do it with some degree of realism, we can assume that they retain some verisimilitude. At the same time, being a highly popular genre, collections of short stories were accessible to a large readership, who could find in them entertaining stories of doubt, among other subjects.

This is the case with two *novelle* by the Bolognese Giovanni Sabadino degli Arienti (c. 1445–1510). The tales come from his most famous work, *Le Porretane*, dedicated to Ercole d'Este, Duke of Ferrara, and record conversations that took place at the thermal location of Porretta, near Bologna. Here, Andrea Bentivoglio (d. 1491), a member of a minor branch of the powerful family that ruled Bologna, had gathered a company of men and women. The conversations from which the *novelle* originated allegedly took place in 1475, and the first printed edition of the work came out in Bologna with the date of 1483.[108] However, scholars have shown that 1483 is a false date; the printed version may only have been completed around 1492, while we possess a manuscript version that could be possibly even later, from around 1498. As has been suggested, the *Porretane* are a sort of work in progress stretching from the 1470s to the 1490s, thus covering a crucial portion of Italian Renaissance history.[109]

The collection includes sixty-one *novelle*; the final *novelle* (nos. 56 to 61) are philosophical in content, and the work concludes with a discourse on the immortality of the soul delivered by the Carmelite theologian and poet Battista Spagnoli (1448–1516).[110] Novella 56 stages a humorous episode, or rather, two connected episodes. In the first section of the tale, the future Pope Paul II (the Venetian Pietro Barbo, then only cardinal of San Marco) discusses Job's patience with a member of his secret chamber, Francesco Malacarne. Malacarne states that probably the devil had not properly tempted Job and that he could have devised much worse trials, such as having Job serve in the cardinal's court. To this point, we have merely an example of anti-courtly sentiment; the cardinal, who was a prudent man and good at dissimulation, too, replies that since Malacarne is a man of such 'subtle and speculative mind', he wants him to examine a heretic who is detained in Castel Sant'Angelo because 'he doubts of the Christian faith'.[111]

The following section of the tale contains the dialogue between Malacarne and the prisoner, in which the latter voices his theological doubts. Malacarne first asks the heretic a general question about the extent to which he believes in the Christian faith. He replies, 'I believe so much, that I doubt it is too much.'[112] Sabadino skilfully plays with the words of doubt; in fact, the verb *dubito* is here employed in its sense of 'to fear, to be afraid'. Shortly before, in his address to the heretic, Malacarne twice employs the word *dubitazione*.[113] One may surmise at this point that the real subject of the *novella* is doubt. Malacarne, turned into an inquisitor (as the modern editor of the text aptly suggests), asks the heretic some further questions. He inquires whether he believes that if there were a huge fire in the room, it would be possible to put it out without water. The heretic replies that he does not believe this would ever be possible. Malacarne agrees with him, laughs, and moves on to the next question. He asks if the heretic believes that a person could reach the midst of the sea on the water, without a boat, and not drown. This, again, the heretic does not believe. Once more Malacarne agrees and proceeds to a further question. Does the accused believe that Christ actually fed the hungry with five loaves of bread? To this he replies that since they cannot be sure of the size of the loaves, he has no idea. Malacarne suggests that the Gospel affirms that along with the bread, Christ also had two fishes. The doubter then claims that he would believe everything if 'the breads were made of a thousand bushels of grain each, and the fishes were two whales'.[114] Again, Malacarne heartily laughs and replies, 'I, too, do not believe this.'[115] When Malacarne reports his examination to the cardinal, the latter is most amused and orders that the prisoner be released. Such is the pleasure that he takes in Malacarne's account that he tells it to the pope and all the consistory, 'so that the Pope and his brother cardinals laughed so much of it, that one still laughs of it'.[116]

Plainly, the heretic's doubts concern miracles in general, and Christ's walking on the water and feeding the five thousand in particular. What is striking is that Malacarne agrees with the heretic's incredulity, and neither the cardinal nor the pope nor the consistory seem to take seriously these admissions of incredulity: quite the opposite. But what is even more disturbing is the subtle impression we get that the heretic seems unfamiliar with Christ's miracles, as if he were hearing of them for the first time. Certainly this is meant to be a funny tale, 'the exemplary tale of a myth of tolerance', as the editor of the text puts it.[117] Other scholars, though, have pointed out that in Sabadino's works, traditional irreverence against friars and churchmen in general seems to broach blasphemy and even heresy.[118] And yet, he seems to be aware of touching upon a delicate matter. In the concluding lines of the *novella*, the pope, after having laughed with the cardinal, 'as a just and most holy shepherd' begs pardon of God and 'has Malacarne officially reprimanded, making him understand that one should not recall the miraculous deeds of our upper King unless with holy glory and utmost reverence'.[119] As if this were not enough, in the concluding remarks Sabadino states that the *brigata* took pleasure in the tale, but then

> the divine honour of our saint and orthodox faith was saved with reverence,
> concluding that, where the divine power blows, all fire, visible and invisible,

would be extinguished without water, and one would sail the sea without boat and without any support, and the whole world, although ravenous, would happily feed on one tiny grain.[120]

This (rather weak) palinode, as well as Sabadino's projecting this anecdote back to the period preceding Paul II's election (1464), signals that voicing doubts in matters of religion was possibly becoming risky in a city that was 'austere' and 'controlled by the Roman curia', marked by the presence of Savonarola, who had entered the convent of St Domenico in 1475.[121] A *novella* could be a safe space to stage otherwise dangerous doubts; a farcical trial could reverse their otherwise dramatic consequences.

In the very same years when Sabadino was drafting his work, a physician by the name of Gabriele di Salò was tried in Bologna 'for asserting that Christ's miracles were natural phenomena', besides denying his divine nature and foretelling the end of Christianity.[122] Gabriele di Salò's case was not probably an isolated one. Debates on the nature of Christ seem to have been going on in Bologna for some time. In his poem *Il Fidele*, the poet Giovanni Filoteo Achillini (1466–1538; he was the brother of Alessandro, a celebrated professor of philosophy at the University of Bologna) devotes special attention to the confutation of Arian ideas denying the divine nature of Christ.[123] It is especially in the third and fifth cantos of this allegorical poem in *terza rima* that Achillini expands on this topic. One may wonder why, in a poem written between *c.* 1513 and 1536 (and never printed; only two manuscript copies survive), well before the dissemination of antitrinitarian ideas, Achillini felt the urge to attack such doctrines.[124] It is likely that voices denying the divine nature of Christ were not uncommon in Bologna. One Aurelio Galterini, a Calabrese who had moved to Bologna to study with the philosopher Pietro Pomponazzi, was an enemy of the clergy, the corruption of which he frequently attacked. In July 1524 he was denounced to the vicar of the bishop for having declared in a public discussion on the incipit of the Gospel of John that Christ had become eternal only at the moment of his conception in Mary's womb, 'because it was in God's mind to make himself a son' ('Jesus Christus filius Dei on fuit aeternus nisi quando incarnates fuit de Virgine, quia in mente divina erat facere sibi unum filium').[125] This was equal to denying the divine nature of Christ. Again, Francesco Panzarasi, a professor of logic at the local university, was tried in 1488 for publicly maintaining in front of illiterate people ('persone ydiote') that earth and heaven were eternal; he managed though to be acquitted from the charge of having deemed the miracles and Moses's words 'vain things and fables' ('fatuitates et fabule').[126] Sabadino's *novelle* were thus grounded in a precise historical context and testify to a spreading attitude of doubt towards religion and its dogma. In turn, reading such texts could contribute to the further spread of said ideas and doubts. As has been suggested, and as my examples prove, dangerous doubts and radical ideas filtered down to the less literate, the above-mentioned 'persone ydiote'.[127]

Sabadino shows some degree of irreverence towards other topics, such as the justice meted out at the Last Judgement (Novella 7) and even the Resurrection. In the eighth *novella*, Sabadino has a priest administer last rites to Salvetto di Sandruzzo, who confesses that he believes in everything but the resurrection of the flesh. This is deemed a 'most great heresy' and a 'false opinion' by the priest.[128] Sabadino also refers in the *novella* to the theory of the *annus magnus* from Plato's *Timaeus*, according to which in 36,000 years everything will return and begin anew. The theory is purely a pretext for a joke and criticism of the priest, who has been trying to force Salvetto to leave his house to the parish. Salvetto cunningly replies that either he will be resurrected or he will come back in 36,000 years: in either case, he does not intend to rent a house after his return. The priest is amused and absolves Salvetto for his folly; in fact, Sabadino calls Salvetto a 'fool' ('pazo'). The mocking of the Last Judgement links Novelle 7 and 8, staging doubts that, even if not Sabadino's own, were probably present in contemporary society. These *novelle* and that of Malacarne and the heretic, however, show 'more doubts than destructive systems', more a willingness to mock 'the old medieval dogmatism' than outright atheism.[129] In sum, the *Porretane* exhibit a push towards new humanistic and Neoplatonic topics, such as the *magnitudo animi* or the ability to counter and overcome astral influence with virtue. Yet Sabatino's sceptical attitude towards miracles testifies to a slowly changing culture, riddled with doubts, as we have also seen in the case of Urceo Codro.[130]

In more or less the same years, another writer from Emilia-Romagna was voicing his unorthodox spirituality and doubts through his works. The Modenese Panfilo Sasso (1455?–1527) was possibly one of the most successful poets in both Latin and the vernacular in the late fifteenth century and early years of the sixteenth century. Sasso spent part of his life in Brescia, where he taught Dante and Petrarch; the Brescian printer Bernardino Misinta published in 1500 the first edition of his vernacular poems, the *Sonetti e capituli*. The work was reprinted nine times between 1500 and 1519; other poems circulated in partial editions or miscellaneous manuscripts. In 1504, Sasso was in Modena and from 1508 in Cesena; in the following years he moved between Modena and Cesena. In 1523 he had to face an inquisitorial trial, following which he was forced to spend a period in Bologna. He was acquitted, thanks to the protection of powerful patrons. After Sasso's acquittal, Count Guido Rangoni appointed him governor of Longiano, where he died on 27 September 1527. His Latin poems appeared in Brescia in 1499 and the final version of his vernacular works in Venice in 1519 (Guglielmo da Fontaneto).

Sasso is well known to historians because of his 1523 inquisitional process, in which he was charged with heresy. In particular, inquisitor Tommaso da Vicenza focused on some dangerous doubts voiced by the poet. Allegedly, Sasso had at various time denied the existence of paradise, purgatory, and hell; the immortality of the soul; the existence of the fire of purgatory; and that demons were in hell. He had denied in a vernacular sonnet the existence of free will and affirmed the human nature of Christ, questioning the possibility of the Incarnation. As if this were not enough, Sasso had practised and taught love spells. Sasso was sentenced to recant and undertake other spiritual penances, among which was to compose a *capitolo* in praise of free will. The sentence was relatively mild, but even so Sasso managed to get away with minor charges, thanks to the protection of Bishop Ercole Rangoni and to the jurisdictional conflicts between the bishop himself and the Holy Office.[131]

Sasso had something of a reputation for his interests in love magic. In 1519, a certain Anastasia la Frappona had been put on trial for witchcraft and confessed that she had made love enchantments using a wax image, needles, and incense dust. She stated that she had obtained the image from Sasso, who had also instructed her on the use of needles, circles, and required fumigations. The name of Sasso recurs in 1531 in the trial of Brighento Brighenti, a warlock from Maranello. As Carlo Ginzburg has pointed out, descriptions of spells and enchantments are frequent in Sasso's Latin poems, and although they were inspired by literary models, they could easily refer to everyday reality. According to Ginzburg, Sasso's Latin and vernacular verses show a personality 'moved by philosophical and religious doubts and anxieties'.[132] Sasso's doubts addressed the main tenets of Christian dogma; in particular, he seems to have denied the divine nature of Christ. In a *carmen* to the 'most erudite' Benedetto Lazioso, Sasso wrote that if one adds marble to wood, marble still remains marble and wood remains wood ('Marmora si iungis ligno non marmora lignum | Sed lignum lignum, marmora marmor erunt'). Similarly, there cannot be two natures — human and divine — in the same person. Therefore, since the person who died on the cross could not have been God (as God cannot die), we must conclude that it was a man who saved us ('genus humanum de Styge traxit homo').[133]

Religious authorities were probably more concerned with Sasso's vernacular poems denying free will and the immortality of the soul: these could easily circulate among a larger readership. In his famous sonnet 'Hor te fa terra, hor te fa smorto' ('Now turn yourself into earth, now become pale'), the poet depicts himself contemplating his own decay and fast-approaching death. In the closing tercets the poet urges his spirit to leave him to put an end to his sufferings; the last lines read: 'Now get, out, since it is time for you to get out: | Do not believe the ignorant crowd | Because there is no other life after death.'[134]

This open denial of eternal life was matched by an equally outright denial of free will. In his sonnet 'Tu me domandi se un predestinato' (You ask me whether a predestined one), Sasso deals with the question of whether a predestined person can be damned. In the first lines, he seems to be aware of the novelty of dealing with such 'doubt' in a poetic text ('sopra Parnaso | Questo dubio non fu mai disputato'). The sonnet brings us into the atmosphere of a theological disputation, as Sasso introduces a distinction between poetry (Parnassus) and philosophy. Poetry should be characterized by sweetness and by a certain and agreeable ornament; those interested in arduous doubts should turn to Scotus's or Aquinas's works.[135] However, he immediately contradicts his own statement, offering in the tercets the resolution to his interlocutor's doubt. Sasso argues that if what God wants has effect, then there is no reason to doubt that if he wants someone to be saved, that person will not be damned ('che dubita, sel vol ch'un salvo sia | Che non serà del popol maledetto').[136]

Sasso was probably not aware that discussing religious doubts in the form of a poetical correspondence was common practice, as we have seen in the case of Feo Belcari. It is nonetheless true that while Belcari's poems circulated only in manuscript form, Sasso's poems, as noted above, enjoyed a large circulation in print. Sasso problematizes Belcari's approach, first establishing the principle that certain topics are genre-specific and then immediately trespassing it. Discussing doubts through the means of poetry deliberately violates poetical norms, thus signalling the desire to extend the realm of poetry to new fields. That this happens while discussing religious or philosophical doubts also seems to hint at the urgency of addressing them outside the dedicated spaces of philosophical or theological treatises, bringing them to the larger public of those who read the vernacular, which seems in line with what we have seen in the case of Sabadino degli Arienti.

Given this dynamic, it was probably not by chance that the Inquisition forced Sasso to recant by writing and printing a *capitolo* in praise of free will, which can be identified as the *Capitolo de predestinatione per il clarissimo poeta Miser Pamphilo Sasso modenese* (A capitolo on predestination by the most famous poet Panfilo Sasso from Modena, published in Brescia by Bernardino Misinta, no date). The text is followed in this print by a sonnet ('Se ben Dio vede ogni cosa futura'). In the opening lines of the *capitolo* the poet admits that in one of his sonnets he had apparently written that men have little power against fate. However, he states, believing such a thing would be nonsense.[137] It is noteworthy that the incipit of the text is borrowed from that of a sonnet ('Se Dio conosce e sa quel ch'è futuro'), also published in the 1519 edition of his poems and also denying free will.[138] In this sonnet, Sasso had boldly declared that 'if you are destined to be blessed, worthy or unworthy, | Fortune makes you fly above the heavens; | If not, virtue is useless, and so is wit'.[139]

Sasso's poems show some of the anxieties spreading at the beginning of the sixteenth century in the Po Valley: a disquiet regarding one's merits and deeds (possibly, but not necessarily, connected to an early reception of Luther's ideas), and doubts concerning eternal life and the divine nature of Christ. At the same time, Sasso's magic beliefs show how the distrust in free will could go along with faith in magic as a means to bend the forces of nature. It is also remarkable that Sasso voiced some of his doubts in vernacular sonnets that underwent several editions and were accessible to a vast public of readers. Even more interesting is that Sasso was forced to recant his ideas through a poem in the vernacular, a detail that reveals the acute perception on the part of religious authorities of the power of vernacular poetry in conveying doubts and 'mistakes' to large audiences.

Notes to Chapter 2

1. Giovanni di Pagolo Morelli, 'Ricordi', in *Mercanti scrittori: Ricordi nella Firenze tra Medioevo e Rinascimento*, ed. by Vittore Branca (Florence: Le Monnier, 1986), pp. 101–339 (p. 311).
2. 'Che l'anima fusse niente o un poco di fiato.' Ibid.
3. Ibid., p. 323.
4. Ibid., p. 324.
5. 'Vidi una donzella bianchissima: e suoi occhi rendeano isplendore, e tenea in mano una palma e dalla sinistra avea una ruota, colla quale mi parea avesse tutta dilacerata questa troia la quale avea veduta.' Ibid., p. 321.
6. 'Da l'altra parte, per non lo lassar quietare in alcuno verso, il diavolo comincia ad tentarlo insino della fede, e dice: "Se io non ti potrò havere per uno verso, io ti harò per uno altro" e metteli nella fantasia che la fede non sia vera e dice: "Che credi tu che sia la fede? Morto el corpo, morta l'anima."' Girolamo Savonarola, *Predica dell'arte del ben morire* (Florence: Bartolommeo de Libri, after 2 November 1496), fol. 15^v.

7. 'Prima ricorri al crucifixo. Guarda la sua bontà che è voluto essere crucifixo e morto per salvarti.' Ibid., fol. 16^r.

8. 'Pertanto el diavolo con tutte le suoi forze si affaticha di disviarlo da essa fede quando muore, inviluppando esso moriente in molti errori e molte superstitioni et heresie.' Domenico Capranica, *Arte del ben morire, cioè in gratia di Dio* (Florence: Bartolommeo di Libri?, 150–), fol. A3^r.

9. 'Non debbe dunche el chatholicho e buono christiano in modo alchuno temere le illusioni o veramente spaventi per grandi o terribili che fussono del diavolo [...]. Esso diavolo è bugiardo e padre delle bugie.' Ibid., fol. A4^r.

10. 'Ancora alla sancta Romana chiesa esser subdito e ubidiente.' Ibid., fol. A3^v. See Alberto Tenenti, *Il senso della morte e l'amore della vita nel Rinascimento (Francia e Italia)* (Turin: Einaudi, 1989), pp. 82–83.

11. On the anti-Christian aspects of fifteenth-century culture see, for further bibliography, Daniele Conti, '"Initium abolendae fidei": Dagli accademici romani a Machiavelli: Una nuova fonte per la storia dell'anticristianesimo quattrocentesco', in *Prima di Lutero: Nonconformismi religiosi nel Quattrocento italiano*, ed. by Lucio Biasiori and Daniele Conti (= *Rivista storica italiana*, 129 (2017)), pp. 984–1021.

12. 'In riso e 'n pianto, fra paura et spene | Mi rota sì ch'ogni mio stato inforsa.' Francesco Petrarca, *Canzoniere*, ed. by Marco Santagata (Milan: Mondadori, 2004), p. 723. I use the English translation in *Petrarch: The Canzoniere, or Rerum vulgarium fragmenta*, trans. by Mark Musa (Bloomington: Indiana University Press, 1999), p. 243.

13. Petrarca, *Canzoniere*, p. 724.

14. See the entry by Eduardo Melfi, 'Collenuccio, Pandolfo', in *Dizionario biografico degli Italiani*, XXVII (Rome: Istituto dell'Enciclopedia italiana, 1982) <https://www.treccani.it/enciclopedia/pandolfo-collenuccio_%28Dizionario-Biografico%29/> [accessed 27 May 2021]; Claudio Varese, *Pandolfo Collenuccio umanista* (Pesaro: Ente Olivieri editore, 1957), p. 11.

15. 'Dubbio è 'l desio fra libertade o morte.' Pandolfo Collenuccio, *Operette morali: Poesie latine e volgari*, ed. by Alfredo Saviotti (Bari: Laterza, 1929), p. 141.

16. 'Chi più schiva il pensier, pur vi s'intrice. | A li occhi nostri 'l ver sempre è nascoso, | Fin che a l'estremo poi quella ne venga, | Che 'l viver nostro ci fa sì dubioso'. Ibid., p. 138.

17. Erasmo Pèrcopo, 'Una tenzone su amore e fortuna fra Lorenzo de' Medici, P. Collenuccio, il Poliziano e G. Benivieni', *Rassegna critica della letteratura italiana*, 1 (1896), 9–14 and 42–46.

18. 'Dal tetto in su è nugolo e sereno, | Come si vede e sole e luna e stelle, | Po' dice Salaiboc e Ismaelle | Che tutto il resto è buio come in seno. | Po' che noi non vedren l'arcobaleno, | Che pensi tu di ritrovar la pelle | In Giusaffà? Ché pentole e scodelle | Ne fie già fatto, o cener sarà almeno. | No' faren gli scambietti affusolati | Cogli occhi chiusi in una scura tomba | E' sensi morti e' membri intirizzati, | E soneren le nacchere e la tromba; | O pazzi spigolistri e smemorati, | O ciechi que' ch'aspettan la Colomba! | Non ti partir da bomba | Con tuo' digiun, perdoni e paternostri | Per ingrassar po' l'orto a frati o chiostri! | E ben ch'alcun ti mostri | Suo' scartabelli iscritti, di che gracchia, | Ch'appena si sa 'l ver fino a Quaracchia? | Vuo'ne tu trar la macchia? | E ricchi stanno dalla state al verno | In paradiso e' poveri in ninferno.' *Lirici toscani del Quattrocento*, ed. by Antonio Lanza (Rome: Bulzoni, 1973), II, 634–35. See Antonio Corsaro, 'Parodia del sacro dal Medioevo al Rinascimento', in *Gli irregolari nella letteratura: Eterodossi, parodisti, funamboli della parola* (Rome: Salerno, 2007), pp. 63–92 (pp. 85–86).

19. The sonnets are published in Paolo Orvieto, 'Uno "scandalo" del '400: Luigi Pulci ed i sonetti di parodia religiosa', *Annali d'italianistica*, 1 (1983), 19–33 (pp. 20–22, here at p. 22).

20. 'Al Belcari già da tempo era riconosciuta la carica ufficiale di "solutore" di dubbi teologici e di correttore di involontarie, o come in questo caso, più che intenzionali deviazioni eretiche.' Ibid., p. 23.

21. See the sonnets in Luigi Pulci, *Opere minori*, ed. by Paolo Orvieto (Milan: Mursia, 1986), pp. 193–201.

22. 'E' ci è tanto romore per un sonetto, | Che pare ch'i' abbia morto colla spada | Coloro che gridan, solo per mio dispetto.' The sonnet is published in Orvieto, 'Uno "scandalo"', p. 30. See also Paolo Orvieto, *Pulci medievale: Studio sulla poesia volgare Fiorentina del Quattrocento* (Rome: Salerno, 1978), Chap. 6.

23. I quote from Feo Belcari, 'Poesie', in *Lirici toscani del Quattrocento*, I, 214–15. The remaining doubts concern (among others) whether God would have chosen to become embodied if Adam had not sinned (Antonio di Guido, ibid., pp. 215–16); whether Mary was marred by the original sin (Francesco di Matteo Orafo, ibid., pp. 216–17); whether the souls of the damned, once rejoined with their bodies, will occupy space on Judgement Day (Giovanni de' Pigli, ibid., pp. 230–31); whether the planet under which one is born determines one's actions (Filippo Lapaccini, ibid., pp. 234–35); why man was not restored to his prelapsarian condition (Niccolò Gesuato, ibid., pp. 238–39); and whether one should follow one's nature or resist it (on the assumption that our nature is corrupted by sin; Giovanni de' Pigli, ibid., p. 239).

24. Ibid., p. 239. Lanza's edition reads 'dubbi passi'; I follow here the version provided in Stefano Cremonini, 'Il linguaggio biblico nelle *Laude* di Feo Belcari', in *Sotto il cielo delle scritture: Bibbia, retorica e letteratura religiosa (secc. XIII–XVI)*, ed. by Carlo Delcorno and Giovanni Baffetti (Florence: Olschki, 2009), pp. 171–92. See also Orvieto, *Pulci medievale*, pp. 230–33.

25. Stefano Cremonini, 'Sui sonetti di Feo Belcari: Intertestualità di una 'poetica theologia', *Studi e problemi di critica testuale*, 68 (2004), 5–36 (pp. 16–17, 32).

26. 'In modo che quasi tutti gli huomini di questi tempi visitano e templi per vergogna et per timore, e prelati li uffitiano, benché in pochi luoghi, per non perder l'entrate; ma non già che né l'una che l'altra spetie creda che sia Idio, che il fig(liuo)lo venissi a incarnare, ecetera, ma che il mondo sia sempre stato, sia et habbia a essere con questa corrutione di tutte le forme e generatione, come sono corpi immobili, vigitativi, sensitivi e rationali, et che l'huomo habbia, per essere più nobile de l'altre forme, a godere tutte le altre, et che morto questo huomo sia finita ogni cosa per lui.' Bartolomeo Cerretani, *Dialogo della mutatione di Firenze*, ed. by Giuliana Berti (Florence: Olschki, 1993), p. 7. See Delio Cantimori, *Eretici italiani del Cinquecento e altri scritti*, ed. by Adriano Prosperi (Turin: Einaudi, 1992), Chap. 3.

27. Cerretani, *Dialogo*, p. 16.

28. 'De ruina mundi', in Girolamo Savonarola, *Rime*, ed. by Giona Tuccini (Genoa: il melangolo, 2015), p. 79.

29. 'Doubt or denial of immortality seems to be more often recorded than direct denial of God and may be just as serious in its implications. [...] Similar thorough-going denials of immortality are said to have been common in early fourteenth century Italy.' Susan Reynolds, 'Social Mentalities and the Cases of Medieval Scepticism', *Transactions of the Royal Historical Society*, I (1991), 21–41 (pp. 33–34).

30. Alison Brown, 'Lucretius and the Epicureans in the Social and Political Context of Renaissance Florence', *I Tatti Studies in the Italian Renaissance*, 9 (2001), 11–62 (p. 560). See also Alison Brown, *The Return of Lucretius to Renaissance Florence* (Cambridge, MA: Harvard University Press, 2010), esp. Chap. 5. Ada Palmer lists fifty-four Renaissance Latin manuscripts of the *De rerum natura* as well as three medieval Latin manuscripts and thirty surviving editions for the period 1471–1600, plus one possible lost edition and one ghost edition; although Lucretius may have been read by hundreds of readers — possibly a few thousand — his text remained accessible to a comparatively small readership; see Palmer, *Reading Lucretius in the Renaissance* (Cambridge, MA: Harvard University Press, 2014), Chap. 5 and Appendices A and C. See also Stephen Greenblatt, *The Swerve: How the World Became Modern* (New York: W. W. Norton & Company, 2012). On Epicurean philosophy during the Middle Ages and the early Renaissance, see Aurélien Robert, *Épicure aux enfers: Hérésie, athéisme et hédonisme au Moyen Âge* (Paris: Fayard, 2021).

31. Marco Sgarbi, *Profumo di immortalità: Controversie sull'anima nella filosofia volgare del Rinascimento* (Rome: Carocci, 2016).

32. Adriano Prosperi, *Infanticide, Secular Justice, and Religious Debate in Early Modern Europe* (Turnhout: Brepols, 2016), pp. 241–50.

33. See Alexander Murray, 'Piety and Impiety in Thirteenth-Century Italy', *Studies in Church History*, 8 (1972), 83–106; Alexander Murray, 'The Epicureans', in *Intellectuals and Writers in Fourteenth-Century Europe*, ed. by Piero Boitani and Anna Torti (Tübingen: Gunter Narr-Brewer, 1986), pp. 138–63. See also Nicholas Davidson, 'Unbelief and Atheism in Italy, 1500–1700', in *Atheism from the Reformation to the Enlightenment*, ed. by Michael C. W. Hunter and David Wootton (Oxford: Oxford University Press, 1992), pp. 63–93.

34. Federico Barbierato, *The Inquisitor in the Hat Shop: Inquisition, Forbidden Books, and Unbelief in Early Modern Venice* (Farnham: Ashgate, 2012), esp. Chap. 2.

35. 'Now Thomas (also known as Didymus), one of the Twelve, was not with the disciples when Jesus came. So the other disciples told him, "We have seen the Lord!" But he said to them, "Unless I see the nail marks in his hands and put my finger where the nails were, and put my hand into his side, I will not believe." A week later his disciples were in the house again, and Thomas was with them. Though the doors were locked, Jesus came and stood among them and said, "Peace be with you!" Then he said to Thomas, "Put your finger here; see my hands. Reach out your hand and put it into my side. Stop doubting and believe." Thomas said to him, "My Lord and my God!" Then Jesus told him, "Because you have seen me, you have believed; blessed are those who have not seen and yet have believed."' John 20. 24–29.

36. Erin E. Benay, 'Touching Is Believing: Caravaggio's *Doubting Thomas* in Counter-Reformatory Rome', in *Caravaggio: Reflections and Refractions*, ed. by Lorenzo Pericolo and David M. Stone (Farnham: Ashgate, 2014), pp. 59–82 (p. 60).

37. Anton Grobler, Angelo Nicolaides, and Clifton Singh, 'The Doubting Apostle "Dydimus" — Saint Thomas: Theological, Psychological and Historical Perspectives', *Pharos Journal of Theology*, 96 (2015), 1–17 (p. 14). As a matter of fact, even Satan believes, as he acknowledges the power of God, yet he lacks faith.

38. Glenn W. Most, *Doubting Thomas* (Cambridge, MA: Harvard University Press, 2005), p. 64.

39. Ibid., p. 58.

40. Ibid., p. 79.

41. Ibid., p. 80.

42. Ibid., pp. 90–100 (p. 98).

43. 'Doubting Thomas seems to have been devised by John largely in order to invoke, exaggerate, and then resolve doubt, and thereby to lay doubt to rest once and for all. [...] Had John not attributed to Thomas so hyperbolic an expression of doubt, he might well have felt that he had not revealed doubt to be so unmistakably godless and senseless an attitude that no reader of his would ever dare to yield to it. If no one ever doubted, Thomas would not have been needed.' Ibid., p. 223.

44. See Erin E. Benay and Lisa M. Rafanelli, *Faith, Gender, and the Senses in Italian Renaissance and Baroque Art: Interpreting the Noli me tangere and Doubting Thomas* (Farnham: Ashgate, 2015). For the medieval representations of the two episodes, see Lisa M. Rafanelli, 'To Touch or Not to Touch: The "Noli me tangere" and "Incredulity of Thomas" in Word and Image from Early Christianity to the Ottonian Period', in *To Touch or Not to Touch? Interdisciplinary Perspectives*, ed. by Reimund Bieringer, Karlijn Demasure, and Barbara Baert (Leuven: Peeters, 2013), pp. 135–73.

45. On the ambivalent early modern attitude towards the sense of touch, see at least Elizabeth D. Harvey, 'Introduction: The "Sense of All Senses"', in *Sensible Flesh: On Touch in Early Modern Culture*, ed. by Elizabeth D. Harvey (Philadelphia: University of Pennsylvania Press, 2003), pp. 1–21; Sharon Assaf, 'The Ambivalence of the Sense of Touch in Early Modern Prints', *Renaissance and Reformation*, 29 (2005), 75–98; Patricia A. Cahill, 'Take Five: Renaissance Literature and the Study of the Senses', *Literature Compass*, 6 (2009), 1014–30; Viktoria von Hoffmann, 'Epistemology of Touch in Early Modern Autopsies', *Renaissance Quarterly*, 75 (2022), 542–82.

46. Benay and Rafanelli, *Faith, Gender, and the Senses*, p. 125.

47. Ibid., p. 126.

48. 'Primi. Toccate il vero com'io e crederete | Ne la somma Iustizia in tre persone, | Che sempre essalta ognun che fa ragione. | Secondi. La mano al vero e gli occhi al sommo cielo, | La lingua intera, ed ogni vostro effetto | Raguardi al ben comune sanza diffetto. | Terzi. Cercate il vero, iustizia conseguendo | Al ben comune, la mente intera e franca | Perch'ogni regno sanza questo manca.' Franco Sacchetti, *Il libro delle rime*, ed. by Alberto Chiari (Bari: Laterza, 1936), p. 285. I use the English translation provided in Benay and Rafanelli, *Faith, Gender, and the Senses*, p. 127.

49. See Lucia Battaglia Ricci, *Palazzo Vecchio e dintorni: Studio su Franco Sacchetti e le fabbriche di Firenze* (Rome: Salerno, 1990), pp. 50–52.

50. Most, *Doubting Thomas*, p. 188.

51. Ibid.

52. Casio was a merchant, a jeweller, and a *poeta laureato*, and is nowadays best known for his interest in painting and for acting as a collector and merchant of art; see Leonardo Quaquarelli, 'Pandolfi, Girolamo', in *Dizionario biografico degli Italiani*, LXXX (Rome: Istituto dell'Enciclopedia italiana, 2014) <https://www.treccani.it/enciclopedia/girolamo-pandolfi_(Dizionario-Biografico)> [accessed 23 August 2022]. I thank Dr Maria Antonietta Garullo for providing me the text of the 1524 *Vite* and for valuable information on Casio's publications.

53. The work was later expanded and published in 1528 under the title *Libro de' fasti giorni christiani*.

54. 'Hieronimo, il scrivere de Amore non è a te più convenente suggetto e anchor troppo in ciò troverai superiori. Ma scrivendo delle cose divine e de epitaphii non tanti, perché mancho sono quelli che scrivono del Cielo e di Morte che quelli di Amore. Del che, preso il parlare di soa Santità per conseglio e commandamento diedi principio con la invocazione della alma Trinitade a compore le vite de' Santi restringendo ogni vita di Santo e Santa in uno petrarchescho sonetto.' Girolamo Casio de' Medici, *Libro de fasti giorni sacri* [...] (Bologna: Benedetto de Hettor Libraro, 1528), fol. 3^r.

55. 'Sepolto Christo con le guardie intorno | Visibilmente da quelle disparve | E a i santi padri e a gli Apostoli apparve, | Disiosi del promesso suo ritorno. | A Luca e Cleophas il terzo giorno | In Emaus da pellegrin comparve | Postosi poi da ortolan le larve | A Maddalena diede gaudio e scorno. | A Thoma sol sue sante piaghe offerse | Et non senza misterio di scrittura | Fe' che il costato con le dite aperse. | Questo più valse a noi che la fé pura | Di Pier, né fur sue opre in India perse | Che i Cristiani acquistò da la cintura.' Ibid., fol. 16^r.

56. *Laude fatte e composte per più persone spirituali* [...]. *Et tutte le infrascripte laude ha raccholto & insieme ridotto Iacopo di maestro Luigi de Marsi Cittadino fiorentino* [...] (Florence: Francesco Bonaccorsi, 1485). The collection was published again in 1495 (Florence: Bartolomeo de' Libri); in 1507–13 (Florence: Bartolomeo de' Libri a petitione di Piero Pacini da Pescia); and in 1512 (Venice: Giorgio Rusconi ad instantia de Nicholò dicto Zopino).

57. 'Chi vuole haver da Dio gran mercede | Ricorra a san Tomaso con gran fede. | O discepol di Christo san Thomaso | Testimonio della fede a tutto 'l mondo | Tu non volesti il vero credere a chaso | Se non toccavi quel corpo giocondo | Di Giesù. Ma toccandolo tu credesti.' Ibid., fol. 45^v.

58. Lily C. Vuong, *The Protevangelium of James* (Eugene, OR: Cascade Books, 2018), p. 69.

59. Ibid, pp. 69–70.

60. Ibid., p. 70.

61. Ibid.

62. The Virgins had been assigned to Mary to keep her company until the day of her wedding with the much older Joseph.

63. R. Bulbeck, 'The Doubt of St. Joseph', *Catholic Biblical Quarterly*, 10 (1948), 296–309 (p. 306).

64. 'The angel does not bring information to remove Joseph's doubt, but brings an order and supports it by repetition of what Joseph already knows. It is the order, not any new information, that solves Joseph's doubt.' Ibid., p. 309.

65. Brian P. McGuire, 'When Jesus Did the Dishes: The Transformation of Late Medieval Spirituality', in *The Making of Christian Communities in Late Antiquity and the Middle Ages*, ed. by Mark Williams (London: Anthem Press, 2005), pp. 131–52 (p. 149).

66. Ibid., p. 151.

67. Joseph was also perceived outside Italy as a 'beloved, revered, venerated, and hilariously ridiculous figure'; see Anne L. Williams, 'Satirizing the Sacred: Humor in Saint Joseph's Veneration and Early Modern Art', *Journal of Historians of Netherlandish Art*, 10 (2018) <https://jhna.org/articles/satirizing-sacred-humor-saint-josephs-veneration-early-modern-art/#citation> [accessed 16 July 2021].

68. ' — Deh dimmi, Giotto, perché è dipinto Iosef così sempre malinconoso? E Giotto rispose: — Non ha egli ragione, che vede pregna la moglie e non sa di cui?' Franco Sacchetti, *Il trecentonovelle*, ed. by Valerio Marucci (Rome: Salerno, 1996), p. 221.

69. See Stefania Colafranceschi, *San Giuseppe nelle sacre rappresentazioni italiane (sec. XIII–XV)* <https://movimentogiuseppino.files.wordpress.com/2011/01/s-giuseppe-nelle-sacre-rappresentazioni-

italiane-sec-xiii-xv.pdf> [accessed 12 December 2017]. See also Tom Flanigan, 'Everyman or Saint? Doubting Joseph in the Corpus Christi Cycle', *Medieval and Renaissance Drama in England*, 8 (1996), 19–48; Marco Piccat, 'San Michele in Piemonte: La "Passione di Revello" (1481)', in *L'arcangelo Michele: Dalla storia alla leggenda*, ed. by Giampietro Casiraghi (Stresa: Edizioni Rosminiane, 2012), pp. 155–88.

70. 'Maria toa mogle, ti so dire, | È grossa, grossa zà da parturire. | À gli oghi morti et la faza obscura, | À le mamelle grosse oltre mesura, | Sta vergognosa perché l'à timore | Che tu non te n'avedi del suo errore. | Tu say bene, bon homo de Dio, | May cognosuta non l'ay più como io, | Un altro ti so dire l'à ingrossata. | Che ferai, o Iosepho, a questa fiata, | Che sey stato iusto sempremay, | Et ày amato iusticia come say.' *La Passione di Revello: Sacra rappresentazione quattrocentesca di ignoto autore*, ed. by Anna Cornagliotti (Turin: Stamperia artistica nazionale, 1976), p. 31.

71. 'O Josepho, povero vegiarello, | Che ferà-tu, tristo poverello? | Dicia bene: "Non voglo mogle, | Per non patire tante amare dogle."' Ibid., p. 32.

72. Roberto L. Bruni and Diego Zancani, 'Antonio Cornazzano: Le opere a stampa', *La Bibliofilia*, 86 (1984), 1–61 (p. 9). One should also add the ten manuscripts listed on pp. 13–14. See Anna Ceruti Burgio, *Studi sul Quattrocento parmense* (Pisa: Giardini, 1988), pp. 99–118.

73. 'Subito fu l'angel del dubbio aveduto.' Antonio Cornazzano, *Vita della gloriosa vergine Maria* (Venice: per Nicolo d'Aristotile detto Zoppino, 1531), fol. B4^v.

74. 'Conobbe anchora el dubbio de l'incarco | L'accorto ambasciator.' Ibid., fol. B4^v.

75. 'Allhora incomincian le vive doglie | Di gelosia, ch'el bestemiò forse | Spesso el baston che mai fè fiori e foglie.' Ibid., fol. B4^r.

76. 'Gioseppe che non fu mai tanto bono | Che non vedesse un spin sotto una rosa | Mira questi atti che gli suoi non sono | [...] E così il pover vecchio | Cominciò a 'mbestiar di gelosia.' Ibid., fol. B7^r.

77. 'Ma come era lui donque tanto cieco | Ch'el pensasse alcun male?' Ibid., fol. B7^v.

78. 'E ragionando sopra el suo partire | La chiosa nel Vangelio l'arguisse | Del pensier suo che la volse fuggire. | Colui ch'è giusto esser Gioseppe disse: | Com'era 'l giusto, sel sapea questo | E che da la sua donna el se partisse? | Poi l'assolve in dui modi, bene e presto: | Over che la lasciava come indegno, | D'appressar lei per atto inhonesto, | Over perché la usanza era in quel regno | La donna lapidar fornicatrice. | Più presto facea disegno di partire, | Onde giustamente giusto il dice. | [...] | Così pien tutto d'amorosa frebbe | Si partì vacillando el vecchio puro | Geloso fu di quel che poi li crebbe.' Ibid., fols B8$^{r–v}$.

79. 'Huomo di bassa fè ben ti dimostri | Che del divin valore ti fidi poco.' Ibid., fol. C1^r.

80. Carolyn C. Wilson, 'The Cult of St. Joseph in Early Cinquecento Venice and the Testimony of Marino Sanudo's *Diaries*', *Studi veneziani*, 47 (2004), 287–312 (p. 289).

81. The altarpieces painted in these decades show 'the extent to which respect is paid to key points of theology and devotion specific to him and to his role in salvation, namely in compositional features or details that signal his Davidicity and nobility, his standing in grace as recipient of God's word in dreams and as first witness to the Incarnation, and his protectorship of Mary and Jesus in carrying out God's commands. [...] That the shepherds are consistently included in Nativity compositions [...] further suggests the saint's perceived function in proselytization'. Carolyn C. Wilson, 'Some Further Evidence of St. Joseph's Cult in Renaissance Italy and Related St. Joseph Altarpieces', in *Die Bedeutung des hl. Josef in der Heilsgeschichte*, ed. by Joannes Hattler and Germán Rovira (Kisslegg: Fe–Medienverlag, 2006), pp. 903–33 (p. 915).

82. Carolyn C. Wilson, 'St Joseph and the Process of Decoding Vincenzo Catena's *Warrior Adoring the Infant Christ and the Virgin*', *Artibus et historiae*, 67 (2013), 117–36 (p. 124).

83. Wilson, 'The Cult of St. Joseph', p. 307.

84. 'What is this Joseph doing and what does he mean? Is he here to protect Our Lady from the exotic warrior, or rather, to assist him in his devotions to her?' Wilson, 'St Joseph and the Process', p. 126.

85. Carolyn C. Wilson, 'Francesco Vecellio's *Presepio* for San Giuseppe, Belluno: Aspects and Overview of the Cult and Iconography of St. Joseph in Pre-Tridentine Art', *Venezia Cinquecento*, 6 (1996), 39–74 (p. 48).

86. Ibid. See also Carolyn C. Wilson, *St. Joseph in Italian Renaissance Society and Art: New Directions and Interpretations* (Philadelphia: Saint Joseph's University Press, 2001), pp. 36–37.

87. Wilson, 'Francesco Vecellio's *Presepio*', 48; Wilson, *St. Joseph in Italian Renaissance Society*, pp. 34–35.

88. For an overview of the evolution of Joseph's iconography, see Wilson, *St. Joseph in Italian Renaissance Society*.

89. On the iconography of sorrow, see Chiara Frugoni, *La voce delle immagini: Pillole iconografiche dal Medioevo* (Turin: Einaudi, 2010), pp. 49–67.

90. Wilson, 'St Joseph and the Process', p. 123.

91. 'Non pensando perhò che la gravedanza fusse da huomo; & stando Ioseph in questo pensiero l'angelo Gabriele li apparve in sogno.' *Biblia vulgare istoriata* (Venice: Giovanni Ragazo a instantia di Luchantonio Giunta, 1490), fol. M^r.

92. Caterina was tried by the Inquisition along with her daughter in 1567/68. See Federica Ambrosini, *L'eresia di Isabella: Vita di Isabella da Passano, signora della Frattina 1542–1601* (Milan: Angeli, 2005); and Federica Ambrosini, *Una gentildonna davanti al Sant'Uffizio: Il processo per eresia di Isabella della Frattina, 1568–1570* (Geneva : Droz, 2014).

93. Erasmus should have used 'più tosto parole risolute che metafore dubbiose', Tomitano complained about his 'trattar le cose importanti sotto scorza de i suoi dubbiosi favellari' and his 'procedere dubbioso e indistinto'. Bernardino Tomitano, *Oratione [...] alli Signori de la Santissima Inquisitione di Vinetia* (Padua: Gratioso Perchacino, 1556), fols 22^r, 24^r, 26^r.

94. 'Però soffre nell'animo occulti pensieri che lo molestano tacitamente; anzi, va imaginando un modo di far divortio onde si potesse divider da lei senza infamia e pericolo della fanciulla. Per la qual cosa fin'hora volse Iddio che l'innocentissimo marito venisse nell'animo a soffrir questi tormentosi affanni e fusse agitato da sì acerbi travagli che così era necessario alla certezza della fede.' *Espositione letterale del testo di Mattheo Evangelista, di m. Bernardino Tomitano* (Venice: Gio. del Griffo, 1547), fol. 6^r.

95. 'Ioseph, figliuolo di David, che suspittione è questa, la quale ti flagella l'animo e ti tormenta con amara passione? Che sospiri son questi tuoi? Che travaglio è il tuo?' Ibid., fol. 6^v.

96. Ibid., fol. 7^r.

97. 'Mentre Giuseppe era confuso da le falsità del sospetto, il Sonno [...] gli aconciò il braccio mancino sopra un desco al quale egli sedeva a lato e, lasciatogli cadere il capo in sul rovescio del gombito, dimenticò le fantasie che lo molestavano nel dormire.' Aretino, *Vita di Maria Vergine*, in *Opere religiose*, II, ed. by Marini, p. 184.

98. 'Non è macula ne l'immaculata donna.' Ibid.

99. 'Dubbio rimane, e poi del dubbio ha pena | E tra 'l senso e la Fede il cor duella. | Alfin la fè s'arrende, e cheto il piede | Ei lungi vuol portar.' Cesare Ripa, *Iconologia [...] notabilmente accresciuta d'immagini, di annotazioni, e di fatti dall'abate Cesare Orlandi [...]*, II (Perugia: Piergiovanni Costantini, 1765), p. 272. On Gigli, see Lucinda Spera, 'Gigli, Girolamo', in *Dizionario biografico degli Italiani*, LIV (Rome: Istituto dell'Enciclopedia italiana, 2000) <https://www.treccani.it/enciclopedia/girolamo-gigli_(Dizionario-Biografico)> [accessed 1 October 2020].

100. The challenge to Aristotle's authority was common from the Middle Ages on, and also within Aristotelian circles; see Luca Bianchi, '"Aristotele fu un uomo e poté errare": Sulle origini medievali della critica al "principio di autorità" ', in *Studi sull'aristotelismo del Rinascimento* (Padua: Il Poligrafo, 2003), pp. 101–24.

101. 'In questo tempo dicono non convenirsi parlare di cose sottili, dubbiose o difficili, anzi ioconde, piacevoli et con dilecto fructuose et utili.' Palmieri, *Vita civile*, p. 170.

102. Antonio Urceo Codro, *Sermones (V–VIII): Filologia e maschera nel Quattrocento*, ed. by Andrea Severi and Giacomo Ventura (Rome: Carocci, 2018); previous quotes from p. 82. On Codro, see Ezio Raimondi, *Codro e l'umanesimo a Bologna* (Bologna: il Mulino, 1987 (1950)).

103. Codro, *Sermones (V–VIII)*, p. 4.

104. 'In hominibus vero raram esse et repertu difficilem et multos vel ignorantia vel sensuum corruptione vel voluptate fortasse etiam utilitate mentiri.' Ibid., p. 92.

105. 'Si fabula est quae nec veras nec verisimiles res in se continet, quid veritatis, quid certitudinis habet haec vita nostra? Quas non potius tenebras, quas non incertitudines?' Antonio Urceo

Codro, *Sermones (I–IV): Filologia e maschera nel Quattrocento*, ed. by Loredana Chines and Andrea Severi (Rome: Carocci, 2013), p. 70.

106. See the passages on religion in ibid., pp. 207–13.
107. Ibid., p. 222.
108. There were five more editions between 1504 and 1540; we also have the autograph manuscript held in Florence, Biblioteca Nazionale Centrale, MS Palatino 503.
109. See Sabadino degli Arienti, *Le Porretane*, ed. by Bruno Basile (Rome: Salerno, 1981), pp. 591–607.
110. On the discourse and its philosophical background, see Sgarbi, *Profumo d'immortalità*, pp. 35–48.
111. 'Subtile e speculativo ingegno'; 'a examinare uno eretico e intendere quello che dubita de la fede cristiana.' Arienti, *Porretane*, p. 487. On anti-courtliness see Paola Ugolini, *The Court and Its Critics: Anti-Court Sentiments in Early Modern Italy* (Toronto: University of Toronto Press, 2020).
112. 'Io credo tanto che dubito non sia troppo.' Sabadino degli Arienti, *Porretane*, p. 488.
113. 'A me è stato imposto [...] ch'io abia a intendere da te l'effecto della toa dubitazione'; 'che eresia è la tua e che dubitazione hai nella nostra fede'. Ibid., p. 487.
114. 'Io credo ogni cosa, se li pani erano de mille stara de grano l'uno e li pessi balene.' Ibid., p. 489.
115. 'Né ancora io el credo.' Ibid.
116. 'El papa cum li suoi fratelli cardinali ne riseno in tal modo, che ancora se ne ride.' Ibid., p. 490.
117. 'Parabola di un mito di tolleranza.' Ibid., p. 484.
118. Marzia Minutelli, *'La miracolosa aqua': Lettura delle 'Porretane novelle'* (Florence: Olschki, 1990), p. 97.
119. 'Come iusto e sanctissimo pastore'; 'fece reprendere il piacevole Malacarne, facendoli intendere che li miraculosi effecti del nostro Re superno non se doveano se non cum diva gloria e summa reverenzia recordare'. Sabadino degli Arienti, *Porretane*, p. 490.
120. 'Fu salvato reverentemente il divino onore de la nostra sancta e ortodoxa fede e concluso che, dove spirasse la potenzia divina, tutto el fuoco visibile e invisibile senza acqua se extinguirebbe, e il mare senza barca e senza alcuno sostegno se solcarebbe, e de uno picol grano tutto el mondo, quando fusse ben famelico, felicemente se ne saciarebbe.' Ibid.
121. Ibid., pp. xlv–xlvi.
122. Davidson, 'Unbelief and Atheism', p. 64; see also Lucio Biasiori, '"Empietà e bestemmie anche alle orecchie dei saraceni infedeli": La condanna di Zanino da Solza tra rafforzamento ecclesiastico e progetti di crociata (1459)', in *Prima di Lutero*, ed. by Conti and Biasiori, pp. 862–86 (pp. 888–89).
123. Arius was a Libyan presbyter (250 or 256–336 CE) who denied homoousian Christology and was therefore condemned by the first Nicaean Council.
124. See Paola Maria Traversa, *Il 'Fidele' di Giovanni Filoteo Achillini: Poesia, sapienza e 'divina' conoscenza* (Modena: Mucchi, 1992), Chap. 3; Guido Dall'Olio, *Eretici e inquisitori nella Bologna del Cinquecento* (Bologna: Istituto per la storia di Bologna, 1999), pp. 42–45. Scholars have noted how the interlocutors of Achillini's dialogue *Annotationi della volgar lingua* (1536) are the same later described by the heretic Camillo Renato in his *Apologia* as the circle of friends that used to gather around him. I will return to this as well as to anti-trinitarianism in Chapter 4.
125. Dall'Olio, *Eretici e inquisitori*, pp. 35–40. We find this idea also in Lelio Sozzini's *Brevis explicatio in primum Iohannis caput* (1561?); cf. Peter G. Bietenholz, *Encounters with a Radical Erasmus: Erasmus' Work as a Source for Radical Thought in Early Modern Europe* (Toronto: University of Toronto Press, 2008), p. 41: 'Lelio sets a radically new standard in that he denies any form of pre-existence prior to Mary's miraculous conception and virgin birth.'
126. Riccardo Parmeggiani, '"Ad extirpandos sortilegiorum, divinatorum ad malleficorum iniquas operationes": Riflessi teorico-pratici della repressione nello specchio di un registro quattrocentesco dell'inquisizione bolognese', in *Prima di Lutero*, ed. by Conti and Biasiori, pp. 842–62 (pp. 848–49).
127. Ibid., p. 850.
128. 'Grandissima eresia'; 'falsa opinion'. Sabadino degli Arienti, *Porretane*, p. 57.
129. Ibid., p. xlvii.
130. One should not forget that it was in Bologna that Pietro Pomponazzi composed his critique

of miracles, the treatise *On Incantations* (*De incantationibus*, completed in 1520; Pomponazzi had moved to Bologna in 1512).

131. On Sasso, see Massimo Malinverni, 'Sasso, Panfilo', in *Dizionario biografico degli Italiani*, XC (Rome: Istituto dell'Enciclopedia italiana, 2017) <https://www.treccani.it/enciclopedia/panfilo-sasso_(Dizionario-Biografico)/> [accessed 16 October 2020]; on his trial, see Umberto Renda, *Il processo di Panfilo Sasso* (Modena: Ferraguti, 1911); Angelo Mercati, *Il sommario del processo a Giordano Bruno: Con appendice di documenti sull'eresia e l'Inquisizione a Modena nel secolo XVI* (Vatican City: Biblioteca Apostolica Vaticana, 1973).

132. Carlo Ginzburg, 'Un letterato e una strega al principio del '500: Panfilo Sasso e Anastasia la Frappona', in *Studi in memoria di Carlo Ascheri* (Urbino: Argalìa, 1970), pp. 129–37: 135; see also Carlo Ginzburg, 'Stregoneria e pietà popolare: Note a proposito di un processo modenese del 1519', *Annali della Scuola Normale Superiore di Pisa: Lettere, storia e filosofia*, 30 (1961), 269–87. Ginzburg observes a peak of twenty-two trials for witchcraft, magic, and superstition in the years 1518–20 (compared to *c.* twelve in 1530–39 and fifteen in 1495–99).

133. *Pamphili Saxi* [...] *Epigrammatum libri quattuor* [...] (Brescia: Angeli Britannici civis Brix. sumptu Bernardinus Misinta impressit, 1499), fol. 11ʳ.

134. 'Hor escie, puoi ch'el te convien uscire: | Non seguir la vulgar e stolta gente, | Ch'altra vita non è da puo' el morire.' I use the critical text published in Massimo Malinverni, 'Sulla tradizione del sonetto "Hor te fa terra, corpo" di Panfilo Sasso', *Studi di filologia italiana*, 49 (1991), 123–65 (p. 163); on the text of Sasso's vernacular poems, see also Massimo Malinverni, 'Lectiones faciliores e varianti redazionali nella tradizione delle rime di Panfilo Sasso', *Studi di filologia italiana*, 56 (1998), 203–28.

135. 'Un parlar dolce, un dir soave ornato | Procede da quel chiaro e sacro vaso | De questo te dirà Scotto e Tomaso | Che l'uno e l'altro è d'argumenti armato.' *Opera del preclarissimo poeta Miser Pamphilo Sasso modenese* [...] (Venice: Guilielmum de Fontaneto de Monferrato, 1519), fol. A3ᵛ.

136. Ibid.

137. This *capitolo* is quite problematic, as Bernardino Misinta, according to the bibliographic catalogue Edit16, stopped printing around 1509 (and in fact the work is tentatively dated 1502). See also Ginzburg, 'Un letterato', pp. 136–37.

138. Sasso, *Opera del preclarissimo poeta*, fol. C3ᵛ.

139. 'Se esser felice dei, degno o non degno | Fortuna sopra el ciel te fa volare; | Se non, virtù non vale, non val ingegno.' Ibid.

CHAPTER 3

Doubting Women and Their Circles

From the end of the fifteenth century and into the first decades of the sixteenth, women were the fulcrum of a rejuvenation of devotional practices. Thanks to their spiritual gifts of prophecy, visions, and other prodigious powers, a number of charismatic women became influential advisors to the ruling elites in cities and at court. Women were also the privileged recipients of writings by spiritual directors, who often addressed their doubts in devotional matters. Doubt entered early sixteenth-century religious experiences in other, more interesting ways. The gifts of charismatic women could be problematic: visions, prophecies, miracles, and ecstasies required proper interpretation. Besides, the very nature of these gifts was problematic, as they could be signs of divine inspiration but also tricks of the devil. This prompted a broader reflection on doubt and on how it could be employed to ascertain the truthfulness of these phenomena while also raising broader concerns regarding truth, reality, and its perception. While exerting control on religious charisma and its gifts was not unusual, linked as it was to the traditional problem of the discernment of spirits, the shifting political and religious realities of early sixteenth-century Italy added layers of uncertainty to the fascinating and disquieting phenomenon of the so-called *sante vive*.

At the heart of this spirituality existed a broader problem — that of women's relation to God — in which doubt played an important role. This chapter explores the connection between doubt, devotional literature, and gender in the early years of the sixteenth century. I will begin with two tales of doubt that circulated in the visual arts and literary texts from the Middle Ages on and reveal how doubt was crucial in assessing, defining, and understanding the relationship between God and women. These two tales — that of the 'Doubting Midwife' and of *Noli me tangere* — will serve as an introduction to this chapter, which then turns to an analysis of some significant spiritual works and characters from the first decades of the sixteenth century.

The Doubting Midwife

Drawing on apocryphal gospels, Jacopo da Varazze tells in his *Golden Legend* that at the moment of Christ's birth, two midwives assisted the Virgin, Zebel and Salome. While Zebel believed in Mary's virginity, Salome was sceptical. Therefore God punished her, turning her hands into stumps. An angel came and ordered her to touch the baby Jesus, and the contact with the miraculous body prodigiously healed her, restoring her to her previous condition of bodily integrity:

> When the hour had come for Mary to be delivered, Joseph called two midwives, the one being called Zebel and the other Salome — not that he doubted that the Virgin would bring forth the Son of God, but that he was following the custom of the country. When Zebel, probing and realizing that Mary was a virgin, cried out that a virgin had given birth, Salome did not believe and tried to find out it for herself, but her hand instantly withered; then an angel appeared and told her to touch the child, and she was cured immediately.[1]

The apocryphal gospels give different accounts of this episode. In Pseudo-Matthew, Joseph returns to the cave with the two midwives, Zebel (or Zahel), and Salome. The episode revolves around three main points: Zebel/Zahel's inspection of the Virgin and her faith; Salome's doubt and her punishment; and Salome's miraculous healing. In Pseudo-Matthew's version we read the following:

> When Mary allowed herself to be scrutinized, the midwife called out in a loud voice and said, 'Great Lord, have mercy! Never before has it been either heard or suspected that the breasts might be full of milk, and yet this newborn makes manifest that his mother is a virgin.' Hearing this cry another midwife named Salome said, 'Certainly I will not believe this unless indeed I verify it.' And Salome went on to Mary and said to her, 'Let me examine you so that I should know if the words that Zahel declared to me are true.' Now when Mary allowed her examination, as soon as Zahel [in fact, Salome] drew away her right hand from the inspection, the hand withered and she began to be most violently stricken by the pain and to cry out, weeping and saying, 'Lord, you know that I have always feared you and have taken care of all the poor without the worry of payment. I have taken nothing from the widow and the orphan and I have never sent the destitute away from me, empty-handed. And behold, I am made wretched because of my unbelief, because I have dared to test your virgin, who gave birth to the Light and after this birth remained a virgin.' And while she was saying these things, a brilliant young man appeared beside her saying, 'Go to the child and worship him, and touch him with your hand, and he will heal you, because this is the Saviour of all who hope in him.' And quickly Salome went to him and worshipped the child and touched the hems of the cloths in which the child was swaddled, and her hand was immediately healed.[2]

The account in the Protogospel of James is slightly different but does not vary in the crucial points of the episode. The main divergence is that the first midwife does not even need to enter the cave to believe, while Salome's doubt is amplified and closely resembles the 'Doubting Thomas' episode:

> And they [Joseph and the midwife] stood in front of the cave. And a dark cloud overshadowed the cave. And the midwife said, 'My soul has been magnified today because my eyes have seen an incredible sign; for salvation has been born to Israel.' [...]
> And immediately the cloud contracted from the cave and a great light appeared within the cave so that their eyes could not bear it. A little time afterwards that light began to contract until an infant could be seen. And he came and took the breast of his mother Mary. And the midwife cried out and said, 'How great is this day for me, for I have seen this wondrous sight.'[3]

Then the first midwife leaves the cave and meets Salome on her way and announces to her the miracle, to which Salome replies:

> 'As the Lord my God lives, unless I insert my finger and examine her physical condition, I will not believe that the virgin has given birth.' The midwife entered and said, 'Mary ready yourself. For there is no small contention concerning you.' And when Mary heard this, she made herself ready. And Salome inserted her finger into her to test her physical condition. And Salome cried out and said, 'Woe for my lawlessness and for my disbelief, for I have tested the living God. And behold, my hand is on fire and falling away from me.'[4]

Finally comes Salome's repentance, followed by her healing:

> And she knelt before the Master, saying, 'O God of my fathers, remember me because I am an offspring of Abraham, Isaac, and Jacob. Do not make me an example to the children of Israel, but place me among the poor.' [...] And behold, an angel of the Lord appeared, saying to her, 'Salome, Salome, the Master of all has heard your prayer. Bring your hand to the child and pick him up and you will have salvation and joy.' And Salome came to the child and lifted him up, saying, 'I will worship him, for he has been born a great king to Israel.' And Salome was immediately healed and went forth from the cave justified.[5]

Scholars have pointed out that Salome is punished 'not for her presumption in touching the mother of God, since touching her patient's genitals was a culturally legitimized act for a midwife [...] but for her lack of faith'.[6] What is at stake in the story of Salome is a distinction between 'faithful verification' and 'doubtful tests' of miracles.[7] Significantly, the Protogospel of James and the Gospel of Pseudo-Matthew offer different reasons for the second midwife's punishment. According to James, Salome is punished for touching the body of the Virgin after Zebel/Zahel had believed in the miraculous birth without actually touching her. In Pseudo-Matthew's version, Salome is punished because of her doubt, as Zebel/Zahel has touched the Virgin without suffering any consequences. In other words, 'both versions interrogate the nature of faith, yet in the first [Protogospel of James], it is the audacity of touching a holy body that is punished, while in the second [Pseudo-Matthew] it is Salome's insistence on corporeal proof'.[8] Salome is a professional who intends to use her skills to ascertain the reality of the birth of Christ. One can clearly distinguish between an 'assisting touch' and a 'testing touch'.[9] This is what ultimately leads to Salome's punishment. Doubt cannot be given any space when the miraculous has taken place: 'The story clearly distinguishes the desire for sensory evidence from the demand for verification; experience can produce valuable spiritual knowledge, but only if it is disassociated from doubt and testing.'[10] Salome's withered hand is her 'doubt made visible'.[11]

This episode had a certain visual presence from late antiquity through the Middle Ages and into the sixteenth century: one finds it in frescoes, paintings, illuminations, sculpture, reliefs, and in many other media.[12] Sometimes the two subjects of the doubting Joseph and the doubting midwife seem to converge, if not overlap, with Joseph represented in his 'melancholic' and pensive pose while the midwife interacts with the Virgin and child.[13] The episode also made its way into popular literary texts: for example, Pietro Aretino inserts it in his aforementioned (and successful) *Vita di Maria Vergine*.[14]

In the period under consideration, one painting stands out for an intriguing detail: Lorenzo Lotto's *Nativity* (or, as some have called it, *The Bath of the Baby Jesus*, 1521–27, Siena, Pinacoteca nazionale). In this painting, the midwife is missing both hands, while the gospels refer to *one* hand having withered. The iconography of the crippled midwife is not unusual; it can be seen in several fourteenth- and fifteenth-centuries frescoes across Italy.[15] It is rooted in another apocryphal gospel, the Arabic Infancy Gospel of the Saviour, where we read that in his search for a midwife, Joseph comes across an unnamed old woman, with whom he enters the cave. Astonished by the supernatural light that signals the birth of Jesus, the woman

> [a]sks the Lady Mary: Art thou the mother of this Child? And when the Lady Mary gave her assent, she says: 'Thou art not at all like the daughters of Eve. The Lady Mary said: As my son has no equal among children, so his mother has no equal among women. The old woman replied: My mistress, I came to get payment; I have been for a long time affected with palsy. Our mistress the Lady Mary said to her: Place thy hands upon the child. And the old woman did so, and was immediately cured. The she went forth, saying: Henceforth I will be the attendant and servant of this child all the days of my life.[16]

And in fact this midwife is the one who, at the time of the circumcision, 'took the piece of skin; but some say that she took the navel-string, and laid it past in a jar of old oil and nard'.[17] This very jar was the one that Mary Magdalene would use to anoint the head and feet of Christ. There was, then, a certain confusion between Salome, the midwife who lost her hand for her unbelief, and this midwife who never doubted but was *already* affected with palsy in both hands. The confusion increased when this unnamed woman came to be identified with St Anastasia, who actually lived long after the events told in the apocryphal gospels. Yet Anastasia was celebrated on 25 December; the pope celebrated the second Mass of Christmas night in her church, and in the same church an extraordinary relic was preserved: the swaddling bands in which Mary had wrapped the baby Jesus. For these reasons, popular tradition came to associate Anastasia with the nativity scene and identify her with the crippled midwife.[18] Several images represented Anastasia — clearly identified as a saint by her halo — assisting Mary, and many literary texts mention her. The thirteenth-century anonymous *Passione lombarda* recalls how she was Mary's nurse ('vostra baila fo santa Nestaxìa').[19] Anastasia is mentioned in the *lauda* that opens the *laudario* of the Modenese confraternity of Santa Maria della Neve, or dei Battuti (the manuscript was completed in 1377).[20] In his *Vita della vergine*, Antonio Cornazzano too recalls the 'assistance of St Anastasia'.[21]

As has been suggested, Anastasia (or, better, the unnamed midwife to whom the saint lent her name) is a sort of positive duplicate of Salome: they share the role of midwife and the miraculous healing of their hands.[22] A certain overlapping between them is thus inevitable, and not only because of the common features of their stories. At least in Lotto's painting, Anastasia too, if only fleetingly, plays the role of doubting midwife. Lotto chooses to represent the exact moment when Mary is handing the baby Jesus to Anastasia before she washes him, while Anastasia stares, puzzled, at Mary. And for good reason, since in that moment, she still does not have hands. How will she be able to hold Jesus? This, it has been argued, is a reversal of Salome's story. It is not Mary who is being tested; instead, she is testing Anastasia's faith.[23]

I surmise that in this story one may read a visual transposition of complex theological categories, and in particular the distinction articulated by Thomas Aquinas between a 'doubt of amazement' ('dubitatio admirationis', or 'discussionis') and a 'doubt of incredulity' ('dubitatio incredulitatis', or 'infidelitatis').[24] These are somehow opposite notions of doubt, which Aquinas discusses in connection with the Virgin Mary. In particular, he discusses a passage of Augustine which suggests that Mary was doubtful at the moment of the death of Christ, which would have been a lack of faith on her part and therefore a sin.[25] Referring to a passage in the prophecy of Simeon on the death of Christ in the Gospel of Luke (2. 35a: 'and a sword will pierce your own soul too', 'tuam ipsius animam pertransibit gladius'), Aquinas concedes that some doctors interpret *gladius* as an allegory for doubt. But, he adds, this is not a doubt of incredulity but rather a doubt of amazement, the soul of the Virgin literally floating ('fluctuabat') between two opposites. On the one hand, she was witnessing the atrocious sufferings of Christ; on the other hand, she was recalling his wonders and miracles from the Annunciation onwards.[26] In this case, doubt was the result of the sense of amazement provoked by these two apparently irreconcilable sets of experiences. Aquinas finds the same 'doubt of amazement' in Mary's reaction to the Annunciation. This doubt does not concern her willingness to do what the angel announces but rather the inevitable puzzlement concerning the supernatural way in which it will happen.[27] In sum, we can say that there is a 'doubt of amazement' that arises when the divinity manifests itself; the story of Anastasia reverses a tale of unbelief into one of amazement. The identification of the believers thus could take place with a positive doubt, the doubt of those who feel astonished and puzzled by the supernatural but do not investigate it but instead confidently accept it.

Noli me tangere

In the early sixteenth century, the episode of *Noli me tangere* — the moment when Mary Magdalene meets the risen Christ disguised as a gardener (also told in the Gospel of John) — began to be represented as an autonomous subject in Italy. As if to signal the increasing importance of the cult of Mary Magdalene, in 1501 the Dominican Silvestro Mazzolini da Prierio dedicated two vernacular works to her.[28] This episode and that of the 'Incredulity of Thomas' form a sort of diptych: Thomas's story relies on touch, and that of the Magdalene centres on seeing and hearing, the two higher senses. As a matter of fact, Magdalene seeks contact with Christ but as soon as she hears his voice forbidding her from touching him, she recognizes her master and calls him 'Rabboni'. This episode troubled the Church Fathers and theologians in general: not only was Magdalene, a woman, the first person to witness the Resurrection, but her reliance on sight and hearing seemed to place her on a higher intellectual level than Thomas, who depended on the lower sense of touch. That this iconography began to spread steadily in the early sixteenth century may reflect the changing status of women in society. As Lisa Rafanelli suggests, in the context of the *querelle des femmes* 'the role of the Magdalene was used by certain writers to demonstrate the equality — if not superiority — of women, their privilege in the eyes of God, the constancy of their faith, and the truth, importance, and reliability of their words'.[29] In the now-lost cartoon by Michelangelo Buonarroti for Vittoria Colonna (1531), this importance was reflected in the 'upright stance and gaze' of the Magdalene, which 'convey her elevated consciousness as well as a surprising level of parity and intimacy in her relationship with Christ'.[30]

Earlier in the century, around 1509–15, Titian had painted another stunning version of the episode (London, National Gallery). Titian's innovative iconography shifts the focus of the story from the apparition of Christ to the Magdalene, and his departure following the moment in which she recognizes Christ. Magdalene is audaciously represented as suddenly refraining from reaching for Christ's groin. Despite such emphasis on the physicality of Christ, Titian conveys the sense that Magdalene does need the lower sense of touch to acknowledge the presence of the risen Christ. Her discernment 'is proof of her intellectual capacity, and her journey towards spiritual enlightenment'. The progression from touch to sight and hearing 'shows her to be making a spiritual journey toward a higher faith'.[31]

Contemporary poetry reflected the evolving importance of the *Noli me tangere* episode, as we can gather, for example, from an interesting short poem (six cantos of *terzine*), the 'Libro intitulato Pascha' by Benedetto (or Benet) Gareth, il Cariteo (*c*. 1450–*c*. 1514). A Spaniard from Barcelona, Cariteo moved early in his youth to Naples, where he undertook a brilliant career in public administration, abruptly interrupted by the French invasion in 1494 and by the following exile of the Aragonese king. Cariteo is nowadays mostly known for his *canzoniere* entitled *Endimione*, but he was also the author of several other compositions in the vernacular.[32] His works were first published in 1506 and subsequently, in an augmented version, in 1509. Although the *Endimione* was mostly composed in the period 1480–93, Cariteo continued to write poetry even after the exile. The poem 'Pascha' features in the 1509 edition of his poems. The poem recounts the deeds of Christ after the Resurrection; in the second *cantico*, Christ appears first to the Virgin Mary and then to Mary Magdalene. While this seems to undermine Mary Magdalene's importance, as she is no longer the first witness to the Resurrection, her relevance to the story of salvation is reaffirmed in the following lines. At first Mary does not recognize her master disguised as a gardener, but as soon as he utters her name, she calls him 'Maestro' and moves closer to him. At this point Christ stops her:

> Do not touch me, for it is not permitted to you.
> To someone else touch, to you only is allowed
> Sight; now behold open my light
> For I removed the thick cloud from your eyes.[33]

Christ then entrusts Mary with the task of proclaiming his resurrection to his brethren. Yet she is dissatisfied with Christ's prohibition to touch his body. Recalling the episode of her washing his feet, she asks, 'How come heaven is so hostile to me | That it does not allow me to at least kiss your feet?'[34] This question prompts Christ to expand on the relationship between faith and doubt: true faith does not require the sense of touch, because faith is not subject to doubt. Cariteo associates then the lower sense of touch with doubt: it is only by touching that those who do not possess perfect faith can overcome doubt:

> It is not necessary — He said — to perfect
> Faith to put your fingers in my wound;
> For faith was never subject to doubt.[35]

Mary is able to see beyond the human veil to the divine nature of Christ, thus proceeding beyond the senses; the 'veil of humanity' she once touched with her 'blonde tresses' no longer impedes her from seeing through it the mystery of the Trinity.[36] Mary's faith has allowed her to move beyond the realm of the lower senses; unlike her, Thomas will not be able to contemplate the divine mystery until the 'shadowy earth' that constitutes the boundary between his limited human nature and divine immensity will be removed. Those who 'move outside the path of faith, as unbelievers' are in fact only able to perceive the human nature of Christ.[37] Yet Thomas's doubt is somewhat independent from his will; in fact it is part of God's providential plan, for God allows this doubt in order to dispel all doubts from others — a passage in line with Glenn Most's conclusion, discussed in Chapter 2:

> For he will not doubt of his own will,
> Since I will permit him to be doubtful,
> So that he will dispel doubt from others.[38]

These two tales point to the gendered nature of doubt: women, too, could be actors in stories of doubt, and their doubt could play an important role in the history of salvation. Works of art and mystery plays, legends, and other easily accessible texts mediated the complex theological meanings of these tales.

Scruples, Again

From the fifteenth century onwards, increasing attention is paid to the multifaceted relationship between women and doubt. For example, Antonino da Firenze was aware that specific social groups — including women — are more inclined to melancholy. Nuns, for example, could easily fall prey to scruple, a 'lighter' — and yet dangerous — form of doubt, as we have seen in Chapter 1. Scruples typically open the path to pusillanimity, an inordinate fear of committing sin. 'An excess of fear and pusillanimity is dangerous and leads a person sooner to lunacy than to perfection': with these words the hermit Hieronymo addressed Cristina Bemba, abbess of St Lawrence in Venice.[39] Hieronymo encouraged Cristina to be vigilant and prevent the nuns in her monastery from examining with exceeding subtlety their conscience, an exercise 'which upsets and afflicts the spirit'.[40] Such exercise impedes one's self-knowledge and the achievement of 'some light of the truth'.[41]

Equally dangerous is putting down in writing one's scruples, an activity that should not be tolerated:

> In the same way should be reprimanded those who spend too much time in self-examination, straining themselves in writing each day not only the words that they deem not appropriately spoken as well as any act of carelessness, but also each thought that crosses their mind, which is far from honesty or from fraternal charity.[42]

Those who embark on such a futile task can be compared to those who try to catch fleas or flies. More than that, it is a temptation from the Enemy, who tries to lead these persons either to desperation or to an excess of self-confidence. The passages above come from the prefatory letter to the vernacular version of a treatise by Jean Gerson. The tract, first published in Italy in Latin, was later republished in the vernacular in 1510 as *De gli remedij contra la pusillanimità, scrupolosità et deceptorie consolationi et suttile tentationi del'inimico* (On the remedies against pusillanimity, scrupulosity, and the deceptive consolations and subtle temptations of the enemy).[43] 'Madness', as the opening of the tract states, is the destiny of those who fall prey to an excess of fear. Scruple is the result of the projection of our ideas of justice onto God. In fact, God's mercy far and away exceeds our comprehension; no one can be saved just because of their good deeds. Instead, Gerson exhorts his readers to believe that 'God wants no more than is in our possibilities' and that 'we are not always forced to do the best and perfect things'.[44] Sexuality and blasphemy were the main sources of scruples: thoughts, words, and images that crossed one's mind, inducing an overwhelming sense of guilt. And yet, one should not feel remorseful for such sins committed against one's will:

> No one should feel exceedingly distressed by such abominable temptations and execrable blasphemy or lustful acts that cross one's mind, for these do not please devotees, rather they torment them, nor come such things from men, rather from the devil who suggests them.[45]

I suggest that Gerson's tract deals with doubt on two levels. On one level, scruple is a form of doubt that needs proper description and cure. However, on another level, scruple is connected to the larger problem of discerning the work of spirits. It is the devil who fools people into having scruples; it is the devil who, with God's permission, plays tricks on these people's minds. It is the devil who blurs the boundaries between good and evil, turning the most pious acts of devotion — even confession — into mortal traps of conscience. Gerson warns his readers to guard against the subtle arts of the Enemy and to be wary of the 'feeling of sweetness and spiritual solace' ('dolceza et consolation spirituale') they may feel, as this does not ensure one is in a state of grace.[46] One therefore should never trust in oneself alone but instead persevere in prayer 'without hesitation or doubt of God's piety', on the assumption that this will be rewarded by God.[47] Spiritual consolation can be sometimes a delusion; therefore, in some cases it is not bad to be deprived of it. This holds true for simple folk ('li simplici') or for those yet unable to distinguish between good and evil or understand how 'the angel of darkness is used to transform himself into an angel of light to deceive them'.[48] Scruple is a variety of doubt, and an excessive amount of it is as dangerous as sin, if not a sin itself, and yet it is a doubtful conscience (although not in the technical, Thomistic sense) that helps one to stay alert against the deceits of the devil.

The concern around the discernment of spirits — that is, how to assess visionary experiences — continues into the sixteenth century and becomes crucial within the circles gathering around 'holy mothers', or *sante vive*. These women, endowed with special charisma and often with a prophetic voice, thrived in the urban and courtly environment of the late fifteenth century and early years of the sixteenth century. They enjoyed the support and devotion of members of the clergy and the ruling elites, often becoming influential advisors to princes. Yet in the eyes of others, their extraordinary performances were suspicious and demanded caution. In those years of wars, shifting allegiances, and political turmoil, the advice of living saints was a precious tool and their prophetic voices often corroborated princely power. Precisely because of their public role, however, these women and their extraordinary gifts required careful assessment. Doubt was instrumental in ascertaining the veracity of their gifts, thus granting that their influence in the political sphere was reliable. Even when women did not play a key role in politics, they could be part of circles, conventicles, or gatherings often led by a spiritual master and marked by intense (and at times, one might say, 'experimental') forms of spirituality, often free from the rules of the church. Interior enlightenment was central to these experiences; again, however, such an intense spiritual condition posed questions and fostered doubts. In these contexts too, therefore, we find traces of reflection on doubt and on how it should be employed on the path to inner enlightenment. The next section will take a close look at one such circle.

A Lost Book

Doubt is often the result of a combination of fear and hope: absolute trust in God is counterbalanced by the incessant fear that his signs may be misunderstood. The discrepancy between appearance and reality urges devotees to exercise caution and adopt doubt as the guiding principle of their spiritual life. In the first decades of the sixteenth century, spirituality was marked by two conjoined and often intertwining phenomena: the so-called *sante vive*, and prophecy.[49] Charismatic persons, especially women, boasted extraordinary spiritual experiences. Yet as we have just seen, the exterior signs of spiritual progress and illumination could be fabricated by the devil, who produced 'revelations, ecstasies, raptures, prophecies, miracles and other wonders' comparable to those coming from God (Jesus Christ famously warned against pseudo-prophets in Matthew 24).[50] A problem that had traditionally troubled the church, the discernment of spirits became especially pressing in early sixteenth-century Italy.[51] The opening lines of Camilla Battista da Varano's autobiography (1491) bear testimony to how visions and prodigious experiences caused anguish and fostered doubts:

> This whole month of February I have been in a great agony and mental battle.
> And the reason was that I had a vehement, warm, and ardent inspiration

which I resisted strongly, for I had doubts and wondered if it was a diabolical temptation.[52]

Or let us consider an episode from the life of Stefana Quinzana (1457–1530). One night while she was in her chamber, an old man appeared and accompanied her along a riverbank where there were angels, some ascending to heaven, some descending. Stefana worried that the vision of the angels could be an illusion sent by the devil. The old man reassured her, as if he could read her mind, that what she saw did not come from the devil. At this point, Stefana began to wonder whether the old man could be her Lord, and she felt great contentment. The vision led Stefana into a supernatural setting, where she would receive an answer to her doubts: 'And that venerable old man told me: "My daughter, you will now receive an answer to your doubts," and he disappeared.'[53] The angels explained to Stefana 'what will make me ascend to the perfect love of my groom, and how will I be able to transform myself into my Lord [...] and what is this transformation'.[54]

Among the many examples of this attitude, the poems of a still little-known churchman, Gabriele Biondo, are of special relevance because they are part of a larger and precocious program of extensive religious doubt. Biondo (d. 1511), the son of the humanist and antiquarian Flavio (1392–1463), was a Camaldolese monk and the prior of the Pieve di Santo Stefano in Modigliana, a little village situated in the Apennines in the area of Emilia subject to Florence. He was also the spiritual guide of a little community of Florentine women. Biondo may have been acquainted with Battista da Crema, who between 1497 and 1499 spent time in Modigliana, in the Dominican convent of Santa Maria delle Grazie, and whose teachings would later prove crucial to the newly established order of the Paolini, to which I shall return soon. In 1501, Biondo was in Florence, while one of his disciples, the physician Giovanni Maria Capucci, was tried in Venice for publicizing his master's book *Ricordo*.[55] Condemned as heretical, the book is now lost. We have partial access to its contents, though, thanks to the philosopher Antonio Trombetta (1436–1517), who in 1504 discussed Biondo's most problematic ideas in order to prove their orthodoxy.[56] Biondo preached a form of spirituality based on a total relinquishment of one's individuality, a form of intense mystical union with God leading to a condition beyond vice and virtue. The true believer did not need the mediation of the church, attendance at Mass, or other exterior 'ceremonies'. In a 1505 letter to his 'spiritual daughters' Maddalena, Caterina, and Dianora, Biondo alluded to their mystical marriage with God that made them free from guilt ('fatte incorruttibile'), specifying that this purity pertained to the body and the mind ('incorruptibilità de mente et de corpo').[57] The Venetian Camaldolese hermit Paolo Giustinian somehow got hold of Biondo's letters and promptly understood the dangers of such ideas. He in turn wrote two letters to Biondo's followers, seeking to persuade them to abandon his dangerous spiritual guidance based on intense mysticism, the notion of *incorruptibilità*, the disdain for ceremonies and exterior signs of piety, and therefore the lack of respect for the ecclesiastical hierarchy. All these ideas are also present in Battista da Crema's works and have their source in medieval spirituality. Yet both Biondo and Battista seem to push them to their extreme consequences.

It is within this context that we should read Biondo's poems, and one in particular, a mystical hymn of 1,508 lines. Biondo's poems, which circulated in manuscript only, revolve around the issue of mystical union with God and the idea that only the *eletti* can enjoy such a condition. The hymn 'Signor Iesu Signore', a dialogue between the author and God, is introduced by a short text that explains how the poem addresses hypocrites, those who live a merely exterior faith. At the same time the author asks God why those with an inauthentic faith seem to enjoy his benevolence. As the author warns, this is a poem full of mystical meanings ('sensi mistici'); the reader must therefore praise God for whatever little truth can be grasped and 'always be afraid ("sempre dubita") that they may have understood imperfectly or incorrectly'.[58] Doubt is, at a preliminary level, the attitude that readers are required to assume when confronting a mystical text of such depth. On a deeper level, Biondo describes doubt as a practice peculiar to those who truly believe. Authentic believers completely surrender themselves, their will, and their reason to God and love him as compelled to do so. Their reason cannot understand this profound form of love or the force that moves it. Nor can intellect understand the mystical union, although God can make it visible. This is why the reason of the true elect 'always doubts | And always fears and, at the same time, hopes'.[59] Doubt is thus a sign of spiritual election: the will ceases to ask questions, reason stops measuring the depth of God's abyss with its inadequate instruments. However, in this world, God willingly (and paradoxically) chooses to fulfill the requests of so-called hypocrites while often frustrating those of real believers and being inexplicably harsh to them.

Doubt was also the almost inevitable by-product of this unstable, whimsical, elusive spiritual world. It will come as no surprise, then, to see Biondo's devotees turn to him and share their doubts. Alessandra degli Ariosti was a nun and a privileged interlocutor and spiritual daughter of Biondo who at some point in the early 1500s sent him seven 'doubts', requesting his explanations.[60] These doubts concerned crucial issues such as the soul's destiny in the afterlife, and in general revolve around the discernment of spirits, the correct understanding of the signs of perfection, and the importance of inner, authentic spirituality as opposed to exterior practices and signs of sanctity. Among these 'doubts', those concerning one's calling take a central position. What Biondo called one's *professione*, the way in which one should fulfill one's vocation, was a highly idiosyncratic matter, 'individual and concrete'.[61] This was by no means unique to Biondo's circle but rather a common feature of early sixteenth-century spirituality, and one that added layers of uncertainty to the religious experience of both laypeople and large numbers of the regular clergy, for whom adherence to the rules no longer granted spiritual perfection or even salvation.

In the first decades of the sixteenth century we witness a spirituality in which sanctity moves in mysterious ways, the mediation of the church is no longer required, the relationship with God transcends reason, and charismatic people claim a peculiar union with the divine, the signs of which could, however, be the devil's forgeries. It is an explosive mix, and one in which doubt legitimately takes a central stance. What is one's place in the world, then? What if someone wanted to embrace the monastic life, for example? Would this be a necessary step to achieving spiritual perfection? Does not one see many people in the world being perfect Christians? And on the contrary, does not one see the decadence of ecclesiastical institutions? And what if one's vocation were merely a diabolical illusion, a mere fancy of a diabolically inflated ego?

These were some of the questions that troubled the mind of Antonio Pagani (1526–1589). In the second half of the century, as a Franciscan, Pagani authored several works, enjoying support from the religious authorities in Vicenza and Venice. However, Antonio Pagani was not entirely the person he claimed to be. In a previous life, under his real name, Marco (or Marco Antonio), he had been a member of the order of the Barnabites and had been one the most fervent followers of the 'holy mother' Paola Antonia Negri, the most influential figure in the communities of the Paolini and Angeliche (the female section of the order) founded by Antonio Maria Zaccaria, Battista da Crema, and Ludovica Torelli.[62] The teachings of Battista verged on a sort of unbridled mysticism leading to the union with God. If a person reached this state of perfection, they could no longer sin (the so-called state of *impeccabilità*). In order to attain this, Battista and later Paola Antonia encouraged devotees to expose themselves to temptation and perform deeds that would be perceived as scandalous in the eyes of the world. In the mid-1540s, Pagani moved from Venice to Milan to live close to Paola Antonia. In 1551, the Paolini were banned from the Republic of Venice, and the following year the doctrine of Battista da Crema was declared heretical by Julius III (although suspicions had arisen as early as 1531).[63] In January 1552, the Inquisition put on trial two members of the Paolini; in July of the same year Pagani adventurously escaped from Milan by climbing down from a window with the help of some bed linens, bringing with him the manuscripts of Battista's works. In November, he went back to Milan to try to help Paola Antonia escape the monastery of Santa Chiara, to which authorities had forced her to retire.

Even though the turmoil around the Barnabites suggested some degree of caution, in 1554 Pagani published his *Rime* in Venice, printed in five hundred copies by Antonio Arrivabene, a printer who had often published suspicious works. The *Rime* featured on the Index in 1559 and in 1564, though not in its entirety: the only prohibited parts were the section in praise of Paola Antonia, titled the 'Trionfo Angelico', and the section of *sonetti diversi* (various sonnets). Pagani kept on working on his *Rime*, partially censoring and rewriting them according to the new religious climate. He published them in 1557 and again in 1570, this time under the title of *Rime spirituali* (another, partial edition had come out in 1560 with the title *L'amorosa giornata*). Pagani never entirely removed the poems dedicated to Paola Antonia from his *Rime*, limiting himself to making the necessary amendments to disguise any explicit references to the 'divine mother' to whose memory and teaching he remained true throughout his life.[64] Failing to understand Pagani's 'enigmatic and obscure' sonnets, the Franciscan inquisitor Marino da Venezia had granted permission for the 1554 *Rime* to be printed.[65]

Pagani's sonnets explored, as he wrote in a sort of apology to the Holy Office, 'the obscure and complex ways of saints and the hidden judgements of God'.[66] According to Battista da Crema's teaching, sanctity should be disguised beneath its contrary; paradoxically enough, behaving immodestly and flaunting arrogance and pride were the ways in which saintly humility revealed itself. Because of its inscrutable nature, causing things to appear as their opposite, sainthood is a mysterious and enigmatic phenomenon that challenges the laws of the church, which in some cases has failed to recognize authentic sanctity. In the sonnet 'Sì varie son le strade ch'Iddio pose' (So various are the ways that God established), Pagani observes that opposite paths have in the past led to the same result: holiness.[67] As we will see in Chapter 5, the possibility that opposite paths may lead to the same result seems to have puzzled and fascinated Renaissance Italians. In building on the idea of diverging, even opposite, and yet equivalent paths Pagani's sonnet embodies the very essence of doubt as we have discussed it. We recognize here the fear that accompanies doubt, for no one is entitled to feel safe about their choice. The ways to sanctity remain beyond understanding, as saints are inspired by a greater grace than are the members of the church.[68]

It is easy to understand the consequences of such statements that in fact partially dismiss the church, its infallibility, and its authority. In another poem, Pagani has Paola Antonia claim that 'I was always subject to the loving flame [i.e., God] | But never to that false yoke [the church's doctrine]'.[69] In other words, true saints reach such a degree of perfection that they are free from every rule. As Pagani writes, true inspiration lies deep in the hearts of the *perfetti*, but the way to these hearts, to the reasons that move them as well as the possibility of understanding them lies beyond human reach and the grasp of the church: 'the whole world | Cannot understand its [i.e., the heart whose "roots" are hidden] silent and internal ways'.[70] Human actions are doubtful, almost impossible to discern; humility is disguised as pride and pride as humility; sanctity hides behind corruption. No rules can be applied to ascertain whether we are dealing with true holiness or its forgery, with a blessed soul enlightened by God or a wretched individual fooled by the devil.

It would be intriguing, but probably impossible to ascertain, whether these reflections were somehow the inspiration for the encomium of doubt that we read at the outset of Pagani's *Ragionamenti*. Addressing various doubts on spiritual matters, this is a work useful for 'the instruction of spiritual people, both ecclesiastics and members of the clergy and secular'.[71] As we read in the foreword, the work is meant to be for the 'universal benefit' of both the literate and the uneducated, as well as for people of all conditions. The foreword opens with some general remarks on doubt:

> It is a certain thing that the more an art or a science is dealt with, practised, investigated, and carried out with new doubts and various questions, the more it is apprehended by learned men, becoming clearer and more perfect. If this is plain to see in the case of mechanical and liberal arts, or of speculative science, it happens even more and more reasonably in the most noble art, or I shall say art of arts, and science above all other sciences, the science of saints and real wisdom through which the inner man is reformed.[72]

It is true that such a positive view of doubt is later counterbalanced in Pagani's text by a critique of the learned who push their curiosity and their doubts too far in the interpretation of Scripture. Such criticism is accompanied by praise for the 'thousands of men and women' who have never cared to investigate the 'high, subtle, and curious' aspects of Scripture and therefore never have doubted it, instead living a simple and authentic faith.[73] Yet apparently for the pious Franciscan, doubt remained a valid means for perfecting the instruction of his spiritual flock.

Holy Women, War, and the Apocalypse

Early sixteenth-century spirituality, and the context of the Barnabites in particular, seems to have been a fertile ground for the development of a reflection on how fruitful a careful practice of doubt could prove. The works of the successful Serafino da Fermo provide a fascinating case study. Serafino Aceti de' Porti, better known as Serafino da Fermo (1496–1540), was a Lateran canon who studied in Padua, where around 1520 he became acquainted with Antonio Maria Zaccaria, later co-founder of the Barnabites. The two cemented their acquaintance during a subsequent sojourn in Milan, around 1530. During his lifetime, Serafino was very close to some living saints, such as Paola Antonia Negri, to whom he dedicated the *Trattato brevissimo della conversione* (A most brief treatise on conversion), and the blessed Margherita Molli from Ravenna and her disciple Gentile Giusti.[74] Serafino perceived the outbreak of the Reformation as a sign of the coming of the Antichrist; he expressed his fears in a work entitled *Breve dichiaratione sopra l'Apocalisse* (A short declaration on the Apocalypse).[75] Serafino was also a successful writer of devotional works, which were reprinted several times throughout the sixteenth century.[76] Many of his works are compendious versions of those by Battista da Crema; because Serafino was able to avoid the most problematic ideas of Battista, or at least tone them down, his writings were the means through which otherwise condemned doctrines could circulate until well into the Counter-Reformation. Serafino's plain and vivid style made these *operette* legible by a wide audience, whom Serafino warned against the delusions of the devil as well as against false prophets and fake miracles.

Serafino called for caution, as God bestows spiritual gifts upon men and women slowly and gradually, as the result of a progressive spiritual growth. If they manifest themselves suddenly, it means they are inspired by the devil. Prophecy could also come from the devil; the way to discern true from false prophecy is to consider its purpose. When this lies in pure 'curiosity and vainglory', one can be sure that prophecy comes from the Enemy.[77] The same applies to miracles; in fact Serafino, who was persuaded that he lived in the time of the Antichrist's return, thought that miracles were the means by which the Antichrist would attract a 'large multitude'.[78] He was therefore sceptical of miracles and other exterior signs of charismatic gifts:

> But the doubt is, in what way is the Lord calling us. I answer that, based on various conjectures, we may draw the conclusion that we should despise now every supernatural means like visions, miracles, excessive fervour, and this in order not to make ourselves similar to the Antichrist. He is very close, and he has already prepared his throne among many people who are inclined to these

signs. And this is why we find countless people who [claim to] have Christ's stigmata and pains.[79]

Like Gabriele Biondo, Battista da Crema, and many other ascetic writers in these decades, Serafino did not trust exterior signs of religiosity, especially when it came to allegedly supernatural phenomena. His treatises take us into a world of swirling visions, signs, prophecies, miracles, feelings that leave us deeply uncertain and puzzled, a world in which the practice of doubt is key in order not to fall prey to the devil's tricks. Doubt, however, is also a feeling that the devotee experiences in less extraordinary circumstances: how can one be sure if one's choices, especially regarding indifferent things, conform to God's will? Serafino suggests a sort of sceptical *epoché*, a suspension of judgement:

> But a great doubt arises: how could we know God's will when something is in itself neither good nor bad? I answer that, in this case, we should suspend our will, so that it does not lean in one direction more than in the other, and then pray to the Lord with firm faith that he condescends to incline our will to the part he approves of.[80]

Serafino is here describing the process of moral decision making in conditions of uncertainty. The situation he pictures is precisely one of doubt, when our mind and will cannot incline towards one or the other of two options. For Serafino, however, doubt extends beyond the realm of moral choices: in a world full of deceit and false appearances, doubt and prudence are the only safeguard against spiritual ruin.

Serafino elaborates on this idea particularly in his account of the life of two 'holy women' Margherita Molli and Gentile Giusti. The spiritual legacy of the blessed Margherita seems to lie in her cautious scepticism, or her practice of doubt. The sign that God guided her spirit was that she did not believe

> in a single thing of which she could doubt, because only those who believe with all their faith can be fooled; and, given that what they believe is true, at least they face the risk without being certain of being tricked: but this exposure to the possibility of being fooled is itself a plain deceit.[81]

Margherita taught her disciple Gentile precisely to believe only in God and in what the Holy Roman Church — the only institution that can sanction supernatural experiences — accepts as authentic. This was a most virtuous precept, particularly in a time when Satan disguised himself as an angel of light. Serafino is aware that such a prudent attitude could be easily equivocated as unbelief and hastens to forestall possible objections:

> And if somebody were to say: 'Now, isn't it an insult to the Holy Spirit not to believe in things divine, when we see that they come from God?' I answer firstly that divine things are of such height that are best understood by those persuaded that they know nothing and understand nothing; hence Petrus Chrysologus affirms that 'he who believes the most, doubts the most'.[82]

The blessed Margherita did not believe the things God revealed to her because they were so deep that had she believed them, her soul would not fit in her body anymore. In a paradoxical twist, doubt becomes a sign of true faith: the more dubious one is, the more profound his or her faith is. The real believer is the strongest doubter, and only those who do not claim to understand or know God have access to his truth.

Serafino feels the need to safeguard himself against any potential accusations of unbelief with a double defence. First, he resorts to authority, quoting a sermon by Petrus Chrysologus (*c.* 380–*c.* 450 CE), Bishop of Ravenna.[83] Then, he reinforces his point with the example of the Virgin Mary. When receiving the announcement that she was to give birth to the son of God, Mary 'remained doubtful of the Angel's words until God reassured her in her heart so that no doubt remained'. Similarly, Margherita 'after a thousand signs remained always doubtful, and the more she was in doubt — yet the doubt induced by humility and not by ignorance — the more the divine light grew inside her'.[84] Two points are worth attention: the first is that the identification between the Virgin and Margherita, also a 'most intact virgin', relies on their being doubtful, as this condition was the sign of their spiritual election.[85] The second point is the distinction between a 'doubt of humility' and a 'doubt of ignorance'. These two expressions encompass the meanings of doubt examined so far, thus proving once more how complex and nuanced the category of 'doubt' was in the early modern time.

The fact that the two holy women to whom Serafino devotes so much attention were from Ravenna should also be considered. The city of Ravenna, on the Adriatic coast, was part of the Venetian Terraferma until the battle of Agnadello in 1509. In 1512 Ravenna was the theatre of one of the most famous battles in the wars of Italy, fought between the French army, led by Gaston de Foix, and the army of the Holy League. Despite Foix's death the French won the day, and the battle was followed by a ferocious sack of the city. It is around this event that the story told in the double biography of Margherita and Gentile revolves. Despite the fact that Margherita died in 1505, seven years before the event, Serafino begins his narrative precisely by recalling that her death happened a few years before the 'horrible slaughter' that took place in 1512 'in the surroundings of Ravenna between the French and the Spanish armies', thus establishing an explicit connection between her and that tragic episode.[86] The battle of Ravenna represents a guiding star of sorts that surfaces multiple times in Serafino's text. Serafino recalls that Margherita had prophesized it, a fact that gives him hope that her prophecy concerning the 'renovation of the church' will also come true.[87] On the other hand, Gentile too had a revelation concerning the conquest of Ravenna, but she did not believe it and thus had to flee the city; in this case, an excess of doubt almost had fatal consequences.[88]

The battle took place in April; a little earlier, in March, a monster had been born. The birth of the 'monster of Ravenna' soon acquired a prophetic meaning, and the creature became known in Italy and throughout Europe thanks to the swift circulation of images and pamphlets. The birth was promptly interpreted as a sign of the church's corruption but also, from an anti-French perspective, as a warning against the potentially schismatic French church. More generally, the monster was seen as a sign of the punishment that awaited the present era because of its corruption.[89] It is not surprising, then, that the city of Ravenna offered Serafino an ideal point of observation on extraordinary events that urged a reflection on doubt. Visions, prodigies, monsters, prophecies and prophets, living saints, miracles: all these experiences challenged the boundaries between reality and illusion. Certainly, such wondrous events prompted numerous questions. Should one acknowledge these prodigious events? In a time when monstrous visions of demonic armies fighting in the sky were heralded by false prophets as apocalyptic signs, one could legitimately nurture doubts concerning everyday experiences.[90] Uncanny phenomena undermined the knowledge that passed through the senses, exposing its liabilities. When Serafino turned his eyes from the microcosm of Ravenna to the macrocosm of contemporary world, he may have sensed that it was even more troubled and problematic.

Serafino was sure that his was a time when the coming of the Antichrist was fast approaching:

> In this time, we see among devotees all the followers of the wretched Antichrist, that is, they are blasphemers of God, horrible sellers of Jesus Christ, manifest heretics, most stubborn superstitious persons, infinite charmers, countless hypocrites, and spiritual persons deluded by the devil more than ever existed. Now, who can doubt that, having all its limbs appeared, soon the head will appear too? And maybe it has just come to light, as we can see from unusual prodigies on earth and in the sky.[91]

One wonders if, when raising the disquieting idea that the Antichrist was already lurking somewhere, as 'unusual prodigies' suggests, Serafino was thinking of the monster of Ravenna. The recent voyages of exploration and the 'discovery' of the Americas also seems to have implicitly confirmed Serafino's apocalyptic anxieties. These previously uncharted lands seemed a compensation sent by God for the territories lost to the Reformation. And yet even if the people who inhabited the 'new world' were rapidly converting, this too may have been a sign of the end of times:

> [I]t will then be in the time of Antichrist, because in that time it will be fulfilled what Paul says: When the plenitude of the people will come, then all Israel will be saved and the Jews, who used to be the first, will be the last. And in order that we know that this time is coming, God has given permission that in the last years the new world be discovered, which, according to faithful written reports, is no smaller than Europe, both in regard of its extension, and of the size of its population. Every year people travel from Spain to those lands, and the gospel is preached where no laws were known before, and many are converting and, just as the blindness of the Jews caused our salvation, our own blindness is forcing Jesus Christ to go to another land. And in the present days we see happening what the Apostles prophesized, that their voice will resonate in every land. In fact, since the Scripture mentions the four parts of the earth, and since the gospel is already known in Asia, Africa, and Europe, it had only to be carried to the fourth, newly found land, called America. You should not wonder if, at the same time, in one place the renovation of faith is underway, while in another the advent of the Antichrist is approaching [...] for now all the evident signs of both have appeared.[92]

Serafino believed that he lived in the age of the *plenitudo temporum*, when the end of time would come. His pessimistic view was somehow mitigated by the recent discoveries of new people (*plenitudo gentium*) who could give birth to new churches.[93] The Reformation had thrown a dark cloak of confusion over Europe. From the 'infernal well', that is to say from 'Ecolampadio, Zuinglio, Carostadio [*sic*], Melantone' had sprung many mistakes.[94] Most of all, the main consequence of the teachings of the Lutheran sect was that 'every sacrament is made doubtful, or openly wiped out'.[95] The Reformation had cast doubt on long-established truths and practices; doubt was an unstoppable and untameable force, ready to bite the very hand that had fed it. Doubt, as one scholar put it, was a 'boundless sea',[96] and the reformers were drowning in the waters of that sea. Confusion, darkness, and instability had also befallen the followers of Luther,

> [w]ho has prepared the seat for the Antichrist, and [the Apocalypse of John] says that his reign became so gloomy, and in fact we see that so much darkness and confusion has arisen among them, that they no longer know what they ought to believe, and they have already changed a thousand times their articles [of faith] and always from bad to worse.[97]

In such troubled times, error, darkness, doubt, and confusion were not a prerogative of the Reformation. Commenting on Chapter 16 of the Apocalypse, Serafino observes that the third head of the Antichrist described therein symbolizes the 'learned and curious men'.[98] The wrath of the third angel will strike

> [t]hose who always practise a curious science and extoll the sect of Aristotle and of his Commentator [i.e., Averroes] and in this way kill the spirit of Holy Scripture because they doubt of the immortality of the soul, on which the whole Christian faith depends.[99]

I would like to draw attention to the word 'curiosity', which Serafino employs twice when defining philosophers and men of science (*curiosi, curiosità*). Curiosity fosters doubts; in turn, doubts in certain matters pose a threat to faith. To sum up, Serafino's works — so widely disseminated — offer an invaluable picture of the many meanings and functions of doubt in the opening decades of the sixteenth century. In his works doubt covers a variety of functions: it is an instrument for assessing extraordinary experiences; a practice of life; an expression of spiritual humility; a dangerous intellectual practice; and a destructive force that once set in motion cannot be stopped.

These surprising beliefs are rooted in early sixteenth-century spirituality, which was characterized by a form of intense mysticism, an inner form of religiosity moving away from external ceremonies and practices. Spiritually elected men and women showed signs of their perfection regardless of the mediation of the church. Yet the signs of spiritual election could be misunderstood, if not counterfeited; true saints and God himself move in mysterious ways, and the devil is always ready to cunningly trick us. As apocalyptic anxieties spread, also because of the corruption of the church, unorthodox paths to salvation began to appear, disclosed by charismatic individuals. Doubt was often a consequence of this heated religious climate, be it as a reaction to the incomprehensible pathways to sanctity, a defence against the signs of fake spiritual election, or an attitude towards the inscrutable abyss of God's will. We have thus moved towards a new dimension of doubt: no longer simply a 'question', doubt has now taken a more existential connotation, if that word can be applied to the sixteenth century.

Notes to Chapter 3

1. Jacobus de Voragine, *The Golden Legend: Readings on the Saints*, trans. by William Granger Ryan, intro. by Eamon Duffy (Princeton: Princeton University Press, 2012), p. 38.

2. Brandon W. Hawk, *The Gospel of the Pseudo-Matthew and the Nativity of Mary* (Cambridge: Lutterworth Press, James Clarke & Co., 2019), pp. 68–70.

3. On the episode, see Lily C. Vuong, *The Protevangelium of James* (Eugene, OR: Cascade Books, 2018), p. 74.

4. Ibid., pp. 74–75.

5. Ibid., p. 75.

6. Denise Ryan, 'Playing the Midwife's Part in the English Nativity Plays', *Review of English Studies*, 54 (2003), 435–48 (p. 441).

7. Alaya Swann, '"By Expresse Experiment": The Doubting Midwife Salome in Late Medieval England', *Bulletin for the History of Medicine*, 89 (2015), 1–24 (p. 3).

8. Ibid., p. 14.

9. Ibid., p. 18.

10. Ibid.

11. Ibid., p. 20.

12. See Guerrino Lovato, *La levatrice incredula nella leggenda della Natività* (Venice: Lupi & Sirene, 2014); Michele Di Monte, 'Vedere, credere, dubitare: Lorenzo Lotto e l'ambiguità', *Venezia Cinquecento*, 25 (2015), 75–113.

13. This is the case, for example, in a eighth-century ivory diptych (Bologna, Museo Civico Medievale); a twelfth-century ivory *paliotto* in the Duomo of Salerno; the 1263 fresco in the Oratorio of Bominaco (L'Aquila); possibly Giotto's *Nativity* in the Scrovegni chapel; the early fifteenth-century *Trittico di Beffi* by the Maestro di San Silvestro (L'Aquila, Museo Nazionale d'Abruzzo); the fifteenth-century silver *paliotto* in the cathedral of Ascoli Piceno; and the 1524 *Nativity* by Domenico Capriolo (Treviso, Museo civico). See Lovato, *La levatrice*, pp. 42–43, 55, 60–61, 64–65, 80–81, 91, 102–03.

14. Pietro Aretino, *Vita di Maria Vergine*, in *Opere religiose*, II, ed. by Marini, p. 191.

15. Di Monte, 'Vedere, credere, dubitare', pp. 94–95.

16. 'The Arabic Gospel of the Infancy of the Savior', in *The Ante-Nicene Fathers*, VIII: *Fathers of the Third and Fourth Century*, ed. by Rev. Alexander Roberts, Sir James Donaldson, and Arthur Cleveland Coxe (New York: Cosimo, 2007 (1886)), pp. 405–15 (p. 405).

17. Ibid.

18. Concetto Del Popolo, 'Anastasia levatrice di Maria', *Lettere italiane*, 57 (2005), 261–71.

19. Ibid., p. 261.

20. 'Sempre virgo ave Maria, | Nato Cristo benedeto | Andè cum sancta Anastasia | E retornò sancto Yosep, | [...] | Da meça nocte Christo nacque, | Vene de çorno: ave Maria'. *Il laudario dei Battuti di Modena*, ed. by Mahmoud Salem Elsheikh (Bologna: Commissione per i testi di lingua, 2001), pp. 7–8.

21. 'Proprio el tempo del parto in questa via | Compisse el frutto suo la donna rese | Con l'aiuto di santa Nastasia | A' vinticinque del decembre mese | Nacque el Salvator nostro'. Cornazzano, *Vita della gloriosa vergine Maria*, fol. C^r.

22. Di Monte, 'Vedere, credere, dubitare', p. 91.

23. Ibid., pp. 104–05.

24. See Roy J. Deferrari, M. Inviolata Barry, and Ignatius McGuiness, *A Lexicon of St. Thomas Aquinas Based on the 'Summa theologica' and Selected Passages of His Other Works* (Baltimore: Catholic University of America Press, 1948), p. 344.

25. The relevant passage is contained in the *Summa theologiae* III, q. 27, art. 4, ad 2.

26. 'Quae tamen non est dubitatio infidelitatis, sed admirationis et discussionis.' <https://www. corpusthomisticum.org/sth4027.html> [accessed 19 May 2020].

27. *Summa theologiae* iii, q. 30, art. 4, ad 2.

28. See Gabriella Zarri, 'La Maddalena nel Cinquecento bolognese: Immagini e contesti', in *Tra archivio e storia: Scritti dedicati ad Alessandra Contini Bonacossi*, ed. by Elisabetta Insabato, Rosalia Manno, Ernestina Pellegrini, Anna Scattigno (Florence: Florence University Press, 2018), pp. 333–54 (pp. 337–38).

29. Lisa M. Rafanelli, 'Michelangelo's *Noli me tangere* for Vittoria Colonna, and the Changing Status of Women in Renaissance Italy', in *Mary Magdalene: Iconographic Studies from the Middle Ages to the Baroque*, ed. by Michelle M. Erhardt and Amy M. Morris (Leiden: Brill, 2012), pp. 223–48 (p. 239).

30. Ibid., p. 231. The cartoon is known through copies by Bronzino, Pontormo, and Battista Franco.

31. Lisa M. Rafanelli, 'Sense and Sensibilities: A Feminist Reading of Titian's *Noli me tangere* (1509–1515)', *Critica d'arte*, 70 (2008), 28–47 (p. 34).

32. On Cariteo's poetry, see Beatrice Barbiellini Amidei, *Alla luna: Saggio sulla poesia del Cariteo* (Florence: La Nuova Italia, 1999).

33. 'Non mi toccar, ché non ti lice. | Ad altro il tatto, a te sola è concessa | La vista; hor mira aperto il lume mio, | Ch'io tolsi a gli occhi tuoi la nube spessa.' Benedetto Gareth, *Le rime di Benedetto Gareth detto il Chariteo* [...], ed. by Erasmo Pèrcopo (Naples: Tipografia dell'Accademia delle Scienze, 1892), p. 386.

34. 'Come hor m'è 'l ciel tanto nemico, | Ch'almen basciarti i pié non mi permetta?' Ibid.

35. ' — Uopo non è, — diss'egli: — a la perfetta | Fede poner la man ne le ferrite, | Ch'al dubbio non fu mai fede subietta.' Ibid., p. 386.

36. 'Tre fiamme in un sol foco inseme unite, | Che tra verdi, incombuste e fresche fronde, | Vide quel primo honor de li Levite; | Hor vedi in me; ché nulla ti nasconde | Questo d'humanità velo condenso, | Che tu toccasti con le treccie bionde.' Ibid., p. 386.

37. 'Né vedrà il mio Thomaso altro che 'l senso, | Fin che tolta gli sia l'ombrosa terra | Che tra lui s'interpone e 'l nostro immenso. | Chi for da via di fede incredulo erra | Solo vede di me l'humana spoglia, | Chiave di fede il mio miglior disserra.' Ibid., p. 386.

38. 'Né quel dubitarà di propria voglia, | Ch'io permetto che sia dubitativo, | A ciò che gli altri poi da dubbio toglia.' Ibid., p. 387.

39. 'El troppo timore e pusilanimità è dannoso e più presto trahe la creatura a dementia ch'a ad alchuna perfectione.' *Gioanni Gerson de gli remedij contra la pusillanimità, scrupolosità et deceptorie consolationi et suttile tentationi del'inimico* (Venice: Simon de Luere, 1510), fol. a^v.

40. 'Deprimme et afflize el spirito'. Ibid.

41. 'Lumme de verità'. Ibid.

42. 'Non altramente adunque sonno da essere represe quelle che attendono troppo a repensare et affaticarsi etiandio in scrivere ogni zorno non solum le parole che a lor parono non così ben ditte, et ogni negligentia, ma anchor ciaschun pensier che si gli offerisse alquanto alieno da la honestà o charità fraterna.' Ibid., fol. a2^r.

43. The Latin title was *Tractatulus de remedijs contra pusillanimitatem, scrupulositatem, contra deceptoria inimici consolationes et subtiles eius tentationes* (Venice: Simon de Luere, 1503). The vernacular edition was reprinted in 1522 (Venice: Ioanne Antonio e fratelli da Sabio) and in 1560 (Venice: per le mani delle convertite). According to Edit16, the press of the Monastery of Santa Maria Maddalena alla Giudecca, or of the Convertite, produced twenty-four editions between 1557 and 1560.

44. 'Dio non vole oltra quello che noi possiamo.' *Gioanni Gerson di gli remedii*, fol. c4^v. 'Notino anchor li pusillanimi et scropulosi che non sempre siamo obligati a far le cose megliore et perfecte.' Ibid., fol. e^v.

45. 'Per queste tale abominevole tentatione et execrande blasfemie over luxurie che ala mente si apresentano niun si debbe turbar troppo, imperhò che queste ali devoti non delectano ma li cruciano, né prociedono tal cose dal'homo ma dal diavolo el qual gli suggerisce.' Ibid., fol. d2^r.

46. Ibid., fol. b^r.

47. 'Senza hesitatione over dubitanza de la pietà de Dio.' Ibid., fol. b2^v.

48. 'Spesse volte lo angelo de le tenebre si sole transformare in angelo de luce.' Ibid.

49. Gabriella Zarri, *Le sante vive: Cultura e religiosità femminile nella prima età moderna* (Turin: Rosenberg & Sellier, 1990).

50. Serafino da Fermo, *Operetta del discernimento de i spiriti*, in *Opere del R. P. Serafino da Fermo* [...] (Venice: Comin da Trino di Monferrato, 1569), fols 392^r–427^r (fol. 395^r).

51. Wendy Love Anderson, *The Discernment of Spirits: Assessing Visions and Visionaries in the Late Middle Ages* (Tübingen: Mohr Siebeck, 2011).

52. 'Tutto questo mese de febraro so' stata in grande agonia e bataglia mentale. E la cagione è stata questa: che ho avuta una veemente, calda e fervente inspirazione alla quale ho fatta grande e forte resistenza, dubitando non fosse tentazione diabolica.' Beata Camilla Battista da Varano clarissa di Camerino, 'La vita spirituale', in *Le opere spirituali*, ed. by Giacomo Boccanera (Jesi: Scuola Tipografica Francescana, 1958), pp. 5–67 (pp. 5–6). On Camilla, see Gabriella Zarri, 'L'autobiografia religiosa negli scritti autobiografici di Camilla Battista da Varano: La 'Vita spirituale' (1491) e le 'Istruzioni al discepolo' (1501)', in *'In quella parte del libro de la mia memoria': Verità e finzioni dell''io' autobiografico*, ed. by Francesco Bruni (Venice: Marsilio, 2003), pp. 133–58; William V. Hudon, '"In the End, God Helped Me Defeat Myself": Autobiographical Writings by Camilla Battista da Varano', *Religions*, 9 (2018) <https://www.mdpi.com/2077-1444/9/3/65≥ [accessed 2 February 2021].

53. 'Essendo una nocte in camera fu menata da uno venerabile vecchio circa la ripa de uno fiume per uno spacio grande caminando, et essendo venuti al fine del fiume, li ge erano Angeli li quali alchuni ascendevano per fino al cielo, et alchuni descendevano. Unde io vedendo questa cosa maravegliosa comenciay a dire nela mente mia: sarìa mai questa illusione del demonio? Dissemi quel venerabile vecchio: Figliola, non temere che questo non è dal demonio. Alhora comenciay a pensare: serìa mai questo el mio Signore? Sentiva uno grande gaudio nel cor mio. Et dissemi quel vecchio venerando: Figliola, adesso sarai certificata de alchuni dubiy tuoi, et disparse lui.' Paolo Guerrini, 'La prima "legenda volgare" de la beata Stefana Quinzani d'Orzinuovi secondo il codice vaticano-urbinate latino 1755', in *Memorie storiche della diocesi di Brescia* (Brescia: Scuola Tip. Istituto Figli di Maria, 1930), pp. 65–186 (p. 159).

54. 'Vogliatime far certa de alchuni dubij li quali molto mi cruciano. [...] Vogliaria sapere, Angelo benedetto, che cosa è quella che me farà ascendere al perfecto amore del mio sposo et a che modo me potrò transformare nel mio Segnore secundo che voi seti transformati, e che cosa è questa transformatione.' Ibid. See Silvia Lorenzini, 'Stefana Quinzani', in *Le stanze segrete: Le donne bresciane si rivelano*, ed. by Elisabetta Selmi (Brescia: Fondazione Civiltà Bresciana, 2008), pp. 11–35.

55. Michele Lodone, 'L'eredità dei francescani spirituali fra Quattro e Cinquecento: Una ricerca in corso su Gabriele Biondo', *Oliviana*, 4 (2012) <https://journals.openedition.org/oliviana/487?lang=en> [accessed 13 May 2019]; Michele Lodone, *Invisibile come Dio: La vita e l'opera di Gabriele Biondo* (Pisa: Edizioni della Normale, 2020).

56. *Antonij Trombette* [...] *opus in Metaphysicam Arist.* [...] (Venice: [Giacomo Penzio], 1504); the discussion of Biondo's twelve theses regarded as heretical (with vernacular excerpts) is at fols 108^r–111^r ('Questio magistri Antonii Trombete super articulos impositos domino Gabrieli sacerdoti'). Trombetta was professor of metaphysics at the University of Padua and later Bishop of Urbino. See Lodone, *Invisibile come Dio*, pp. 104–34. Trombetta's text is now published in Michele Lodone, 'Un teologo, un medico e un libro (Padova, 1502)', *Riforma e movimenti religiosi*, 6 (2019), 141–84 (pp. 154–78).

57. Michele Lodone, 'Direzione spirituale e autorità eremitica: Paolo Giustiniani e le seguaci fiorentine di Gabriele Biondo', *Aevum*, 90 (2016), pp. 523–45 (p. 539).

58. 'Lauda Dio di quella parte che te haverà concesso intendere et sempre dubita de havere o imperfectamente o male inteso.' Michele Lodone, 'L'opera poetica volgare di Gabriele Biondo', *Interpres*, 35 (2017), 39–97 (p. 74).

59. 'Però dubita sempre | Et teme et spera insieme.' Ibid., p. 87.

60. They are now in Seville, Biblioteca Capitular y Colombina, MS 325 (7-1-9), fols 13^v–20^r. I heartily thank Michele Lodone for sharing with me his transcription of the text.

61. 'Individuale e concreto'. Lodone, *Invisibile come Dio*, p. 101.

62. For the life of Pagani, see Rita Bacchiddu, 'Pagani, Marco (in religione Antonio)', in *Dizionario biografico degli Italiani*, LXXX (Rome: Istituto dell'Enciclopedia italiana, 2014) <https://www.treccani.it/enciclopedia/marco-pagani_%28Dizionario-Biografico%29/> [accessed 16 October 2020]. On Negri, see Massimo Firpo, 'Paola Antonia Negri, monaca Angelica (1508–1555)', in *Rinascimento al femminile*, ed. by Ottavia Niccoli (Rome: Laterza, 2008 (1991)), pp. 35–82; on Torelli, see Attilio Toffolo, '"Servire a Dio in l'habito mio seculare": Ludovica Torelli e l'esperienza religiosa dei primi Barnabiti', *Barnabiti studi*, 30 (2013), 21–78.

63. On the Barnabiti, see Massimo Firpo, *Nel labirinto del mondo: Lorenzo Davidico tra santi, eretici, inquisitori* (Florence: Olschki, 1997), pp. 1–67; Bonora, *I conflitti della Controriforma: Santità e obbedienza nell'esperienza religiosa dei primi barnabiti* (Florence: Le Lettere, 1998); P. Renée Baernstein, *A Convent Tale: A Century of Sisterhood in Spanish Milan* (New York: Routledge, 2002).

64. Whatever his inner convictions were, in 1557 Pagani chose to become a Franciscan, teaching canonical law at San Francesco alla Vigna in Venice, preaching, and fighting heresy. In 1562, he took part in the Council of Trent and in 1569 he became *consultore* of the Holy Office in Vicenza. In Vicenza he also founded the order of the Dimesse and that of the Santissima Croce, a congregation of lay people who lived in common. From the 1560s to the 1580s he authored a number of spiritual works, among which was the *Ragionamenti*. Elena Bonora (*I conflitti della Controriforma*, Chap. 10) has argued that much of Battista da Crema's original teaching remained disguised under the surface of these apparently perfectly orthodox treatises.

65. Because of this and other errors, Fra Marino later had to defend himself before the Inquisition; see Bonora, *I conflitti della Controriforma*, pp. 574–75; on the *Rime*, see Elena Bonora, 'Nei labirinti della censura libraria cinquecentesca: Antonio Pagani (1526–1589) e le "Rime spirituali"', in *Per Marino Berengo: Studi dagli allievi*, ed. by Livio Antonelli, Carlo Capra, and Mario Infelise (Milan: Franco Angeli, 2000), pp. 114–36; Franco Tomasi, 'Le "Rime" di Marco Antonio Pagani', *Bollettino della Società di Studi Valdesi*, 218 (2016), 71–102.

66. 'Le vie de' santi oscure et difficili et li iudicii di Dio nascosti.' Quoted in Bonora, 'Nei labirinti', p. 124.

67. 'Sì varie son le strade ch'Iddio pose | Per gir al ciel, che l'una all'altra appare | Opponersi.' The text is published in Tomasi, 'Le "Rime"', p. 88.

68. 'L'intera Chiesa ebbe Lorenzo a schivo; | Error perciò non fu ne i lor pensieri, | Ma gli è ch'un maggior lume par che appanni | Un ch'è minor e d'ugual gratia privo.' Ibid.

69. Quoted in Bonora, 'Nei labirinti', p. 127.

70. 'Così non facilmente si discerne | Vera humiltà di un cor che nel profondo | Nascoste ha le sue radici e tutto il mondo | Capir non può sue vie tacite e interne.' Ibid., p. 126.

71. *Ragionamenti di diverse notabili materie ne i quali si contengono le risolutioni di vari dubbi, intorno a cose molto giovevoli per l'ammaestramento, & per l'essercitio pratico di persone spirituali, così ecclesiastiche e religiose, come secolari* [...] (Venice: appresso Domenico Farri, 1587), fol. ★3ᵛ.

72. 'Egli è cosa certa che ogni arte e ogni scienza tanto più s'apprende, s'illustra e si fa perfetta nell'huomo studioso quanto maggiormente vien trattata, pratticata e con nuovi dubbi e varie questioni investigata e essercitata. Il che se palesemente si vede avenir delle arti meccaniche o liberali, over delle speculative scienze, molto più suol succedere e più ragionevolmente riuscir della nobilissima arte, anzi arte delle arti, e scienza sopra le altre scienze, scienza de' santi e vera sapienza per la qual si riforma l'huomo interiore.' Ibid., fol. ★3ʳ.

73. Ibid., pp. 102–03.

74. See Raoul Manselli, 'Aceti de' Porti, Serafino', in *Dizionario biografico degli Italiani*, 1 (1960) <https://www.treccani.it/enciclopedia/aceti-de-porti-serafino_%28Dizionario-Biografico%29/> [accessed 15 November 2022]; Gabriele Feyles, *Serafino da Fermo canonico regolare lateranense (1496–1540)* (Turin: SEI, 1942).

75. First printed in Milan in 1538, dedicated to Lucrezia Pico Rangona, and subsequently printed in Venice in 1541.

76. Beside the editions of single works, miscellaneous editions of Serafino's works appeared in 1541, 1543 (twice), 1548, 1556, 1562, 1569, 1570, 1587, and 1596; see Gabriella Zarri, 'Note su diffusione e circolazione di testi devoti (1520–1550)', in *Libri di spirito*, pp. 103–46.

77. Serafino da Fermo, *Operetta*, fol. 402^r.

78. Ibid., fol. 415^r.

79. 'Ma il dubbio sta, qual è quel modo col quale il Signore hora chiama. Io rispondo che per varie congetture si può concludere che hora bisogna disprezzar ogni mezo sopranaturale come sono visioni, miracoli, fervori eccessivi, e questo è per non asimigliarsi a Antichristo, il quale è molto vicino, e già ha preparato sedia in molti che sopra tal cose s'appoggiano. Onde si trovano senza numero persone che hanno le stimmate e i dolori di Iesu Christo.' Ibid., fol. 419^r.

80. 'Ma nasce un dubbio molto grande, come si potrebbe sapere il voler di Dio quando una cosa è indifferente e può essere buona o cattiva? Al che rispondo che in tal caso dobbiamo sospendere ogni nostro volere, tal che non più pende dall'una parte che dall'altra, e poi con ferma fede pregar il Signor che si degni inchinarci da quella parte che a lui piace.' Ibid., fol. 421^v.

81. 'Ad alcuna cosa della qual dubitar si potesse, perché sol chi crede e impegna la fede sua può esser ingannato e poniamo che creda il vero almen si espone al pericolo non havendo ferma certezza d'esser illuso e questo esponersi al poter esser ingannato è un manifesto inganno.' Ibid., fol. 424^r.

82. 'E se alcun dicesse: "Hor non si fa ingiuria al Spirito santo non creder alle cose divine quando si vedono essere da Dio?" Rispondo prima che le cose divine son di tanta altezza che colui meglio le comprende il quale fermamente niente conosce, niente comprendere, onde dice Pietro Crisologo che chi più altamente crede, più altamente dubita.' Ibid., fol. 424^v.

83. The quote comes from Sermon 79, 'De resurrectione Christi'. Cf. *Patrologia latina*, LII, cols 423–24. Serafino spent the period of his preparation for preaching in Ravenna.

84. 'Stette alle parole dell'angelo dubiosa mentre da Dio fu talmente nel cuor accertata che dubbio alcun non vi rimase'; 'dopo mille segni sempre restò dubbiosa e quanto più era dubbiosa di quel dubbio che l'humiltà e non l'ignorantia induce, tanto più il divin lume cresceva in lei'. Serafino da Fermo, *Operetta*, fol. 425^r.

85. 'Integrissima vergine'. Serafino da Fermo, *Vita di due beatissime donne, Margarita e Gentile*, in *Opere del R. P. Serafino da Fermo* [...] (Venice: Comin da Trino de Monferrato, 1569), fols 365^r–391^r (fol. 366^r). The work was first printed in Mantua, possibly by Venturino Ruffinelli, in 1545.

86. Serafino da Fermo, *Vita di due beatissime donne*, fol. 366^r.

87. Ibid., fol. 371^r.

88. Ibid., fol. 380^v.

89. Niccoli, *Prophecy and People*, pp. 35–51.

90. Ibid., Chap. 3. See also Lorraine J. Daston and Katharine Park, *Wonders and the Order of Nature, 1150–1750* (New York: Zone Books, 1998), Chap. 5.

91. 'In questo tempo si vede tra' fideli tutti i membri del pessimo Antichristo cioè sono biastematori di Dio, horribili venditori di Iesu Christo, manifesti heretici, ostinatissimi superstitiosi e incantatori infiniti, hipocriti senza numero, spirituali illusi dal demonio più che mai sian stati. Hor chi dubita che essendo comparse tutte le sue membra presto apparirà il capo? E forsi a questa hora è comparso, come per insoliti prodigi dal cielo e dalla terra si vede.' Serafino da Fermo, *Breve dichiaratione*, fol. 344^v.

92. Serafino comments on the tenth chapter and the prophecy of a new preaching: 'questa predicatione non può essere quella de gli Apostoli [...] sarà adonche nel tempo di Antichristo peroché allhora s'ademprirà quel che dice san Paolo quando la plenitudine delle genti sarà intrata allhora tutto Israel sarà salvo e così gli Hebrei quali furono primi saranno gli ultimi; e perché si conosca questo tempo avicinarsi ha permesso Dio che da pochi anni in qua si sia ritrovato il nuovo mondo, qual secondo la fidel relatione di molti che scrivono non è menor che tutta l'Europa, così di grandezza de sito, come di copia di persone, dove ogn'anno navigano dalla parte di Spagna e hora se vi predica l'Evangelio, dove mai fu cognitione d'alcuna legge e già molti si convertono accioché, come la cecità de gli Hebrei fu occasione della salute nostra, così la cecità nostra constrenga Iesù Christo andar in altro paese e al presente si verifichi quel che da gli apostoli fu profetato, che in ogni terra la lor voce penetraria. Che essendo spesso nelle Scritture nominate le quattro [...] parti della terra, e havendo già l'Evangelio penetrato l'Asia, l'Africa e l'Europa, restava solo che alla quarta parte novamente ritrovata, chiamata America, fusse transportato. Non ti maravigliare se in un tempo medesimo s'apparecchia dall'una parte

la renovatione della fede, dall'altra la dispositione alla venuta di Antichristo e hora [...] sono comparsi gl'inditij evidenti dell'uno e dell'altro.' Ibid., fol. 338^{r-v}.

93. Adriano Prosperi, 'America e Apocalisse: Note sulla "conquista spirituale" del Nuovo Mondo', in *America e Apocalisse e altri saggi* (Rome: Istituti Editoriali e Poligrafici, 1999), pp. 15–63 (pp. 46–49).

94. Serafino da Fermo, *Breve dichiaratione*, fol. 333^{v}.

95. 'Ogni sacramento over è posto in dubbio, over appertamente annichilato.' Ibid., fol. 334^{r}.

96. Don Cameron Allen, *Doubt's Boundless Sea: Skepticism and Faith in the Renaissance* (Baltimore: Johns Hopkins Press, 1964).

97. 'I quali hanno preparato la sedia a Antichristo e dice che 'l suo regno diventò tenebroso, come si vede che tanta tenebra di confusion è nata tra loro che non sanno più quel che credere si debbia e già hanno fatto mille mutation d'articoli e sempre di male in peggio.' Serafino da Fermo, *Breve dichiaratione*, fol. 350^{v}.

98. 'Huomini scientiati e curiosi'. Ibid., fol. 349^{v}.

99. 'Quelli che sempre correno d'una scientia curiosa, e magnificano la setta d'Arist[otele] e del Commentatore, e per tal modo occideno il spirito delle Scritture sacre e perché pongono in dubio l'immortalità dell'anima dalla qual dipende tutta la fede Christiana.' Ibid., fol. 350^{r}.

CHAPTER 4

Doubt and the
Challenge to Orthodoxy

Within the spiritual crisis of the early cinquecento, doubt seems to have become a privileged instrument for shaping one's relationship with God. Doubt allowed the individual to explore and map the realm of what should or should not fall within the boundaries of 'true' faith. Doubt could be a fearful enemy or a precious ally in the quest for one's true vocation. In questioning traditional devotional practices, doubt could lighten their burden, helping shape a more simple and direct relationship with the divine. Yet doubt could also prove an unstoppable force that left one contemplating a world devoid of certainties, to the point that the very idea of God seemed to dissolve. The consoling message of the *beneficio* of Christ, that true believers are saved by his willing death, opened the way to new doubts: How could one be sure of being among the saved? How far could one go in leaving behind traditional practices of devotion? Should one live in the world, or devote oneself to spiritual contemplation? At a time when all religious certainties seemed to be shaken, it is not surprising that doubt came to play a pivotal role. Practices, beliefs, institutions were scrutinized; one's interiority often became the theatre of a psychomancy that could turn into a quasi-pathological condition. Within the polyphonic religious world of early sixteenth-century Italy — where a drive to reform the Catholic church from within coexists and sometimes overlaps with Valdésian, Reformed, and more radical ideas — doubt became a privileged tool for rethinking the issue of salvation.

It was the written word that once more turned doubt from an individual condition into a shared cultural object, the centre of a field of discourse. Thus, much of the disquieting and destructive aura of doubt was lost. Doubt shifted from being a condition experienced in isolation into an object that could be described and explored in writing (poems, pamphlets, tracts, etc.) and in conversation. Writing allowed the dangers of doubt to be neutralized — or made sense of — and its positive functions shared. In a sense, defining doubt through the written and spoken word allowed not only a defence to be built against it but also a conscious — proactive, one may say — use of doubt as a tool in shaping one's own and others' spirituality and, as we will see, one's self.

This chapter does not aim to shed new light on religious life in the first decades of the sixteenth century. Instead, it looks at the complexity of religious life through the particular lens of how doubt changed from being an overwhelming external force to an asset that could be consciously directed and employed. This happened within the shared social space of the written and spoken word, in which doubt became alternatively an object and/or a method of reflection. This use of doubt as a kind of strategic mechanism did not happen in ego-documents such as those studied by Alec Ryrie. Even when doubt seemed to be mostly self-doubt, it emerged as a fulcrum for shared discourses meant from the start to target specific audiences, be it the reading public, a particular group of individuals, or religious authorities. Dialogues (actual or literary), poems, letters, tracts built a common space in which doubt could be discussed. As we will see, however, there is no teleology at work here: the uncanny power of doubt is always lurking, undermining the hope of salvation. Italian devotees walked a fine line between the 'doubt of desperation' and the 'doubt of enlightenment' or, in other words, between a doubt that threatened the space of interiority and that which allowed one to rise to higher forms of spirituality.

This chapter will move through three different areas of Italian spirituality: the first is connected with the dawning push towards a renewal of the Catholic church as voiced in the 1510s by Paolo Giustinian and his acolytes; the second is that of the so-called *spirituali*; and the third is the broad arena of more radical dissent.

Gloomy Thoughts and Lanterns in the Night

It is April 1512, and a man sits at his desk in the Camaldoli hermitage in Tuscany. He is writing to two friends in Venice, Niccolò Tiepolo and Gasparo Contarini, debating the choice of monastic life over worldly life. Although he himself has abandoned the second to embrace first, he does not think that this is the only way to lead a spiritually pure life. After signing the letter, he adds a postscript inviting his friends to come and visit him at Camaldoli. He encourages them not to be frightened by the ongoing wars, which will not last forever. The postscript could be finished thus, but he feels compelled to add a few more lines: 'Shortly after writing [these lines], I hear cries, broken formations, retreats, captures, death of people: things that should move to tears stones, let alone us.'[1]

The sounds of the battle of Ravenna are recorded almost in real time on the page of Vincenzo Querini, and their echo spreads from Camaldoli to Venice (although some days must have elapsed before the news of the battle reached Camaldoli). The terrible echo of the battle of Ravenna — which later resonates in the works of Serafino da Fermo, as we have seen — also found its way to the private letters exchanged by a group of Venetian noblemen who were reflecting on how to pursue spiritual perfection. In these letters, one finds some of the same topics as those discussed by Serafino and Antonio Pagani. The anxiety over the choice of one's spiritual path, the fear of illusions, the anguish related to possible temptations that may be hiding even at the heart of apparently impeccable choices were in fact not specific to the spiritually intense circles gathering around 'holy mothers' and spiritual directors. Even persons born into aristocratic families and possessing a humanistic background shared such concerns. A fine example is provided by the letters that Gasparo Contarini (1483–1542) sent to Tommaso Giustinian (later known as Paolo, 1476–1528) and Vincenzo Querini (later Pietro, 1478/79–1514). Giustinian and Querini were among the friends of the writer Pietro Bembo (1470–1547), all members of the so-called Compagnia degli Amici, a sort of academy open to men and women 'to discuss the abandonment of worldly ambition, the life of contemplation, and love poetry'.[2] Bembo himself drafted in 1502/03 the rules of this society of fellows devoted to poetry and friendship, the cult of art, and Platonic love. However, Giustinian and Querini soon felt the need to devote themselves to an entirely religious life and entered the Camaldolese order; Giustinian even took on the task of revising Bembo's rules, giving them a spiritual cast.[3]

Despite both Querini's and Giustinian's hopes that Bembo would embark on the same reclusive life they pursued, these expectations were soon frustrated by Bembo's decision to move first to Urbino and then to Rome, where he was appointed secretary of the *brevi* by Leo X. Giustinian and Querini shared the belief that the Roman Church was in need of some reform from within; to this purpose, they penned a book directed to the newly elected Pope Leo X (*Libellum ad Leonem X*, 1513) in which they made their suggestions to this effect.[4] The turning point in their lives had been in 1510/11, when Giustinian and Querini decided to abandon worldly life. Although Querini had felt a spiritual pull towards eremitic life since the early 1500s, his decision to join Giustinian was a tormented one. For a few years he remained actively involved in Venetian politics as a man of his standing was expected to do. While performing his ambassadorial duties in Burgundy in 1504–06, Querini had the chance to travel across Europe and observe the state of religion in several countries. He was especially impressed by the piety of the Burgundians, as testified to in his report (*relazione*) to the Venetian Senate. His words of praise for the men and women of Burgundy drew an implicit comparison with the mores of other contemporary Europeans. Querini wrote, in fact, that among Flemish people '[o]ne does not find lust, nor corruption, nor blasphemy, nor envy nor hatred, as one finds in many other places, nor incredulity in matters of faith'.[5] This is followed by a long passage in praise of Burgundian women and their virtue. The portrait of Flemish people is one of simple men and women, perhaps inclined to the pleasures of eating and drinking and to a merry life but with no proclivity whatsoever to lust. In sum, they were in Querini's eyes 'good Christians'; in particular, he had not found among them any trace of the incredulity that, in his view, was sweeping over other European countries.

Querini, Giustinian, and Contarini experienced the same climate of anxiety over the corruption of the church and the impending ruin of Christian religion that one perceives in the works of Serafino da Fermo and of many other contemporary writers and preachers.[6] Despite the general inclination towards a withdrawal into eremitic life in early sixteenth-century Venice, Giustinian's and Querini's choice to join the hermits of Camaldoli in Tuscany in 1510/11 was not an easy one. In a letter dated 22 January 1511, Querini writes to Giustinian, who by that time was already in Camaldoli, saying that although all their friends send their regards, '[S]ome of them consider you as affected by melancholy, some call you desperate, a man of little prudence, a fool, even crazy.'[7] Querini's own decision was no less difficult and required a good deal of examination of conscience before he finally made his profession on 22 February 1512. Querini's letters to Giustinian testify to his doubts and perplexity. One in particular, a very long letter written presumably in January 1511, is a veritable theatre of the soul. Querini stages the conflict between two opposite sides of his personality, one that aspires to a spiritual life and the other that insinuates doubts and presents obstacles of all sorts. Querini dons in this letter the mask of Licenope, a persona that 'gave playful voice to all of Querini's doubts and hopes about the monastic life', or, as other scholars have put it, reveals 'his better self who would like to follow Giustiniani and overcome Vincenzo's doubts, weaknesses, and hesitations'.[8]

In the opening paragraphs of the letter, Querini compliments Giustinian on his spiritual advancement and encourages him to persevere on his path to perfection, despite the falls and moments of despair that he will inevitably face. Querini quickly realizes, however, that he is unworthy of giving advice to his friend, who is far ahead of him on his spiritual path. His elaborate apology is of interest to us:

> But how can I, a man of the world, wrapped up in my sins and engulfed by my foul deeds (as I have always been), show the light to a man who, in every respect, will be able to see through darkness better than I could see in plain light? If I ponder this all, it happens to me what happens to those who walk carrying a light, that they show the way to others without being themselves able to see it.[9]

The image of the man who walks in the night with a lantern without being able to see his way recalls Ripa's first allegory of doubt, discussed in Chapter 1. Querini is probably referring to Dante, and in particular of Statius's speech to Virgil in *Purgatory*, xx. 64–73. Here Statius expresses his gratitude to Virgil not only for having inspired him to become a poet, but also, and mostly, for having shown him, through the prophetical verses of the fourth Eclogue, the way to Christianity. Even though Virgil was not a Christian, his inspired words revealed to others the coming of the new faith. Virgil himself remained in the darkness of paganism, despite being able to show to others the enlightened way to Christianity. It is in this context that Dante employs the image of the man who walks in the dark carrying a lantern for those who follow him.[10] Querini implicitly compares himself to Virgil walking in the dark and Giustinian to Statius, both of them on the safe and enlightened path of true religion. It is against this background of aspirations to renew the church as well as a knot of complex interpersonal dynamics that we must set the letters between Giustinian, Querini, and Contarini.

Giustinian in particular was a highly regarded figure, and Contarini, despite being only a few years his junior, looked on him with admiration. In his letters to Giustinian and Querini, Contarini describes his painful spiritual condition and the difficulties connected with the choice of an eremitic life, also voicing his perplexity concerning the appropriateness of Querini's decision to pursue it. Contarini's letters open a window onto a deep spiritual crisis, a protracted moment of doubt and uncertainty, a nearly pathological condition of intense melancholy broaching insanity. These letters, spanning a little over a decade, bear witness to the difficulties connected to the quest for an authentically spiritual life. Contarini first writes to Giustinian on 1 February 1511, lamenting his 'heart of stone' and his feeling of being almost 'like a ship on the sea without guidance'.[11] On 24 April of the same year, he declares that he had considered his way of living and was deeply discontent and 'almost desperate' about it. He thus consulted with a friar, 'who began to tell me that the way to salvation is broader than many may think. [...] So I understood that, even if I did all possible penitence, and more again, that would not suffice'. The contemplation of the crucified Christ has led him to think that 'his passion has been enough, and even more than enough'. Yet the thought of his faults led him 'into sadness and almost desperation'.[12] This is a key moment in Contarini's spiritual labour, for he finds out that the way to salvation is broad and rests solely on Christ's passion and not on our deeds; later in the century these ideas will become two main staples of the theology of the Italian evangelical movement.

A few months later, Contarini introduces in his letters another key term: *beneficio*. In his letter to Giustinian of 10 August, he declares that when he reflects on the 'innumerable benefits' of Christ he is astonished that he does not die of both pain and love; yet despite this joyous thought, he is still oppressed by 'a severe and mortiferous lethargy'. Worldly life seems to him 'a shadow or a dream', and although he tries to change his way of living he is unable to do so, as if he 'were lethargic'.[13] Little more than a month later, he speaks about his 'distressed soul'; a soul that is, at the same time, 'asleep'.[14] The stark contrast between a conflicted soul, moved by passions, doubts, and fears, and a form of spiritual drowsiness is peculiar to Contarini's letters. At this stage of his life, he is unable to make a decision and definitively embrace the appropriate path. The distress (perturbation) of the mind reappears in a letter to Vincenzo Querini in late November 1511. This time, however, Contarini places his disquiet in a larger context. He voices his concerns about Querini's choice to pursue a spiritual life, since he feels his friend does not possess the required strength. Querini, and Contarini with him, are standing at the crossroads between a solitary religious life and a worldly one: the dilemma is that neither does religious life lead with certainty to salvation, nor civil life absolutely to damnation — both can lead to either result. Unfortunately, not one of us, 'being blind', knows which is the right choice.[15] Contarini warns Querini that even if he is persuaded that eremitic life is his vocation, he should not deem every other option or any occurring impediments as a diabolic temptation.

Contarini further expands upon these topics in a long letter to Querini, written on 26 December 1511. After declaring that his soul is 'perplexed', that is, deeply doubtful, he muses on the topic of eremitic life. If, he argues, one has felt for a long time a calling, then that vocation should be followed. One should make sure that this vocation comes from God, otherwise choosing a monastic life over the worldly one would be equal to tempting God; in fact, the 'cunning of the Enemy' is far more powerful than our intellect, and he can easily deceive us. Many a person has embraced eremitic life without the necessary strength and, as a consequence, has fallen prey to either melancholy or 'some diabolical delusion'.[16] To strengthen his point, Contarini tells the story of one Tommaso Moro, a friar in the convent of San Pietro Martire of Murano. Prompted by the devil, he had begun to fast, live alone, and inflict on himself harsher penances than his body could sustain. As a result, after a few months he fell into such a strong 'melancholic disposition' ('disposition melancolica') that his fellow friars feared that he might lose his mind. After some time spent in this dreadful condition, poor Tommaso suffered a fever and died.

The 1500s to the 1520s are years of religious enthusiasm, be it that of holy mothers or of aspiring hermits. The downside of this frenzy was the sudden bursts of melancholy, delusion, physical illness, and possibly death. Caution was required on the part of the person who decided to embrace religious life; no reliable signs granted confidence in one's choice. Doubt was an inevitable condition, as if many early modern Italians were sleepwalking into a realm of visions and delusions, a theatre of shadows that could equally lead to eternal salvation or to desperation (although this condition was widespread in fifteenth-century spirituality). Contarini was scarcely prone to such enthusiasm, as he saw himself unfit to embrace monastic life. His attempt to pursue religious life led him to melancholy and even produced physical disease. The reading of Scripture caused him a 'great distress of the body because of the melancholic humour, and a great disturbance of the soul', as he writes to Giustinian on 26 February 1512.[17] In the same letter Contarini recalls how he had lately read St Matthew, St Gregory, and St Augustine, and that 'through their reading, I felt rising in my soul some vain and crazy fears'. He had then decided to read only Thomas Aquinas and 'low-profile speculations by philosophers and theologians'.[18] Contarini provides an interesting reason for this, connected to the widespread suspicion towards mysticism and its risks:

> My weakness does not sustain [the reading of] the works by the more ancient theologians, who always interpret mystically the Scripture and give warnings concerning the way of life and the feelings of the soul which one should pursue, and to which I cannot rise. In fact, if I study those works, I move from fear to discontent and from discontent back to fear. So it is that, while I think that through this study I can free my soul from all perturbation, I always feel I am little by little descending to an even greater perturbation and then to some superstition and some foolish form of credulity, which are all caused by the pusillanimity of the soul produced by this reading.[19]

In this extraordinary passage — relevant also to the history of reading — Contarini explains the bodily and mental effects of reading. Constance Furey has spoken of an 'affective failure', also connected to a shift in the practice of reading to '[focusing] less on reading techniques than on the reader's emotional response'.[20] Mystical interpretations of the Bible, as well as the too-demanding and unattainable standards of behaviour set by some fathers of the church, cause melancholy, and this in turn causes forms of superstition and credulity, or the belief in vain ideas. The 'therapeutic effects' of the written word turn into their opposite, eliciting a sort of emotional as well as physical illness.[21] The word pusillanimity is also interesting, and somewhat surprising to find in the writing of a person who will rise to become one the most powerful cardinals of the Roman church. It is the same pusillanimity we have considered in Chapter 1, the excessive fear of sin, associated in this case with the *credulità paze*, the belief in what may be pure illusion. Also in Contarini's world, then, the boundaries between dreaming and wakefulness, reality and imagination are anything but clear-cut. The obsessive presence in his letters of terms such as 'sleep', 'dream', 'lethargy', and 'melancholy' hint not merely at an individual condition but to a more widespread *mal du siècle*.

The 'crazy' images of Contarini's mind could turn into openly frightful ones. We have a letter to Querini and Giustinian, written on 17 July 1512, in which Contarini recalls how in 1509 he had moved from Padua to Venice because of the wars, and how he had then studied philosophy and Christian doctrine, subsequently moving to the study of mathematics and of Thomas Aquinas's works. As a consequence of these studies, he had fallen into the melancholic disposition we have already discussed. From the letter, it seems possible to infer that after the violent onset of melancholy that befell Contarini in 1511, a recurrence, if possibly less fierce, of the illness took place in 1512. Contarini affirms that melancholy disturbs him 'with such sad and gloomy thoughts, with such dreadful phantasies (dreadful, I say, because they are about such things that reason deems almost impossible) that only a few people, I believe, can be found in the whole world with a more troubled soul than me'.[22] It is notable that melancholy raises the ghosts of things perceived as real and threatening, although according to reason they should not and could not exist. Contarini seems to describe a scenario of diabolical temptation very much in the style of contemporary depictions of the temptations of St Anthony. The devil's work becomes evident when Contarini claims that he has come to 'hate my studies and the only thing that previously used to bring me joy, reading Holy Scripture, now causes me great annoyance'.[23] Again, he talks of 'these gloomy thoughts that molest me' and of how 'the Holy Scripture nowadays does not give me any consolation and I doubt the time will ever come when it will please me'.[24]

In the same letter, Contarini mixes the description of his spiritual illness with some of the formulae that will later become well-known tenets of evangelical spirituality. Although he does not and will never despair of the 'merits of Jesus Christ crucified', he also hopes in his friends' prayers.[25] He claims to be sure that Christ allows him to doubt the impossibility that 'bitter thoughts' ('pensieri amari') could ever arise from the contemplation of the Crucifix. He is, however, persuaded that the 'Divine Majesty' made him fall into his affliction to make him aware that 'making myself quiet and peaceful' does not depend on himself, but solely on Christ.[26]

Throughout Contarini's letters one perceives the coexistence of desperation and hope in the merits of Christ's passion. Contarini seems to anticipate the argument of *sola fide* salvation, which he will champion later in the century. As I have suggested, Contarini's letters do not merely describe an individual state of mind; they fit into a broader concern over the decadence of the church and the challenges that lie ahead. In a letter to Querini, written on 13 June 1514, he admits that he had placed high hopes in the election of the new pontiff, Leo X, but then realized that a man alone could not heal the church. The pope was in need of 'good men' ('homeni boni') able to help him to carry out this task.[27] Years later, under the reign of Paul III, Contarini himself will become one of these 'good men'. Besides, the letters we have examined are part of a polyphonic dialogue between a group of friends who share their doubts with each other. The technical words they use — 'perplexity', 'pusillanimity' — show that we are in the realm of doubt as elaborated by contemporary theology. Although these letters may appear at first glance to be private documents, they are in fact part of a broader reflection. Doubt is projected against a social background, as it arises not only from the uncertainty concerning one's choices and the interpretation of the signs of one's calling but also from the friction between social expectations and personal choices. As in the case of the holy mothers (with all due differences), here it is not only a matter of internal enlightenment but of its social and even political consequences.

The Ambiguity of Doubt: Juan de Valdés

Mid-cinquecento spirituality was largely shaped by the teaching of Juan de Valdés, a Spaniard who had moved to Italy in 1531, first to Rome and then in 1535 to Naples, where he died in 1541. He soon became the centre of a network of men and women seeking spiritual relief. In his teaching, Valdés mixed Erasmian and Lutheran ideas with the tradition of Spanish *alumbradismo*, a mystical doctrine based on interior enlightenment. His teachings placed a strong emphasis on subjectivity, so that the enlightened person was free of norms and orthodoxy.[28] There were degrees to Valdés's doctrine, and only the more proficient had access to his most radical ideas. While his doctrine was meant to have a soothing effect on his followers, stressing inner faith and salvation by grace, it was radically alternative to that of the Roman Catholic Church, which provided its devotees with a set of rites that would lead them along the path to salvation. Reformed believers could not be certain of election and therefore of salvation, but 'anxious Christians could outsource their concern about themselves to the ministers who policed them'.[29] Loosely organized circles of devotees, their beliefs founded almost exclusively on an interiorized form of faith, did not offer the same guarantees: self-scrutinizing devotees might fear that their faith was not strong enough, that they were not bound to salvation, or in more direct terms, not of the elect. While the devotion of Italian evangelism, following ideas set out by Erasmus in *De immensa Dei misericordia* (1524), came to rely largely on the 'broad way' to salvation, that is, the idea that Christ through his sacrifice has saved us all, painful doubts could nevertheless arise. Ethan Shagan has recently reconstructed the evolution of the category of 'belief' in Europe, stressing the importance of the Reformation in shaping a new meaning of belief which came to be identified with believing in salvation through faith. Relying on doctrine or following exterior practices imposed by a church were no longer sufficient guarantees of being a true believer. If belief had been up to that point a datum, after the Reformation it became a goal, an ideal that common pessimism concerning human nature rendered, if not unattainable, certainly stressful and psychologically demanding. This was true also of the Catholic version: both Catholics and Protestants made belief increasingly difficult as they 'determined that only particular doctrines, and only particular ways of holding those doctrines, and only particular sources of assurance of these doctrines, constituted Christian belief'.[30]

The combination of a newly 'hard' conception of belief and the pessimism about the spread of unbelief gave birth to the question of 'how safe or reliable could any belief be'.[31] This new scenario was especially challenging for Protestants, who were left alone with their inner faith, without the assurance of Catholic rituals: 'if [...] belief in God was belief that you yourself were saved by believing, it followed that doubt about your own salvation amounted to doubting God'.[32] Shagan highlights the inherent paradox of Reformed belief: on the one hand, 'an understanding of "belief" as utterly incompatible with doubt'; on the other hand, 'a theology of human depravity demanding that even the elect remain mired in uncertainty'.[33] This contrast generated sizable anxiety in Reformed believers. Shagan speaks of the 'psychic turmoil generated by predestination';[34] such turmoil was the result of the scrupulous examination of conscience demanded of believers and the awareness that all sins are violations of the first commandment ('I am the Lord thy God') and therefore an act of doubt and unbelief. Reformed believers thus came to realize 'their incapacity for the sort of utter reliance on God and immaculate freedom from doubt that they had been taught was the definition of authentic belief'.[35]

Valdés approached doubt from a different perspective, devoting considerable attention to it as a crucial step on the path to interior enlightenment. He did so in a work titled *Le cento e dieci divine considerazioni* (The hundred and ten divine meditations; the first Italian version appeared in Basel in 1550), whose editor was Celio Secondo Curione (1503–1569), an exile *religionis causa* who had fled Italy for Switzerland in 1542. Curione's introduction to Valdés's work was addressed to those who are 'sanctified by God the Father' and 'saved and called' by Christ.[36]

In his prefatory letter, Curione sketches a brief biographical and intellectual portrait of Valdés, recalling how this should have been the first in a series of editions of Valdés's works.[37] Curione claims that after the Evangelists and the Apostles themselves, no one has possibly written in a manner 'more firmly and more godly' than Valdés himself.[38] The Spanish reformer stands out, in Curione's words, as the one who opposed the many writers and 'doctors' who have complicated authentic religion, making it unrecognizable and subject to doubt, to the point 'that we trust more the so-called doctors [...] than the pure doctrine of Christ'.[39] The many subtle disputations of the theologians have led to a form of religious scepticism, making the otherwise plain teaching of Christ subject to doubt:

> First of all, because they wrote huge books, they could not help the lies, the follies, the foolishness [...]. Then, these great writers have torn Scripture into questions and disputations and turned it into an Academy, *doubting almost everything*, so that they rendered entirely *doubtful* the doctrine of the son of God and of his apostles as well as the unerring and most certain hope in eternal life.[40]

Contrary to these scholars, in his reasoning Valdés 'shows the origin, the reasons, the progress, and the conclusion; and this from the clear, certain, and undoubted principles of Holy Scripture'.[41]

While Curione emphasizes the destructive effects of doubt, which he considers the result of scrutinizing Scripture with exceeding subtlety, Valdés takes instead a different and more articulated stance on doubt, describing its ambiguous role in our path to salvation. Valdés deals with doubt especially in *Considerazioni* 101 and 103. *Considerazione* 101 addresses the difficulty, or the impossibility, of believing.[42] More specifically, Valdés explores the seeming paradox that pious devotees face difficulties in believing, whereas the superstitious believe easily. According to Valdés's categories, pious devotees are those who have accepted the 'general pardon', as stated in Chapter 13:

> There are other people who know themselves as being rebels to God and who put their whole faith and credit in the general forgiveness that God preaches to them in the Gospel; and so immediately, without giving more thought to it, because they accept the general forgiveness, they enter the reign of God, giving up the reign of the world and the rule of human prudence. Those, although they may have doubts at the beginning — they doubt forgiveness, they doubt God's governance and rule — by keeping themselves under God's reign, begin to ensure that God is restoring to them the image and likeness of Him, which the first man lost because of his rebellion.[43]

This is precisely what the 'superstitious' do not believe in: 'They do not believe that which is the foundation of all true things, i.e., the pardon of sins and the reconciliation with God, thanks to God's justice carried out through Christ.'[44] The superstitious are accustomed to believe 'out of opinion' ('per opinione') and 'out of habit and use' ('per usanza e costume'); in doing so, they deem it foolish and impious to question tradition and cast doubts on it, 'taking doubt as an impiety'.[45] In other words, this category of devotees accepts religion as it is, with its mix of true and false beliefs, following exterior practices but failing to grasp the fundamental teaching of our redemption through Christ's sacrifice. In this light, doubt can be a useful tool to get rid of all superimpositions that prevent believers from reaching the true heart of Christian revelation.

Nonetheless, doubt can also impede and retain pious believers along their path. Doubt can be fostered by three main causes. The first is 'bad conscience' ('mala conscientia'), the awareness that humans are enemies of God as a consequence of the Fall. The second is the difficulty of accepting what the gospel announces — the general pardon of all sins and that God 'holds us for friends'. The third reason is lust, or our inclination towards carnal pleasure. In addition, doubt can be the result of an excess of scruple, or of the will to ascertain whether all sins have been pardoned. By contrast, with a peaceful conscience one 'is confirmed in the faith so that one is little inclined to doubt'.[46] In other words, doubt is a consequence of the impossibility or unwillingness to accept the infinite mercy of God, his salvific grace, or the result of an excess of scrutiny of God's grace. The pious should 'stop being in love with themselves and the world' ('desinnamorarsi di se medesimi e del mondo') and fall in love with God. One can easily achieve this condition by contemplating the wickedness of the world and of human nature, as opposed to the good that can be found in God and in Christ.

Valdés expands even further on doubt in *Considerazione* 103, where he distinguishes among different kinds and degrees of doubt. According to Valdés, humans are unable to have sufficient faith to be entirely free of doubt. But while those who do not pursue the path of authentic faith do not feel the urge to doubt ('solicitatione al dubitare'), those who by virtue of the Holy Spirit are beginning to accept the general pardon are powerfully stimulated by doubt. Because Christ's justice exceeds our comprehension, true believers feel inclined to doubt it. This inclination appears to be a diabolical temptation causing disquiet and annoyance. It is precisely from these negative feelings, however, that a person can obtain the certainty that her or his faith is authentic, thus reaching a condition of tranquillity. In fact, Valdés provides five suggestions on how to overcome disquiet and doubt; I will briefly mention the first two. The first is that those who experience this kind of doubt must realize that doubt is a sign of spiritual improvement; it is because they want to believe that they have doubts. The second suggestion is directed to those who think that their doubt is the same as that of those who 'doubt without spirit' ('dubitano senza spirito'). These persons should be aware that 'those who doubt without spirit do not feel any nuisance in their doubt, nor do they desire to be free, whereas I feel a nuisance in my doubting, and I desire to be free from it'.[47]

When Valdés arrived in Naples, he found a city where heterodox ideas circulated and where books destined to end up on the Index of Prohibited Books were being widely disseminated and openly discussed by people from all social classes.[48] One preacher in particular caused a sensation: the Capuchin preacher Bernardino Ochino, who first preached in the city in 1536 and then again in 1538–40 and who would soon flee Italy to avoid religious persecution. Ochino's sermons exerted a strong intellectual and emotional pull on Neapolitans. The opening pages of Valdés's *Alfabeto cristiano* (Christian alphabet) bear witness to Ochino's impact. The *Alfabeto* consists of a dialogue between Valdés himself and Giulia Gonzaga (1513–1566), a noblewoman of exceptional intellectual distinction and close to Valdés and many of the Italian *spirituali*, such as Pietro Carnesecchi and Marcantonio Flaminio.[49]

Following Lent of 1536, Gonzaga had gone through a deep spiritual crisis. She had attended Bernardino Ochino's sermons, and his words had shaken her conscience. This was, for Gonzaga, an experience of conversion and spiritual rebirth that nonetheless carried with it a phase of acute spiritual crisis. It was thanks to her conversations with Valdés that the crisis subsided. In his dedication letter in the *Alfabeto*, addressed to Gonzaga, Valdés recalls their common attendance at Ochino's sermons and the conversations that followed: 'I have written in form of dialogue all that religious conversation in which we were so deeply interested the other day when returning from the sermon that only the night made it necessary for us to break it off.'[50]

In the opening lines of the dialogue, Gonzaga voices her dissatisfaction with herself. She laments that in her heart there lies only 'confusion, uneasiness, and perplexity'.[51] Her spiritual search seems destined never to be fulfilled: 'I cannot conceive what can not be offered to me, sufficient to remove this, my confusion of mind, appease my uneasiness, and resolve this perplexity.'[52] This condition has been going on for many years. Ochino's words, while disclosing a glimpse of the peace she craves, have caused her to sink into an even deeper condition of confusion, adding new reasons for her anxiety. Gonzaga herself sketches her painful condition in a passage that deserves attention:

> Besides this, you know that at the first sermons I heard from our Preacher he persuaded me by his words that, by means of his doctrine, I should be able to calm myself and bring peace to my mind; but now, at last, I find it altogether the reverse of what I thought. And although I attribute this more to my own imperfections than to any defect in him, yet altogether it gives me pain to perceive that my hopes have not succeeded. [...] The sermons of the Preacher have produced this conflict in my mind. Through them I see myself violently assailed, on the one side by the fear of hell and the love of paradise, and on the other by the dread of people's tongues and the love of world's honor.[53]

We find here and in the previous quotations the unmistakable words and emotions of doubt: perplexity, the inability to make a decision, the pain created by two equally powerful options. Gonzaga describes her state as an 'infirmity', an ailment that often brings her to tears. This condition is immediately defined as one of 'confusion, doubt, and perplexity', a 'tempest of affections and appetites, of imaginations and diversities of will'.[54] In the dialogue, Valdés will soothe Gonzaga's anxieties, showing how the instructions laid out in the *Cento e dieci divine considerazioni* could be effectively applied. In this context, doubt seems to characterize a condition in which the believer is at the crossroads of two paths. On the one hand, Gonzaga has the option of staying with the life that had caused in her, up to that moment, dissatisfaction and anxiety. On the other hand, she is tempted to adhere to the new ideas, which seem to offer spiritual solace and yet would prove unacceptable in the eyes of society and would therefore have a cost. The radical new spiritual experiences caused an inevitable clash with the social horizon within which a person was expected to act. In this regard, the new ideas did not add new layers of doubt to the anxieties of Italian devotees; they nonetheless heightened such anxieties while also causing more dramatic consequences. A few years later, the tragic story of Francesco Spiera, a lawyer who had to renounce his Calvinist faith and consequently died of desperation, was to show how destructive these consequences could be.[55] Letters, dialogues, and tracts provided an ideal space in which to voice doubt and one's views on its role in spiritual life. Poetry could also prove an effective means to share one's anxiety, especially in the hands of one the most skilled poets of the cinquecento, Vittoria Colonna. Colonna (1492–1547?), Marchioness of Pescara and wife of the late *condottiero* Francesco Ferrante d'Avalos (1490–1525), began to change her poetical style as early as 1536, recasting traditional Petrarchan love poetry in a spiritual key. A fervent admirer and follower of Bernardino Ochino, Colonna voiced Valdés's teachings in her poems — whether she knew them directly or through Ochino is not entirely clear — as well as the theology of the benefit of Christ, that is, the idea of salvation by grace. Colonna's spirituality was nevertheless complex and developed over the years; it may also appear contradictory in its ambivalence towards Catholic 'ceremonies'. As Gigliola Fragnito has suggested, Colonna may have adopted a double standard of communication, disguising the more nuanced and delicate aspects of her spirituality under the surface of a formal observance of traditional religiosity. The same quality might apply to her poetry, so that only the learned among her readers would have recognized the allusions to salvation *ex sola fide* and similar ideas, while common readers would have simply enjoyed the spiritual solace offered by her poems.[56] As recent scholarship has pointed out, Colonna's *Rime* enjoyed a broader circulation than has been commonly acknowledged. Several of her works — of both poems and letters — circulated in cheap books printed and sold by street hawkers.[57] As for the scribal dissemination of her poems, Abigail Brundin has argued that in general, Colonna tended to exert a strict control over her spiritual sonnets, which circulated mainly within her inner circle.[58]

In her poems, Colonna situates doubt at the intersection between her acute awareness of the fragility of human nature and the certainty of Christ's grace. In the sonnet 'Riverenza m'affrena e grande amore' ('Reverence holds me back, but great love'), Colonna writes: 'The ice of my own sins and the burning fire | Of his love for us confuse my mind'. If the consciousness of her guilt seems to weaken her desire to welcome God into her heart, Christ's ardent charity appears to be stronger than fear. Thus, personified faith makes its bold appearance amidst doubts, begging the Lord to feed her the food of the soul ('Ma la fede fra i dubbi ardita e franca | Chiede il cibo de l'alma').[59] It is God who takes away from the poet's burning heart the doubts inspired by cold fear: 'That great and divine Eye, whose virtue | Has not seen, nor will see, rather always sees, | Takes away from my breast, out of his piety, | The doubts of my cold and slavish fear.'[60]

In the sonnet 'Doi modi abbiam da veder l'alte e care' ('Two ways we have to see the high and cherished'), Colonna muses on the ways God has given us to know him and, particularly, his grace. Among these ways is reading Holy Scripture. The other, and most effective, way is raising the eyes of one's heart to the book of the cross. Both ways lead to God, but the second is more straightforward, more secure, and more effective. In fact, if the first escort, Scripture, leads us to salvation — which is not entirely certain — it does it so only on a doubtful path. But if the soul is filled by Christ, it will run 'fast and sure' to its destination, heaven:

> With such escort, she proceeds uncertain
> So that, if she reaches to her desired destination,
> She passes through a long and dubious path;
> But with this one often, enlightened
> By divine lights, and inflamed by a beautiful fire,
> Runs fast and sure to her true destination.[61]

In this sonnet, we perceive the presence of Valdésian ideas such as the pre-eminence of the spiritual and mystical union with God over the study of Holy Scripture. In general, however, Colonna 'holds the Cross and the Bible together as she tries to navigate [...] the tension between spiritual discernment (*lectio domini*) and meditative reading (*lectio divina*)'.[62]

The perception of life as an earthly labyrinth is expounded in a beautiful sonnet (no. 69, 'Ovunque giro gli occhi o fermo il core', 'Wherever I turn my eyes or halt my heart'), in which Colonna defines her existence as a 'dark life' and a 'dead life' where one cannot distinguish the true from the false path. The soul lacks 'vital consolation' unless it enters the safe harbour of Christ's wounds. There, the soul 'si sta romita': Christ's wounds are compared to a hermit's cave, where the soul, shaken by doubts and uncertainty, can finally find shelter.[63] Ironically enough, despite such a tormented attitude towards the human spiritual condition, contemporaries perceived Colonna as both a spiritual and literary model who, having left behind her all doubts, was safely proceeding on the path to eternity. The poet Bernardo Tasso (1493–1569) wrote in a sonnet dedicated to Colonna: 'Merry you, that with such beautiful thoughts | Out of every dubious path, gladly see | All roads that lead to immortality.'[64] Michelangelo Buonarroti too looked at Colonna as 'a safe guide to follow in the labyrinths of doubt'.[65] This is nicely illustrated in his madrigals 'Per qual mordace lima' and especially 'Ora in sul destro, ora in sul manco piede'. Although not all of Michelangelo's doubts or requests are doctrinal in nature, referring mostly to his perception of human fragility and the inadequacy of works and will, Colonna emerges as a spiritual authority.[66]

Interlude: Doubts and Giants

In fact, Michelangelo's voicing of doubts predated his encounter with Colonna (around 1536). In a series of undated *ottave*, he had provided an unprecedented — to the best of my knowledge — allegory of doubt, as if to make sense not of particular doubts but of the troubling nature of doubt per se. The allegory is found among Michelangelo's *Rime*, in some *ottave* that appear in two separate series in Enzo Noè Girardi's critical edition (nos. 67 and 68). As scholars have subsequently pointed out, however, these octaves should be published together as the remaining fragment of a longer text, possibly an allegorical poem.[67] In the latest edition of Michelangelo's poems the *ottave* appear together.[68] Michelangelo's text was most likely composed at the end of the 1520s or at the beginning of the 1530s. Its interpretation — and that of its prophetic nature — is rather obscure. Scholars agree that it represents a critique of power, perhaps of the Medici (in particular, of Duke Alexander and of Pope Clement VII). The description of giants in the *ottave* is reminiscent of Dante's *Commedia* as well as of the Apocalypse of John, all blended with Pasquinesque satire and Savonarolian ideas.[69]

The text opens with the description of a pastoral and bucolic landscape where shepherds live a peaceful life, happy with what they possess. They do not desire gold (l. 18) and among them one finds neither envy nor pride (ll. 25–26); hoes and shovels are their 'golden vases' (l. 32). The reference to gold leads to the second section of the poem, a long tirade against the vices fostered by Avarice. By contrast, the good shepherds find their solace in praying and honouring God. Their simple faith prevents them from being exposed to intellectual sophistries and from being led astray from the path of virtue. These sophistries that poison the lives of those who follow them are represented as personifications of abstract logic categories:

> Doubt and Perhaps and How and Why can never
> Spoil him, for he is not involved with them:
> If he adores and prays to God and heaven
> With simple faith, he'll bind one and bend the other.[70]

Michelangelo's allegorical description of Doubt and his companions is uncanny, since they act in a nocturnal setting and are represented as dangerous outlaws. Michelangelo's Doubt has the unique feature of being armed and lame:

> Doubt is depicted armed and crippled,
> And moves around by jumping, like the locust,
> Quivering all the time by his very nature,
> Just as a marsh reed will do in the wind.[71]

'Doubt is depicted' ('si figura'): there is no mistaking that Michelangelo is here talking of how Doubt is or should be represented in painting. The fact that he is described as both lame and armed alludes to his nature, which is both destructive and unstable. As such, Doubt leaps about and shakes, because as soon as he is dispelled he is reborn. Doubt's friends Why, How, and Perhaps are no less troubling:

> And Why is thin, and all around his belt
> Has many keys, but they don't fit at all;
> So he must pick the lock of every door,
> And travel by night, with darkness as his escort.
> How and Perhaps are close relatives,
> And they are giants of so great a height
> That both seem to delight in reaching the sun,
> But have been blinded by gazing at its brightness.[72]

Why is represented as a thief, only walking around at night and carrying keys. Both Doubt and Why are characterized as dangerous (armed) and outlaws. Why's keys do not fit locks; he therefore has to force them, as if to imply that our inquiries are not able to open the secrets of nature. Forcing locks and carrying weapons thus are the features of Why and of Doubt. Violence is their way because doubting and pushing knowledge too far is a violation or a theft, in clear contrast with the pure evangelical faith of the shepherds. In their edition of the *Rime*, Antonio Corsaro and Giorgio Masi point out that in his description of How and Perhaps, Michelangelo conflates two myths connected to arrogance: that of Dedalus and Icarus, who flew too close to the sun; and that of the tower of Babel, built by the giants to reach the sky. The underlying idea is that one should not stare into the sun (of God), lest one be blinded.[73] One should limit one's desire for knowledge and avoid inquiring into the abyss of God's mystery.

Michelangelo builds a refined counterpoint between the darkness that characterizes the allegory of Why and the excess of light that belongs to the allegories of How and Perhaps. However, obscurity comes into play again as the giants keep the sun away from the cities with their might: 'With their fierce breasts they keep it away from the cities, | Overshadowing its beauty everywhere.'[74] As suggested by Corsaro and Masi, the speculations of How and Perhaps — possibly philosophical or even theological ones — negatively affect the political life of cities, resulting in vain and ineffective discussions.

Michelangelo includes another personification in his *ottave*, the only positive allegory among so many negative characters. Truth goes around 'poor and naked and alone' and is 'greatly valued among humble people'.[75] Truth shares some features with Doubt but their meaning is, of course, reversed. If Doubt goes leaping as a locust, thus implying that as soon as he is dispelled from a place he arises in another,[76] Truth 'is born in a thousand places if he dies in one'.[77] While Doubt quivers all the time, Truth has a golden body and a diamond heart (traditional symbols of stability) and 'is firm and constant to his faithful followers'.[78] If Truth wanders solitary and naked, Falsehood lives in the courts with her maidens Fraud, Discord, and Mendacity.

The last allegory of the fragment is represented by Adulation, but the fragment is abruptly interrupted here. Its second section opens with the image of a giant who reaches for the sun and builds a tower and has more than once destroyed a city while walking. It is clearly the same *imagérie* of the preceding octaves. He lives with a giantess who has given birth to seven children (most likely, the seven deadly sins). Michelangelo's allegories in this section are thick and rather obscure: every detail in the description of the two giants and of their deeds is highly symbolical and entails a series of literary references (especially Dantesque). Doubt no longer features in this section of the text, but it is undeniable that Michelangelo has not only invented an allegory of doubt, he has also placed it within a complex discourse on truth, faith, and the corruption of civic life. Michelangelo provides possibly one of the first allegorical representations of doubt, one that is totally negative. Before Ripa's 1593 *Iconologia*, considered in Chapter 1, to the best of my knowledge only Michelangelo and Daniele Barbaro (to be discussed in Chapter 5) had tried their hand at creating personifications of doubt, trying to visualize it and give it a recognizable shape. In both cases, the result is a disquieting and dysmorphic creature whose distressing qualities are foregrounded, suggesting that in those decades doubt was mainly perceived as a potentially disruptive force.

The Spaces of Doubt: Camillo Renato's *Apologia*

As ideas challenging orthodoxy spread in Italy, doubt evolved from being exclusively a condition that one experienced, whether one liked it or not (most of the time not) to an active instrument that one could and must master. Doubt could be instrumental in dismantling Catholic dogma (and therefore, in proselytising); it could also play a defensive role, turning into a useful rhetorical strategy. Many Italians tried by the Inquisition resorted to the stratagem of declaring that whatever they may have believed or affirmed, they did so as a form of doubt, as a question or a possibility; doubt was a means of affirming and denying at the same time.[79] Some of Valdés's most radical followers became masters in the use of religious doubt.

It was not only pamphlets and treatises that signalled doubt as an emerging object of discourse within the circles of Italian dissidents. In 1540, Camillo Renato penned a stunning reflection on the ambiguities of doubt, one that deserves some scrutiny, for it reveals the refined strategies of doubt within Italian circles of religious dissent. Renato was born in Sicily as Paolo Ricci at the beginning of the sixteenth century; we know little of his early years.[80] He was a churchman, possibly a Franciscan and an esteemed preacher; he moved quite early in his life to Padua and then to

Venice, where he was jailed for his heretical ideas at some point between 1526 and 1531. He was eventually absolved from all charges, but he probably left holy orders. He resurfaced in Bologna as a layman around 1538–39 under the name of Lisia Fileno. In Bologna he seems to have been acquainted with noble families and intellectuals. Bologna was receptive to heterodox ideas, which was helped by its proximity to Modena, a hotbed of heresy.[81] As we have already seen, Bologna was a peculiar environment in which humanistic disputes and religious debates could easily go hand in hand.[82] This is what happened in the case of Renato, who would mix humanistic debates with heterodox ideas, 'persuading them [his students and followers] not to believe in what the Roman Church believes'. Because of his teaching, which combined ideas drawn from Luther and Erasmus with more radical doctrines, close to those of the Anabaptists, he was denounced to the Inquisition in 1540; he therefore thought it more prudent to move to Modena, where he continued to spread his ideas, not only among students but also among peasants in the countryside. In October 1540, Fileno-Renato was arrested in Nonantola, near Modena, upon order of Duke Ercole II of Ferrara, and after a brief quarrel between the Duke and the inquisitor of Bologna was tried in Ferrara.[83]

Renato was very effective at addressing peasants and simple folk. On 26 October, Giovanni Domenico Sigibaldi, the vicar of the bishop of Modena, informed Bishop Giovanni Morone that 'a former friar preacher of St Francis, who has left the order [...] has been arrested here in the Modenese after fleeing from Bologna: he was subverting the peasants'.[84] Another chronicler, Alessandro Tassoni, wrote that at the beginning Renato limited himself to reading Scripture and the letters of St Paul to a restricted number of people who already shared his ideas. Then he began to proselytise, attracting people of all kinds, including women. These persons began to dispute 'in squares, in pharmacies, in churches', tearing apart Scripture, quoting the Gospels and the Apocalypse of John along with 'all the doctors' which 'they had never seen'.[85] If a form of social subversion was the main effect of Renato's teaching, another equally significant result was the sudden spread of systematic doubt. On 22 December, the Modenese chronicler Tommasino Bianchi wrote in his *Cronaca modenese* that 'it seems that he said and did bad things, and he has engulfed in erroneous ideas the brain of many a person in Modena, who presently walk with their heads bowed and nurture even worse doubts'.[86]

Before his trial, Renato drafted an *Apologia*, a defensive memoir aimed at confuting the charges raised by forty witnesses.[87] What he offered the inquisitors was a meditation on the nature of doubt, the matters to which it can legitimately apply, and who — and in what context — is allowed to nurture doubts. Renato might have had in mind Erasmus's *On the Freedom of the Will* (1525), in the opening section of which he could find similar reflections on the legitimacy and boundaries of doubt. Renato certainly went farther than Erasmus ever dreamt of, and his radical views put him in trouble with both the Catholic Church and the Protestant community.[88]

In the *Apologia*, the same person accused of stirring up peasants and raising disquieting doubts seems suddenly conscious that doubt can be problematic when practised by commoners. Renato is aware that in a time of greater availability of printed books, it is only too common for people of both sexes to care more about what they read and say than about what they understand, Renato bitterly observes.[89] People even read profane texts — among which he explicitly mentions the works of Pietro Aretino — thus learning all sorts of vices.[90]

By contrast, he has always urged both men and women to read in common the New Testament, a gift from the Holy Spirit and a book about which it is not permitted to have any doubts ('de quo non licet [...] vel tantillum dubitare'). Among all books, this is the best, the safest, and the truest ('optimus, tutissimus, verissimus'). This is especially so in the current bad times ('his praesertim temporibus malis'), in which everyone feels entitled to shamelessly question and call into doubt without reverence even the works of the Church Fathers.[91] However fundamental to one's spiritual advancement, though, the reading of the New Testament requires some precautions. Renato stresses repeatedly that before turning to Scripture one should beg the Holy Spirit's assistance in order to understand properly the word of God. Renato suggests an exercise in humility as well as in scepticism: no one, in fact, should trust their own intelligence when it comes to reading Scripture ('nihil sibi tribuant aut fidant in intelligendis scripturis sacris').[92]

The naive and somewhat dangerous enthusiasm of commoners is contrasted, in Renato's narrative, with the example of the learned and careful discussions he has entertained with a select group of friends and students. In a passage where he confronts the charge of having denied the importance of confession, Renato admits that he has in fact debated the issue, but not in front of common people ('non enim ego haec in vulgus iacto'). Rather, Renato repeatedly stresses, doubts emerged during conversations with educated people whom he knew very well and who were 'curious' about everything and eager to know.[93] Even when it came to thorny questions such as the 'sleep of the blessed', Renato stuck to his narrative that the question had originated in the curiosity of scholars, who presented him with passages taken from the works of the most distinguished Church Fathers such as Augustine and Ambrose. Despite having consulted with a preacher who had preached in the church of St Petronio in Bologna in previous years, he had remained doubtful ('visus sum aliquantum de hac re dubitare').[94]

Renato therefore introduces a series of cultural and social distinctions that set the boundaries of doubt. Throughout his *Apologia* one finds the idea that more than doubt itself, one should consider the person who voices those doubts, their context, and their goals; the performance of doubt is as important as its content. Doubt, like a Janus figure, can be dangerous in the mouths of the uneducated and a sign of intellectual distinction in those of the learned — or at least this is what Renato wanted his prosecutors to believe. So, for example, when addressing his alleged denial of the existence of purgatory, he stresses that in his research he has acted as a theologian and not as a canonist (that is, he never aimed to establish definitive rules). It is in fact the practice of theologians to doubt everything, so that the truth can shine.[95] Renato affirms boldly that he does not believe in any kind of otherworldly justice, as Christ has saved us with his merits.[96] Yet he claims he has drawn this belief not from Lutheran books but from theologians such as Augustine. There are in fact many controversial and uncertain beliefs ('incerta et contraria') allowed by the church, and the existence of purgatory is among these beliefs. Since the question of purgatory does not concern an *articulus fidei*, one is permitted to harbour doubts about it ('videtur licere dubitare').[97]

The first section of the *Apologia* is in fact conceived as a general introduction, laying out the spaces of doubt (words such as 'doubt' and 'to doubt' recur at least thirteen times from fols 1^r to 5^r). Renato suggests that criticism of Catholic doctrine can be legitimate, if not in some cases required. He recalls, on the authority of Thomas Aquinas, that all human judgements concerning God are doubtful ('iuditia omnia dubia sunt de veritate divina').[98] He then claims that it is not in the power of the church ('in potestate ecclesiae') to assert what is true and what is false in questions regarding God ('in rebus divinis'). The church can only state what has been done on the authority of Scripture ('declarare quod factum fuerit [...] ex scripturae auctoritate').[99] This opens the path to doubt: it is safe ('sine periculo') to doubt what the church has established, even through councils, if this goes against Scripture and the authority of the doctors. Sometimes councils set forth wrongful interpretations of Scripture or were not inspired by the Holy Spirit, as in the case of the Council of Florence. Renato clearly aims to separate doubt from heresy. Doubting articles of faith is certainly heretical; doubting decrees issued by councils of the church that are based on a solid interpretation of Scripture verges on heresy ('haeresim sapit'). But it is not heresy to doubt the councils' decrees that are based on a wrongful interpretation of Scripture, nor, Renato argues, does it count as heresy to doubt in matters on which theologians do not agree. In this case, though, one should not be obstinate in sticking to one's position (tellingly, Renato's example here is the conception and sanctification of the Virgin).

Renato's overarching strategy is to establish a boundary between Scripture, which is beyond doubt, and its interpretations, which can and sometimes must be doubted. In in the *Apologia* Renato has to confront charges pertaining to some serious but not uncommon staples of Reformed belief: purgatory, confession, vows, saints and their cults, Lent and fasting, free will, and so on, the most troubling issue being that of the destiny of blessed souls. However, subjecting as Renato does virtually all tenets of Catholic doctrine — except articles of faith — to doubt and scrutiny forces a crack in the wall of orthodoxy. Through this crack doubt can carve its way in and undermine fundamental beliefs such as the divine nature of Christ, the immortality of the soul, or the role of sacraments. Renato was forced to recant his ideas on all these points in his 1551 abjuration.[100]

The Consequences of Doubt: Identity and Severance

In 1567, one Oddo Quarto, tried and sentenced to imprisonment for life, declared to his judges that he did not want to be curious in matters of religion and preferred to sin out of ignorance. He wanted his conscience to be 'clean and safe as possible from all scruples and doubts that plague the soul and do not do any good so that one goes from scruple to scruple and it never ends, and this is the way the devil sets his snares for us'.[101] Going from scruple to scruple or from doubt to doubt was precisely what some reformers required of neophytes. Perfectly conscious that coming to terms with dissenting ideas — especially when these exceeded 'Lutheran' ideas — could prove a long and troubling process,[102] in some cases reformers would introduce their ideas by gradually raising doubts on increasingly serious matters. This proved especially true within the most radical circles. In his 1551 trial before the Inquisition, Pietro Manelfi recalled how the Anabaptist known as Tiziano, together with Lorenzo da Modiana and Giuseppe da Asola, had introduced him to Anabaptist doctrines. These included the refusal to baptize children; the idea that sacraments were merely signs and did not retain any value; that the Roman Church was 'diabolical and anti-Christian' ('diabolica et antecristiana'); and that those who had already been baptized were not Christian and needed therefore to be rebaptized. Manelfi, who already shared Lutheran ideas, reacted in shock, refusing to accept these points. For many months, he did not believe in this new doctrine ('stetti alquanti mesi che non volsi credere questa dottrina'). When he finally brought himself to assent to Anabaptist ideas, he discovered a world in which voicing and discussing doubts was accepted practice.

In November 1551 Manelfi was tried in Rome; there he described the Anabaptist council held the previous year, when nearly fifty or sixty Anabaptists had gathered to discuss the main tenets of their doctrine. Manelfi's description is a vivid picture of meetings in which everyone was entitled to suggest possible topics of discussion. Apparently, there were many doubts that needed a solution; among them, the most urgent regarded the true nature of Christ:

> It is true that the first time we gathered I spoke after the oration suggesting a doubt concerning the incarnation of our Lord Jesus Christ. I said that we had gathered because we did not want to go blindly in matters regarding this master of ours, Christ, but in order to decide whether he was merely a man, generated by human seed, or God, conceived by the Holy Spirit.[103]

The council decided that Christ was not the son of God, therefore sharing his divine nature, but 'merely a man, generated by human seed, and yet full of all God's virtues'.[104] The Anabaptists from Italy and Switzerland had gathered to discuss doubts that affected fundamental tenets of Christian doctrine, yet among them it soon appeared that some people were going far beyond their already bold claims. As Manelfi confessed, there was in Naples a 'new sect' of heretics, belonging to the highest echelons of society, who believed

> [t]hat Christ is not God but a great prophet and he did not come as a Messiah but as a prophet and he died for the Truth and he has not resuscitated yet, but he still has to resuscitate and come as a Messiah; and after him, the elect

will resuscitate according to their order [...]. And they deny the whole New Testament and they say it is an invention of the Greeks and of the heathens, and that Paul did not understand a word of the old Scripture, in particular for what concerns justification and resurrection.[105]

Manelfi had in mind a select group of Valdés's followers who had been introduced to some of their master's doctrines that did not find their way to the public sphere, doctrines that were dangerous and 'diabolical'.[106] Among them was Lorenzo Tizzano, alias Benedetto Florio, a friar of the order of 'monte Oliveto' who appeared before the Venetian Inquisition on 30 December 1553.[107] Eighteen or twenty years earlier he had left the monastery and served Caterina Sanseverino, sister of Pietrantonio, Prince of Bisignano, as her chaplain for nine years. Following this he moved to Venice and, after a month, to Padua, where he still was when he re-converted to 'find peace and solace in the arms of the Holy Mother Roman Catholic Church'.[108] Tizzano's story was simple: ten years after he had left the monastery, he had had some conversations with Valdés. Valdés was friendly but would not communicate much of his ideas. It was one Juan de Villafranca who instead handed down to him some of Valdés's works and taught him new opinions. Tizzano divided these ideas into three categories: Lutheran ideas, Anabaptist ideas (in fact, a form of proto-antitrinitarianism), and diabolical ideas.[109] These 'diabolical ideas' are certainly the most intriguing, for they included the notion that Christ was not the Messiah but rather a prophet, although he had 'a greater spirit and a greater gift from God than the other prophets'.[110] Besides this, Tizzano learned that the soul dies with the body, but God will resurrect the elect. Finally, he was taught that the Bible is false because of its many contradictions. Tizzano came only gradually to share these radical ideas, moving from the most common Lutheran tenets, then to Anabaptist or antitrinitarian ideas, and eventually accepting even more radical views. Two years passed before he moved from Lutheran to Anabaptist ideas, and two more years elapsed before he moved from these to the 'diabolical' opinions.[111] Tizzano shared these ideas only with a restricted circle of companions, since 'these opinions were so diabolical that they could not be spread among many people'.[112] We can gather further information about these opinions from the interrogations of Tizzano's acolytes.[113] It is interesting to notice the relevance accorded to the critical and philological analysis of the Bible, and the influence of Erasmus's textual analysis that led these people to discuss supposed interpolations in the biblical text.[114] Their conclusions were that

> the Gospels and the letters of St Paul quoted many authorities from the Old Testament mistakenly and not in accordance with the meaning they had in the Old Testament, and that such authorities were not quoted by the evangelists, or by St Paul, but by other people who had added them.[115]

Nowhere can we better witness the gradual and unstoppable action of doubt as in the trial of Giulio Basalù.[116] Basalù, a doctor of law, appeared voluntarily before the Inquisition in Venice on 2 March 1555. As a matter of fact, the inquisitors had been gathering information on him since at least 1548. To them, it was no mystery that Basalù had gone far beyond Lutheran ideas: from 1552 it was known that, among others, he denied the divine nature of Christ. Many witnesses had provided detailed lists of his beliefs. Matteo d'Aversa declared that Basalù was 'very suspicious' ('molto sospetto', 17 July 1553) and that Girolamo Capece had told him that 'he [Basalù] believed only what was in accordance with both laws, i.e., Jewish and Christian, in other words in what was accepted by both laws'.[117] Raffaele da Roccaguglielma reported on 14 June 1554 that Basalù 'had some different opinions from the other heretics, i.e., that Christ was to come again to reign, so that he could save all the Jews'.[118]

Familiar with Lutheran ideas from at least 1538, Basalù had tried for four years to suppress his doubts on justification by faith alone. These doubts were of little importance, however, compared to those he began to nourish when he returned to Naples from a sojourn in Padua and made the acquaintance of some disciples of Valdés. In particular, it was the Spaniard Juan de Villafranca who led him through a path of progressive denial of any truth. Among the depositions against Basalù, that of Matteo Busale on 5 July 1553 is crucial in reconstructing the role of doubt in Villafranca's teaching and in the erosion of orthodox belief. Busale recalls that he had made the acquaintance of Villafranca and since the same Villafranca had fallen ill, Busale began to pay him visits at his home. During their conversations, Villafranca would slowly introduce his teaching, beginning with heretical ideas with which Busale was already acquainted. It was only then that

> [h]e showed me some authorities, and he showed that he doubted and said: 'Well, how would you explain this?' And first he made me doubt the authority and then, as soon as I had fallen into doubt, he would say: 'Well, if we were to interpret this thing in this way, wouldn't you think it would be correct?' And thus he persuaded me of many false opinions [...] and then he persuaded me that the Trinity did not exist but [there was] only one God, that Christ was not God but God inhabited in Christ.[119]

As for his own position, Basalù had already made a rather surprising statement:

> Even if I was familiar with the aforementioned people, and they had different opinions during the discussions in which I took part, in truth not only I did not believe them, but I did not even understand them. This is because when I accepted the opinion that once the body is dead everyone's soul is dead too, every other opinion fell to the ground. I came to believe that every religion was an invention of men to induce other men to live well, so that I did not want to take pains to understand the different opinions in matters of religion [...] [and] if at the beginning I believed in justification *ex sola fide, et cum consequentibus*, once I entered this other opinion [i.e., the mortality of the soul] that belief too fell to the ground.[120]

Probably Basalù felt that a declaration of seeming atheism was preferable to admitting to having believed in the radical ideas held by his companions (although in a letter to the inquisitors dated 9 July 1555, the day of his abjuration, he denied ever having been an atheist).[121] Luca Addante has called attention to this letter, in which Basalù lamented that in the squares of Venice people talked about him as someone who denied God. These discussions, as Addante argues, show how these 'diabolical' ideas were no longer the object of secret discussions but were available on the streets. Basalù sketched a path of doubt as the force leading him first to a belief in justification by faith and from there to the denial of the immortality of the soul and, eventually, to unbelief; we cannot but perceive the sense of isolation of a person who had pushed his doubts too far, becoming remote even from his close associates. Basalù had first become acquainted with justification through faith in 1538 in Padua and it had taken him four years to accept it. When he went back to Naples he was still grappling with this opinion. It was then that he met Villafranca, who, following his usual method, moving 'from consequence to consequence, with the only foundation of said opinion', convinced him of Lutheran ideas concerning the intercession of saints, purgatory, images, confession.[122] After four months, Villafranca moved to 'opinions of greater importance', namely that the Eucharist is merely a sign and that Christ had only human nature.[123] Villafranca taught him that the souls of reprobates die, and from this opinion Basalù had come to the conclusion that the soul is always mortal, 'founding [this opinion] on natural reason and my own chimeras'.[124] It was then easy for him to come to 'deny to myself every religion, both Christian and Jewish [...] and I laughed at everything'. He denied the creation of the world, the divine nature of Christ, the sacraments, the miracles: in sum, all the tenets of Catholic religion.[125] Basalù specified that the 'majority of my reasonings weren't based on Scripture but on my fantasy, because I have never read any of the Gospels nor an entire letter by Paul'.[126] He had read, however, among others, Luther, Calvin and Curione, Lorenzo Valla and Erasmus, the *Beneficio di Cristo*, and some of the Qur'an.[127]

As Addante has pointed out, Basalù was never a proper atheist but rather a libertine and a 'proto-deist' who believed in materialism and rationalism.[128] For him, assenting to what both Villafranca and his own reason suggested to him proved a traumatic experience. If it had taken him four years to accept the doctrine of justification, in just eight months Villafranca dismantled what remained of his beliefs. After the revelation that the soul of the reprobate dies, Basalù stopped meeting Villafranca for some time, and for two months he could not bring himself to accept this idea. His was a path in which doubt was at the same time a method, a sort of intellectual stimulus, and a reaction — sometimes excruciatingly painful — to what he was discovering. The discussions he and his fellows described point to a social dimension in which doubt, as both a practice and a state of mind, brought together high-born women, humanists, former monks, students of law, and other people of diverse social backgrounds. Unorthodox conventicles were not uncommon in those years, and yet one senses that the scope and sheer number of opinions, the extent of doubts and their potential consequences made these gatherings unique.

These exercises in systematic doubt entailed, however, other, even more disturbing consequences. Let us consider the story of Giovanni Laureto, who appeared voluntarily before the Venetian Inquisition on 2 October 1553.[129] In the summer of 1548, he had found protection under Isabella Breseña, wife of Piacenza's Governor Don Garcia Manriquez and protectress of members of heterodox circles. An intimate friend of Giulia Gonzaga, Isabella was part of the Valdésian circles of

Naples. Laureto followed her to Piacenza, where he met another Neapolitan, the abbot Girolamo Busale (brother of the aforementioned Matteo), who was serving as secretary to the duchess. It was Busale who introduced Laureto to radical ideas, sharing with him his many doubts:

> I found out that he doubted of Christ's divinity; and while he was reasoning with me about this, we began to read and turn upside down the Scripture in order to have this point clear. And he knew very well Hebrew and Greek, and he encouraged me to learn these languages because, he said, they were necessary to grasp the truth: in fact, he suspected also that the Gospels had been tampered with and corrupted.[130]

At the beginning of 1550, Busale left and went to study in Padua, where Laureto later joined him. He began studying Hebrew and was converted to Anabaptism by two Anabaptists named Benedetto and Nicola, who rented a house that soon became a place where the Anabaptists met to discuss the main issues related to their faith.[131] According to Laureto's words, this was a space for free discussion:

> And having rented a house [...] to hold meetings and gatherings, we used to meet all in the said house, where we discussed this Anabaptist doctrine, and everyone said whatever he pleased.[132]

Addante has stressed how this freedom of saying 'quel che li pareva' could not be limited by any principle of authority and was supported by unrestrained critical doubt.[133] When Nicola and Benedetto left, Busale was appointed bishop of the community because of his doctrine. Having overheard that he was suspected of taking part in these meetings, he decided to leave for Naples (in February 1551), and Laureto accompanied him. Along their way, Laureto realized that Busale had developed prophetic ideas and seemed out of his wits.[134] Busale foresaw great persecutions that were to befall the Anabaptists; he himself would be burnt, and his house and family ruined. The habit of intellectual freedom was slowly turning into a prophetic posture that could indeed turn out to be dangerous.

In Naples, Girolamo Busale's family was disappointed by this turn of events, and also by his insistence on publicly preaching his ideas. His brother Matteo immediately realized that Girolamo wasn't his usual self. He insisted that Laureto persuade him to take a trip to Alexandria, Egypt, where the family had some acquaintances. Girolamo agreed (he eventually died in Damascus) but he did not want Laureto around. Laureto thus stayed in Naples in the service of Giulia Gonzaga for less than a month; he then left for Rome and again for Padua. In early 1551, Laureto left for Salonicco (Thessaloniki), where he met many former brethren, including the Nicola who had first converted and then excommunicated him because he had 'contradicted their many superstitions'.[135] For these reasons, Laureto decided to remain isolated from the community.

At this point, Laureto's life took a most extraordinary turn. Convinced that all he needed to make sense of his doubts was to understand Hebrew, he began to spend time with the local rabbis until he converted to Judaism, even getting circumcised. He obtained a room where he could study, but the initial enthusiasm gave way quickly to bitter disappointment: '[T]he more I studied, the more I realized their many mistakes and superstitions.'[136] After four or five months, he came to the conclusion 'that theirs were foolish ideas, superstitions, and lies, and not only those of the said Jews, but also those of all the sects I had followed so far'.[137] It was then — he claimed — that he made the decision to return to the 'womb of the Holy Roman Church and to reconcile with her'.[138] After an adventurous journey he returned to Venice; there he met Giulio Basalù, who suggested he turn himself in to the Inquisition.[139] Laureto's confession was deemed insufficient, and he was arrested and detained in the hope he would provide more detailed information on the content of his ideas and on his networks. Yet he somehow managed to escape from prison and disappear, never to be heard of again. The story of Giovanni Laureto, who had embraced Catholicism, Lutheran, and Anabaptist ideas as well as Judaism until his final re-conversion, suggests how doubt and intellectual unrest prompted unbelief not only towards Catholic orthodoxy but also eventually towards all forms of faith. Ironically, these radical doubts seemed to push people back to the Catholic Church. At the beginning of the 1550s, the Inquisition began its campaign of trials, and heterodox networks were discovered and dismantled across Italy. Trying to prevent possible charges and accusations or limit their consequences by denouncing one's past mistakes and declaring the will to atone for them was a convenient move. Laureto and others were probably aware that the Inquisition possessed information on them and was ready to use it. Still, it seems possible to capture something more in Laureto's and his fellows' declarations to the authorities. If one considers their deep intellectual and spiritual disquiet, the solitude they experienced, even the apparent insanity as in the case of Girolamo Busale, one may surmise that returning to the church provided some stable ground after such disrupting experiences. This may be sheer speculation, and yet their stories show how doubt could be an exhilarating experience of intellectual emancipation as well as one of spiritual anguish, like staring into an empty abyss.

The extent of these ideas and doubts is certainly mesmerizing, and so is their social dimension, the urge to meet and discuss them. Yet even more intriguing, because of the questions it raises, is the complexity of doubt that emerges from these stories. Doubt was a state of mind; an intellectual response to certain beliefs; and, most of all, a method, an effective tool for proselytising and dismantling Catholic dogma. All these layers overlap and interact with each other, testifying to the complexity of early modern doubt. The stories of Laureto, Tizzano, Basalù, and Busale suggest that we take into consideration questions connected with and raised by doubt. We have seen, for example, the violent emotions triggered by radical doubt and the impact it had on social and familial ties, which were often severed, a phenomenon not unknown to other European radical doubters.[140] When Tizzano claimed that he was looking for 'peace and solace' ('pace et refrigerio') in the arms of Holy Mother Church, he was probably seeking the inquisitors' benevolence. Yet the choice of his words is intriguing: on the one hand he mentions peace, the end of his inner war and of his ceaseless quest for truth; on the other hand, he speaks of *refrigerio*, relief, but also literally 'refreshment', as if a flame were burning inside him. Laureto instead wanted to go back to the womb of Mother Church: a standard expression, certainly, but also one that in this context could have a deeper meaning of security and protection. Busale died alone and forgotten after having prophesied his own ruin; Basalù was derisive of everything, but his laughter was a bitter one.

Certainly, for these people going back to the Roman Church meant burying the past; the church offered the chance to start afresh and maybe, as Addante points out, a space for simulating belief.[141] Besides, established rules and rituals may help avoid desperation and offer a safe road to salvation; at the very least, they provide some firm ground. Moreover, these stories seem to provide excellent testimony to John Jeffries Martin's notion of the Renaissance's 'anxious identities'. The stories of Tizzano and Laureto speak to a fluid 'relation between belief and identity' and of the 'extraordinarily restless and [...] apparently protean character' of many reformers' lives.[142] Laureto and Tizzano were looking for a life that would allow them to manifest their internal convictions, 'a quest for a religious idiom and a community' where one could 'present himself without compromise, without equivocation'.[143] Issues of identity, self-expression, and emotional response to a new set of circumstances are intertwined in the stories we have examined. Again in Martin's words,

> [T]he stressful fragmentation of religious beliefs and the anxieties about salvation that developed in the Renaissance, especially as the Reformation began to make itself felt, complicated the issue of identity for many of those men and women who were caught up in the religious ferment of the time.[144]

We can push Martin's argument further, suggesting that if convictions and personal identity are related in some way, the hyperbolic doubt that undermined all these people's convictions equally destroyed their selves. More than looking for spaces wherein they could express their self, they were looking precisely for this self. The loss of Busale's inner identity, his insanity, is an extreme and emblematic outcome of the effects of radical doubt. In this light, the return to the Roman Church also appears as the means to retrieve a form of identity, a space in a world that at that juncture was not prepared for unrestrained unbelief. In some cases, dissimulation and compromise could be more reassuring than freedom, and wearing a mask less traumatic than staring into an empty mirror.

Notes to Chapter 4

1. 'Doppo scritto odo rumori, rotture di campi, fughe, pressure, morte de genti; cose da movere e saxi a lachrimare, non che noi.' Nelson H. Minnich and Elisabeth G. Gleason, 'Vocational Choices: An Unknown Letter of Pietro Querini to Gasparo Contarini and Niccolò Tiepolo (April, 1512)', *Catholic Historical Review*, 75 (1989), 1–20 (p. 16).
2. Stephen Bowd, *Reform before the Reformation: Vincenzo Querini and the Religious Renaissance in Italy* (Leiden: Brill, 2002), p. 37.
3. Alessandro Gnocchi, 'Tommaso Giustiniani, Ludovico Ariosto e la Compagnia degli Amici', *Studi di filologia italiana*, 67 (1999), 277–93.
4. Eugenio Massa, *L'eremo, la Bibbia e il Medioevo in umanisti veneti del primo Cinquecento* (Naples: Liguori, 1992).
5. 'Né lussuria, né latrocinj, né biastemme, né invidia, né odio, come in moltri altri luoghi si ritrova, né incredulità circa alla fede.' Vincenzo Querini, 'Relazione di Borgogna [...]', in

Relazioni degli ambasciatori veneti al Senato, ed. by Eugenio Alberi, serie 1, 1 (Florence: Tipografia all'insegna di Clio, 1839), p. 13. On religious life in Burgundy, see Johan Huizinga, *The Autumn of the Middle Ages*, trans. by Rodney J. Payton and Ulrich Mammitzsch (Chicago: University of Chicago Press, 1996 (1921)), esp. Chaps 6–9.

6. See Michele Lodone, *I segni della fine: Storia di un predicatore nell'Italia del Rinascimento* (Rome: Viella, 2021).

7. 'Degli amici vostri, tutti vi salutano, peraltro chi vi ha spacciato per malinconico, chi per disperato, chi per poco prudente, chi per scempio, chi in tutto pazzo vi nominan.' Johannes Benedictus Mittarelli and Anselmus Costadoni, *Annales Camaldulenses ordinis sancti Benedicti*, t. IX (Venice: aere monasterii sancti Michaelis de Muriano, 1773), col. 508.

8. Bowd, *Reform before the Reformation*, p. 72; Minnich and Gleason, 'Vocational Choices', p. 5.

9. 'Ma che vado io, mondano, ne' peccati come prima involto, nelle scelleratezze raviluppato, mostrando il lume a chi per ogni rispetto potrà meglio nelle tenebre vedere, ch'io non farei nella viva luce? Ma si ben riguardo il tutto, a me quello istesso addiviene, che suole a coloro avvenire, che portando il lume seco mostrano ad altri la via, senza ch'essi la possino punto vedere.' Mittarelli and Costadoni, *Annales Camaldulenses*, col. 498.

10. A similar passage, but opposite in its meaning, is the episode of Bertran de Born in Dante's *Inferno*, XXVIII. 118–25; Dante represents the French poet walking around Malebolge and holding in his hand his severed head, which he uses as a lantern. All scholarly commentaries highlight the impossibility of the scene. I wish to thank Giuseppina Brunetti and Elisa Brilli for pointing out these passages to me.

11. 'Cor di sasso'; 'hora quasi nave in mezo al mar senza governo rimasto'. Hubert Jedin, 'Contarini und Camaldoli', *Archivio italiano per la storia della pietà*, 2 (1959), 51–117 (p. 61). On this exchange of letters, see also Constance Furey, 'The Communication of Friendship: Gasparo Contarini's Letters to Hermits in Camaldoli', *American Society of Church History*, 72 (2003), 71–101; Constance Furey, *Erasmus, Contarini, and the Religious Republic of Letters* (Cambridge: Cambridge University Press, 2006), pp. 86–98.

12. 'Men che quasi disperato'; 'me cominciò a ragionar che la via de la salute era più ampia di quel che molti se persuadeno. [...] Et compresi veramente che se io fessi tute le penitentie possibile et molto più anchora, non serìa bastante'; 'la passion sua è stà sufficiente et più che bastante'; 'me induceva in una tristitia et una quasi desperation'. Jedin, 'Contarini und Camaldoli', pp. 63–65.

13. 'Innumeri beneficii'; 'di dolor et di amor'; 'da un grave et mortifero lethargo'; 'una ombra over uno sonnio'; 'quasi come se fosse letargico'. Ibid., pp. 66–67.

14. 'Diverse perturbation d'animo'; 'mio adormentato animo'. Ibid., p. 68.

15. 'Ciaschadun de nui essendo cieco.' Ibid., p. 70.

16. 'Son con l'animo molto perplexo'; 'la astutia de l'inimico'; 'qualche suggestion diabolica'. Ibid., pp. 73–74.

17. 'Indispositione grande nel corpo per questo humore melancholico et perturbation grande ne l'animo.' Ibid., p. 77.

18. 'Mi sentiva nascere per quella lectione alguni timori ne l'animo, vani et pazzi'; 'speculatione basse de philosophi et theologi'. Ibid.

19. 'Quelle altre cose de li theologi più vechi, li quali sempre in interpretatione mystice de la Scriptura over in admonitione di uno modo di vivere et di uno affecto di animo, al qual non posso inalzarme, la debellezza mia non sostene, immo, se io in quelle cose verso, di timore in discontento, et di discontento in timore ritorno. Et così, onde che per quella doctrina penso liberarmi l'animo da perturbatione, mi sento di continuo in maggiore perturbatione, et a poccho a poccho descendere poi ad algune superstitione et algune credulità paze, de le quali tute è causa la pusillanimitade di animo che tale lectione mi genera.' Ibid., p, 78.

20. Furey, *Erasmus, Contarini*, p. 93.

21. Ibid., p. 94.

22. 'Mi molesta con sì tristi et turbidi pensieri, con tali imagination paurose (paurose, dico, di cose che la ragion discorre esser quasi impossibili) che pocchi, credo, se trovi al mondo con l'animo più inquieto di me.' Jedin, 'Contarini und Camaldoli', p. 87.

23. 'Me son venuti in odio li studii, et quella sol cosa che a l'altra volta mi ralegrava, cioè la lection de la Scriptura Sacra, hora me dà grande molestia.' Ibid.

24. 'Questi foschi pensieri me molestano'; 'le Sacre lettere, hora non me danno alguna consolation, et dubito che mai non vegnirà quel tempo che le mi dilettano'. Ibid.

25. 'Li meriti de Iesu Christo crucifixo'. Ibid., p. 88.

26. 'Farme quieto et tranquillo non sta in me.' Ibid., p. 88.

27. Ibid., p. 94.

28. Massimo Firpo, *Riforma protestante ed eresie nell'Italia del Cinquecento* (Rome: Laterza, 1993), pp. 115–27; Massimo Firpo, *Juan de Valdés and the Italian Reformation* (London: Routledge, 2016); on the *alumbradismo* see Stefania Pastore, *Un'eresia spagnola: Spiritualità conversa, alumbradismo e Inquisizione (1449–1559)* (Florence: Olschki, 2004).

29. Ryrie, *Unbelievers*, p. 110.

30. Ethan Shagan, *The Birth of Modern Belief: Faith and Judgment from the Middle Ages to the Enlightenment* (Princeton: Princeton University Press, 2018), p. 132.

31. Ibid.

32. Ibid., p. 133.

33. Ibid., p. 135.

34. Ibid., p. 140.

35. Ibid.

36. 'Celio Secondo Curione, servo di Gesù Cristo, a tutti quelli i quali sono santificati da Dio Padre, e salvati, e chiamati da Gesù Cristo nostro Signore; la misericordia, la pace e la carità di Dio vi sia moltiplicata'. Juan de Valdés, *Le cento e dieci divine considerazioni*, ed. by Teodoro Fanlo y Cortés (Genoa: Marietti, 2004), p. 155. Curione had received the manuscript of the work from Pietro Paolo Vergerio, former bishop of Capodistria and also a religious exile. In November 1551, Pietro Manelfi (*c.* 1519–post 1552), a Marchigian priest who had initially shared Lutheran ideas before turning to Anabaptism and who had appeared earlier in October before the Bolognese inquisitor Leandro Alberti to denounce heterodox networks all over Italy, offered some relevant information on the manuscript's history. According to Manelfi's narrative, 'Vergerio had printed in Basel [the *Cento e dieci divine considerazioni*] [...] which *Consegli* don Pietro sent in manuscript from Padua to said Vergerio' ('Gli quali fece stampare il Vergerio in Basilea, quali *Consegli* don Pietro mandò scritti a penna da Padova al detto Vergerio'). Carlo Ginzburg, *I costituti di don Pietro Manelfi* (Florence: Sansoni; Chicago: Newberry Library, 1970), pp. 58–59. It was thus Manelfi himself ('don Pietro') who had passed a manuscript copy of the *Cento dieci considerazioni* to Vergerio, who in turn gave it to Curione.

37. 'Or di questo sì grande e celeste tesoro ne siamo tutti debitori a m. Pietro Paolo Vergerio, come stromento della Divina Provvidenza in farlo stampare.' Valdés, *Le cento e dieci considerazioni*, p. 157. Curione does not mention Manelfi.

38. 'Più saldamente e più divinamente'. Ibid., p. 155.

39. 'Siamo venuti a tanto, che più e maggior fede si dà a quei che si chiamano dottori [...] che alla semplice dottrina di Christo.' Ibid., p. 156.

40. 'In prima adunque perché hanno scritti de' grandissimi libri, non hanno potuto fuggir le menzogne, le follie, e le vanità [...]. Poi questi gran scrittori hanno tutta la Scrittura tirata a questioni e disputazioni e ne hanno fatto una Accademia, *dubitando quasi di ogni cosa*, talmente che *hanno renduta tutta dubbiosa* la dottrina del figliuol di Dio e delli apostoli suoi, e la infallibile e certissima speranza della eterna vita.' Ibid., pp. 155–56; my italics.

41. 'Mostra la origine, la caggione, i progressi ed il fine; e tutto ciò da chiari, certi e *indubitati* principii delle Scritture sante.' Ibid., p. 157; my italics.

42. 'Donde procede che gli impii non ponno creder, che li superstiziosi credono con facilità e che li pii credono con difficultà.' Ibid., p. 438.

43. 'Sono altri che si conoscono ribelli a Dio, e donano intera fede e credito al perdono generale che nel Evangelio gli è predicato da parte di Dio, e così subito, senza pensar più oltre, accettando il perdono, se ne vengono al regno di Dio, renonziando al regno del mondo e al governo della prudenza umana. Costoro, se ben al principio in alcuna maniera dubitano — dubitano del perdono, dubitano del governo e reggimento di Dio —, non appartandosi dal regno, si vanno certificando che Dio gli va restituendo quella imagine e similitudine di Dio, la quale il primo uomo perdette per la sua ribellione.' Ibid., pp. 202–03.

44. 'Non credono quella che è il fondamento de tutte le [cose] vere, questa è la remission delli peccati e la reconciliazione con Dio, per la giustizia di Dio eseguita in Cristo.' Ibid., p. 440.
45. 'Tenendo per impietà il dubitare'. Ibid., p. 439.
46. 'Sta confirmato nella fede di tal maniera che poco è sollecitato a dubitare.' Ibid., p. 440.
47. 'Coloro che dubitano senza spirito non sentono fastidio nel dubitare, né desiderano d'esser liberi, e io sento fastidio nel dubitare e ne desidero d'esser libera.' Ibid., p. 446.
48. For an overview, see Marco Faini, 'Reading, Devotion and Religious Print in Early *Cinquecento* Naples: The Case of Francesco Sovaro's *Christiade*', *Italian Studies*, 72 (2017), 238–55.
49. The work was composed between 1536 and 1538, its Italian translation was ready in the summer of 1543, and the book was printed in Venice in 1545. Giulia Gonzaga owned a copy of the Spanish original version of the text. Manuscript copies of the Italian translation survive in Hamburg, Basel, and, most notably, a copy in Rome, Biblioteca Apostolica Vaticana, MS Vat. Lat. 12921, which bears inquisitorial annotations that can be traced back to 1558–59. Valdés, *Le cento e dieci considerazioni*, pp. 34 and 58–60. On Gonzaga, see Guido Dall'Olio, 'Gonzaga, Giulia', in *Dizionario biografico degli Italiani*, LVII (Rome: Istituto dell'Enciclopedia italiana, 2001) <https://www.treccani.it/enciclopedia/giulia-gonzaga_(Dizionario-Biografico)> [accessed 15 November 2022]. See also Susanna Peyronel Rambaldi, *Una gentildonna irrequieta: Giulia Gonzaga fra reti familiari e relazioni eterodosse* (Rome: Viella, 2012); Gennaro Tallini, '*La piccola Athene*: Giulia Gonzaga e il circolo di Fondi tra letteratura ed eterodossia (1526–1566)', in *La donna nel Rinascimento: Amore, famiglia, cultura, potere*, ed. by Luisa Secchi Tarugi (Florence: Cesati, 2019), pp. 303–19.
50. Juan de Valdés, 'Christian Alphabet', in *Spiritual and Anabaptist Writers*, ed. by George H. Williams and Angel M. Mergal (Philadelphia: Westminster Press, 1957), pp. 351–90 (p. 354); see the Italian text: 'Ho scritto in dialogo tutto quello ragionamento cristiano, nel qual l'altro dì tornando da la predica di fra Bernardino da Siena scappuccino tanto ci [inebbriammo] che fu necessario che la notte il conchiudesse.' Juan de Valdés, *Alfabeto cristiano*, ed. by Adriano Prosperi (Rome: Istituto Storico Italiano per l'età moderna e contemporanea, 1988), p. 20. Significantly, the reference to Ochino is present only in the manuscript version of the dialogue, now in Rome, Biblioteca Apostolica Vaticana, MS Borgiano Lat. 194; in the 1545 print the reference is to an anonymous preacher.
51. Valdés, 'Christian Alphabet', p. 357. 'Confusione, perplessità et inquietudine'. Valdés, *Alfabeto cristiano*, p. 23.
52. Valdés, 'Christian Alphabet', p. 357. 'In modo che non posso pensare che cosa mi si potesse offerire il [dì] d'oggi che bastasse a togliermi questa confusione et acchetarmi questa inquietudine e risolvermi questa perplessità'. Valdés, *Alfabeto cristiano*, p. 24.
53. Valdés, 'Christian Alphabet', p. 358. 'Oltra ciò, sappiate che nelle prime prediche le quali udii dal vostro fra Bernardino Scappuccino mi persuase con le sue parole che per mezzo della sua dottrina io potrei serenare e mettere in pace l'animo mio, ma fin ad'ora m'è successo al roverscio di quello che io pensava. E benché io attribuisca più questo ad imperfettione mia che a difetto suo, tuttavia mi dà pena in vedere che la mia speranza non m'abbia successo. [...] Questa contradditton hanno ingenerato nell'animo mio i sermoni del predicatore, mediante li quali mi veggio fortemente combattuta, da una parte dal timore dello inferno e dall'amore del paradiso, e dall'altra dal timore delle lingue delle genti e dallo amor dell'onor del mondo'. Valdés, *Alfabeto cristiano*, p. 24. Again, the explicit reference to Ochino is present only in the manuscipt version.
54. Valdés, 'Christian Alphabet', pp. 358–59. 'Confusione, dubbio e perplessità'; 'in questa tempesta d'affetti, d'appetiti, d'imaginationi e di diversità di volontadi'. Valdés, *Alfabeto cristiano*, p. 25.
55. For an overview of Spiera's story and the sources that relate it, see Silvano Cavazza, 'Una vicenda europea: Vergerio e il caso Spiera, 1548–49', in *La fede degli Italiani: Per Adriano Prosperi*, ed. by Guido Dall'Olio, Adelisa Malena, and Pierroberto Scaramella, 1 (Pisa: Edizioni della Normale, 2011), pp. 41–51; see also John Jeffries Martin, *Venice's Hidden Enemies: Italian Heretics in a Renaissance City*, 2nd edn (Baltimore: Johns Hopkins University Press, 2004), Chap. 5.
56. Gigliola Fragnito, ' "Per lungo e dubbioso sentero": L'itinerario spirituale di Vittoria Colonna', in *Al crocevia della storia: Poesia, religione e politica in Vittoria Colonna*, ed. by Maria Serena Sapegno (Rome: Viella, 2016), pp. 177–213.

57. Tatiana Crivelli, 'Godere di cattiva stampa: Spunti per una rilettura della tradizione editoriale delle rime di Vittoria Colonna', in *Al crocevia della storia*, pp. 137–57. See also Tatiana Crivelli, 'The Print Tradition of Vittoria Colonna's *Rime*', in *A Companion to Vittoria Colonna*, ed. by Abigail Brundin, Tatiana Crivelli, and Maria Serena Sapegno (Leiden: Brill, 2016), pp. 69–139.

58. 'Colonna's mature, spiritual Petrarchism did not move very far from the poet herself and a close group of associates during her lifetime [...] the evidence suggests that it was her later, more focused spiritual production that was tightly controlled and prevented from reaching a wider readership, perhaps because of its reformed religious bent.' Abigail Brundin, 'Vittoria Colonna in Manuscript', in *A Companion to Vittoria Colonna*, ed. by Brundin, Crivelli, and Sapegno, pp. 39–68 (p. 49). One hundred and three spiritual sonnets were contained in the gift manuscript she sent around 1539/40 to Michelangelo (now Rome, Biblioteca Apostolica Vaticana, MS Vat. Lat. 11539); to those she later added forty more, which Michelangelo probably bound with the Vatican manuscript. See Vittoria Colonna, *La raccolta di rime per Michelangelo*, ed. by Veronica Copello (Florence: Società Editrice Fiorentina, 2020).

59. 'Il gel de le mie colpe e 'l vivo ardore | Suo verso noi fan dubbio a l'intelletto.' Vittoria Colonna, *Rime*, ed. by Alan Bullock (Rome: Laterza, 1982), p. 95; Vittoria Colonna, *Sonnets for Michelangelo: A Bilingual Edition*, ed. and transl. by Abigail Brundin (Chicago: University of Chicago Press, 2005), p. 103.

60. 'L'Occhio grande e divino il cui valore | Non vide, né vedrà, ma sempre vede, | Toglie dal petto ardente, Sua mercede, | I dubbi del servile freddo timore.' Colonna, *Rime*, p. 125.

61. 'Con quella scorta ella se 'n va sospesa, | Sì che se giunge al desiato fine | Passa per lungo e dubbioso sentiero; | Ma con questa sovente, da divine | Luci illustrata e di bel foco accesa, | Corre certa e veloce al segno vero.' Ibid., p.167.

62. Furey, *Erasmus, Contarini*, p. 112.

63. Colonna, *Rime*, p. 119.

64. 'Felice voi, che con sì bei pensier | For del dubbio camin lieta scorgete | De l'immortalità tutti i sentieri, | Tal che senza temer l'ira di Lete, | Tra i rari spiriti, e più di fama alteri, | Vivo exempio d'onor sempre sarete.' Bernardo Tasso, *Rime*, ed. by Domenico Chiodo (Turin: RES, 1995), I, 160.

65. 'Emerge piuttosto la distanza spirituale che Michelangelo avvertiva nei confronti della Colonna, a cui si rivolgeva come a una guida sicura da seguire nei labirinti del dubbio.' Colonna, *La raccolta di rime*, x.

66. They are, respectively, nos. 5 and 6 of the 'Rime spirituali e religiose' in Michelangelo Buonarroti, *Rime e lettere*, ed. by Antonio Corsaro and Giorgio Masi (Milan: Bompiani, 2016), pp. 298–301. Antonio Corsaro stresses the 'senso della debolezza dell'uomo' and the 'inadeguatezza e incapacità di far fronte al peccato senza l'aiuto divino (la grazia)'. See Corsaro, 'L'artista, l'opera, l'anima: Sul dialogo poetico fra Michelangelo e Vittoria Colonna', in *Michelangelo e Vittoria Colonna: Amicizia, arte, poesia, spiritualità dall'assedio di Firenze all'apertura del Concilio di Trento*, ed. by Veronica Copello and Andrea Donati (Todi: D'Arte, 2022), pp. 121–33 (p. 133); and in the same volume, Veronica Copello, 'Lettere a un "singularissimo amico": Le epistole di Vittoria Colonna a Michelangelo', pp. 135–44.

67. Guglielmo Gorni, 'Le ottave dei giganti', in *Michelangelo poeta e artista*, ed. by Paolo Grossi and Matteo Residori (Paris: Istituto Italiano di Cultura, 2005), pp. 41–52 (p. 43). Gorni suggests an earlier date for the fragment, which may have been composed around the beginning of the century; see also Carlotta Mazzoncini, 'L'occhio nel calcagno: Fioritura e fortuna di un'immagine delle "ottave dei giganti" di Michelangelo', *L'ellisse*, 10 (2015), 111–32.

68. They are no. 30 in the 'Frammenti e abbozzi' section in Buonarroti, *Rime e lettere*, pp. 410–17 (pp. 1088–94 for commentary).

69. See Ida Campeggiani, *Le varianti della poesia di Michelangelo* (Lucca: Pacini Fazzi, 2012), pp. 69–115. As pointed out by Richard Popkin, Savonarola was interested in Sextus Empiricus's scepticism; Savonarola 'apparently knew enough about Pyrrhonian scepticism to perceive the value of it from what he heard from some of the humanist scholars at San Marco, probably including Gianfrancesco Pico'. Popkin, *The History of Scepticism*, p. 25. Gianfrancesco Pico della Mirandola, nephew of Giovanni Pico, turned ancient scepticism against classical philosophy to

show that all human knowledge is 'open to grave doubts', whereas there is a 'special revealed prophetic knowledge which is absolutely certain' (ibid.). See also Gian Mario Cao, 'L'eredità pichiana: Gianfrancesco Pico tra Sesto Empirico e Savonarola', in *Pico, Poliziano e l'Umanesimo di fine Quattrocento*, ed. by Paolo Viti (Florence: Olschki, 1994), pp. 231–45.

70. *The Poetry of Michelangelo: An Annotated Translation*, ed. and trans. by James M. Saslow (New Haven, CT: Yale University Press, 1991), p. 167. 'El Dubbio, el Forse, el Come, el Perché rio | No 'l può ma' far, ché non istà fra loro: | Se con semplice fede adora e prega | Iddio e 'l ciel, l'un lega e l'altro piega.' Buonarroti, *Rime e lettere*, p. 412.

71. *The Poetry of Michelangelo*, p. 168. 'El Dubbio armato e zoppo si figura, | E va saltando come le locuste, | Tremando d'ogni tempo per natura, | Qual suole al vento far canna palustre.' Buonarroti, *Rime e lettere*, p. 413.

72. *The Poetry of Michelangelo*, p. 168. 'El Perché è magro, e 'ntorn'alla cintura | Ha molte chiave, e non son tanto giuste, | Ch'agugina gl'ingegni della porta. | E va di notte, e 'l buio è la suo scorta. | El Come e 'l Forse son parenti stretti, | E son giganti di sì grande altezza, | Ch'al Sol andar ciascun par si diletti, | E ciechi fur per mirar suo chiarezza.' Buonarroti, *Rime e lettere*, p. 413.

73. One may find here a reminiscence of the last lines of Petrarch's *Rerum vulgarium fragmenta* 339, 'Conobbi, quanto il ciel li occhi m'aperse'.

74. *The Poetry of Michelangelo*, p. 168. 'E quello alle città co' fieri petti | Tengon, per tutto adombran lor bellezza'. Buonarroti, *Rime e lettere*, p. 413.

75. *The Poetry of Michelangelo*, p. 168. 'Povero e nudo e sol ne va 'l Vero, | Che fra la gente umìle ha gran valore.' Buonarroti, *Rime e lettere*, p. 413.

76. As Corsaro and Masi write: 'Scacciato da un luogo, cioè superato riguardo a un argomento, ne raggiunge subito un altro.' Buonarroti, *Rime e lettere*, p. 1090.

77. *The Poetry of Michelangelo*, p. 168. ''n mille luoghi nasce, se 'n un muore'. Buonarroti, *Rime e lettere*, p. 413.

78. *The Poetry of Michelangelo*, p. 168. 'sta co' suo fedel costante e saldo'. Buonarroti, *Rime e lettere*, p. 413.

79. Silvana Seidel Menchi, *Erasmo in Italia (1520–1580)* (Turin: Bollati Boringhieri, 1987), Chap. 8.

80. For the sake of simplicity, I will refer to Ricci as Renato, the nickname (literally meaning 'reborn') that he took in 1542 when he fled to Valtellina; see Luca Addante, 'Renato, Camillo (Paolo Ricci, Lisia Fileno)', in *Dizionario biografico degli Italiani*, LXXXVI (Rome: Istituto dell'Enciclopedia italiana, 2016) <https://www.treccani.it/enciclopedia/camillo-renato_%28Dizionario-Biografico%29/> [accessed 15 November 2022].

81. See Matteo Al-Kalak, *L'eresia dei fratelli: Una comunità eterodossa nella Modena del Cinquecento* (Rome: Edizioni di Storia e Letteratura, 2011).

82. See Antonio Rotondò, 'Per la storia dell'eresia a Bologna nel secolo XVI', *Rinascimento*, 13 (1962), 107–54; Dall'Olio, *Eretici e inquisitori*, esp. pp. 101–08.

83. As in the case of Panfilo Sasso, there was a jurisdictional quarrel over which authority had the right to deal with the case, with powerful families intervening in the conflict; Count Ercole Rangoni protected Renato against the Dominicans, praising his virtue in a letter to Ercole d'Este. Cf. Camillo Renato, *Opere: Documenti e testimonianze*, ed. by Antonio Rotondò (Florence: Sansoni; Chicago: Newberry Library, 1968), pp. 168–69.

84. 'Già frate predicatore de santo Francesco, sfratato [...] fugito da Bologna et è stato preso qua sopra il Modenese, che andava suvertendo li villani.' Ibid., p. 170.

85. 'Sed posteaquam venit, auctus est numerus et primi confirmati ab ipso sunt, et non solum homines cuiuscumque conditionis, docti et indocti et ignari literarum, sed et mulieres, ubicumque occasionem dabatur, in plateis, in apothecis, in ecclesiis, de fide et lege Christi disputabant et omnes promiscue scripturas sacras lacerabant, allegantes Paulum, Matthaeum, Johannem, Apocalypsim, et omnes doctores, quos, numquam viderant.' Ibid., pp. 193–94.

86. 'E pareva ch'el dicesse, come e' faceva, male, et già ha involupato el cirvello a molti de Modena, li quali al presente vano con el capo chino e dubitano de pegio ancora de loro.' Ibid., pp. 192–93.

87. Today preserved in a manuscript in Bologna, Biblioteca dell'Archiginnasio, MS B 1928.

88. In 1542 Renato fled to Valtellina and joined the local Protestant community; in 1547 the pastor of Chiavenna, Agostino Mainardi, attacked him for his radical views; in 1550 he was

excommunicated and the following year he was forced to abjure his radical ideas. Renato was thus persecuted by both the Catholic and the Protestant church; doubt led him to share radical views that did not fit within any orthodoxy, either Catholic or Protestant. He was instead close to the Anabaptist communities of the Veneto: it was within these circles, outside any organized church, that religious doubt reached its extreme consequences.

89. 'Summo studio quaerere quid dicant, quid legant magis quam quod intelligant.' Renato, *Opere*, p. 66.

90. 'Item videmus, et utinam mentiar, luce meridiana clarius fere omnes, tam mares quam foeminas, summo studio quaerere quid dicant, quid legant magis quam quod intelligent, in rebus praesertim divinis. Secus enim res habet in lectione prophana aut Petri Aretini aut cuiusvis alterius; ita enim quaeruntur ut diligenter intelligantur et ut legentis animum optabili voluptate afficiant immo erudiant ad omne genus vitiorum ac scelerum.' Ibid., p. 66.

91. 'Etiam sanctorum patrum volumina tam insolenter, tam impudenter ab omnibus in dubium ac suspicionem revocantur.' Ibid., p. 68.

92. Ibid., p. 69.

93. 'Sed inter peritos et iuditio praeditos aut viros aut scholares quibuscum est mihi fere consuetudo perpetua, ut sunt rerum omnium curiosi ac cupidi sciendi, ut scilicet consilium hominum hac opera in rebus dubiis evocemus.' Ibid., p. 45.

94. 'Statim consului concionatorem divi Petronii superioribus annis et in spetie anni 1540.' Ibid., p. 65. We do not know who the preacher was in 1540, but in 1539 it was Tommaso da Carpineto and, interestingly, in 1538, Serafino da Fermo. Renato had to defend himself against the charge of having maintained that the souls of the saints do not reach heaven immediately after their death. This matter had an obvious connection with the doctrine of the 'sleep of the blessed', a staple of Anabaptist faith. Put simply, it was about whether the souls of those who are destined to salvation go directly to heaven or whether they sleep until Judgement Day.

95. 'Ut theologorum mos est frequentissimus omnia in dubium revocare ut magis veritas eluceat.' Ibid., p. 40.

96. 'Nullum esse purgatorium, nullum infernum, nullam legem, nullam legis poenam, nullum peccatum, nullam mortem, nullum satanam.' Ibid., p. 39.

97. Ibid., p. 43.

98. Ibid., p. 35.

99. Ibid., p. 36.

100. Ibid., pp. 235–41.

101. 'Et haver più che si può la conscientia sicura et netta da ogni scrupulo et dubitatione, che tengono infestato l'animo et altro ben non fanno et si va da scrupulo in scrupulo et mai si finisce, et per questa via il diavolo cerca d'illaquearci.' Quoted in Aldo Stella, *Anabattismo e antitrinitarismo in Italia nel XVI secolo: Nuove ricerche storiche* (Padua: Liviana, 1969), p. 198.

102. 'Lutheran' was an umbrella term of sorts, covering some of the most widespread tenets of Reformed belief in Italy, including the denial of Purgatory, the intercession of the saints, and images, and the belief in saving grace.

103. 'Vero è che la prima volta che si congregassimo che io ragionai da poi l'oratione proponendo il dubio della incarnatione del signor Giesu Christo, dicendo che quivi eravamo ragunati per non andare alla ciecca di questo nostro maestro Christo, ma per rissolversi se era solo huomo generato di seme o pur Dio concetto di Spirito santo.' Ginzburg, *I costituti di don Pietro Manelfi*, p. 66.

104. 'Sol'huomo generato di seme humano, pieno però de tutte le vertudi da Dio.' Ibid., p. 83.

105. 'Christo non essere Dio ma gran propheta et non essere venuto come messia ma come propheta, et essere morto per la verità, et che non è anchora risuscitato ma che ha da risuscitare et venire come messia, et doppo esso risuscitarano li eletti per ordine [...] anzi negano tutto il testamento novo et dicono essere inventione di Greci et Gentili et che Paolo non ha inteso niente delle scritture vechie, maxime circa la giustificatione et resurrecione.' Ibid., p. 69.

106. Stella, *Anabattismo e antitrinitarismo*; Seidel Menchi, *Erasmo in Italia*, esp. Chap. 8; Luca Addante, *Eretici e libertini nel Cinquecento italiano* (Rome: Laterza, 2010); Luca Addante, '"Parlare liberamente": I libertini del Cinquecento tra tradizioni storiografiche e prospettive di ricerca', *Rivista storica italiana*, 123 (2011), 927–1001; Luca Addante, 'Radicalisme politique et religieux:

Les libertins italiens au XVIe siècle', in *Libertin! Usage d'une invective au XVIe et XVIIe siècle*, ed. by Thomas Berns, Anne Staquet and Monique Weis (Paris: Garnier, 2013), pp. 29–50; Luca Addante, 'Dal radicalismo religioso del Cinquecento al deismo (e oltre): Vecchie e nuove prospettive di ricerca', *Rivista storica italiana*, 127 (2015), pp. 770–807. See also George H. Williams, *The Radical Reformation*, 3rd edn (Kirksville, MO: Sixteenth Century Journal Publishers, 1992), pp. 860–64 (and in general, the entire Chap. 22); Martin, *Venice's Hidden Enemies*, Chap. 4.

107. The trial is published in Domenico Berti, 'Di Giovanni Valdes e di taluni suoi discepoli secondo nuovi documenti tolti dall'Archivio Veneto', *Atti della R. Accademia dei Lincei*, 275 (1887/88), 61–81. The original is in Archivio di Stato di Venezia (= ASVe), *Sant'Uffizio*, Processi, b. 11. See also Addante, *Eretici e libertini*, pp. 15–25.

108. 'Essendo molto mal sano dela vita mia'; 'trovare pace, et refrigerio nelle brazzie dela Santa madre Chiesia Catholica Romana'. Berti, 'Di Giovanni Valdes', p. 69.

109. Addante, *Eretici e libertini*, p. 22.

110. 'Magior spirito et maggior dono di Dio, deli altri profeti.' Berti, 'Di Giovanni Valdes', p. 70.

111. Ibid., 71.

112. 'Perché queste opinioni erano così diaboliche non caminavano per molte persone.' Ibid., p. 72.

113. For a detailed analysis of these opinions, see Addante, *Eretici e libertini*, pp. 20–24.

114. Berti, 'Di Giovanni Valdes', p. 78.

115. 'Che li evangeli et epistole di S. Paolo allegasseno molte autorità del testamento vecchio quali fossero allegate stortamente, et non secondo la mente che nel testamento vecchio erano dette, et che tali authorità non erano allegate né dalli evangelisti né da san Paolo ma da alcuni che l'haveano agionte.' Ibid., p. 80.

116. The trial is recorded in ASVe, *Sant'Uffizio*, b. 13, fasc. III and b. 159, fasc. II; see Addante, *Eretici e libertini*, 25–40; Luca Addante, 'Hérésie radicale et libertinage: Le valdésien Giulio Basalù et Domenico Scandella dit Menocchio', in *Dissidence et dissimulation*, ed. by Antony Molho and Jean-Pierre Cavaillé (= *Les dossiers du Grihl*, 3–2 (2009)), <https://journals.openedition.org/dossiersgrihl/3779≥ [accessed 7 June 2021].

117. 'Giulio Basalù era molto sospetto et mi par che don Geronimo Capece mi dicesse che lui credeva solo quello che concordava con l'una et l'altra legge, cioè hebrea et christiana, cioè in quello che accettava l'una et l'altra legge.' ASVe, *Sant'Uffizio*, b. 13, fasc. III, fol. 6^v.

118. 'Giulio Basalù haveva alcuna opinione differente alli altri heretici, cioè che Christo doveva venir un'altra volta a regnar onde poi salvar tutti li hebrei.' Ibid., fol. 10^v.

119. 'Et poi mi monstrava con alcune autorità et monstrava de dubitar et diceva: 'bene, come intenderesti questo?' Et inanzi mi faceva dubitar nell'autorità et come era cascato nel dubio diceva: 'ben, quando se intendesse così, non vi pare a voi che stesse bene?' Et mi persuase in questo modo molti errori [...] et di poi mi persuase che non era la Trinità ma un solo Dio, che Christo non era Dio, ma che Dio habitava in Christo.' Ibid., unnumbered fol.

120. 'Et ben praticavo con li nominati et che quelli havesseno diverse opinioni a li ragionamenti de le quale mi son trovato presente, io in verità non solamente non le credevo, ma non le intendevo, perché essendo intrato in opinione che morto il corpo morisse l'anima di ognuno, ogni opinione andò per terra, credendo che tutte le religione fossero inventione di homini per indur li homini al ben vivere, onde non volevo affaticarmi per intender le diverse opinion di religione [...] se ben da principio io credevo la iustificatione *ex sola fide, et cum consequentibus*, intrato in questa altra opinione anche quella andò per terra.' Ibid.

121. The letter is in ASVe, *Sant'Uffizio*, b. 13, fasc. III, and follows Basalù's confession.

122. 'De consequentia in consequentia con el fondamento solo de ditta oppinione'. ASVe, *Sant'Uffizio*, b. 159, fasc. II, fol. 112^v.

123. 'D'oppinion di maggior importanza'. Ibid., fol. 113^r.

124. 'Raggion natural et mie chimere'. Ibid.

125. 'Venni a negar tra me medesimo ogni sorta di religion, così christiana come hebrea [...] et mi ridevo d'ogni cosa.' Ibid.

126. 'La maggior parte delli mei ragionamenti era senza Scrittura ma de fantasia perché mai ho letto né uno Evangelio, né una epistola de S. Paolo integra.' Ibid., fol. 115^r.

127. Ibid., fol. 115^v.

128. Addante, *Eretici e libertini*, pp. 31–32.
129. Although Laureto, like his fellows, probably wanted to benefit of the two benign *brevi* issued in 1550 by Jules III, which granted a fair treatment to those involved in matters of heresy. He was born in Cava de' Tirreni, near Salerno, in 1518 and was a member of the Benedictine Olivetan order, which he subsequently left. At the time of his trial, he was around thirty-five years old and affirmed that he had entered the order when he was around seventeen or eighteen, around 1535 or 1536. He had then entered the Augustinian monastery of S. Anello in Naples; his acquaintance with Lutheran or, more likely, Valdésian ideas dates from 1545/46. The trial is recorded in ASVe, *Sant'Uffizio*, b. 11, and published in Édouard Pommier, 'L'itinéraire religieux d'un moine vagabond italien au XVIᵉ siècle', *Mélanges d'archéologie et d'histoire*, 66 (1954), 293–322 (p. 318). See also Addante, *Eretici e libertini*, pp. 7–15.
130. 'Lo scopersi che egli dubitava della divinità di Christo; et ragionando cum meco di questo, comenzamo a lezer et rivoltar le Scritture per chiarir questo puncto. Et lui era molto dotto nella lingua hebrea et greca, et esortò anche me ad imparar le ditte lingue, perché diceva che erano necessarie per haver la verità, perché lui dubitava anche che li Evangelii fossero stati alterati et coroti.' Pommier, 'L'itinéraire religieux', p. 318.
131. 'Stando qui in Padoa, in compagnia del ditto abate, et studiando la lingua hebrea, venero in quella città alcuni Anabatisti, tra li quali era uno chiamato Benedeto, credo che fosse da Axolo, et un altro Nicola, credo che sia da Treviso [...] et ci scoprirno la loro doctrina anabatistica, et fecero si che si persuasero a ribaptizarsi.' Ibid.
132. 'Et havendo pigliata una casa [...] per far riduti et congregationi, ci reducevamo tutti in ditta casa, et qui ragionavamo di questa doctrina anabattistica, et ogniun diceva quel che li pareva.' Ibid.
133. Addante, *Eretici e libertini*, p. 11.
134. 'Io mi accorsi che lui incommenciava ad uscir di sé' ('I realized that he began to be beyond himself'). Pommier, 'L'itinéraire religieux', p. 319.
135. 'Perché io contradiceva a molte loro superstitioni, come saria che non vollevano che si legesse altra scritura che quella del Testamento vecchio et novo.' Ibid., p. 320.
136. 'Quanto più io studiava, tanto più mi veniva accorgendo delli loro molti errori et superstitioni.' Ibid.
137. 'Che le sue erano baie, superstitioni et ciancie, et non solamente quelle de ditti hebrei, ma anche tute le altre sette che io havea seguitato fino alhora.' Ibid., p. 321.
138. 'Gremio della S. Chiesa Romana et riconciliarmi cum lei.' Ibid.
139. This suggests that Laureto's confession was not entirely spontaneous, as he had declared to the inquisitors.
140. See for example the experience of the English Seekers described in Ryrie, *Unbelievers*, pp. 162–67.
141. Addante, *Eretici e libertini*, p. 14.
142. John Jeffries Martin, *Myths of Renaissance Individualism* (Basingstoke: Palgrave Macmillan, 2004), pp. 43, 45.
143. Ibid., p. 57.
144. Ibid., p. 48.

CHAPTER 5

The Sociability of Doubt

This chapter explores some aspects of what I suggest we call the 'sociability of doubt' in the sixteenth century. As we have already seen, doubt was not always a solipsistic and sometimes traumatic experience, as we often tend to think of it (although the previous chapter provides some evidence for this). Sometimes, doubt could become the fulcrum in a series of cultural practices that brought together individuals through academies or games. In the case of academies, the individuals involved were mostly social elites, although some academies promoted vernacular culture in an attempt to serve the public good. Games, texts produced within academies, and other works featured in this chapter were designed to reach larger audiences, including women, who appear integral to the sociability of doubt. I start by reviewing the genre of 'love doubts' before turning to discuss a game of chance, a refined creation of the printer Francesco Marcolini and the artists and intellectuals who gathered around him. I then analyse the role of doubt within two academies, the Infiammati and the Dubbiosi. Finally, I present a story that shows how a work designed within an academy could enter religious debates and how doubts examined therein could resonate with religious anxieties and help nurture dangerous questions. All the works discussed in this chapter point to the entertaining nature of discussions of doubts and of talking about doubt in the vernacular, in academies (real or virtual) and social gatherings. We see here the pleasure of exploring the variety of human events, the ambiguities, shortcomings, and contradictions of knowledge — also of everyday knowledge — and the intellectual delight of penetrating beneath the surface and appearance of things. At the same time, we discover a society that at the crucial juncture of the 1540s and early 1550s learns to use doubt as an instrument of self-defence. This lively vernacular culture of doubt appears to be distinct from that of universities; the point here seems less to use doubt as a tool against intellectual authorities than as a means to act upon a complex reality, a way to build forms of useful social interaction.

Playing with Doubt

Love Doubts

That doubt could have an entertaining side was well known in courtly culture, wherein 'love doubts' were a favourite entertainment, as testified to by a flourishing literary tradition. Giovanni Boccaccio (1313–1375), in the fourth book of his *Filocolo*, has a group of young men and women discuss love questions. Since this episode was loosely connected to the main plot, it was often detached and published independently. As such, it enjoyed a large European circulation thanks to Spanish, French, and English translations.[1] The humanist Mario Equicola (c. 1470–1525), in his *Libro de natura de amore* (Book on the nature of love, 1525), reports that the Mantuan writer Giovan Giacomo Calandra, in his now-lost *Aura*, had proposed 'some seventy doubts on love'.[2] Love doubts are discussed by another Mantuan, Baldassar Castiglione, in his *Book of the Courtier* (1528). The habit of asking questions in matters of love was not restricted to the courts: members of academies seem to have enjoyed it as well. In the early 1550s, the Florentine Benedetto Varchi (1503–1565), a good friend of Fortunato Martinengo (to whom we shall return), devoted four lessons to love questions, which he recited in the Florentine Academy.[3] Love doubts were also a favourite pastime with the Sienese Academy of the Intronati. Girolamo Bargagli (1537–1586) suggests several versions of this kind of game. In one version, two young men are called to discuss 'a question or doubt of love'; as in academic disputes, each proposes reasons in favour or against that particular doubt until a lady pronounces the winner.[4] A variant of this is the game of riddles, where one presents doubts in the form of poems, making sure that they 'apparently mean something dishonest'.[5] Another variation of this game consists in inventing a love story from its very beginning and debating various doubts concerning its possible developments. In this version, instead of debating different subjects, the participants stick to just one story, and doubts arise 'one after the other' following the possible solutions provided by players — in other words, players and readers are faced with a series of crossroads and according to the path they choose, new doubts arise.[6] It is clear that in all these cases — as in other games involving doubts, such as those presented in Innocenzo Ringhieri's *Cento giuochi liberali, et d'ingegno* (A hundred noble and ingenious pastimes, 1551) — doubts are merely pretexts for polite games and conversation. As we will see, however, the distinction is not always so clear-cut, and sometimes authors could suggest the overlap between their 'pastimes' and more serious genres dealing with uncertainty.

The flourishing genre of love doubts, which continued into the late sixteenth and seventeenth centuries, was fortunate enough to become the object of parody. The *Dubbi amorosi* (Love doubts) attributed to Pietro Aretino were in fact composed in the early seventeenth century, probably before 1618. Some eighteenth-century scholars have suggested that their author could be one Marco Lamberti (mid-1500s–1637), a poet and man of the church who enjoyed some popularity in his day and had a penchant for scurrilous and obscene verses. As an ecclesiastic and a doctor of law and theology, he had certainly mastered both the civil and canon law that was often quoted in these doubts, which are eight-line poems followed by an answer of the same length. The poems are thus a parody of the lofty courtly and academic tradition of love questions, and at the same time they target questions and disputes of canonical and civil law. They also draw on a third tradition, possibly the most interesting to us. An eighteenth-century manuscript now in the Biblioteca Marucelliana in Florence (C 214) carries the pseudo-Aretinesque *Dubbi amorosi* as well as poems by Lamberti; however, the title announces it as *I dubbi o siano i casi di coscienza di Marco Lamberti* (The doubts, or cases of conscience of Marco Lamberti).[7] Whether Lamberti was the author of the *Dubbi amorosi* or whether he simply appropriated and enlarged a pre-existing corpus is up for debate among philologists. What is remarkable is that these obscene doubts are called 'cases of conscience'. This choice of title points to the contemporary overflow of treatises of casuistry and moral philosophy discussing cases of conscience. Starting from the 1570s it was mostly the Jesuits who dominated this field, pushing the originally Dominican theories of probabilism to their extreme consequences. In other words, these seemingly marginal, pseudo-Aretinesque poems merge the tradition of courtly love questions with casuistic literature and moral theology. Far from being naive exercises in obscene poetry, they masterfully target the 'high' traditions of love doubts and moral doubts (but then again, sexual matters were central in cases of conscience).[8] As is often the case with doubt, even apparently disengaged exercises can reveal a hidden and somewhat troubling side.

A Garden of Doubts

The *Dubbi amorosi* may have not been penned by Aretino, but it was within Aretino's circle that a work deeply imbued with doubt came into being. Francesco Marcolini's *Le sorti, o sia giardino di pensieri* (The chances, or a garden of thoughts, 1540; reprinted with variations in 1550) is one of the best known *libri di ventura* or *libri di sorti*, divination games that often functioned as 'a surrogate for actual gambling'.[9] These games were generally endowed with allegorical meanings and allowed players to delight in the different paths of fortune, providing them at the same time with the thrill of its inconstancy and the illusion of controlling it, thanks to the combinatory rules of the game.[10] The book of *Sorti* is a game of fortune in which a series of images — attributed to such outstanding artists as Francesco Salviati, Giuseppe Porta, Lambert Sustris, and Francesco Menzocchi[11] — are matched with oracles in answers written by Ludovico Dolce.[12] The artists chosen to realize the more than one hundred woodcuts that adorn the book are a monument to the innovative nature of Marcolini's editorial enterprise. The Florentine Francesco Salviati (1510–1563) had moved to Venice in 1539, setting up a productive collaboration with Marcolini and his best-selling author, Pietro Aretino. Salviati's arrival in Venice acquainted Venetians with the Tuscan manner (the so-called *bella maniera*). During the same period that Marcolini published the *Sorti*, Salviati, Porta, Sustris, Menzocchi were all busy decorating the Palazzo Grimani in Santa Maria Formosa.[13] The artists involved in the book's production were thus at the cutting edge of contemporary artistic experimentation. Marcolini himself was a highly innovative printer whose several personal interests ranged from mathematics to engineering and architecture, and whose catalogue also included works on music and figurative arts.[14]

The *Sorti* displays a lavish frontispiece by Giuseppe Porta, a student and follower of Salviati's, showing philosophers and astronomers (one is holding an armillary sphere) disputing among ruins, while in the background we see a landscape

FIG. 5.1. Frontispiece to Francesco Marcolini, *Le sorti*. [...] *intitolate giardino di pensieri* (Venice: Francesco Marcolini, 1540). Archivio Storico Civico Biblioteca Trivulziana, Milan. © Comune di Milano.

(Figure 5.1). Augusto Gentili has called attention to the figures of two philosophers in the foreground, who are pointing to a young man represented according to the iconography of melancholy. A smiling young woman is sitting next to him and holding a half-open book, the *Sorti* itself, inviting the young man to look at it. Entering Marcolini's symbolic 'garden' and playing his game of chance will help the young man to exorcise his own melancholy, while taking delight in the cultural project underlying the work.[15] In front of the two young people we see a deck of cards. This detail breaks the barrier between the image and its beholder (in this case, the reader), who is invited to glance through the book and take part in the conversation and in the game. A similar visual device (Figure 5.2) is featured on the frontispiece of the 1557 Venetian edition 'per Mattio Pagan in Frezaria' of Lorenzo Spirito's *Libro de la ventura* (The book of chance).[16]

The use of elaborate allegorical frontispieces was a distinctive feature of the genre, as shown by Sigismondo Fanti's *Trionfo di Fortuna* (The triumph of Fortune, 1527) (Figure 5.3). The engraving shows the pope sitting on top of the world, at the crossroads between virtue (*virtus*) and pleasure (*voluptas*, standing for vice). On the left-hand side we see Good Fortune and on the right-hand side, an evil spirit. The scene is thus clearly divided into two sections, morally signified. Underneath Good Fortune we see a young man holding dice; he represents the immutable time of eternity as well as Fortune, here shown as a 'metaphysical, superior, and absolute entity'.[17] In other, words, we see here the unalterable course of fortune as established by eternal cosmological laws. Next to the figure of Fortune-Eternity, the image includes an astrologist or philosopher interpreting the perennial laws of nature that fall beyond historical time. On the other side of the engraving, directly under the influence of the evil spirit, we see a city with a clock tower. This is the time of history, and the city is Rome, as we can gather from the Pantheon in the middle ground. The book appears in 1527, the year of the sack of Rome, and the engraving is a memento of the damages of fortune and the instability of human endeavours.

For us, the image is relevant because the figure of the pope standing between *virtus* and *voluptas* — echoing the topos of Hercules at the crossroads — serves to install at the heart of the work the idea of a crossroads and therefore, of doubt. Games of chance are based on a series of crossroads, paths from which different stories originate, therefore taking into account the doubtful and precarious nature of the human condition. Marcolini shows that 'two or more different paths have the same outcome and that, conversely, two or more similar paths can lead to just as many different outcomes'.[18] We recognize here a pattern of sixteenth-century reflection on fortune. The idea that similar means bring opposite outcomes or that opposite means bring the same outcome puzzled Niccolò Machiavelli, for example, in his 'Ghiribizzi al Soderini' (1506), a draft of a letter to Giovan Battista Soderini, nephew of Pier Soderini, *gonfaloniere* of Florence.[19] In this text Machiavelli, drawing on examples taken from ancient and contemporary history, muses on why the same goal can be attained through opposite means. Machiavelli is interested in how a ruler aiming at a given purpose can be faced with equivalent options, with no

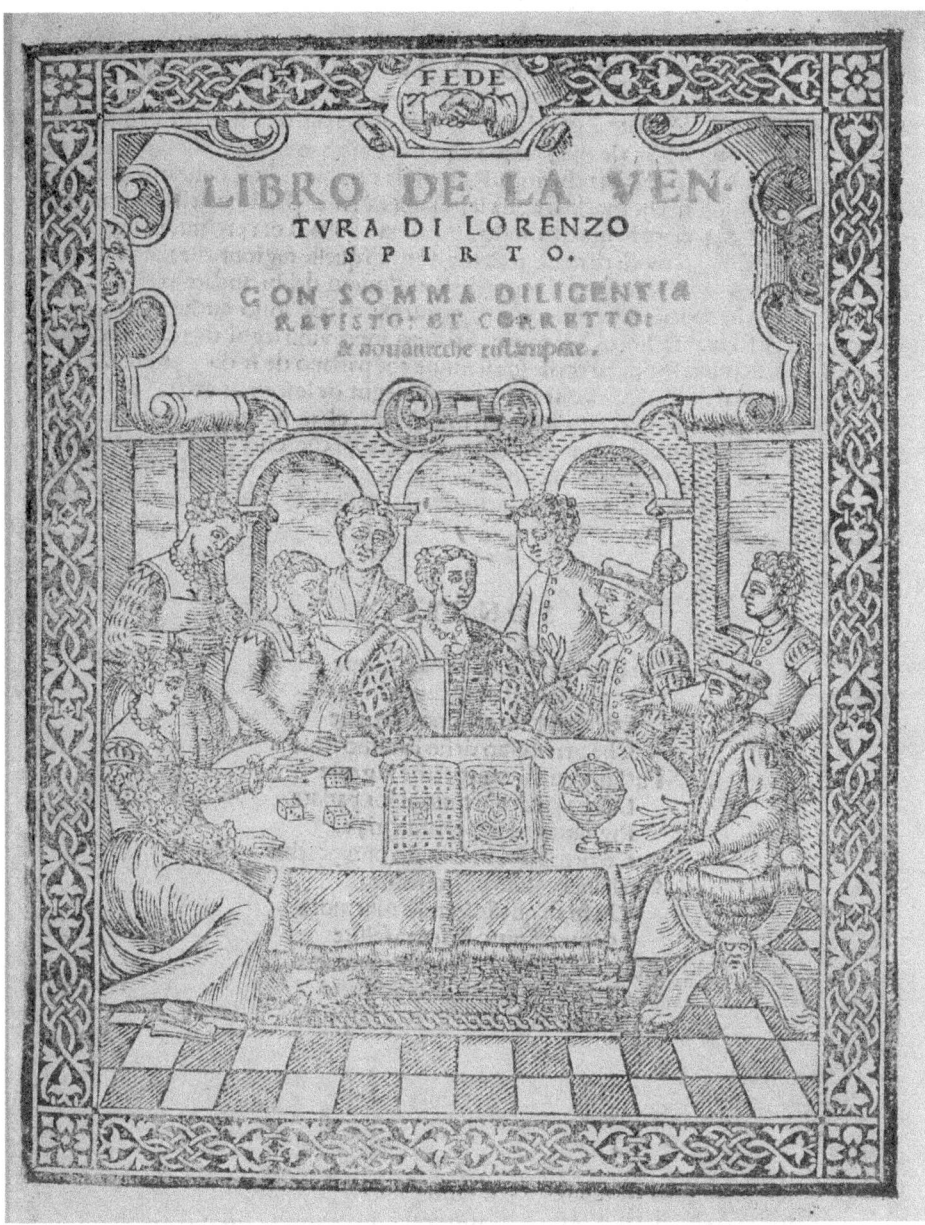

FIG. 5.2. Frontispiece to Lorenzo Spirito, *Libro de la ventura*
(Venice: per Mattio Pagan, 1557). © Fondazione Giorgio Cini, Venice.

FIG. 5.3. Frontispiece to Sigismondo Fanti, *Triompho di fortuna*
(Venice: Agostin da Portese ad instantia di Iacomo Giunta, 1527).
Archivio Storico Civico Biblioteca Trivulziana, Milan. © Comune di Milano.

special reasons to choose one over the other. Such hesitation can be resolved only by resorting to circumstances: it is the ability to act according to what is required and to bend one's personality to what the moment requires that allows successful choices. Certainly, there exist universal rules, but as to their efficacy, one can never be sure. Special circumstances can turn an otherwise wrong decision into a successful one, and the other way around. Perhaps not by chance, this is the topic of the first of Montaigne's *Essays*: 'By diverse means we arrive at the same end'.[20]

Arriving at the same goal through different if not opposite paths, or at opposite goals by the same path: this is the quintessence of doubt, the moment when taking one course of action over another is a seemingly arbitrary step. Christian Rivoletti has suggested that this pattern of thought is at the basis of the narrative mechanism underlying Ludovico Ariosto's *Orlando furioso* and can also be found in Anton Francesco Doni's *I marmi* (1552).[21] As this is also the mechanism at the basis of Marcolini's *Sorti,* we can say that doubt is brought directly into the structure of the work, as its very essence. On a more exterior level, doubt is ubiquitous in the responses to the questions asked by players. It is time, then, to see how the game works.

First of all, we should make clear that this is not a gambling game, although the boundary between parlour games and proper gambling were all but clear-cut. Marcolini himself explains in his dedication letter to the reader that the work can also be used as a game of cards in which money can be waged. In point of fact, in 1556 Doni accused his former friend and patron Aretino of having spread false rumours concerning the origin of this game. Allegedly, Aretino had made insinuations that the game had been invented by some players in a gambling house on the island of Murano and then appropriated by Marcolini. We cannot trust Doni's argument, as it comes from a violent pamphlet against Aretino titled *Teremoto* (Earthquake, written after Aretino's death). However, this curious story is a witness to the hybrid nature of these and similar games 'enabling players to perform virtue while enjoying the pleasure of gambling'.[22]

The *Sorti*, dedicated to Ercole d'Este, Duke of Ferrara, contains a series of fifty allegorical images of virtues and vices, and fifty images of ancient philosophers.[23] Each allegory is displayed on a page (along with forty-five small boxes containing combinations of two cards) associated with four moral categories, or *quadri*, shown on the facing page and divided by a 'cross'. Each player must pick a question from one of the three lists provided at the beginning of the work (there is a series of questions applying to men, one to women, and one to both). Each question will direct the player to one of the allegories (Ignorance, Sleep, Envy, Sin, etc.); at this stage the player picks two cards from a deck of thirty-six. The combination of the two cards will be found in one of the forty-five small boxes that accompany each allegory, along with the instructions to pick one card and proceed to a given *quadro*. Each *quadro* is subdivided into nine boxes and each box shows a card; according to the card that the player has picked, she or he will be directed to one of the philosophers. Here the player will pick one more card and finally receive an answer to the question that was initially selected.[24]

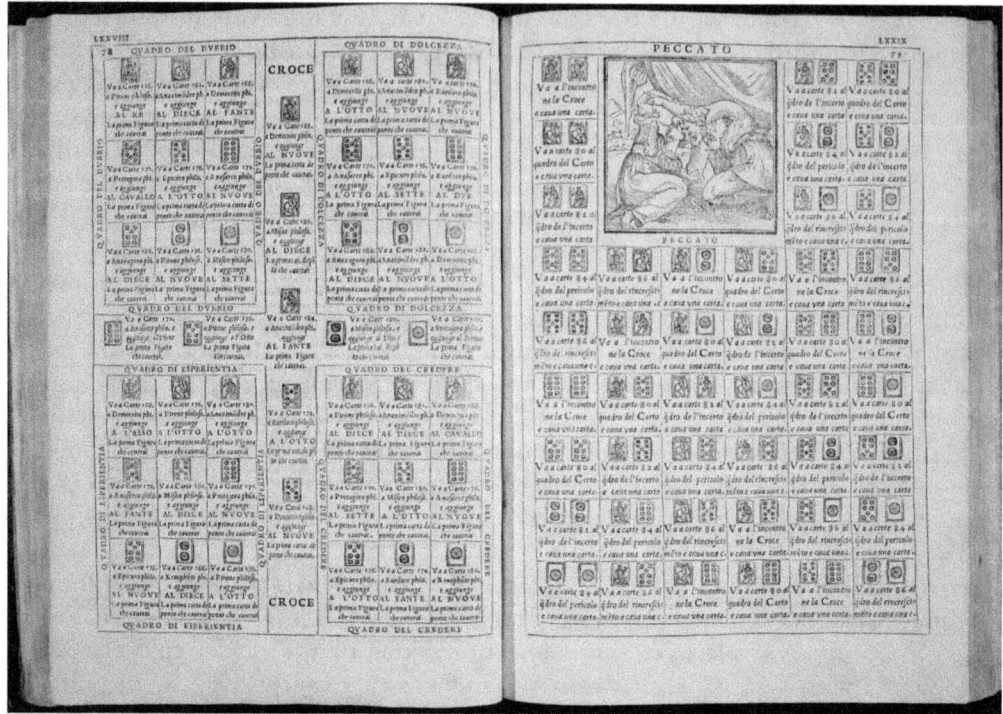

FIG. 5.4. *Quadro* of 'Dubbio' and 'Peccato', in Francesco Marcolini, *Le sorti.* [...] *intitolate giardino di pensieri* (Venice: Francesco Marcolini, 1540), pp. 78–79. Archivio Storico Civico Biblioteca Trivulziana, Milan. © Comune di Milano.

In the 1540 edition, doubt is one of the four categories, or *quadri*, associated with the allegory of Sin, together with experience, sweetness, and belief (*credere*) (Figure 5.4). In the 1550 edition, it is instead associated with the Parcae, the personifications of destiny (while retaining the same associations with the other *quadri*). In both editions the player could reach the *quadro* of doubt only from the allegory of Fear ('Timore'): those who reached Fear would in fact be asked to pick two cards and, depending on their combination, they then (and only then) could be directed to doubt. Doubt was thus associated with sin and fear as well as with destiny. The allegory of Sin has a prominent sexual connotation, as it shows an old man who seems to reach for a woman's genitalia. The association between doubt and sin is interesting, as it may suggest, through the visual image of the old man trying to grope the woman, that doubt is somehow connected with a form of violation. If so, doubt could be identified, as is often the case in the mid-sixteenth century, with an excessive will to knowledge, a violation of the boundaries set to our understanding. That sexuality is used in the *Sorti* to debate matters of knowledge has been suggested by Marie-Cécile Van Hasselt, who highlights the pervasive references to syphilis in the *Sorti*. In fact, these references should be read in the light of Marcolini's and Dolce's reflection on the dialectic between appearance and reality. The *Sorti* displays a pessimistic view of existence, in which appearance and reality only rarely and randomly match. There seems to be no divine or providential plan guiding our actions, and if there is one, it remains unfathomable to us.[25] The projections of our desires and expectations seem to hinder our perception of reality and are bound to be frustrated. Syphilis, associated in the text especially with courtesans, comes into play in this context. Courtesans are represented as attractive young women hiding a secretly repulsive nature,[26] and the courtesan affected by the French disease aptly embodies the gap between appearance and reality.[27] A strong tie between sexuality, false appearances, and doubt is thus established. The connection between doubt and fear, as we have seen in Chapter 1, has always been present ('to doubt' also means 'to be afraid of'); in Marcolini's network of images, fear is connected to the assault on the woman but also to the discovery of a dangerous secret, the mortal disease lurking underneath the pleasant physical appearances.

The *Sorti* highlights how the consequences of our deeds are often unpredictable and unforeseen: things are not as they seem and neither are people (hence a certain devaluation of physiognomy throughout the text).[28] All this must be projected against a radically negative background, in which faith and justice seem to have abandoned this earth and peace lies in a remote and most uncertain future.[29] Doubt and unbelief are thus most useful precautions against the delusional nature of what we call reality. Doubt is not only an intellectual practice but a pragmatic habit of self-defence against the blows of Fortune. Unsurprisingly, quite a few answers in the *Sorti* suggest the systematic practice of doubt. Among the responses attributed to Anaxarchus (*c.* 380–*c.* 320 BCE), for example, we find the following two (implausible as the first is):

> I like that creed of Margutte's
> Which was useful and healthy: and oftentimes
> *It is a great virtue not to believe to others.* (XXXIII. 30)

> Belief, my son, is oftentimes harmful.
> If you want to live safely, *do not believe in anything*,
> I tell you this shouting it out loud. (XXXIII. 33)[30]

Two answers are devoted to the idea that people should not be trusted and that trust can only be placed in God:

> It is all tall tales, my son,
> Fables and vain talk: *and do not believe*
> *In anyone who lives*, other than God. (XXXI. 14)

> Faith you must have only in God.
> As for the rest, to say it fair and square
> *You will not believe even my father.* (XXXV. 41)[31]

Two further answers, attributed respectively to Eurilochus (fourth century BCE) and Anaximander (*c.* 610–546 BCE), explicitly lay out a programme of radical doubt wherein incredulity becomes a form of self-defence against the pitfalls of existence:

> Even if someone swears on the sacred God
> *Be always doubtful and live cautiously,*
> And, in this way, you shall never be fooled. (XXXIV. 16)

> To trust people was always judged
> Dangerous: and if you love me
> *Be always incredulous and doubtful.* (XXXVIII. 19)[32]

Incredulity is openly praised in an answer attributed to Myson, who according to some sources was one of the Seven Wise Men of Greece:

> Among the rarest and most wonderful things
> I find, in some books in our language,
> That always believes less he who knows more. (XXXVII. 44)[33]

Unbelief is a rare and 'most wonderful' attitude, a sign of true wisdom. What then of the idea of Truth, that beautiful young woman who became Marcolini's printer's mark with the motto *Veritas filia temporis* (Truth, daughter of time)? In Marcolini's emblem, Time is lifting Truth to the sky, while a snake-tailed woman, symbolizing Ignorance, is trying to get hold of her (Figure 5.5).[34] In Marcolini's work not only is truth threatened by ignorance: through the contradictory responses to the same questions, which sometimes implies a reversal of the moral order based on the allegories, truth shows its 'fragility and its precariousness'. In the process of the game, it 'loses its identity and its certainty about itself', being 'destitute from its ontological, universal foundations'.[35]

FIG. 5.5. *Veritas filia temporis*, Francesco Marcolini's printer's mark. Archivio Storico Civico Biblioteca Trivulziana, Milan. © Comune di Milano.

Dreams and Doubts

Two years after the *Sorti*, Marcolini published Daniele Barbaro's *Predica dei sogni* (A sermon on dreams, 1542). There are connections between Barbaro's and Marcolini's works, as scholars have pointed out.[36] Enrico Parlato has analysed the allegory of Knowledge ('Sapere') in the *Sorti*, calling attention to the dark setting in which Knowledge is depicted (Figure 5.6). This is at odds with the brightness and light usually associated with knowledge. The male figure on the right seems to be sleeping and could be the personification of Sleep itself. This may hint at the idea of dreams (or a specific kind of dream) as a privileged vehicle for knowledge. The general context of the image is provided by the opposition between waking and sleeping.[37] The woodcut establishes a connection between knowledge and action, as Knowledge is setting its foot on a ship while holding by its hair the figure in the bottom left of the picture (recalling the iconography of Fortune held by the lock of its hair by those who are able to seize opportunity). What holds together Marcolini's and Barbaro's works is the preoccupation with the future: while the *Sorti* is a mechanism to tame its unpredictability, the *Predica* is preoccupied with how dreams foretell future events. There is an underlying anxiety concerning the instability of human condition that both works make apparent.

It is precisely on this anxiety that Barbaro reflects in the concluding section of the *Predica dei sogni*. His pessimistic view explores the commonplace of life as a dream:

> This world
> Is a dream, and we mortals,
> Wretched, blind, and frail
> Are nothing but
> Smoke and shadow
> And dust that the wind
> Blows from the face of the earth.[38]

Even more interestingly, our frail condition and the inversion of dreaming and being awake seem to be a consequence of our post-lapsarian condition:

> An apple made us dream
> What we see as awake
> [...]
> Now consider within thyself
> Often and deeply
> If you can see other than dreams
> In the works of the heirs
> Of the first Father, Adam.
> Dark and blackened images
> That fool our mind
> And make people dream
> And believe that among us
> With all its blessings
> There lies Heavens.[39]

What we call 'life' is nothing but a dream that deceives us, making us believe that we live in a heaven on earth, while our life is merely a shadow of true life.

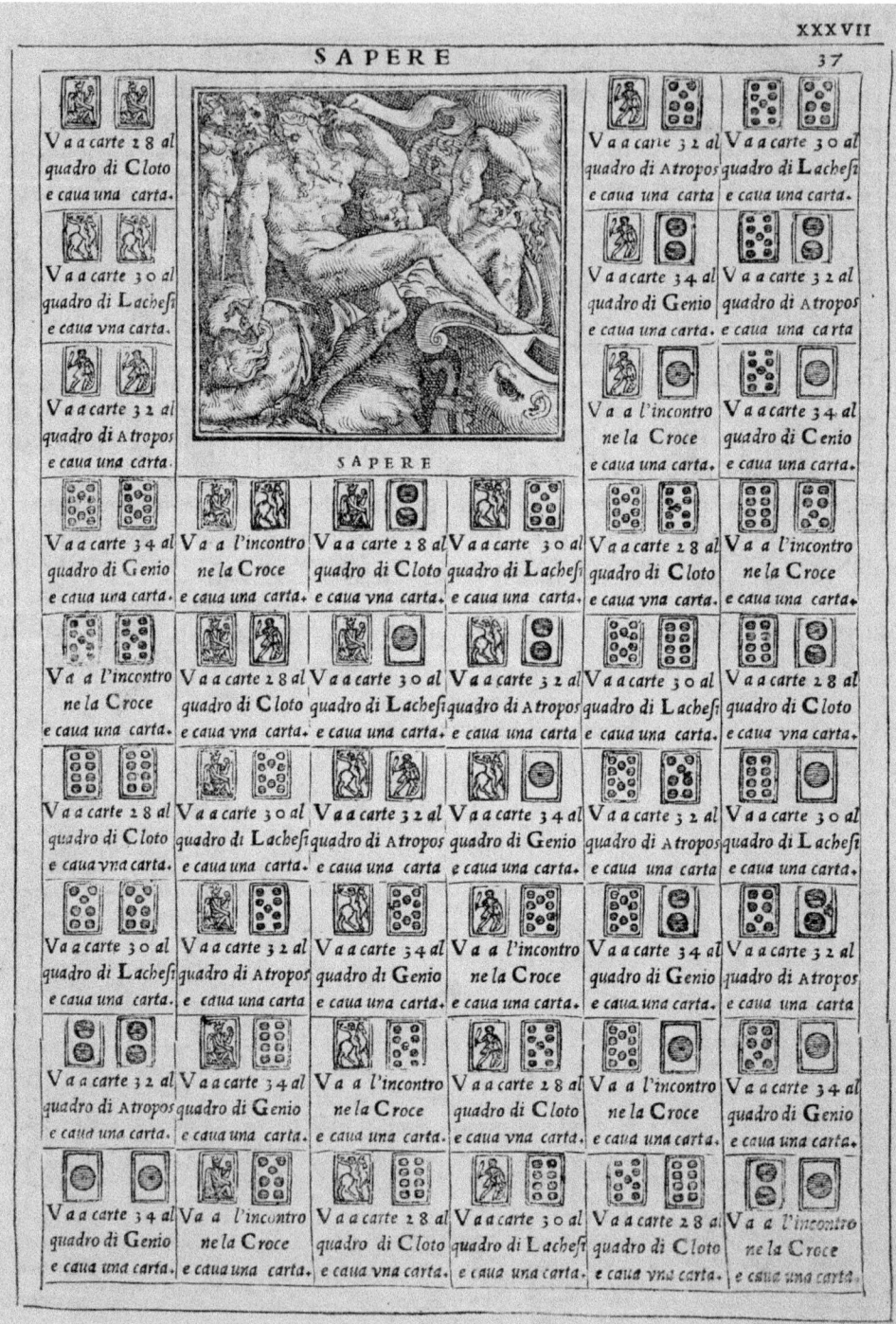

FIG. 5.6. 'Sapere', in Francesco Marcolini, *Le sorti.* [...] *intitolate giardino di pensieri* (Venice: Francesco Marcolini, 1540), p. 37. Archivio Storico Civico Biblioteca Trivulziana, Milan. © Comune di Milano.

A scholar of perspective like Barbaro may have been intrigued by this game of false appearances. One of the first to write about anamorphosis, in *La pratica della perspettiva* (The practice of perspective, 1568), Barbaro suggested that a painter be able 'to shadow and cover with several brush strokes the subject of his painting so that it shows a different appearance from what is actually drawn, showing landscapes, water, mountains, rocks, and other things different from what is painted. He can, indeed must, also deceive by cutting and separating lines that should be straight and continuous'.[40] In this landscape of deceit, aberrations of the gaze, false appearances, and doubts give the sense of a labyrinthine world. Barbaro was something of a pioneer but was not isolated. His studies on anamorphosis are consistent with a broader interest in this practice, which has been connected with 'a new sense of instability', in turn part of a larger, Europe-wide 'fascination with the disunity or incoherence of reality'.[41]

Certainly, in his *Predica*, Barbaro may be building on commonplaces, and yet some passages of his work are strongly emotionally charged, as when he suggests that everything is unstable and as dreadful as a dream. Thus is revealed the true nature of the dreams that make up our existence: they are fearful, nightmarish visions. Since we are lost in our dreams, we can infer that humanity is wandering in a maze of uneasy dreams, forever detached from truth, forever unable to abandon its condition of uncertainty:

> Underneath the moon
> One finds no
> Stability, nor something
> Which is not fearful
> Like a dream.[42]

Whoever is able to look beyond our sublunary world to the celestial skies where eternity rules will discover that it is only those who are there that are really alive, while we are in fact dead: 'asleep, | No, dead, is whoever | Lives here'.[43] This reversal of life and death, a displacement of the point of observation, is indeed an anamorphosis that reveals the presence of death beneath the surface of what appears to be life, much in the style of Hans Holbein's *The Ambassadors*, where a distorted skull lurks below a 'visual order' that is 'painstakingly naturalistic'.[44] Barbaro's interest in defining the nature of dreams gives way to the urge to describe human existence as a dreadful dream. All philosophical distinctions among the different kinds of dreams showcased in the previous sections of the *Predica dei sogni* make space for a reflection on dreaming as the painful, death-like condition that befell humankind after the fall of Adam. Unsurprisingly, the work closes with an invocation to God, begging delivery from the monsters that crowd our dreams:

> Please, Lord, remove
> Entirely from our eyes
> These infinite monsters
> That are the dreams we dream.[45]

It is probably not surprising, then, that Barbaro chose to include in the *Predica* a series of five sonnets on doubt titled 'Del dubbio' (On doubt), a unique treatise on doubt placed immediately after the main body of the work, as if to stress that doubt represents the most authentic aspect of our human condition. How else could it be, if life and death, dreaming and waking, illusions and reality dissolve into each other, leaving us struggling in that theatre of dark and painful shadows we call existence?

Barbaro's sonnets explore doubt from the psychological and intellectual point of view, stressing its potentialities but also its risks. The first sonnet explains how doubt originates from wonder and from the contrast between two seemingly irreconcilable explanations of a fact. This, however, leads to discovery of the truth. Doubt can dissolve long-lasting beliefs, boldly denying them ('negation ardita'); it has thus a positive, rejuvenating function. 'Wise doubting' ('saggio dubitar') prepares the intellect to deny what is wrong and give its assent to what is right.[46]

The second sonnet introduces some negative elements into the picture. The doubting intellect mixes true and false and can no longer discern one from the other. The impossibility of acting 'makes thought for him sad and murky' ('tristo gli rende e torbido il pensiero'). Doubt is 'weak and imperfect' ('debile e imperfetto'), impairing our judgement. If doubt is exceedingly protracted it annoys ('noia produce'); however, it may also result in joy and solace if it manages to grasp the truth ('ma s'al ver si piega | Allegrezza ne genera e conforto').[47]

The third sonnet expands on these feelings of happiness and accomplishment produced by doubt. Doubters are compared to those knitters who manage to find the end of a thread in a knot and with that suddenly undo the knot. Likewise with a doubter who grasps a glimpse of the truth: their 'invalid and lame' ('infermo e zoppo') intellect is then able to reach the whole truth. Like someone who wanders in the night, if one is able to find a light then one will be able to reach its origin; so too those who are able to discover a glimpse of truth will also be able to find its origin.[48]

Doubt is again highly praised in the fourth sonnet, where it is defined as the 'father of invention' ('padre all'inventione'). Doubt spurs those who are 'slow and lazy' ('tardo e pigro') to find answers and reasons; it also brings order to our knowledge, binding together that which is loose ('in dubitando si ritrova | Il modo di legar le cose sciolte'). What is more, doubt has the positive function of 'making peace where there is a perpetual war' ('e pace porre, ove sia guerra eterna').[49] Barbaro may be referring here to a figurative war between conflicting interpretations and reasons. It is hard not to connect this definition to Erasmus's use of doubt to tone down doctrinal controversies, the irenic function of doubt that will inspire Sebastian Castellion's *De arte dubitandi*.[50]

Compared to this positive assessment of doubt, the following sonnet, the last of the series, comes as an abrupt reversal. Here Barbaro seems to return to the negative connotations described in his second sonnet (and alluded to also in the other poems). Barbaro builds a shapeless monster without recognizable physiognomy — no hands, no feet, no face. It is Doubt, depicted in a way that would have challenged many a painter:

> If doubting had feet and life
> One would never see it moving forward or backward.
> If (it had) a tongue, it would not be able to either speak or be silent,

Either successfully or unsuccessfully.
If it had shoulders, arms, hands, and fingers
It would never want to begin or end a piece of work
And finally, placed between life and death
It would neither die nor live.
Hence it would be a displeasure to nature,
Hell, the world and heavens
To see such a stolid creature.
So it was wisely decided by the College
That it be shapeless, without a figure,
Without feet, without hands, without a face.[51]

Reading through these sonnets, one is compelled to mark the insistence on obscurity and darkness, often but not always counterbalanced by light. A whole of set of images also seems to point to melancholy. Even the shapeless figure described in the fifth sonnet recalls the monstrous nightmares produced by melancholy. There is no denying, then, that for all doubt's positive effects, Barbaro conveys an overall gloomy picture. As we have seen in the previous chapter, the decade of the 1540s seems to see an increased interest in doubt, especially in the Veneto. This appears to be related on the one hand to the new vernacular culture produced within the academies, where discourses on doubt seem to be flourishing. On the other hand, it is hard not to also connect this interest with ongoing religious discussions and the response from religious authorities. It may be only a coincidence, but it is certainly a significant one, that Barbaro's sonnets on doubt were published the same year the Tribunal of the Roman Inquisition was established. It seems undeniable that Barbaro's sonnets take the connection between doubt and vernacular poetry to a new level. While discussing specific doubts in poems was by no means uncommon, here is a series of sonnets dedicated to doubt itself. As in the case of Michelangelo, who in his poem hinted at the representation of doubt itself rather than to that of a specific story of doubt, we perceive here the urge to make sense of the very nature of doubt. In the 1530s and 1540s, attempts at rejuvenating vernacular culture began to clash with attempts at regulating this very culture. It is against the background of this increasingly fragile balance that we should project mid-sixteenth-century discourses on doubt. Academic culture was central in the elaboration of the culture of doubt to which Barbaro contributed; it is to this culture that we now turn our attention.

From the Infiammati ...

I will focus especially on Barbaro's membership in the Academy of the Infiammati, which promoted the use of the vernacular to read, comment, and translate the classics (among which Aristotle's *Ethics* and *Rhetoric*). Rhetoric, eloquence, and poetry were the basis of a programme focused on shaping the new political elite; unlike other academies, the Infiammati pursued forms of knowledge that could be fruitfully applied in civil life. It has been suggested that the academy's goal was not only 'innovation and dissemination' but also 'the research of truth, which should be explored, especially in philosophical meditations, with a mind free from all rigid respect of the principle of authority'.[52] Many people flocked to the Thursday and Sunday lectures, and external attendees were more assiduous than the academicians themselves.[53] Among the members of the Infiammati, Sperone Speroni, who was its *principe* between the fall of 1541 and the spring of 1542, played a pivotal role in advocating the use of the vernacular. It is important to understand the academy's intellectual agenda, and how it may have had an impact on one of its members in particular, Fortunato Martinengo.

First, however, we must step back in time to the winter of 1529, when a group of humanists and patricians who had gathered in Venice to discuss the immortality of the soul ended up instead debating whether an active life was preferable to a contemplative one. This little crowd of distinguished people, including Cardinal Ercole Gonzaga, Giovan Francesco Valier, Luigi (Alvise) Priuli, and the poet Antonio Brocardo, were gathered in the *palazzo* of Gasparo Contarini, whom we met in Chapter 4. This was around the time that Pope Clement VII met Charles V in Bologna to give him the imperial crown. Contarini had been an ambassador to both Clement VII and Charles V and was therefore well informed about what was happening behind the curtains of this historical meeting in Bologna. What was at stake in those days was no less than an end to the Italian Wars, and in that game Contarini played a crucial part, as Cardinal Gonzaga acknowledged: 'I know [...] that at present your virtue should rather concern itself in putting an end to the wars of Italy.'[54]

The conversation that supposedly took place in Venice between Contarini and his friends is recorded in a dialogue by Sperone Speroni titled *Dialogo della vita attiva e contemplativa* (A dialogue on active and contemplative life), probably composed a few years later in the mid-1530s and not completed. The dialogue explores a recurring topic in Speroni's works. In it, Valier supports the pre-eminence of an active life and Contarini, a contemplative one. The conversation, however, originates from Valier's 'doubt' regarding his own attitude to this problem. In his words, he is actually 'drowning in this doubt', to which Contarini replies, highlighting the positive function of doubt: 'You should thank the Lord for enlightening you enough to doubt, because doubt is nothing else than the occasion for discovery.'[55] Speroni depicts Contarini as yearning for the contemplative life he has always desired, as if civic duty were a mere, somewhat unpleasant interlude within a life of study. He speaks of his present condition as a 'prison in which I hope I will not stay much longer', a prison he has chosen because of social pressure and his peers' judgement.[56] It is not necessary to follow all the arguments in favour of one or the other choice; it is enough to note that Speroni has Valier voice ideas he himself will expound in other works. Among them is the idea that humans are created by God half-way between animals and angels, and that what is peculiar to the human race is being able to act virtuously (virtue meaning essentially civic virtue: *operar civilmente*); while speculation, especially in matters pertaining God and metaphysics, is vain, since the truth is unattainable and we cannot fully know things as they are.[57] Human knowledge is just a shadow of God's understanding, whereas virtue is a special attribute of humanity:

> Understanding through speculation does not entail a perfect understanding of
> truth, but it is a shadow and an imitation of the perfect knowledge that God has
> of the truth; but being perfectly good, i.e., possessing good and virtuous habits,
> is a special privilege of man's nature.[58]

Speroni's position reflects a fundamental distrust towards what he calls the
'incertitude' of knowledge.[59] For Speroni, given the general imperfection of our
understanding, its weakness and ambiguity, it is important that we turn our efforts
from speculative sciences — accessible only to a restricted elite of philosophers, and
possibly not even to them — to more practical and useful forms of knowledge.[60]

   Speroni expounded on these ideas to a greater extent in his *Dialogo della retorica*
(A dialogue on rhetoric), where he suggested that the knowledge of the orator 'is
not a science of truth but an opinion and a likeness of truth'.[61] In this work Speroni
goes even further when discussing the utility of rhetoric in civic life. Orators act as
mediators of truth, presenting their audiences with a verisimilitude of it. Although
orators act merely on probable and uncertain opinions, they nevertheless deserve
praise, for these opinions are the only ones accessible to the majority of the citizens,
and thus the only effective ones in civic life.[62] Within political and social life we
deal, in fact, with things whose nature varies, so that they can be either good
or bad, a vice or a virtue, depending on the evolution of laws and customs. The
ability to argue in favour of or against the same thing is thus more productive than
scientific knowledge, which relies on immutable demonstrations:

> For if the same act in different times can be banned or praised by the city's
> authorities, it can be vice or virtue, it is good and reasonable that our republics
> are wisely ruled not according to demonstrative sciences, true and certain in
> all times, but by rhetorical opinions, which are variable and changeable (as our
> deeds and laws are).[63]

There is thus a radical difference between philosophers, who are used to dealing
with eternal truth(s), and those who administer the *rem publicam*, who are supposed
to resort to *prudentia*, or the ability to discern the best course of action while taking
into account the mutability of contexts. It is also worth noting that philosophers
are by nature characterized by a certain degree of scepticism: 'And it is true that
philosophers [...] the more they know, the less they believe.'[64] One perceives in
these passages from *Della retorica* the influence of sophistry on Speroni's thought,
and in fact some of the points discussed in this treatise are also touched upon in a
short text titled 'In difesa dei sofisti' (In defence of sophists).[65] Here Speroni claims
that sophists are the masters of imperfection and can 'teach us to live imperfectly',
which is what we are left to do, since our 'civilization' is in itself 'imperfection'.[66]
Sophistry thus becomes the mirror of our human (one is tempted to say 'existential')
condition, of our own being:

> Our very being is a sophist, because it is not but looks like it is: it is not because
> the present being is an indivisible moment that rather was, and perhaps it will
> not be again, and only what is immortal truly is.[67]

Speroni's disquieting remarks open a window on the vacuum lying at the heart of
our human condition, which is a mere imitation of life (we have seen something

similar voiced by Daniele Barbaro from a different standpoint). Speroni wrote 'In difesa' in 1542, the same year that Aretino, himself member of the Infiammati, published his comedy *Lo Ipocrito* (The Hypocrite), with a double dedication to the Duke of Urbino and Daniele Barbaro. The almost obsessive refrain of the comedy was 'nada es todo, todo es nada' (Spanish for 'nothing is all, all is nothing'). All is nothing: a bitter remark on the part of the Scourge of Princes. The failure of the Diet of Ratisbon (1541), and with it, of the hopes of peace between the Catholic and the Reformed worlds, and the establishment of the Tribunal of the Inquisition in that very year probably exacerbated an already existing sense of anxiety and hollowness. If nihilism were an applicable category, one would be tempted to use it to describe some of these intellectuals' statements. Certainly, Speroni reinstates uncertainty and probability at the centre of civil life. In doing so, however, he embraces it and turns it into a viable option for intellectuals and citizens. Leaving aside lofty philosophical speculations, his rhetoric tinged with sophistry and exposed in the vernacular becomes a weapon in the hands of the people, the *vulgo*; and 'what Speroni calls "vulgo" is the Venetian merchants and people working with material goods, who can build, maintain, and increase the wealth of their republic'.[68] Whatever value Speroni assigns to rhetoric — scholars have conflicting views on this point — I would argue that his discussion of it goes beyond the mere purpose of providing a tool for shaping a new ruling class.[69] Immediately beneath the surface of the academic discussions on rhetoric and the contemplative life lies the sense of instability, imperfection, uncertainty, even the hollowness of human life.

Daniele Barbaro, who was also a member of the Infiammati, shared Speroni's interest in eloquence and rhetoric. In his treatise *Della eloquenza* (On eloquence) Barbaro too reflects on doubt, which at this stage should come not as a surprise. We have already considered his sonnets on doubt; to this, we could add that in the early 1540s Barbaro was busying himself with sceptical philosophy, as his discussion of Cicero's *Academica* of around 1542/43 shows.[70] The publication history of *Della eloquenza* is interesting in itself because it connects the Academies of the Infiammati and the Dubbiosi (to which I shall come back shortly): the ideas discussed in the work are comparable to those of Speroni, while the people who took care of its editorial process were members of the Dubbiosi.

The dialogue was printed in 1557, when Girolamo Ruscelli finally got hold of Barbaro's manuscript, handed to him by his fellow *Dubbioso* Francesco Maccasciola (or Maccasola). The dedication letter claims that the *Della eloquenza* was drafted much earlier, in 1536, although we could push its origin to an even earlier period.[71] The first part is a dialogue between Nature, Art, and Soul, which aims to embody itself as an eloquent man. Again, I will not follow all of Barbaro's at-times convoluted arguments, but limit my analysis to the role of doubt, which comes into play in connection with persuasion, the main object of eloquence. One can obtain persuasion only when the soul is at rest and not troubled by any passion. This is the ideal condition for the soul to experience the pleasure that accompanies learning. This state of mind is attained through a sort of sceptical suspension of judgement, and this can be done effortlessly [by] placing oneself in between yes and no, as does the person who is in doubt. For it is easier to reach a conclusion and admit the truth moving from doubt than if one has an already existing opinion.[72]

Doubt appears to be a precondition of knowledge, necessary to distinguish among different opinions. Opinion seems to retain the meaning examined in Chapter 1, unsurprising given that Barbaro studied Aristotelian philosophy at Padua. Opinion is thus a 'doubtful knowledge', but only those who possess real wisdom perceive its uncertain nature.[73] To all others, opinion is indistinguishable from truth. Opinion is neither ignorance nor science. Rather, it is an intermediate form of knowledge that differs from doubt because it 'leans more towards one part than towards the other', whereas doubt keeps the mind suspended between denial and assent.[74] But precisely because it suspends our assent to already existing opinions, doubt predisposes the mind to accept new questions and new explanations.[75] This opens the path to persuasion, which moves from 'the similitude of things' rather than addressing directly 'the depth of things'.[76] Doubt and opinion together shape a form of knowledge that despite its uncertainty is more useful than that of natural and moral philosophers, whom Barbaro does not spare from his lampooning. Like his friend Speroni, Barbaro targets the vain speculations of philosophers, to which he prefers persuasion, which if based on reason can even turn into science.[77] However Barbaro, also not unlike Speroni, shares a certain pessimism: if we are born with an inclination towards truth, we are nonetheless unable to attain it. This is because of the weakness of our constitution, in which the senses prevail over sheer reason, thus making our knowledge weak and confused.[78]

One finds similar ideas aired by another member of the Infiammati, Alessandro Piccolomini. In his preface to *La seconda parte de la filosofia naturale* (The second part of natural philosophy, 1554), he chastises the attempts of philosophers and scientists to know what should remain inaccessible. These arrogant researchers of truth 'move from doubt to doubt' without reaching a point where the exceedingly curious intellect can eventually rest.[79] The 'greedy doubts' ('ingorde dubitationi') of those who try to transcend the set boundaries of the human intellect become particularly embarrassing when dealing with God, the understanding of which requires something other than opinion or science.[80] Piccolomini seems sceptical of the power of human reasoning in other works as well, an attitude that can be traced back to Pomponazzi's teaching. In general, the 'crisis of trust' in human reason led at this juncture to privileging an active and civic life over a contemplative one.[81]

There was, therefore, among the members of the Infiammati a common understanding of the limits of human reason, and the drive towards new, more flexible forms of knowledge able to take into account such limitations as well as the provisional nature of laws and institutions. With the common good of the community as their lodestar, the Infiammati acknowledged the importance of doubt as part of our experience of reality. Even more, they were able to turn it from a liability into the driving force at the basis of a rejuvenation of science.

... to the Dubbiosi

Around 1550 a gentleman from Brescia, Count Fortunato Martinengo (1512–1552), founded an academy which he called 'dei Dubbiosi' (the Doubtful). Martinengo was the first to choose this name for an academy, although other academies by the same name were founded in the following decades.[82] The academy was short-lived, as was Martinengo himself: he died two years later, and the academy did not continue without him. Little is known about this academy other than what we can gather from the two main works its members produced and other desultory sources. It was based in Venice, although Fortunato also resided in his hometown of Brescia. Martinengo has been a long-forgotten figure, and only recently has scholarship begun to reassess his role as a man of letters and a patron of artists and writers alike.[83] Martinengo was born into one of the most prominent feudal families in all of the Serenissima Republic and one of the most steadily involved in religious dissent.[84] He himself was deeply engaged in the religious debates of his time. Among his friends and acquaintances, one finds some of the most innovative and influential intellectuals of the mid-cinquecento: Anton Francesco Doni, Girolamo Ruscelli, Sperone Speroni, Bernardino Tomitano, Ortensio Lando, Pier Paolo Vergerio, Pietro Aretino, Niccolò Franco, and many others. His intellectual background was shaped by his attendance at the University of Padua and, most notably, by his membership in the Paduan Academy of the Infiammati.[85]

Besides being a patron of the arts, Martinengo was the author of a handful of poems and some letters.[86] His poems disclose a tormented spirituality and an acute, somewhat melancholic awareness of the disastrous workings of time and death. Martinengo usually describes life as vain, a mere shadow, a brief illusion rushing towards its end. 'I walk step by step to my end | Nay, I rush to it, without even realizing it': this is the beginning of one of his sonnets that concludes thus: 'When will it be that, to leave her suffering | She [the soul] will unburden herself and fly away | From this false to the other, true life?'[87] The vanity of this world is the subject of another sonnet, whose first quatrain runs as follows: 'Alas, how did these and the previous years go | Without my realizing their passing | Alas, that I now know this vain and short | Life that is nothing but shadow and grief.'[88]

Martinengo's letters offer precious glimpses into the evolution of his spirituality and on the growing importance of the study of Scripture over his previous philosophical interests. The dedication letters of the several works addressed to him as well as the numerous references to him in some of his friends' works provide us with a rich picture of Martinengo's many and diverse intellectual interests. The portrait by Moretto now in the National Gallery in London reveals not only the external features of Count Martinengo — a somewhat hefty man, clad in a luxurious ermine-hemmed robe — but also something of his psychology. Despite the opulent setting and the antiques displayed around him, bearing witness to his refined taste, the count shows an unmistakably melancholic attitude, reinforced by the gesture of resting his cheek on the palm of his hand. Scholars have hypothesized that Martinengo was mourning the loss of his beloved wife, Livia D'Arco. A certain melancholy is, however, characteristic of Martinengo, who is otherwise described as a jovial and pleasant man, capable of making jokes.

When he founded his academy, Martinengo had been acquainted with Speroni and Barbaro for years. To this background he added his own religious anxieties. The name of his academy, 'the Dubbiosi', reflects the somewhat playful element that academies' names often entailed, but we would not be far off the mark in saying that it also reflected Martinengo's genuine interest in doubt.

The Academy of the Dubbiosi gathered intellectuals gravitating around Padua and Venice, although it had strong ties with the Kingdom of Naples. Only two works can be connected to the academy with certainty. The first, by the polygraph Girolamo Ruscelli, is a *Lettura* (A reading, 1552) on a love sonnet in praise of Maria d'Aragona, Marchioness of Vasto. The work aims to prove women's perfection while also explaining the 'Platonic ladder' for ascending from earthly love to spiritual contemplation. The second work connected with the academy is a collection of poems in praise of Maria's sister Giovanna d'Aragona, titled *Del tempio alla divina signora Giovanna d'Aragona* (The temple to the divine lady Giovanna d'Aragona, 1554).[89]

Maria and Giovanna d'Aragona were the daughters of Ferdinando of Castellana, illegitimate son of King Ferrante I of Aragona, and Castellana Cardona. Maria (1503–1568) was familiar with Giulia Gonzaga and Vittoria Colonna as well as with Juan de Valdés, Bernardino Ochino, and Pietro Carnesecchi, the Florentine humanist and reformer tried by the Inquisition and eventually beheaded in 1567. Giovanna (1502–1575) was the wife of the powerful Ascanio Colonna (1500–1557) and therefore Vittoria Colonna's sister-in-law.[90] The academy's ties with Naples were particularly tight: the driving force behind the *Tempio* was in fact the poet Ferrante Carafa (1509–1587), who wanted it to be dedicated to both Maria and Giovanna. The academicians discussed the request and eventually rejected it, resorting to the classical *exemplum* of Marcus Claudius Marcellus, who wanted to dedicate the same temple to Virtue and Honour but was prevented from doing so by the Roman pontiffs. The academicians decided that Ruscelli's *Lettura* should function as a temple in honour of Maria, while the *Tempio* should be devoted exclusively to Giovanna. As Ruscelli boasted in an introductory text, poems had been sent and, as he was writing, were still pouring in from all over the world; members of the Dubbiosi could in fact count on 'poems in every language, and we already have [poems] in German, Flemish, French, Slavic, Moresque or Arab, Hungarian, Polish, Chaldaic or Indian, Hebrew, and in other languages'.[91] Ruscelli was perhaps overselling his book, but it is true that the *Tempio* includes poems in Italian, Latin, ancient Greek, and Spanish.

In the mid-1540s Martinengo had travelled to Naples, where he made the acquaintance of the Valdésian intelligentsia and become a member of the local Academy of the Sereni (of which Carafa was one of the founders), which explains the Dubbiosi's privileged relationship with Naples. During his journey, Martinengo had the chance to meet Vittoria Colonna and Giulia Gonzaga, whom he enthusiastically praised in a letter of June 1546 to the Bishop of Capodistria, Pietro Paolo Vergerio. He described Colonna as 'burning with the love of Christ'; the 'power of her reasoning' was such that 'it is almost as if from her mouth came out chains attracting the spirits of her listeners'. But it was possibly Giulia Gonzaga who made the strongest impression on Martinengo: 'I will only say this, that never has the presence of any other woman stunned me like hers.'[92]

When he founded the Academy of the Dubbiosi, Martinengo was well advanced on his spiritual path. Besides his acquaintance with Neapolitan Valdésians and with reformers such as Vergerio, Martinengo counted among his friends the little-known intellectual and poet Giovanni Andrea Ugoni, tried twice by the Inquisition. Unfortunately, we know too little about the academy and its intellectual programme to propose hypotheses concerning possible religious debates among its members. What we know suggests that discussions concerned love, poetry, commentaries on Petrarch, and the *querelle des femmes*, with the academicians maintaining the superiority of women.[93] The solemn beginning of the *Lettura*, a hypertrophic Neoplatonic reading of a sonnet by Giovanni Battista d'Azzia, immediately proposes a 'high and above any other most important doubt'. This doubt troubles the minds of those who consider

> [h]ow it is that, God having created the universe, this wondrous machinery, out of the sheer infinite richness of His love [...] and placed man at its centre, [and made him] the master of all things belonging to this inferior world [...] to no other purpose than, after his brief pilgrimage down here, he could ascend to Heaven walking on the feet of his holy works, still the majority of us are so crooked that, like the Prophet cries out, no one is to be found who does any good.[94]

The pages that follow will teach the stages of spiritual ascent to God's vision and contemplation. Sight is key to reaching this stage, as, platonically, the contemplation of God moves from earthly beauty. However, since sight, like fire, is good in itself but dangerous in the hands of those who cannot properly handle it, we need someone who can teach us how to turn it in the right direction, 'this greatest of all secrets'.[95] Ruscelli feels he is up to this demanding task: the rest of the work will address precisely the 'secret' of turning our contemplation to God. We are still at the threshold of the text, and at this point Ruscelli discloses a glimpse of the academy's activity:

> And because last Sunday I was commanded by order of the most illustrious and right honourable sir, the President of this perpetually glorious Academy that, following the established order, today I should take this place and read the sonnet by Petrarch that follows those we have already read, it seemed to me apt that, instead of a sonnet by Petrarch, I should bring to your Lordships today a new sonnet by the most illustrious sir the Marquis della Terza, addressed to the Marchioness of Vasto.[96]

From this emphatic declaration, we learn that the academy gathered weekly, possibly on a Sunday, in order to read and comment on Petrarch's poems. We do not know which sonnets had been read when Ruscelli decided to disobey Martinengo's orders, but we can certainly assume that the academicians discussed love doubts — a preferred entertainment of courtly culture, as we have seen — from a high spiritual and philosophical perspective. Around Martinengo, however, other figures promoted different forms of doubtfulness.

A Master Doubter: Ortensio Lando and His Virtual Academies

One such figure was the polygraph Ortensio Lando (born at some point between 1500 and 1512 and died between 1556 and 1559), with whom Martinengo enjoyed a long-lasting friendship. Lando presents a challenge to scholars, who are still grappling with the many pseudonyms he used and with the gaps in his biography. He is best known today for his *Paradossi* (Paradoxes, 1543). Paradoxes are, broadly speaking, part of the culture of doubt, as they present alternative ways to look at reality, suggesting that opposite interpretations of the same phenomenon are always possible.[97] Lando certainly inclined to heterodox ideas, although he was a master at dissimulating them. Some scholars have suggested that he shared the radical Anabaptist ideas that spread in the Veneto in the 1540s and early 1550s. His multifarious output included funeral sermons and paradoxes, books of doubts and collections of letters, moral dialogues, catalogues of notable things, and much more. Lando also authored the first Italian translation of Thomas More's *Utopia*, printed in Venice in 1548 by Anton Francesco Doni. Lando travelled extensively throughout Italy and Europe, and his immense network of friends and acquaintances would be hard to summarize. Saying that Lando was one of the most fascinating and enigmatic characters in the first half of the sixteenth century is no exaggeration.

We do not know when Lando first came in contact with Martinengo, but we know that he praised him as early as 1540 in a work titled *Desiderii Erasmi funus* (The funeral of Desiderius Erasmus), an ambiguous text describing Erasmus's funeral that has divided scholars as to its interpretation, although it should be regarded as a satirical attack on Erasmus.[98] After that, Martinengo features in many of Lando's works, as do many of the people gravitating around Martinengo and the Dubbiosi. For this reason, it is not too far-fetched to turn to Lando's works to understand more of what may have interested the academicians. Two works in particular stand out, which may be read as something like virtual academies devoted to the discussion of doubts and questions. The first is the *Lettere di molte valorose donne* (Letters of many valorous women, 1548; 1549, revised) and the second is the *Quattro libri de dubbi* (Four books of doubts, 1552, lacking the fourth book; 1556, complete).

The *Valorose donne* is a textual conundrum, as is often the case with Lando's works. Scholars are divided as to the real authorship of these letters supposedly exchanged by 181 women of generally high social standing. Although the most plausible and generally accepted hypothesis is that the letters are Lando's invention, the suggestion that he could draw on original material should not be entirely ruled out.[99] While the historical identity of many of the women involved in these literary exchanges is beyond dispute, that of others is less sure. All scholars agree, however, that finding an overarching plan that ties the letters together is seemingly impossible. Lando seems to endorse conflicting ideas, resorting to his usual style based on doubt and paradox, to cover the traces of his ideas. According to Meredith K. Ray, if a plan underlies the collection it is that of bitter criticism of humanistic culture. The display of exempla and *auctoritates*, the lists of episodes and anecdotes, mostly coming from Jean Ravisius Textor's *Officina* (a famous reference book), serve the purpose of parodying a sterile humanistic culture that Lando, a religious dissident, 'had come to find empty, inferior to the one true source of knowledge, scripture'.[100] Ray, building on Paul Grendler's intuition, stresses that Lando's insistence in the text on arguing from both sides of the same issue (Lando had studied theology and medicine in Bologna and was therefore familiar with the tradition of the *disputationes in utramque partem*) serves a double purpose: to ridicule humanistic rhetoric, and eventually 'to cast doubt on the importance of the question'.[101] Lando capitalized on the growing importance of the *querelle des femmes*, on the role that women assumed in Reformed circles (religion is one the main threads of the letters), and on the appetite in the print market for collections of letters. The encomiastic sonnet by Pietro Aretino — the inventor of the 'book of letters' — placed at the end of the collection, along with those of other famous writers, is in this sense a guarantee of the work's excellence. Nonetheless, what drives Lando's publication is not merely the desire to exploit a promising niche of the print market or the patronage of ladies of high social standing. Many of the subjects discussed in the letters are paramount in both Lando's output and mid-sixteenth-century culture.

One may wonder whether it is legitimate to draw conclusions from a male-authored collection of letters by women. The *Valorose donne* should be considered in the context of Lando's production, especially in the period between the mid-1540s and the early 1550s. In 1544 he published a work titled *Della vera tranquillità dell'animo* (On the true tranquillity of the soul) under the name of Isabella Sforza (1503–1561; she belonged to a minor branch of the Milanese Sforza family). In the dedicatory letter, Lando explains that he himself had been writing a similar work but had then come across Isabella's text. Lando was ready to acknowledge its superiority and decided to publish it instead that his own work. In fact, the *Della vera tranquillità* is a work by Lando, although in the dedication letter he presents himself as a mere editor. In 1552 Lando published a dialogue on Holy Scripture, in which he acts as a sort of master of and spiritual counsellor to Lucrezia Gonzaga. In the same year, however, Lando edited Gonzaga's *Lettere*. It is possible, as Ray suggests, that Lando 'assisted the novice writer with the publication and perhaps even the composition of the *Lettere*'.[102] It is undeniable, however, that in the *Lettere* Lucrezia 'has become the teacher, assuming the active role played by many women (such as Vittoria Colonna) within the evangelist movement in Italy'.[103] The *Valorose donne* therefore falls into a period when Lando was promoting innovative projects of women writing in different forms. Women's letter-writing in print was at that juncture one such innovative project. Ray has perfectly captured the main difference between the *Valorose donne* and Gonzaga's *Lettere*:

> As the first *epistolario* to be published under a female name following the *Valorose donne* [...] Gonzaga's *Lettere* cannot help but draw comparison to their Landian predecessor. [...] The *Lettere* are largely devoid of the 'female' content so important to the *Valorose donne*. Instead, they focus almost exclusively on constructing Gonzaga as an exemplary, authoritative female figure.[104]

The 'female content' to which Ray refers is represented by the many letters in the *Valorose donne* that touch on domestic life as well as the feminine sphere, from marriage and childbirth and childrearing, to beauty secrets and recipes. In these portions of the work, Lando 'grants the reader a seemingly intimate glimpse into the private world of women, a female network of mothers, sisters, and friends in which advice, comfort, and support are passed from one to the other'.[105] It is certainly female experience as seen by a man, but it is also true that Lando often uses it to indicate 'that women's knowledge which comes from direct experience is superior to that of men', at least for all that concerns the female body.[106] If this is a fundamental point — since here women become spokespersons for Lando's critical attitude towards academic culture — it is also crucial to stress the reference to the 'female network' created in the *Valorose donne*. Lando's collection of letters revolves around real, partially real, or imagined networks of women that often coincide with Lando's own networks. The exhibition of sociability is key in Lando's works, and if it serves as a means to seek and reinforce protection, it can also serve, given the religious content of his works, as a 'call to arms' to people who share his ideas of spiritual renewal. We will never know to what extent Lando lends his voice to his characters (men and women alike) or borrows their voices, but certainly he brings to the fore ideas, names, and voices that otherwise would have been restricted to private circles.[107]

With a paradoxical twist, a fictional text such as the *Valorose donne* brings in an element of realism, while its ventriloquism in a way reinforces women's voices. Again, as Ray has suggested, Lando's 'impersonations' resulted in 'public fame and recognition for the women who inspired them. Lando played a fundamental role in what we may call the manufacture of female cultural reputation'.[108] In this process there were certain shadows and contradictions, and Lando was aware that he would benefit from these literary attempts. Undeniably, nonetheless, in both the *Valorose donne* and the *Quattro libri de dubbi*, women play a role whose importance can hardly be underestimated: that of calling into question official narratives. Their intellectual brilliance comes to the fore, and while we may argue that their voices served to shield Lando's own ideas when it came to embarrassing religious themes, the historical importance of women in religious discussions confers a realism on Lando's works.

Important as the questions and contradictions in *Valorose donne* are, they should not prevent us from looking for traces of a 'sociability of doubt' in the letters. Whether this sociability was real, an imitation of reality, or merely imagined by Lando as he would have liked it to be is a matter we can leave unanswered, since we lack sufficient evidence and sometimes these levels are conflated. Because virtually all aspects of Lando's style are meant to raise doubts, I will limit myself to the explicit references to doubts or conditions of doubt. Lando stages a sort of long-distance conversation between interlocutors. Even if the letters are not, in the large majority of cases, followed by an answer, they are nevertheless morsels of an ongoing dialogue: they allude to events familiar to the writer and to the addressee, and they often seem to follow up on real conversations, meetings, or other forms of communication. The result is a kaleidoscopic conversation touching upon various matters, from love and married life to art and religion, from the superiority of women over men to ancient history and erudition.

This form of virtual sociability often discloses glimpses of real-life aggregation. An exchange of letters between Ottavia Baiarda and Camilla Testa is one such example. Ottavia was born in 1524 into a noble family from Parma, while Camilla Testa was a learned woman from Rome.[109] Ottavia writes from Pavia (she had married Manfrino, a member of the local Beccaria family), asking for 'the solution to some doubts that the other day were discussed in my house by ingenious women'.[110] More than the content of these twenty-some doubts, all pertaining to love, it is important to pay attention to this form of sociability, a sort a domestic academy where 'ingenious' women convened to discuss doubts. Only one year before the *Valorose donne* was published, Tullia d'Aragona (1501/04–1556) had printed her *Dialogo dell'infinità d'amore* (Dialogue on the infinity of love, 1547) a text allegedly recording 'a certain discussion, which took place in my home some months ago', as she claimed in her dedication to Cosimo de' Medici. The same house is described by one of the interlocutors of the dialogue as 'a universal and prestigious academy'.[111] Lando may have had in mind this and similar experiences, although Ottavia's doubts are not original: she (or Lando on her behalf) draws them from the *Aura* by Gian Giacomo Calandra, known to sixteenth-century readers (and to us) through Mario Equicola's *Libro de natura de amore*, as noted at the beginning of this chapter.[112]

In her reply to Ottavia, Camilla, who claims to be too old to talk of love, playfully rebukes her: 'You suggest to me an Iliad of obscure questions so that I can solve them for you.' However, she goes on to say that because in Ottavia's house 'learned and ingenious people meet', she will in turn propose some questions. Interestingly, and probably in keeping with Camilla's age, her questions verge on love from a more 'physiological' and sexual perspective; we may even identify them as problems of natural philosophy.[113] Yet Camilla debases love, warning Ottavia to avoid it, for love 'is an evil thing that turns us from wise into fools, it deprives us of our free will, it turns us away from the love of our husbands'.[114] Isabella Pezzini has stressed the parodic effect of this reply, put as it is in the mouth of someone who represents herself as so old that 'these wrinkles of mine, these huge and shaky teeth of mine make love run away a thousand miles'.[115] Camilla's caricatured self-description raises questions about her 'doubts' ('Why men with thin legs are more lustful. Why birds that fly less are more lustful', etc.; we will see Lando deal with this kind of 'doubt' in the *Quattro libri de dubbi*).[116] Although Lando was drawing on pre-existing encyclopedic sources, we cannot fail to perceive in Camilla's questions what Pezzini calls 'a morbid tone' that 'invests with parody and desecrating irony also the medical-philosophical tradition of sixteenth-century culture'.[117] In other words, whatever meaning we assign here to 'doubt', it seems clear that doubts per se are less important than the strategy within which Lando uses them. As we have seen and will see again, the context of doubts is often more significant than their content.

Other letters include questions or doubts that sit at the intersection of ancient history and what we may call 'religious history'. A letter written by Lucrezia Picinarda Crotta from Cremona to Cinzia Vannini opens with a recap of a series of problems previously posed by Vannini to Picinardi (we do not have a reply, but the opening lines hint at an ongoing discussion):

You would like to know from me [...] how comes it that women are represented by ancient writers as less perfect than men. Why there is the saying that once you take away or put out the lamp, all women have the same nature and the same will. For what reason Romans forbade wine to women; why Love was painted winged; why in Caria women acting as priests grow a beard; and who suggested to Phydias that he paint Venus on a tortoise. For the time being, I will answer these present questions of yours to the best of my knowledge.[118]

More significant is a letter written by Emilia D'Arco to Costanza Borella. Emilia was perhaps a sister of Livia D'Arco, Fortunato Martinengo's wife. The letter, once again, suggests an ongoing discussion, a habit or practice of meeting, either in the real space of salons or in the virtual space of letters, to discuss doubts and questions:

The other day I begged of you that you send me the solution to the following doubts, i.e., for what reason Romans greeted the gods with their head uncovered and man with their head covered; and in the same vein, what pushed them to make sacrifices to Saturn and Honour without wearing anything on their head. I also prayed of you that you explain through some letters for what reasons sons accompanied their fathers to their tomb wearing a veil on their head and daughters with a naked head. I wait for your answer to these doubts.[119]

We may see in these doubts a form of merely erudite curiosity, but they imply also a certain attention to contradictions and inconsistencies in ancient sources and the desire to make sense of apparently problematic passages. More than an antiquarian and philological preoccupation with the past, we can see here at work the parodic erudition that scholars have observed in Lando's *Valorose donne*. There is a further level of reading: these doubts seem to mock Roman ceremonies and their inconsistencies. The accumulation of conflicting and seemingly unreasonable practices casts a veil of barely perceptible irony on Emilia's antiquarian preoccupations. And for anyone familiar with Lando's (or, for that matter, with Fortunato Martinengo's) views on religion, irony about religious ceremonies would immediately suggest criticism of the Roman Church. That such doubts are voiced by a relative of Fortunato Martinengo is all the more significant.

However, doubts in the *Valorose donne* were not confined to this form of learned entertainment. When it came to religious matters, doubts became far more serious and could concern such delicate issues as conversion, or the choice of evangelical purity over worldly temptations. In these cases, the meaning of 'doubt' switches back to its more familiar connotation of 'state of mind' or 'spiritual condition'. At the opening of the collection, we find a letter by Isabella d'Este Gonzaga, Marchioness of Mantua, written to a Jewish woman also from Mantua, Pazienza Pontremoli. Isabella would like Pazienza to convert, since everyone knows 'the fame, resounding everywhere, of your virtue and of your goodness'. Isabella goes on to promise that all the women of the ruling family will act like mothers to Pazienza. What is more, she promises to find for her

[a] nice little husband, shrewd but not deceitful, bold but not reckless, whose eloquence is free and clear, but not annoying and tiring; his bites, with which he gladly pierces the priests' avarice, are neither those of a dog or a wolf, but those of a tame lamb. [...] Your house will never be home to any melancholic feeling.[120]

The chosen husband was one Marco Antonio Sidonio, a sort of actor and buffoon, whom Lando himself praised despite including him on a list of 'flatterers, buffoons, and parasites'.[121] Pazienza's reply is a display of both biblical and classical erudition. It is also a precious document — despite and beneath the literary patina — concerning her perplexity. Whether this is a real document or an attempt on Lando's part to represent the possible scruples and state of mind of a person considering conversion, it depicts a condition of doubt and distress:

> On the other hand, I remain doubtful [worried] that, by converting to Christianity, I may offend the divine Majesty. I live in anguish that, should I confess that Christ is the true Messiah, I may provoke Moses's disdain and the curse of the whole Synagogue against me. I do not know (wretched me) where I can turn to find help and advice. Your letters have moved me infinitely [...] but I ponder, my Lady, on the Holy Scripture's promises that when the Messiah will come, he will resurrect Israel and we, poor Jews, are still in our diaspora. [...] What is more, I see that our Law was given publicly by God through Moses's hands on Mount Sinai [...] whereas yours was given secretly by the hands and the confession of twelve poor and barefooted people; besides, I cannot but fully trust our Rabbis, who have a very different opinion of your Messiah than yours [...]. You, while I wait for the Spirit to reveal me what I am to do, pray for me.[122]

This bold and at times harsh letter opens with a statement of doubt and anguish and, circularly, closes with a hint at a condition of doubt. Confessors suggested that when in doubt one should refrain from acting; Pazienza seems to choose this course of action. She declares she will hope for the Spirit's inspiration and, on a more conciliatory note, invites Isabella to pray for her. Establishing the authenticity of these two letters is perhaps less important than recalling Lando's interests in cabbalistic culture, or noting that in 1552 he dedicated his *Dialogo* [...] *nel quale si ragiona della consolatione, & utilità, che si gusta leggendo la Sacra Scrittura* (A dialogue [...] where one reasons on the consolation and usefulness that one enjoys reading Holy Scripture) to the Jewish *conversa* Beatrice di Luna.[123] A letter by Girolamo Ruscelli follows the text, in which he extolls Beatrice's and Ortensio's merits, and reminds readers how it was he, Ruscelli, who had persuaded Lando to print his treatise.[124] At the same time, Lando, who claimed to have met several *marrani* (Spanish Jews forcibly converted to Christianity) in Naples and likely held anti-Trinitarian views, often questioning the divine nature of Christ, could certainly sympathize with certain strands of Judaism.[125]

In other letters, more traditionally, doubt emerges as the inevitable and reproachable result of the philosophers' vain speculations, in the context of evangelical invitations to leave aside all worldly knowledge and focus exclusively on the Bible. Giovanna Cavalleria, writing from Venice to Clara Gualanda, asks her why she wonders that she, Giovanna, has claimed that she could no longer stand reading any book other than the Bible. Her praise of the Bible is at the same time a devaluation of all disciplines, not surprising if we consider that Lando himself, in one of his paradoxes, had praised ignorance over knowledge. Certainly, the vanity of sciences was a staple of evangelical doctrine, especially for a man like Lando familiar with Heinrich Cornelius Agrippa and his *De incertitudine et vanitate scientiarum et omnium artium* (Of the vanity and uncertainty of sciences and of all the arts, 1530), a recurrent presence in his œuvre.[126] Despite the fact that Lando was a master of doubt, in this particular letter doubt appears as one the most fearful consequences of humanity's vain pursuit of knowledge:

> Does it [the Bible] perchance make you unbelieving and doubtful of immortality like philosophers do? Neither does it offer the vain knowledge of doctors, mathematicians, students of law, historians.[127]

Doubt is described as the condition of the 'superstitious' in a letter written by Margherita Pellegrini to Camena Landriana, in which she addresses the recipient by wishing her 'peace and salvation in the Lord' ('pace et salute nel Signore'). The letter is deeply rooted in evangelical spirituality, and 'superstition' should be probably understood in the sense that reformers gave to this word — in other words, the practice of exterior rituals.[128] Margherita praises Camena: 'I rejoiced in hearing that you left the world and gave yourself entirely to Jesus Christ.' She then warns her that 'religion is very close to superstition' and that she therefore should pay attention not to be 'tainted' by it. Doubt comes into play as the condition of fear that superstitious believers experience in proximity to the altar: because they are unable to experience the vivifying power of Scripture, the more they are close to God, the more they tremble, scared by the God of law and punishment. In her words, '[A] superstitious believer is more afraid in a church, is more doubtful near the altar than elsewhere; but if you want to get free from its hands [i.e., of superstition], turn your soul to Holy Scripture.' Camena should instead read Scripture with such attentiveness that it is converted into 'her juice and blood'.[129]

Whatever we make of Lando's fiction, we cannot but notice the importance that he gives to a form of sociability revolving (also) around doubt, as well as the complex rhetorical strategies that he displays in order to suggest in a covert way his criticism of official (humanistic, social, and religious) narratives. Doubt serves several functions, denoting curiosity towards love or matters of erudition; the state of mind of those who are facing dramatic personal choices such as conversion; the spiritual condition of fear and uncertainty of those who trust exterior devotion; and, of course, the oblique attack on official narratives.

A few years after the appearance of the *Valorose donne*, Lando decided to fully exploit the potential of doubt, publishing in 1552 — the same year that his friend Martinengo died — the *Quattro libri de dubbi* (Four books of doubts, 1552). Initially the volume contained only three books, since at the time of printing the publisher, Giolito, had not yet received permission to issue the section on love doubts. In a short note to the reader placed at the conclusion of the volume, Giolito promised to print the full work shortly. In fact, four years elapsed before he was able to fulfil his promise, although Lando's love doubts had appeared in 1552 in another work, titled *Varii componimenti* (Miscellaneous writings, also published by Giolito). The *Libri de dubbi* are no less of a textual conundrum than the *Valorose donne*. In the 1556 edition, Giolito addresses the reader with a short letter in which he claims that the four books are a sort of spiritual journey, moving from love and sensuous things

(Book I) to arrive at 'the contemplation of higher and divine things' (Book IV). It is the same trajectory followed by Ruscelli's *Lettura*, but in the case of Lando's work the philosophical content is more apparent than real. Certainly the answers to the doubts contain the 'most great secrets and most beautiful advice', but these are meant 'to make a man seem wise and prudent despite his not being an expert in the studies of philosophy or theology'.[130] The target reader of the *Libri de dubbi* is less interested in ruminating on the text to achieve inner wisdom or solid knowledge than in finding a shortcut to brilliant social conversation.

In fact, things are more complex than Giolito believed or wanted us to believe. For a start, Lando is cleverly using a new and catchy title for a work rooted in an old genre, the so-called book of problems (a tradition that goes back to antiquity, as we have seen in Chapter 1). However, he is the first one to use 'doubts' — a word that contains layers of intricacy that competing terms do not — instead of 'questions' or 'problems' on the frontispiece.[131] The book of problems genre goes back to the (pseudo)-Aristotelian tradition of the *Problemata* and the *Secreta secretorum*. From these works stems a production of encyclopedic works in the question-answer form; generally, these works are either medical encyclopedias or collections of *mirabilia* and wonders. Some of the most popular works in this specific field were produced in northern Europe (Germany and Bohemia) and, drawing on a variety of sources, were intended as a tool for table talk, in order to 'transform the banquet into an occasion of intellectual and spiritual progress'. However, entertainment often prevails over spiritual progress, even if these works succeed in showing that 'science can be transformed into a subject of conversation'.[132]

In Italy, the most successful of such works was the *Libro del perché* (The book of why), written by the Bolognese humanist Girolamo Manfredi (1430–1493), first published in 1474 and printed several times until 1650, besides being translated into Castilian and Catalan. This best-seller of the genre contained two sections: a health regime (*regimen sanitatis*), and a tract on physiognomy.[133] The *Perché* is not, strictly speaking, a book of medicine, as it does not contain notions of pharmacology, anatomy, surgery, or pathology; nevertheless, it has an undeniably medical background. Instead of the format of standard medicine treatises, Manfredi, using the question-answer method, recreates for his readers the process of scientific discovery.[134] This aspect certainly intrigued those who followed Manfredi's example in the mid-sixteenth century, notably Ortensio Lando, who plagiarized (although the word does not accurately describe Renaissance rewriting) the *Perché* in the first of his *Libri de dubbi*, and Girolamo Garimberti, author of the *Problemi naturali, e morali* (Natural and moral problems, Venice, 1549 and 1550). Manfredi, Garimberti, and Lando (and their predecessors) made a clever move: starting from traditional genres such as the dialogue or the academic *quaestio*, they invented a genre that would captivate the reader, covering a wide variety of everyday matters. These works did not require cover-to-cover reading, and the usually short explanations to the questions could be easily memorized. Besides, the contents usually considered medical and scientific matters traditionally overlooked in lofty treatises — questions that concerned the most basic functions of the human body, curiosities, phenomena that are apparently mysterious despite being before everybody's eyes (why is it hard for elderly people to sneeze? why do people hold their breath when they have hiccups? why is wolf's liver good for those who suffer from liver illnesses? etc.). What these authors discovered and offered their readers were the wonders of everyday life, the 'everyday marvellous'.[135]

Lando and Garimberti extended the realm of problems covered by these works to ethics and religion: they both understood that the pleasure of discovering hidden wonders in all spheres of human experience would attract readers. Thus, they were able to offer entertaining instruction to those with little education. Garimberti, for example, claimed to have written 'for the benefit of the common people' in the vernacular, lamenting his 'prolixity, for with uneducated persons one cannot leave behind certain principles'. He also had to embellish the discourse with 'delectable and easy things to facilitate the obscure senses and amuse the readers, and while amusing them, invite them to read'.[136] Bartolomeo Paschetti, who published two books of *Dubbi morali et naturali* (Moral and natural doubts) in 1581, claimed to have written for the benefit of the busy tradesmen and merchants of Genoa who had little spare time to read and yet enjoyed vernacular books:

> In this city, which is all devoted to commerce, those who know Latin are only but a few although it does not lack of ingenious men and women who gladly spend the free time from their work reading vernacular books, which bring them entertainment and benefit.[137]

Despite its potential, the genre declined starting in the 1560s.[138] Nonetheless, Lando was quick to understand how a public accustomed to reading the wondrous tales of paladins, monsters, and dragons could be attracted to scientific curiosities.[139] A gifted writer, Lando introduced some novelties into the genre; first of all, the fiction connected to what I call a 'virtual academy'. What we read are not disembodied answers and questions, but (allegedly) real questions asked by real people, identified by their name and (often) their social rank by the author, Lando himself, who often intervenes in the text as 'I'. There are dozens of people asking hundreds of questions, and for each of them Lando seems to have an answer (although he sometimes phrases it in ambiguous and uncertain terms). This answer is often very precise in terms of both history and geography, connecting certain habits and practices to cities or people, thus adding layers of realism to the explanations in an attempt to further entice readers.[140]

More than that, however, Lando creates a veritable labyrinth where different characters often ask the same question, receiving different if not opposite answers.[141] For example, the question about who is steadier in love receives two diametrically different answers, depending on whether it is men or women. Women are more stable because of their cold nature, since cold is more stable than heat; at the same time, men are said to be more stable because, being more 'robust' in general, they are also steadier in their affections. In the same way, it is easier to persuade a man of being loved because women, when someone claims to love them, usually think that they are being fooled. At the same time, it is easier to persuade women of being loved because they 'hold their merits in higher esteem than they should'.[142]

Such examples could easily be multiplied, but the question is, what are we to make of them? First, we may safely say that Lando is playing with a corpus of received knowledge, showing its contradictions and its weaknesses. Second, he is presenting the reader with a *mise-en-abyme* of his work: in a work of doubts, the reader is often in a situation of doubt, that is, unable to choose among two equivalent answers. In doing so, Lando conflates the two main meanings of doubt considered so far (question, and condition of uncertainty). There are two more strategies at work in Lando's *Dubbi*. One becomes most effective in the last book, where Lando advances his religious ideas, in some cases close to those of the Anabaptists and certainly not in line with the Roman Church's orthodoxy.[143] In this case, multiplying different and conflicting answers discourages the potential censor, while the reader patient enough to follow Lando's rhetorical strategies will learn to discover his red herrings, distinguishing what is purely smoke and mirrors from the author's authentic convictions.[144] The other point is that uncertainty is for Lando a sort of existential condition, connected with the necessity to dissimulate on the one hand and with the effects of sin on the other.

As for Lando's covering his tracks, consider a series of three consecutive and apparently unrelated questions asked by Monsignor Da Silva, followed by their replies:

> Why are the necks of pigeons and the peacock's feathers so pleasant to our eyes?
> Because of the variety and uncertainty of colours.
> What is the work of the human heart?
> To simulate and dissimulate.
> Why is the chameleon wondrous?
> For it receives all colours.[145]

We have here a specimen of Lando's method: short questions followed by equally short answers, without an apparent common thread. The first and the third questions concern animals, while the second is a moral doubt, and rightly so since we are in the third book, about moral doubts. We should not be deceived, then: even when talking of peacocks, pigeons, and chameleons, Lando is indeed talking about morals, and particularly about the ability to simulate and dissimulate that is so peculiar to the human heart. The changing colours of the peacock's and pigeon's feathers, as well as of the chameleon's skin, are thus the equivalent of the changing nature of the human heart, of its ability to disguise itself. We should not forget that these words come from the mouth of someone who was also known as Geremia da Milano (when he was an Augustinian friar), Ortensio Tranquillo, Filalete citizen of Utopia, Hortensius Appianus, Andronico Collodio ... So many identities for one of the most controversial and elusive writers of the sixteenth century, someone on whom not even the Inquisition was able to lay its hands. Even Lando's religious ideas, despite falling well outside the bounds of Catholic orthodoxy, remain something of a mystery because of his ability at simulating and dissimulating. Be that as it may, it seems that uncertainty and simulation cause pleasure (the feathers that are 'grate', the 'maraviglioso' chameleon).

Yet (and this is the other point) uncertainty, as a condition that befell humankind after Cain's slaughter of his brother Adam, is anything but pleasant. Among the religious doubts, a question asked by Caterina Colonna Gonzaga opens a window onto Lando's view of uncertainty:[146]

> Did God give Cain any penance for his fault other than that he had to move from land to land?
> This would have been a light affliction, for this Abraham too and many other saints had to endure. But the penance that was to distress him was that his mind was to be unsettled and uncertain about all his deeds or decisions, and that everything he tried turned out to be harmful to him.[147]

Doubt and uncertainty are thus the state of those who live outside grace: instability of mind, distress, and inner turmoil are a curse we have to endure if we do not possess 'proper faith'. In fact, what is proper faith (as Franceschina Dressino inquiries), if not 'a certain science conceived in the mind, alien from all doubtful opinions'?[148]

Ortensio Lando's works mediated the access to otherwise intricate doctrines — natural, philosophical, religious — by a vast public of curious men and women. Whatever we may nowadays think of his impersonations or of his ventriloquizing of others' voices, his was a successful formula. Readers could identify with the crowd of curious doubters and interlocutors featured in his works who asked doubts and questions that may have crossed their own minds. Some of these readers — the more attentive, the more skilled — may have seen, beyond the maze of dead alleys created by Lando, his real purposes, from the deconstruction of humanist culture to the suggestions concerning radical religious ideas. All must have probably been under the impression of taking part in some academic gathering, sitting among the public of a virtual assembly of doubters. If the speakers in Lando's works belonged to the elite class, his readers could potentially come from all social classes, provided they had some education. Democratizing a quintessentially elitist institution such as an academy was likely a by-product of Lando's strategy that transformed doubt, even when potentially disruptive, into a social game.

Voicing Doubts, Cutting Tongues

The final section in this chapter turns to a story about the doubts of a priest who was eventually executed because of his scandalous beliefs, many of which he drew from literary works. The story emerges from the trial of the Brescian priest Francesco Calcagno in 1550.[149] On 7 February 1550, one Giovanni Antonio Savaresi made a deposition against Calcagno, articulated in ten points. Among the accusations were that Calcagno had affirmed that Christ had never existed, and that the person whom people call 'Christ' was a man made of flesh, who had often had sexual intercourse with St John the Apostle. Calcagno had then denied the reality of Eucharist, further expanding on this point by affirming that a 'nice arse was his altar, his mass, his host, his chalice'.[150] In fact, he would rather 'carnally adore' a nice boy than worship God.[151] While some accusations concerned sexual misbehaviour and blasphemy, the sixth point on the list was interesting in other ways: '[He said] that one should rather have faith in Ovid's Metamorphosis than in the Gospel'.[152] Another witness, the bookseller Pietro delle Grazie, specified in his testimony that Calcagno 'had repeatedly stated that the Bible and the Gospels are Metamorphosis'.[153] The identification between Scripture and Ovid is here complete: the two texts are interchangeable and, one may infer, both are mere fables. In fact, Calcagno had not simply denied the divine nature of Christ: a third witness, Lauro Glisenti, claimed that he had 'repeatedly affirmed that neither God nor the soul exists, and that once the body is dead, so is the soul'.[154] Glisenti had probably retained more of Calcagno's alleged ideas; with regard to point six, he was able to go far beyond what the authorities already knew:

> Ovid is more veritable than Scripture, and he said that those [who] have written this Scripture were minions of the devil, and he often told me that this was in order to make people scared, and rule the world according to their own rule, and he repeated to me often the line from Lucretius: 'It was fear that first created the gods in the world.'[155]

As if this were not enough, Calcagno also added that the 'the pope and these great men share my same belief that there is no God, and that there is no heaven nor anything else, and that once the body is dead, the soul is dead too, and that the whole universe is ruled by chance'.[156] The line attributed to Lucretius was in fact to be found in Statius's *Thebais*, although Statius himself was probably quoting (the verse was also attributed to Petronius), and by the sixteenth century it had likely become a proverb. Even if Calcagno did not read Lucretius, he may have read Machiavelli, possibly the *Discourses on Livy*, where the idea of *religio instrumentum regni* is outlined. Other witnesses recalled how Calcagno also used to say at times that he believed everything the church believed, while at other times he asserted he believed nothing the church maintained.[157] Interestingly enough, these statements were expressed in conversations that took place in the bookshop of Pietro delle Grazie, next to the door of the cathedral ('nella mia botega apresso la porta del Domo').[158] The group that gathered in this *bottega* was a conventicle of proto-atheists, at least according to Calcagno's self-defence. Lauro Glisenti would say that he did not believe in anything other than what he saw, and the priest Nicolò Ugoni said that he believed 'in the Scripture as much as he believed in Aesop's fables'.[159]

Calcagno may have released these statements merely with the goal of sharing with others the burden of the accusations. What is certainly remarkable is the part that literature plays in them: from the Bible to Ovid to misquoted Lucretius to Aesop. The case of our priest could have prompted exercises in what we might call 'comparative religion', suggesting for example that the Bible and some of the most famous texts of classical antiquity shared similarities and could find their place on the same shelf of an ideal library. But there is one work that deserves special attention. We have seen that Calcagno was accused of declaring he preferred to 'carnally adore' a young boy over worshipping God. He denied the accusation, admitting only that 'I said that a nice ass was heaven and God, and I saw these words in a book called la *Cazzarìa*'.[160] Thus we learn that Calcagno in all likelihood had read Antonio Vignali's *Cazzarìa*, written in the mid-1520s, a homoerotic dialogue originating from the cultural humus of the Academy of the Intronati in Siena. The *Cazzarìa* is a parody of academic and Scholastic culture, a praise of homoerotic sexuality as well as a sexualized political allegory staging the inner conflicts that ravaged the Sienese body politic. Scholars have highlighted its libertine and sceptical stance towards religion as well as official culture. The passage alluded to by Calcagno was more problematic than reported in his trial, as it entailed a full denial of any otherworldly reality:

> And if the opinion of Discreto Intronato is correct, that paradise, hell, and purgatory are to be found in this world, and that paradise is your house, where you live surrounded by servants, master of all your goods, and the angels are beautiful young men, and all the circumstances that make man content are the elements of the angelic hierarchy, and on the other hand prison is purgatory, poverty is hell, and worn-out wretches are the devils, then I would like to believe that ambrosia and nectar are nothing but the sweet tongue of a beautiful young man and the profound secret pleasure that is to be found in his soft delicate asshole.[161]

A text such as the *Cazzarìa* was deliberately intended to raise doubts on two levels. On one level, explicit passages like the above could lead one to question religious truth. On another level, 'the discussion [...] is divided into a series of *quaestiones*, which appear in the margins of the earliest editions. This method of structuring a text is typical of a medieval Scholasticism which by Vignali's time was coming to seem stuffy and outdated'. The questions in the margins, which are addressed in the main text, 'are ridiculous and bawdy parodies'.[162] In fact, most of them concern low bodily functions, for which the text offers 'comic and facetious explanations': thus, the *Cazzarìa* 'mocks intellectual methods and modes of argumentations by applying them to sexual and bodily knowledge'.[163] The explanations of bodily functions, again, 'make fun of Scholastic logic as well as mocking the tradition of argumentation *pro et contra*' in which students address seemingly futile questions.[164] In this regard, the *Cazzarìa* finds its place in a line of Sienese culture, expressed by the local academies of the Intronati (which had among its 'laws' one that said 'Nemini credere', 'Do not believe anyone') and the Rozzi. This cultural strand centred around paradox and 'curious' questions, as shown by the *Dieci paradosse degli academici intronati* and the *Quistioni e chasi di più sorte*.[165] In a way, Vignali's work merges these two interests but takes them to another level.

In doing so, Vignali draws on another textual tradition, that of books of questions, or doubts, that addressed a variety of questions concerning basic bodily functions without being proper medical treatises. The most famous of these was possibly Manfredi's *Libro del perché*, mentioned earlier in this chapter. It was natural that in a work openly dealing with sexuality at a time when obscene literature was not yet fashionable, Vignali would be attracted to a genre that asked questions on matters traditionally excluded from high literature. As Cherchi suggests, 'the technique of "perché" elevated the obscene discourse to the dignity of academic language', finding 'a new and "curious" way to talk about prohibited issues'.[166] Thus the book market could drive unintended developments: in the hands of skilled humanists, books of questions (or problems, or doubts) could become the template for works such as the *Cazzarìa*, which voiced more serious and disturbing doubts. An appealing, amusing, and apparently accessible text, Vignali's work could in turn end up in the hands of people like Calcagno, igniting or reinforcing their doubts. Besides this, an example like that of Calcagno's trial shows how hard it is to disentangle the different levels and meanings of 'doubt'.

In the case of Calcagno, if it is interesting that the men who gathered in the bookstore of Pietro delle Grazie shared such audacious ideas, it is even more striking that two of them were clergymen, while Pietro probably had some connections with the local clergy, too, if his store was next to the cathedral.[167] Books provided these people with useful tools to deconstruct Christian tenets; even if Calcagno was formally charged of being a Lutheran, his ideas stretched far beyond heresy. On 16 August 1550, local authorities sent a letter to the Council of Ten in Venice providing information on Calcagno and two other heretics, in which they reported that Calcagno had uttered 'words so nefarious and repugnant [...] that neither Turk nor Jew [nor] the demons themselves have ever come not only to say, but even to imagine [them]'.[168] Calcagno's story ended tragically: the executioner cut off a piece of his tongue, beheaded him, and, for good measure, burned his body.

The story of Calcagno can be read on many levels, but for the purposes of this book it shows the complications that could arise from putting doubts into writing and the unforeseen consequences that could follow. It also shows how dangerous it had become to voice doubts in the 1550s. That the founding of the Academy of the Dubbiosi and Calcagno's trial happened in the same year, 1550, is again a coincidence. That they both originated in the Venetian Terraferma (in this case, the city of Brescia) is perhaps less of a coincidence. The cutting of Calcagno's tongue is in fact a highly symbolical act that signals the will to silence not only dissenting voices but also expressions of doubt. For these reasons, it seems suitable to close my exploration of discourses around doubt at this turning point: doubt does not disappear in the period we call the Counter-Reformation, but takes new forms and new spaces that would require a whole other study to fully understand and appreciate.

Notes to Chapter 5

1. Pio Rajna, 'L'episodio delle questioni d'amore nel *Filocolo* di Boccaccio', *Romania*, 31 (1902), 28–81.
2. Mario Equicola, *Libro de natura de amore*, ed. by Enrico Musacchio (Rome: Aracne, 2018), p. 160.
3. Ireneo Sanesi, *Il Cinquecentista Ortensio Lando* (Pistoia: Fratelli Bracali, 1893), pp. 235–47. See Maiko Favaro, *Ambiguità del petrarchismo: Un percorso fra trattati d'amore, lettere e templi di rime* (Milan: Franco Angeli, 2021), pp. 31–104.
4. 'Una questione o dubitazione d'amor'. Girolamo Bargagli, *Dialogo de' giuochi che nelle vegghie sanesi si usano di fare*, ed. by Patrizia D'Incalci Ermini, intro. by Riccardo Bruscagli (Siena: Accademia Senese degli Intronati, 1982), p. 95. The dialogue, originally published in 1572, was printed seven times by 1609.
5. 'Mostrino qualche cosa poco onesta di significare'. Ibid., p. 62.
6. 'L'una dubitazione dopo l'altra facendo nascere'. Ibid., p. 117.
7. In this manuscript, the traditional corpus of doubts is augmented by other, similar poems; additionally, the pseudo-Aretinesque doubts present a high number of variant readings.

8. For the discussion of the *Dubbi amorosi*, I follow Giuseppe Crimi, 'Per l'edizione dei *Dubbi amorosi* attribuiti ad Aretino: Nuove acquisizioni e qualche indizio di paternità', *Filologia e critica*, 40 (2015), 3–46. On probabilism and casuistry, see Tutino, *Uncertainty in Post-Reformation Catholicism*.

9. Suzanne Karr Schmidt, *Interactive and Sculptural Printmaking in the Renaissance* (Leiden: Brill, 2017), p. 332.

10. See Elide Casali, 'Libri di ventura e divinazione nel Cinquecento', in *Un giardino per le arti: 'Francesco Marcolino da Forlì': La vita, l'opera, il catalogo*, ed. by Paolo Procaccioli, Paolo Temeroli, and Vanni Tesei (Bologna: Editrice Compositori, 2009), pp. 315–35; Paolo Procaccioli and Silvia Urbini, 'Fortuna donna di palazzo: Libri di sorte da Lorenzo Spirito a Giuseppe Maria Mitelli', in *Dea Fortuna: Iconografia di un mito*, ed. by Manuela Kahn-Rossi (Carpi: Edizioni del Comune di Carpi, 2010), pp. 28–37; Paolo Marini, 'Un libro di sorti nella Romagna post-tridentina: Il manoscritto I 66 della Biblioteca Comunale "Aurelio Saffi" di Forlì', *Rara volumina*, 20 (2013), 23–50; Jessen Kelly, 'Predictive Play: Wheels of Fortune in the Early Modern Lottery Book', in *Playthings in Early Modernity*, ed. by Levy, pp. 145–66; Kelli Wood, 'Chancing It: Print, Play, and Gambling Games at the End of the Sixteenth Century', *Art History*, 42 (2019), 450–81.

11. Enrico Parlato, 'Le allegorie nel giardino delle "Sorti"', in *Studi per le 'Sorti': Gioco, immagini, poesia oracolare a Venezia nel Cinquecento*, ed. by Paolo Procaccioli (Treviso: Fondazione Benetton-Viella, 2007), pp. 113–37; Enrico Parlato, 'Abecedario iconografico marcoliniano', in *Un giardino per le arti*, ed. by Procaccioli, Temeroli, and Tesei, pp. 249–68; Augusto Gentili, 'Marcolini, Doni e le immagini della "maniera" veneziana', ibid., pp. 339–52.

12. Lodovico Dolce, *Terzetti per le 'Sorti': Poesia oracolare nell'officina di Francesco Marcolini*, ed. by Paolo Procaccioli (Treviso: Fondazione Benetton-Viella, 2006).

13. Enrico Parlato, 'L'editoria veneziana e Marcolini', in *Francesco Salviati 'spirito veramente pellegrino ed eletto'*, ed. by Antonio Geremicca (Rome: Campisano, 2015), pp. 75–85.

14. Paolo Procaccioli, 'Marcolini autore "ingegnoso"', in *Studi per le 'Sorti'*, ed. by Procaccioli, pp. 3–18.

15. Augusto Gentili, 'Il problema delle immagini nell'attività di Francesco Marcolini', *Giornale storico della letteratura italiana*, 157 (1980), 117–25 (p. 120).

16. Originally printed in Perugia in 1482, Spirito's work was immensely popular in Italy and beyond. In the 1557 edition, its frontispiece shows a company of men and women sitting around a table in an elegant domestic interior. Two groups of four people stand on either side of a woman sitting at a table, on which we see an armillary sphere, dice, and an open book — the same book that the reader is about to peruse, which the woman is holding open for the reader to see.

17. 'Un'entità metafisica, superiore e assoluta'. Gentili, 'Il problema', p. 120.

18. 'Due o più percorsi diversi abbiano lo stesso esito e che, viceversa, due o più percorsi analoghi possano giungere ad altrettanti esiti differenti.' Christian Rivoletti, 'L'uno e il molteplice: Il sistema dei destini incrociati tra Ariosto, Marcolini e Calvino', in *Studi per le 'Sorti'*, ed. by Procaccioli, pp. 99–110 (p. 102). As Marcolini writes, 'havendo io a mostrare l'arteficio della sorte ho voluto che [...] in questa opera mia [...] quantunque si cavi lo istesso punto, vengano i versi variati, e che cavando punti diversi scontrino i terzetti medesimi'. *Le sorti di Francesco Marcolino da Forlì intitolate giardino di pensieri* [...] (Venice: Francesco Marcolino, 1540), p. 4.

19. The 'Ghiribizzi' are kept in Rome, Biblioteca Apostolica Vaticana, MS Capponi 107, II, fols 221^r–222^v. The section on the mutability of circumstances is originally contained in a marginal note; I use the text as reconstructed in Nicolò Machiavelli, 'Ghiribizi scri<pti> <in> P[eru]gia al Soderin<o>', appendix to Carlo Ginzburg, 'Diventare Machiavelli: Per una nuova lettura dei "Ghiribizzi al Soderini"', in *Nondimanco: Machiavelli, Pascal* (Milan: Adelphi, 2018), pp. 43–65.

20. *The Complete Essays by Montaigne*, trans. by Donald M. Frame (Stanford, CA: Stanford University Press, 1965).

21. Rivoletti, 'L'uno e il molteplice'.

22. Wood, 'Chancing It', p. 460; on the story told by Doni, see Procaccioli, 'Marcolini autore "ingegnoso"', pp. 10–11.

23. The *Sorti* are perhaps, after Alciato's *Emblemata* (1534), the first work that provides visual allegories of moral categories; it is little wonder that some of the representations of virtues and

vices also exerted an influence on Ripa's *Iconologia*, besides being employed in Anton Francesco Doni's works. See Enrico Parlato, 'Le *Sorti* nell'*Iconologia*, l'*Iconologia* nelle *Sorti*: Un percorso tra immagini e parole all'ombra di Anton Francesco Doni', in *Cesare Ripa e gli spazi dell'allegoria*, ed. by Sonia Maffei (Naples: La Stanza delle Scritture, 2010), pp. 39–60.

24. See Serena Berrettini, 'Le "Sorti" come macchina ludica: Regole e procedure', in *Studi per le 'Sorti'*, ed. by Procaccioli, pp. 21–38.

25. 'Dieu est source du bien, mais sans que l'on puisse sonder sa rationalité. Il n'y a pas de référence au Jugement dernier et il est rare que la Justice divine intervienne dans le cours des événements. Les *Sorti* témoignent donc d'un manque générale de dessein.' Marie-Cécile Van Hasselt, 'Être/paraître, de fausses perceptions sous l'enseigne de la vérité', in *Studi per le 'Sorti'*, ed. by Procaccioli, pp. 85–97 (p. 89).

26. According to a long-standing tradition of feminine creatures hiding their monstrous nature; see, for example, the 'stammering woman', the *femmina balba*, in Dante's *Purgatory*, xix. For the topos of the courtesan as internally disfigured by ailment, see Deanna Shemek, '"Mi mostrano a dito tutti quanti": Disease, Deixis, and Disfiguration in the *Lamento di una cortigiana ferrarese*', in *Medusa's Gaze: Essays on Gender, Literature, and Aesthetics in the Italian Renaissance in Honor of Robert J. Rodini*, ed. by Paul A. Ferrara, Eugenio Giusti, and Jane Tylus (Lafayette, IN: Bodighera, 2004), pp. 49–64; Robert Buranello, 'The *Zoppino* Dialogue: Malice, Misogyny, and Meretricious Misrepresentation', *Rivista di studi italiani*, 23 (2005), 45–62; Paola Ugolini, 'The Satirist's Purgatory: *Il Purgatorio delle cortegiane* and the Writer's Discontent', *Italian Studies*, 64 (2009), 1–19; and Ugolini, *The Court and Its Critics*, pp. 82–83, which also shows how the topos could serve anti-courtly purposes.

27. 'Étant donné les caractéristiques de l'illusion (l'attrait et le désenchantement), la courtisane personnifie l'illusion: elle a des attraits physiques, mais elle n'a point de pureté [...]. On comprend finalement l'intérêt des *Sorti* pour le mal contagieux. Ce mal, dévorant le corps du malade sans que l'on en aperçoive les symptômes, s'apparente aux souffrances causées par l'illusion fondées sur les fausses apparences et perceptions [...]. Il y a donc une rupture profonde entre l'"être" et le "paraître".' Van Hasselt, 'Être/paraître', p. 90.

28. Ibid., p. 89.

29. Dolce's *rime* have sometimes apocalyptic connotations: see, for example, v. 30 and x. 10; Dolce, *Terzetti per le 'Sorti'*, pp. 58, 83.

30. 'A me piace quel credo di Margute, | Ch'era utile e sano; e spesse volte | *Il non creder ad altri è gran virtute*'; 'Il creder, figlio, spesse volte nuoce. | Se vuoi viver secur, *non creder nulla*, | Io te 'l dico gridando ad alta voce.' Ibid., p. 200. Anaxarchus lived in the fourth century BCE. Significantly, we have testimony on him from Sextus Empiricus, according to whom he 'likened existing things to stage-painting and took them to be similar to the things which strike us while asleep or insane'. The passage is quoted in Richard Bett, 'Pyrrho', in *The Stanford Encyclopedia of Philosophy* (Winter 2014), ed. by Edward N. Zalta <http://plato.stanford.edu/archives/win2014/entries/pyrrho/> [accessed 28 October 2016]. The so-called credo of Margutte refers to Luigi Pulci's poem 'Morgante' and especially the declaration of sceptical incredulity, verging on atheism, by Margutte in Canto xvii. However, as Alessandro Polcri has shown, Pulci's alleged atheism should be reconsidered, as the whole poem can be interpreted as based on Christian allegory; see Polcri, *Luigi Pulci e la Chimera: Studi sull'allegoria nel Morgante* (Florence: Società Editrice Fiorentina, 2010); see also Chap. 2, this volume.

31. 'Le sono fanfaluche, figliuol mio, | Chiacchiere e fole; *e tu non prestar fede* | *Ad huom che vive*, fuor ch'a solo Dio'; 'La fede solo si conviene a Dio. | Nel resto a dirti il vero e chiaro e piano, | *Non crederai perfino al padre mio*.' Dolce, *Terzetti per le 'Sorti'*, pp. 188, 211. The first is attributed to Democritus, the second to Pyrrho.

32. 'Anchor che a *sacra Dei* ti sia giurato, | Dubita sempre, e vivi cautamente, | E a questo modo non sarai ingannato'; 'Il prestar fede altrui pericoloso | Fu sempre giudicato; e tu se m'ami | Mostrati sempre incredulo e dubbioso.' Ibid., pp. 203, 223.

33. 'Fra le cose rare e più stupende | Io trovo, in certi libri in lingua nostra, | Che sempre crede meno chi più intende.' Ibid., p. 221. Van Hasselt, 'Être/paraître', p. 90, suggests that the tercet 'se réfère à *La dotta ignoranza* de Nicolò de Cusa'.

34. Stefano Pierguidi, 'Verità e menzogna: I motti e le marche tipografiche di Aretino, Marcolini e Doni', *Venezia Cinquecento*, 33 (2007), 5–21.

35. 'Fragilità e precarietà'; 'può smarrire quindi l'identità e la sicurezza di sé'; 'la Verità è destituita dai suoi fondamenti ontologici universali'. Amedeo Quondam, 'Nel giardino del Marcolini: Un editore veneziano tra Aretino e Doni', *Giornale storico della letteratura italiana*, 157 (1980), 75–116 (p. 112).

36. Lucia Nadin, *Carte da gioco e letteratura tra Quattrocento e Ottocento* (Lucca: Pacini Fazzi, 1997), pp. 35–85, esp. pp. 82–85.

37. Parlato, 'Le *Sorti* nell'*Iconologia*', pp. 48–51; Enrico Parlato, 'Sogno e conoscenza nella Venezia del Cinquecento: Daniele Barbaro, alias Hypneo da Schio, e Francesco Marcolini', in *Forme e storia: Scritti di arte medievale e moderna per Francesco Gandolfo*, ed. by Walter Angelelli and Francesca Pomarici (Rome: Artemide, 2011), pp. 505–14; see also Angelo Papi, 'Le perigliose sorti del duca Ercole: Considerazioni a margine di una dedica', in *Studi per le 'Sorti'*, ed. by Procaccioli, pp. 157–71.

38. 'Questo mondo | È un sogno e noi mortali | Poveri, ciechi e frali | Altro che fumo e ombra | Non siamo | Et polve che disgombra | Il vento da la faccia de la terra.' [Daniele Barbaro], *Predica de i sogni composta per lo reverendo padre d. Hypneo da Schio* (Venice: Francesco Marcolini, 1542), fol. C4^r.

39. 'Un pomo fe' sognare | Ciò ch'in vigilia appare. [...] | Hor va considerando | Tra te stesso | Profondamente e spesso | S'altro che sogni vedi | Nell'opre de gli heredi | D'Adamo primo padre. | Effigie oscure e adre | Ch'ingannano le menti | E fan sognar le genti | E creder che fra noi | Con tutti i beni suoi | Si trove il Paradiso.' Ibid., fol. C4^v.

40. 'Nescessario è per ascondere meglio quello che si dipigne con le predette pratiche, che il pittore perspettivo [...] sappi adombrare, e con diversi tratti di penello coprire la pittura, acciò che dia una apparenza lontana dalle cose figurate e dimostri paesi, acque, monti, sassi e altre cose diverse da quelle che sono dipinte. Può e deve anche ingannare, tagliando e separando le linee che devono essere dritte e continuate.' Daniele Barbaro, *La pratica della perspettiva* [...] (Venice: Camillo et Rutilio Borgominieri, 1569), p. 161.

41. Jennifer Nelson, *Disharmony of the Spheres: The Europe of Holbein's 'Ambassadors'* (University Park: Pennsylvania State University Press, 2019), pp. 7, 11.

42. 'Sotto della Luna | Non si ritrova alcuna | Stabilitade, o cosa | Che non sia paurosa | Come un sogno.' [Barbaro], *Predica de i sogni*, fol. D^v. See Parlato, 'Sogno e conoscenza', p. 510.

43. [Barbaro], *Predica de i sogni*, fol. D^v.

44. Clark, *The Vanities of the Eye: Vision in Early Modern European Culture* (Oxford: Oxford University Press, 2007), p. 92 (but see the whole Chap. 3); see also Jurgis Baltrušaitis, *Anamorfosi o Thaumaturgus opticus* (Milan: Adelphi, 1990).

45. 'Horsù, Signor del tutto | Leva da gli occhi nostri | Quest'infiniti mostri | De i sogni che sognamo.' [Barbaro], *Predica de i sogni*, fols D2^v–D3^r.

46. Ibid., fol. D3^r. In Dante's *Divine Comedy* (*Paradiso*, IV) doubt is the propulsive force that fuels this desire of understanding, and Dante devotes the concluding lines of the canto to praising it: 'I now see clearly that our intellect | Cannot be satisfied until that truth enlighten it, | Beyond whose boundary no further truth extends. | In that truth, like a wild beast in its den, it rests | Once it has made its way there — and it can do that, | Or else its every wish would be in vain. | Like a shoot, doubt springs | From the root of truth, and its nature | Urges us toward the summit, from ridge to ridge. | It is this, lady, that invites, and assures me | To ask You, with reverence, about another truth | That still remains obscure to me.' Dante Alighieri, *Paradiso*, verse trans. by Robert Hollander and Jean Hollander (New York: Anchor Books, 2007), pp. 98–99. 'Io veggio ben che già mai non si sazia | Nostro intelletto, se 'l ver non lo illustra | Di fuor dal qual nessun vero si spazia. | Posasi in esso, come fera in lustra, | Tosto che giunto l'ha; | e giugner puollo: | Se non, ciascun disio sarebbe *frustra*. | Nasce per quello, a guisa di rampollo, | A piè del vero il dubbio; ed è natura | Ch'al sommo pinge noi di collo in collo. | Questo m'invita, questo m'assicura | Con reverenza, donna, a dimandarvi | D'un'altra verità che m'è oscura.' Dante Alighieri, *Paradiso*, ed. by Anna Maria Chiavacci Leonardi (Milan: Mondadori, 1994), pp. 122–23.

47. [Barbaro], *Predica de i sogni*, fol. D3^v.

48. Ibid., fol. D3^v.

49. Ibid., fol. D4^r.

50. Enrico Pasini, 'Dubbio e scetticismo in Erasmo da Rotterdam', in *Erasmo da Rotterdam e la cultura europea/ Erasmus of Rotterdam and European Culture*, ed. by Enrico Pasini and Pietro B. Rossi (Florence: Sismel-Edizioni del Galluzzo, 2008), pp. 199–250.

51. 'S'il dubbitar havesse piedi e vita | N'innanzi o indietro si vedrebbe gire. | Se lingua, né tacer saprebbe o dire | O con buona o con trista riuscita. | Se spalle havesse, braccia, mani e dita | N'incominciar vorrebbe opra o finire | E posto alfin tra 'l vivere e il morire | Non morrirebbe e non starebbe in vita. | Però n'increscerebbe alla natura, | Allo abisso e al mondo e al paradiso | Veder così intronata creatura. | Onde ben fu nel colleggio deciso | Che senza forma sia, senza figura, | Senza piè, senza man, e senza viso.' [Barbaro], *Predica de i sogni*, fol. D4^v.

52. 'Innovazione e divulgazione'; 'la ricerca della verità da indagare, soprattutto nelle meditazioni filosofiche, con la mente sgombra da qualsiasi rigido vincolo al principio d'autorità'. Valerio Vianello, *Il letterato, l'accademia, il libro: Contributi sulla cultura veneta del Cinquecento* (Padua: Antenore, 1988), p. 84. On Italian academies, see *The Italian Academies 1525–1700: Networks of Culture, Innovation and Dissent*, ed. by Jane E. Everson, Denis V. Reidy, and Lisa M. Sampson (Oxford: Legenda, 2016); on their role in a later period, see Edward Muir, *The Culture Wars of the Late Renaissance: Skeptics, Libertines, and Opera* (Cambridge, MA: Harvard University Press, 2007).

53. So we read in a letter sent by Alessandro Piccolomini to Benedetto Varchi on 24 May 1541; see Florindo Cerreta, *Alessandro Piccolomini: Letterato e filosofo senese del Cinquecento* (Siena: Accademia Senese degli Intronati, 1960), pp. 266–68.

54. 'Conosco [...] che al presente la virtù vostra più tosto si dee adoprare in dar fine alle guerre d'Italia.' Sperone Speroni, *Dialogo della vita attiva e contemplativa*, in *Opere* [...] *tratte da' mss. originali*, II (Venice: Domenico Occhi, 1740), pp. 1–43 (p. 5).

55. 'Nel qual dubbio mentre io sono sommerso.' Ibid., p. 8. 'Ringraziate pure Dio che vi dia lume da dubitare, con ciò sia cosa che 'l dubitare non è altro che occasione di sapere'. Ibid., p. 10.

56. 'Nella quale prigione ho speranza di non istar lungo tempo'. Ibid., pp. 21–22. Contarini strongly feared that his lacking the 'honours' usually bestowed upon men of his rank 'could be thought as coming from my not being able to obtain them, rather than from my not desiring them' ('fortemente temea che 'l mancarne [...] fosse stimato dover procedere anzi dal non valere ottenerli che dal voler rifiutarli'). Ibid., p. 21.

57. Ibid., p. 15.

58. 'Lo 'ntendere speculando non è intendere perfettamente la verità, ma è ombra e sembianza della perfetta scienzia che ha Iddio della verità: ma l'esser buono perfettamente, cioè dotato di buoni abiti virtuosi è special privilegio della natura dell'uomo.' Ibid., p. 16.

59. 'La nostra scienzia per la sua incertitudine rispetto a quella di Dio sia come l'ombra alla verità.' Ibid., p. 17.

60. Maria Rosa Davi, 'Filosofia e retorica nell'opera di Sperone Speroni', in *Sperone Speroni*, ed. by Antonio Daniele (Padua: Programma, 1989), pp. 89–112.

61. 'Non è scienzia di verità ma openione e di vero similitudine.' Sperone Speroni, *Dialogo della retorica*, in *Trattatisti del Cinquecento*, I, ed. by Mario Pozzi (Milan and Naples: Ricciardi, 1978), pp. 637–82 (p. 648). This dialogue, composed in the first half of the 1530s, forms a sort of tryptich with the *Della vita attiva e contemplativa* and the dialogue *Delle lingue*; see Alessio Cotugno, *La scienza della parola: Retorica e linguistica in Sperone Speroni* (Bologna: il Mulino, 2019), pp. 38–43.

62. 'Il qual vulgo non avendo vertù di digerir le scienzie e in suo pro convertirle, de' loro odori e delle loro similitudini, gli oratori ascoltando, suole appagarsi; e così vive e mantiensi. Dunque, io non vedo per qual cagion la retorica debbia sbandirsi delle repubbliche, sendo arte che ha per subietto le nostre umane operazioni, onde hanno origine le republiche: ché, avvegnadio che l'oratore con ragioni probabili e anzi incerte che no, dilettando e persuadendo, giudichi e regga le civili operazioni; nondimeno sommamente è da commendare e d'aver cara la sua solerzia, dalla quale le cose nostre perfettamente e propriamente, in quel modo che a loro essere si conviene, sono trattate e considerate.' Speroni, *Dialogo della retorica*, p. 678.

63. 'Ché se una opra medesima, in varii tempi dalle leggi cittadinesche or vietata e or commendata, può esser vizio e vertù, ragione è bene che le nostre republiche non da scienzie demostrative, vere e certe per ogni tempo, ma con retorice openioni variabili e tramutabili (quali son l'opre e le leggi nostre) prudentemente sian governate.' Ibid., p. 678.
64. 'E nel vero il filosofo [...] tanto men crede quanto più sa.' Ibid., p. 679.
65. On the connection between sophistry and *Della retorica* (and on the relevance of sophistry in Speroni's thought in general), see Teodoro Katinis, *Sperone Speroni and the Debate over Sophistry in the Italian Renaissance* (Leiden: Brill, 2018), pp. 66–74.
66. 'Ci insegni di vivere così imperfettamente'. Sperone Speroni, 'In difesa dei sofisti', in Katinis, *Sperone Speroni*, pp. 153–60. I am using Katinis's translation.
67. 'Sofista è lo esser nostro, perché non è e pare essere: non è, perché il presente dello essere è instante indivisibile, che fu piuttosto, e forse non sarà, che non è; e solo lo immortale è veramente.' Ibid., p. 156.
68. Ibid., p. 71.
69. Marco Sgarbi argues in favour of a negative function of rhetoric in Speroni's thought; see Sgarbi, *The Italian Mind: Vernacular Logic in Renaissance Logic (1540–1551)* (Leiden: Brill, 2014), Chap. 3. For a more positive view, see Stefano Jossa, 'Verso il barocco: Sperone Speroni e Carlo Borromeo (tra retorica e mistica)', *Aprosiana*, 11–12 (2004), 11–34. See also Valerio Vianello, '*Res e verba* nel "Dialogo della retorica" di Sperone Speroni', *Atti dell'Istituto Veneto di scienze, lettere ed arti*, 138 (1979–80), 231–53.
70. Barbaro's writing on the *Academica* is held in Florence, Biblioteca Nazionale, MS Magl. VIII 1492. This short work (nine folios) includes a dedication letter to the Cardinal of Ravenna, Benedetto Accolti the younger (1497–1549), and is dated 'Venetijs idibus Februarij mdxlii'. If the date were interpreted according to common use, the work should have been finished by 13 February 1542. Were the date instead interpreted *more veneto*, the work would be slightly later, i.e., finished in early 1543. Charles B. Schmitt has somewhat dismissively interpreted this work not only as 'a preliminary version of a more finished piece which Daniele hopes to complete', as Barbaro himself writes in the dedication, but as 'merely a workmanlike condensation of selections of the *Lucullus*, hardly worthy of an intelligent schoolboy beginner in Latin'; see Schmitt, *Cicero Scepticus: A Study of the Influence of the 'Academica' in the Renaissance* (The Hague: Martinus Nijhoff, 1972), pp. 67, 69. On Barbaro, see the essays gathered in *Daniele Barbaro (1514–1570): Letteratura, scienza e arti nella Venezia del Rinascimento*, ed. by Susy Marcon and Laura Moretti (Crocetta del Montello: Antiga Edizioni, 2015).
71. According to Lucia Signori, the first part of the work could be older, dating back to 1530–35, while the second part could have been completed or revised in a later period, between 1554/55 (when the manuscript was passed from Maccasciola to Ruscelli) and 1557, when it was printed. A further possibility, as suggested by Signori, was that the work was actually completed by 1536 and only subsequently did Ruscelli himself insert a series of references to works appearing later; see Maria Teresa Girardi and Lucia Signori, 'Daniele Barbaro letterato e il *Della eloquenza*', *Aevum*, 71 (1997), 651–89 (pp. 662–65).
72. 'E questo agevolmente si può fare ponendosi prima di mezzo tra il sì et il no, come chi sta in dubbio. Però che più prontamente si prende partito e si ammette il vero dubitando che portando seco alcuna opinione.' Daniele Barbaro, *Della eloquenza, in Trattati di poetica e retorica del Cinquecento*, ed. by Bernard Weinberg, II (Bari: Laterza, 1970), pp. 335–451 (p. 354).
73. 'Dubbiosa conoscenza'. Ibid., p. 361.
74. 'Piega più in una che in un'altra'. Ibid., p. 362.
75. 'Abito mezzano tra il vero intendimento e l'ignoranza, differente dal dubitare in questo, che la opinion piega più in una che in un'altra parte. Il dubitare tiene in egual bilancia la mente tra l'affermare et il negare, e però bisogna rivocare in dubbio le cose già ammesse e dimostrar quanto pericolo sia il giudicare. Da questo ne nascerà la questione e la dimanda, la quale disponendo la mente alle ragioni, quanto leverà della prima opinione tanto porrà di quella che tu vorrai.' Ibid., p. 362.
76. 'Le simiglianze delle cose'; 'profondità delle cose'. Ibid., p. 362.
77. 'Se la opinione con la ragione sarà legata [...] non più opinione ma scienza si potrà nominare.' Ibid., p. 365.

78. 'Perché la naturale cognizione del vero è molto debile e confusa, come quella che ai sensi piegando, lascia da parte la ragione e lo intelletto. [...] Questi sentimenti a sé la ragione traendo, fanno fallace et incostante il giudicio.' Ibid., p. 365.

79. 'E tant'altre spesse volte procedono questi tali con la curiosissima arrogantia loro, che di dubbio in dubbio trapassando, e di causa in causa prosuntuosamente cercando di porre il piede, a nissun termine vengon mai, dove l'ingordo loro intelletto quietare e posare si possa.' Alessandro Piccolomini, *La seconda parte de la filosofia naturale* [...] (Venice: Vincenzo Valgrisi, 1554), p. 7.

80. 'E d'intorno a i divini articoli che ad altro nostro assenso che d'opinione o di scientia son posti innanzi, eglino in modo s'affannano per fargli quadrare a i lor sensi propri che non trovando mai quello che cercano, inviluppatissimi in cotal ingorde dubitationi, menan tutta la vita loro. E in somma cosa alcuna quanto si voglia profonda o nascosta dentro a la mente di Dio potentissimo non si ritruova che essi non sperino e tentino di trarnela fuori e porsela finalmente manifesta dinanzi a gli occhi.' Ibid., p. 8.

81. Davi, 'Filosofia e retorica', pp. 101–02. See also Antonino Poppi, 'Il prevalere della "vita activa" nella paideia del Cinquecento', in *Rapporti tra le università di Padova e Bologna: Ricerche di filosofia, medicina e scienza*, ed. by Lucia Rossetti (Trieste: Lint, 1988), pp. 97–125; Eugenio Refini, 'Struggling with Power: Alessandro Piccolomini between *vita activa* and *vita contemplativa*', in *Penser et agir à la Renaissance/Thought and Action in the Renaissance*, ed. by Philippe Desan and Véronique Ferrer (Geneva: Droz, 2020), pp. 265–82.

82. See Michele Maylender, *Storia delle accademie d'Italia*, II (Bologna: Cappelli, 1927), pp. 222–25.

83. *Fortunato Martinengo: Un gentiluomo del Rinascimento fra arti, lettere e musica*, ed. by Marco Bizzarini and Elisabetta Selmi (Brescia: Morcelliana, 2018).

84. See Roberto Andrea Lorenzi, 'Per un profilo di Massimiliano Celso Martinengo, riformatore (1515–1557)', *Bollettino della società di studi valdesi*, 122 (2005), 23–68; Elisabetta Selmi, 'Tendenze erasmiane e calviniste tra i Martinengo nel '500', in *Fortunato Martinengo*, ed. by Bizzarini and Selmi, pp. 273–94. On the family, see Paolo Guerrini, *I Conti di Martinengo: Una celebre famiglia lombarda: studi e ricerche genealogiche* (Brescia: Geroldi, 1930).

85. Although he was only in Padua, where he had studied, between November 1541 and January 1542.

86. See Marco Faini, 'Fortunato Martinengo, Girolamo Ruscelli e l'Accademia dei Dubbiosi tra Brescia e Venezia', in *Girolamo Ruscelli: Dall'accademia alla corte alla tipografia: Itinerari e scenari per un letterato del Cinquecento*, ed. by Paolo Procaccioli and Paolo Marini (Manziana: Vecchiarelli, 2011), II, 455–519.

87. 'Vommene passo passo verso il fine, | Anz'a gran fretta e mai non me n'accorgo'; 'Deh, quando fia che per uscir d'affanni | Ella si scuota e fuor s'inalzi a volo | Da questa falsa, a l'altra vera vita?' Ibid., p. 505.

88. 'Oimé com'iti son questi e quegli anni | Senza che di lor fuga mi si' accorto | Oimé ch'or io conosco il lieve e corto | Viver ch'altro non è ch'ombra e affanni.' Ibid., p. 508.

89. Girolamo Ruscelli, *Lettura* [...] *sopra un sonetto dell'illustriss. signor marchese della Terza alla divina signora marchesa del Vasto. Ove con nuove et chiare ragioni si pruova la somma perfettione delle donne; et si discorrono molte cose intorno alla scala platonica dell'ascendimento per le cose create alla contemplatione di Dio* [...] (Venice: Giovan Griffio, 1552); Girolamo Ruscelli, ed., *Del tempio alla divina signora Giovanna d'Aragona* [...] (Venice: Plinio Pietrasanta, 1554). See Diana Robin, *Publishing Women: Salons, the Presses, and the Counter-Reformation in Sixteenth-Century Italy* (Chicago: University of Chicago Press, 2007), Chap. 4; on this typology of texts, see Maiko Favaro, 'Duttilità di una metafora: Note sui "Templi" letterari profani del Cinquecento', in *Le carte e i discepoli: Studi in onore di Claudio Griggio*, ed. by Fabiana di Brazzà et al. (Udine: Forum, 2016), pp. 201–09.

90. Giuseppe Alberigo, 'Aragona, Maria d'', in Dizionario biografico degli Italiani, III (Rome: Istituto dell'Enciclopedia italiana, 1961) <https://www.treccani.it/enciclopedia/maria-d-aragona_(Dizionario-Biografico)/>; Giuseppe Alberigo, 'Aragona, Giovanna d'', ibid., <https://www.treccani.it/enciclopedia/giovanna-d-aragona_(Dizionario-Biografico)/> [both accessed 26 September 2020].

91. *Del tempio*, pages not numbered.

92. 'Molto accesa dell'amor di Christo'; 'Ella ha tal forza ne' ragionari che par quasi che dalla sua

bocca escan catene colle quali tragga i sensi de gli ascoltanti. [...] Della s. Donna Giulia [...] sol questo dirò che non mi sbigottì mai presenza di donna alcuna coma la sua.' *Delle lettere di diversi autori raccolte per Venturino Ruffinelli* [...] (Mantua: [Venturino Ruffinelli], 1547), fols 25^v–26^r.

93. The second section of Ruscelli's *Lettura* lists all the most virtuous and outstanding Italian ladies living in the most important cities.

94. 'Alto veramente, et sopra ogni altro importantissimo dubbio, dottissimi e honoratissimi Signori, si dee credere che assai spesso discorra per la mente a ciascuno in considerare onde avenga che havendo Iddio per sola infinita ricchezza dell'amor suo creata questa miracolosa fabrica dell'universo [...] e posto nel centro suo l'huomo, signoreggiatore di tutte le cose di questo inferior mondo [...] non ad altro fine se non perché peregrinando per qualche tempo qua basso venisse tuttavia co i piedi delle sante opere [...] a condursi al cielo, non dimeno si camini dalla maggior parte di noi così a traverso che, come grida il Profeta, non si trovi pur uno che faccia bene.' Ibid., fol. 1^r.

95. 'Un grandissimo secreto sopra di ciò'. Ibid., fol. 4^r.

96. 'Là onde essendo per comandamento del molto illustre e honorato signor Presidente di questa gloriosa Academia l'altra domenica statomi imposto che seguendo l'ordine incominciato io dovessi oggi tener questo luogo e leggere il sonetto del Petrarca che segue a gli altri già letti, non sonetto del Petrarca mi è paruto recar oggi alle Signorie vostre davanti ma un nuovo sonetto dell'illustriss. s. Marchese della Terza alla gran Marchesa del Vasto.' Ibid., fol. 4^v.

97. See Letizia Panizza, 'The Semantic Field of Paradox in 16th and 17th Century Italy: From Truth in Appearance False to Falsehood in Appearance True: A Preliminary Investigation', in *Il vocabolario della République des Lettres: Terminologia filosofica e storia della filosofia — Problemi di metodo*, ed. by Marta Fattori (Florence: Olschki, 1997), pp. 197–220; Rosalie Cole, *Paradoxia Epidemica: The Renaissance Tradition of Paradox* (Princeton: Princeton University Press, 1966).

98. See Marco Faini, 'Fortunato Martinengo e Ortensio Lando: Dubbi e dubbiosi alla metà del Cinquecento', in *Fortunato Martinengo*, ed. by Bizzarini and Selmi, pp. 74–97.

99. This is what Serena Pezzini and Francine Daenens have argued. See Pezzini, 'Dissimulazione e paradosso nelle "Lettere di molte valorose donne" (1548) a cura di Ortensio Lando', *Italianistica: Rivista di letteratura italiana*, 31 (2002), 67–83; and Daenens, 'Donne valorose, eretiche, finte sante: Note sull'antologia giolitina del 1548', in *Per lettera: Scrittura epistolare femminile tra archivio e tipografia — secoli XV–XVII*, ed. by Gabriella Zarri (Rome: Viella, 1999), pp. 181–207. On the other hand, Meredith K. Ray and Elisabetta Simonetta point to Lando's authorship. See Ray, 'Textual Collaboration and Spiritual Partnership in Sixteenth-Century Italy: The Case of Ortensio Lando and Lucrezia Gonzaga', *Renaissance Quarterly*, 62 (2009), 694–747; Ray, *Writing Gender in Women's Letter Collections of the Italian Renaissance* (Toronto: University of Toronto Press, 2009), Chap. 2; and Simonetta, 'Il dissidente segretario delle valorose donne: Ortensio Lando tra *camouflage* epistolare e retorica del paradosso', *Bruniana & Campanelliana*, 22 (2016), 553–63.

100. Ray, 'Textual Collaboration', p. 706.

101. Paul Grendler, *Critics of the Italian World (1530–1560): Anton Francesco Doni, Nicolò Franco and Ortensio Lando* (Madison: University of Wisconsin Press, 1969), p. 148. Quoted also in Ray, *Writing Gender*, p. 62.

102. Ray, *Writing Gender*, p. 83.

103. Ibid., p. 118.

104. Ibid., p. 119.

105. Ibid., p. 72.

106. Ibid.

107. In reference to women's voices, I find especially convincing what Ray has argued: 'By focusing on themes such as family and household, in addition to broader problems like learning and religion, the *Valorose donne* allowed specifically feminine aspects of women's experience to become part of the public literary realm. On one level, this publicization of women's private experience expanded the parameters of epistolary discourse for women. [...] Whether we read them as serious compositions or not, the *Valorose donne* bring these issues to the forefront in a literary form. In spite of the frequent element of satire, this focus on the private sphere does lend,

at times, a certain dignity to a wholly female culture. For all its contradictions, impersonations, and idiosyncrasies, the *Valorose donne* are a valuable example of a male author's representation of the female epistolary realm. On the other hand [...] no other collection approaches the *Valorose donne* in terms of this detailed, intimate attention to the so-called "women's issues." The epistolary of Lucrezia Gonzaga, Veronica Franco, Isabella Andreini, and Arcangela Tarabotti [...] uniformly avoid such detailed consideration on childbirth, laundry, cosmetics, and home remedies, concentrating rather on careful literary self-presentation.' Ibid., p. 80.

108. Ray, 'Textual Collaboration', p. 695.

109. Ottavia's grandfather was the poet Andrea (*ante* 1459–1511). She was celebrated for her beauty: Ruscelli mentions her in his *Lettura*, and the Brescian writer Bartolomeo Arnigio (1523–1577) dedicated to her a work titled *Lettera, rime, et oratione* [...] *in lode della bellissima et gentilissima signora Ottavia Baiarda* (A letter, poems, and an oration [...] in praise of the most beautiful and most gentle lady Ottavia Baiarda) (Brescia: Ludovico Britannico il vecchio, 1558); she is mentioned in Ruscelli, *Lettura*, fol. 66^v. Ottavia, who married at the age of fourteen in 1538, has been identified as the young woman portrayed by Parmigianino in his so-called *Antea* (Naples, Capodimonte). The portrait could have been painted on the occasion of her marriage. See Giuseppe Bertini, 'Una proposta di identificazione dell'*Antea* del Parmigianino: Ottavia Baiardi Beccaria', *Aurea Parma*, 86 (2002), 361–68. On Andrea Baiardi, see Ceruti Burgio, *Studi sul Quattrocento parmense*, pp. 15–50, esp. pp. 47–50 for the relationship between the Baiardi family and Parmigianino. On Camilla, see Marcello Alberti, *Istoria delle donne scientiate*, 1 (Naples: Felice Mosca, 1740), p. 20.

110. 'La solutione di alcuni dubij che l'altro giorno nella mia casa di ingegnose donne si trattarno.' Ortensio Lando, *Lettere di molte valorose donne* (Venice: Giolito, 1548; rev. edn 1549), fol. 49^r.

111. Tullia d'Aragona, *Dialogue on the Infinity of Love*, ed. and trans. by Rinaldina Russell and Bruce Merry (Chicago: University of Chicago Press, 1997), pp. 54, 108. Cornelio Frangipane sets his *Dialogo d'amore* (written in August 1541 but published only in 1588) in Tullia's house. On Tullia, see Julia Hairston, 'Tullia d'Aragona', in *Dizionario biografico degli Italiani*, XCVII (Rome: Istituto dell'Enciclopedia italiana, 2020) <http://www.treccani.it/enciclopedia/tullia-d-aragona_%28Dizionario-Biografico%29/> [accessed 13 May 2020].

112. Pezzini, 'Dissimulazione e paradosso', pp. 75–77.

113. 'Voi mi proponete una Iliada de oscuri quesiti perché ve li solva [...] ma poiché nella vostra casa si ragunano delle persone dotte e ingegnose fatemi voi gratia di propor loro perché [...].' Lando, *Lettere*, fol. 50^r.

114. 'L'è una mala cosa: egli ci fa di savie doventar pazze, ci spoglia d'arbitrio, ci disvia dall'amore de' mariti.' Lando, *Lettere*, fol. 50^r.

115. 'Le mie grincie con questi miei scalzati dentoni fanno fugir Amore lontano mille miglia.' Lando, *Lettere*, fol. 50^r.

116. 'Perché sono più lussuriosi quei huomini c'hanno le gambe più sottili. Perché sono più lussuriosi quei uccelli che meno volano.' Lando, *Lettere*, fol. 50^r.

117. 'Un tono morboso [che] investe con la parodia e l'ironia dissacrante anche il filone medico filosofico del sapere cinquecentesco'. Pezzini, 'Dissimulazione e paradosso', p. 78.

118. 'Vorresti da me sapere [...] onde nasca che la femina sia dalli antichi scrittori reputata più imperfetta del maschio. Per qual rispetto si soglie dire che levata o spenta che sia la lucerna tutte le femine sieno d'un animo et d'un volere. Per qual cagione i Romani ci vietassero il vino; perché fusse l'Amore depinto con l'ali; perché naschi la barba a quelle donne che in Caria fanno l'ufficio de sacerdoti e così chi mosse Phidia a pingere Venere sopra di una testuggine. Alle presenti questioni per hora risponderoti il meglio che saprò.' Lando, *Lettere*, fol. 46^r.

119. 'L'altro giorno io vi pregai che mi volessi mandar la solutione delli infrascritti dubbi, cioè per qual causa gli Romani salutavano li Dei col capo scoperto e li huomini col capo coperto; e così qual cosa li moveva a sacrificare a Saturno et all'Honore senza havere alcuna cosa in capo; vi pregai anchor anche per lettere mi significaste da qual ragione mossi i figliuoli portavano il padre alla sepoltura col capo velato e le figliuolo con il capo ignudo. Aspetto di questi dubbi vostra dichiaratione.' Lando, *Lettere*, fol. 75^v.

120. 'Un consortino astuto, non frodolento, audace e non temerario, di una eloquentia libera e chiara ma non importuna e satievole; i suoi morsi co' quali trafigge volentieri l'avaritia de' preti

non sono di cane né di lupo ma di mansueto agnello [...]. Non albergarà mai nella casa vostra alcuno humore maninconico.' Lando, *Lettere*, fols 4^v–5^r.

121. 'Faceto è Marco Antonio Sidonio, dotato di buon tenore di voce, di molta audacia e di chiara pronuntia; esso solo piacque ad Hercole cardinal di Mantova cui poche cose sogliono piacere per lo suo troppo dilicato gusto.' Ortensio Lando, *Sette libri de cathaloghi a varie cose appartenenti* [...] (Venice: Gabriel Giolito de' Ferrari, 1552), p. 501.

122. 'Dall'altro canto, stammi dubbiosa di non offender col farmi christiana la divina Maestà; vivo in angoscia se Christo per il vero Messia confesso, di non provocarmi contra il sdegno di Mosè et la maledittione di tutta la Sinagoga; non so (misera me) dove mi volga per aiuto e per consiglio. Le vostre lettere mi hanno infinitamente commossa [...] ma considero, Signora mia, le promesse della Scrittura sacra che quando verrà il Messia, l'Israel sarà riscosso, e noi poveri Hebrei siamo pur anchora tuttavia dispersi [...]. Veggo di più che la nostra legge fu data pubblicamente da Iddio per mano di Mosè sul monte Sinai [...] là dove la vostra è data celatamente per mano e per confessione de duodeci poveri scalzi, oltre che non mi posso contenere di non prestare intiera fede a' nostri Rhabini, li quali hanno nel vostro Redentore molto diversa opinione da voi [...]. Voi, fra tanto che lo Spirito non riveli ciò che ho da fare, pregate per me.' Lando, *Lettere*, fols 5^v–6^r.

123. Venice: Al Segno del Pozzo [Andrea Arrivabene], 1552. Beatrice, also known as Gracia Nasi, left the following year Italy for Constantinople, where she returned to her pristine Jewish faith; see Maria Giuseppina Muzzarelli, 'Beatrice de Luna, vedova Mendes, alias donna Gracia Nasi: Un'ebrea influente (1510–1569 ca.)', in *Rinascimento al femminile*, ed. by Ottavia Niccoli (Rome: Laterza, 1991), pp. 83–116.

124. Simonetta Adorni Braccesi, 'L'"Agrippa Arrigo" e Ortensio Lando: Fra eresia, cabbala e utopismo: Ipotesi di lettura', *Historia philosophica: An International Journal*, 2 (2004), 97–113, (esp. p. 107).

125. Silvana Seidel Menchi, 'Chi fu Ortensio Lando?' *Rivista storica italiana*, 106 (1994), 501–64, (esp. p. 557).

126. See Adorni Braccesi, 'L'"Agrippa Arrigo" e Ortensio Lando'. Agrippa's *De incertitudine* was translated into Italian by Ludovico Domenichi and published in 1549 in Venice by Anton Francesco Doni.

127. 'Forse ch'egli vi fa miscredente e dubbioso dell'immortalità come fanno i philosophi? Né offre il vano sapere di medici, matematici, legisti, storici.' Lando, *Lettere*, fol. 19^r.

128. 'For Lando, the misuse of religion verges on superstition, and superstition in all forms is anathema to him.' Ray, *Writing Gender*, 60.

129. 'Mi è molto piaciuto d'intendere che habbiate abbandonato il mondo e vi siate data tutta a Giesù Christo [...] ma perché la religione è assai vicina alla superstitione [...] guardatevi [...] che non ne restiate in parte alcuna macchiata [...] il superstitioso più teme in chiesa, più dubita presso l'altare che altrove non fa; ma se volete dalle sue mani liberarvi, svolgete l'animo alle sacre lettere.' Lando, *Lettere*, fol. 47^{r-v}.

130. 'Contemplatione di cose alte e divine'; 'grandissimi secreti e bellissimi avvertimenti possibili a far parere un huomo savio et accorto ancor che non fusse molto pratico ne gli studi di filosofia o di Scrittura'. [Ortensio Lando], *Quattro libri de dubbi con le solutioni a ciascun dubbio accommodate* [...] (Venice: Gabriel Giolito de Ferrari, 1556), fol. A2^v.

131. See Procaccioli, 'Un cultore del dubbio nell'Italia del Cinquecento', pp. 189–206.

132. Iolanda Ventura, '*Per modum quaestionis compilatum*', pp. 286, 288.

133. Antònia Carré and Lluís Cifuentes, 'Girolamo Manfredi's *Il Perché*: I. The *Problemata* and Its Medieval Tradition', and 'Girolamo Manfredi's *Il Perché*: II. The *Secretum secretorum* and the Book's Publishing Success', *Medicina & Storia*, 10 (2010), 13–38, 39–58.

134. Paolo Cherchi, 'Il quotidiano, i *Problemata* e la meraviglia: Ministoria di un microgenere', in *Ministorie di microgeneri*, ed. by Chiara Fabbian, Alessandro Rebonato, and Emanuela Zanotti Carney (Ravenna: Longo, 2003), pp. 11–48 (p. 25).

135. Ventura, '*Per modum quaestionis compilatum*', p. 298; Cherchi, 'Il quotidiano'; Emanuela Zanotti Carney, 'I *Dubbi* di Ortensio Lando e il *Perché* di Girolamo Manfredi', *Giornale storico della letteratura italiana*, 185 (2008), 64–78.

136. 'Dove che io volendo giovar al volgo, sono stato astretto di scrivere volgarmente et etiamdio con prolissità: percioché con gli indotti non si possono lasciar a dietro alcuni principii, i quali si presuppongono ne i litterati, né si poco pretermettere cert'altre cose dilettevoli e facili, per facilitar i sensi oscuri, e dilettar i lettori, e dilettando invitar loro a leggere e per consequente levar il velo dell'ignoranza loro.' Girolamo Garimberto, *Problemi naturali, e morali* (Venice: Vicenzo Valgrisi, 1550), fol. 3^{r-v}.

137. Bartolomeo Paschetti, *Dubbi morali et naturali* [...] (Genua: [Antonio Roccatagliata], 1581), pages not numbered, from the dedication letter to Giovan Pietro Crollalanza. Paschetti's work 'nearly constituted a complete translation of the *Omnes homines*'; Carré and Cifuentes, 'Girolamo Manfredi's *Il Perché*: I', pp. 26–27. The *Omnes homines* is a collection of problems written in Germany between the end of the thirteenth and the beginning of the fourteenth centuries. Paschetti was a doctor and a philosopher who studied in Padua and moved to Genoa; he was active from 1578 to 1616, the year of his death.

138. For example, Garimberti has an interesting 'doubt' about why the inhabitants of the recently discovered 'Western Indies' have laws and habits in common with Europeans without their knowing anything about Europe, and the other way around (Garimberto, *Problemi naturali, e morali*, fol. 119^{r}). While the question could have prompted interesting comparative anthropological reflections, in the hands of, say, Montaigne, Garimberti does not even try to understand cultural differences, talking about 'foolish idolatry' and reporting curious habits of the inhabitants of the Eastern and Western Indies, and even resorting to the myth of Atlantis to explain possible encounters of civilizations. Probably, this inability at problematizing questions and instead treating them as mere curiosities, at a time when the 'new science' was blossoming, caused the genre to slowly disappear; see in particular Cherchi, 'Il quotidiano', pp. 34–40.

139. Zanotti Carney, 'I *Dubbi*', p. 78.

140. Ibid., pp. 75–77.

141. Although internal contradictions are not unusual within this genre; see Ann Blair, 'The *Problemata* as a Natural Philosophical Genre', in *Natural Particulars: Nature and the Disciplines in Renaissance Europe*, ed. by Anthony Grafton and Nancy Siraisi (Cambridge, MA: MIT Press, 1999), pp. 171–204.

142. [Lando], *Quattro libri*, pp. 22 and 29, 25 and 29 ('stimansi di più valore e di più alto merito di quel che sono').

143. See Seidel Menchi, 'Chi fu'; Silvana Seidel Menchi, 'Sulla fortuna di Erasmo in Italia: Ortensio Lando e altri eterodossi della prima metà del Cinquecento', *Schweizerische Zeitschrift für Geschichte*, 24 (1974), 537–634; Silvana Seidel Menchi, 'Spiritualismo radicale nelle opere di Ortensio Lando attorno al 1550', *Archiv für Reformationsgeschichte*, 65 (1974), 210–77. Some of the doubts concerned the nature of baptism and of the Eucharist as pure signs, the critique of miracles, the divine nature of Christ, the universal salvation of the elect, salvation by faith, and the regeneration of human nature thanks to Christ's sacrifice.

144. Seidel Menchi has argued that doubt allows light to be cast on the same problem from two or more perspectives and undermine dogma under the false pretence of inexperience that requires proper instruction: doubt allows either ambiguous or adamant answers to compromising questions. See Seidel Menchi, 'Spiritualismo radicale', p. 259; and her *Erasmo in Italia*, Chap. 8.

145. 'Perché sono sì grati agli occhi nostri i colli de i colombi e le penne de i pavoni? Per la varietà e incertitudine de i colori. Quale è l'ufficio del core humano? Egli è di simulare e dissimulare. Perché è maraviglioso il camaleonte? Per ricevere tutti i colori.' [Lando], *Quattro libri*, p. 278. Da Silva may possibly be the same Miguel da Silva to whom Baldassare Castiglione dedicated his *Book of the Courtier*.

146. Caterina was the daughter of Prospero Colonna and the wife of Massimiliano Gonzaga, Signore of Luzzara. The first three books feature only four women, whereas the last one has twenty-two. This seems consistent with Lando's attitude to act as counsellor of or collaborator with women in spiritual matters.

147. 'Diede Iddio altra pena al fallo di Caino salvo che egli dovesse mutar paesi? Cotesta sarebbe stata leggiera afflittione percioché tal cosa sostenne anche Abraamo e molti altri santi; ma la pena che l'haveva da affliggere si era ch'ei dovesse esser di mente perturbata e incerta di tutti i suoi fatti

e consigli e tutto quello ch'egli isperimentasse nocevogli [*sic*] gli fosse.' [Lando], *Quattro libri*, pp. 357–58.

148. 'Che cosa è propriamente fede? Ella è una certa scientia conceputa nella mente, aliena da ogni dubbia opinione.' [Lando], *Quattro libri*, p. 390. Franceschina belonged to the powerful Trissino family of Vicenza.

149. Calcagno's story is reconstructed — along with a transcription of the trial — in Giovanni Dall'Orto, '*Adora più presto un bel putto, che Domenedio*: Il processo a un libertino omosessuale: Francesco Calcagno (1550)', *Sodoma*, 6 (1993), 43–55. See also Stella, *Anabattismo e antitrinitarismo*, p. 44. Lucia Felici, 'Ateismo e sodomia nella Repubblica di Venezia. Ancora sul caso di Francesco Calcagno (1528-1550)', *Riforma e movimenti religiosi*, 8 (2020), 59–80. Lucia Felici, 'A Sixteenth-Century Libertine Priest. Francesco Calcagno', in *Cursed Blessings. Sex and Religious Radical Dissent in Early Modern Europe*, ed. by Umberto Grassi (London-New York: Routledge, 2024), pp. 21–39.

150. 'Un bel culo era el suo Altare, la sua messa, l'hostia, calice, et la pathena.' Dall'Orto, '*Adora più presto*', p. 46.

151. Ibid.

152. 'Se doveria più presto dar fede alle Metamorphosi d'Ovidio, che al'Evangelio.' Ibid.

153. 'Esso prete più volte ha detto che la Bibia et li Evangeli sono Metamorphosi.' Ibid., p. 47.

154. 'Più volte ha detto che Dio non è, né anima, et che morto el corpo, è morta l'anima.' Ibid.

155. 'Esso Ovidio è più verace che non è essa scrittura, et me diceva che quelli [che] hanno scritta questa scrittura erano persone del Diavolo, et che facevano questo per far star la gente in timore, et governar il mondo a loro modo, et me diceva spesso quel verso de Lucretio "Primus in Orbe deos fecit Timor"'. Ibid., p. 48.

156. 'Il papa, et questi huomini grandi credevano come lui, cioè che non vi è Dio, et che non vi era né paradiso né altro, ma che morto il corpo, è morta l'anima, et che il Tutto se governava a caso.' Ibid.

157. 'Hora negava ogni cosa, et hora diceva che credeva ogni cosa.' Ibid., p. 50.

158. Ibid., p. 47.

159. 'Dicendo Messer Lauro di Glisenti da Vestone ch'el non credeva in cosa alcuna, se non quel che se vedeva [...]. E da poi in ottobre [...] dicendo detto prete Nicolò che credeva tanto alla scrittura, quanto alle fabule de Isoppo.' Ibid., pp. 50–51.

160. 'Io ho detto che un bel culo, era el paradiso, et Domenedio, et queste parole [le] vidi in un libro chiamato *La cazzarìa*.' Ibid., p. 52.

161. Antonio Vignali, *La Cazzaria — The Book of the Prick*, ed. and trans. by Ian Frederick Moulton (London: Routledge, 2003), p. 93. The original Italian reads as follows: 'e se è vera la openion del Discreto Intronato, cioè che 'l paradiso, l'inferno e 'l purgatorio siano in questo mondo, e che il paradiso sia la tua casa, ove vivo e con tutti e beni padrone ti trovi, e gli angioli i bei giovani, e l'altre circonstanze che fanno l'uomo contento l'altre gerarchie, e così per il contrario la prigione sia il purgatorio e la povertà l'inferno e gli affanni i diavoli, io voglio pensare che non altro sia ambrosia e nettare che la dolce linguina e 'l chiuso piacere che è nel dolce e delicato culo d'un bel giovane.' Antonio Vignali (Arsiccio Intronato), *La Cazzaria*, ed. by Pasquale Stoppelli, intro. by Nino Borsellino (Rome: Edizioni dell'elefante, 1984), p. 61. On the texts, see Maria Teresa Ricci, 'Antonio Vignali e *La Cazzaria*', in *Extravagances amoureuses: L'amour au-delà de la norme à la Renaissance/Stravaganze amoureuses: L'amore oltre la norma nel Rinascimento*, ed. by Élise Boillet and Chiara Lastraioli (Paris: Honoré Champion, 2010), pp. 181–90; Robert Buranello, 'The Hidden Ways and Means of Antonio Vignali's *La Cazzaria*', *Quaderni d'italianistica*, 26 (2005), 59–76.

162. I quote from Ian F. Moulton, 'The Greatest Tangle of Pricks There Ever Was: Knowledge, Sex, and Power in Renaissance Italy', introduction to Vignali, *La Cazzaria*, pp. 1–70 (p. 22).

163. Ibid., 5 and 22.

164. Ibid., 24.

165. *Dieci paradosse degli academici intronati* (Milan: Gio. Antonio degli Antonij, 1564); Congrega dei Rozzi di Siena, *Quistioni e chasi di più sorte*, ed. by Claudia Chierichini (Siena: Accademia dei Rozzi, 2019). On the *ingannati*, see Franco Tomasi, 'L'Accademia degli Intronati e Alessandro Piccolomini: Strategie culturali e itinerari biografici', in *Alessandro Piccolomini (1508–1579): Un*

siennois à la croisée des genres et des savoirs, ed by Marie-Françoise Piéjus, Michel Plaisance, and Matteo Residori (Paris: Cirri, 2011), pp. 23–38.

166. 'La ricerca e la tecnica del "perché" elevava il discorso osceno alla dignità del linguaggio accademico, o meglio trovava una piattaforma insolita o un modo nuovo e "curioso" di parlare di cose proibite.' Paolo Cherchi, 'La *Cazzaria* di Vignali e *Il libro del perché* di Manfredi', *Annali Online di Ferrara — Lettere*, 1 (2007), 106–16 (p. 113).

167. The social composition of this conventicle is also interesting. Among its members were Ludovico Calini and Giovanni Paolo Boldrino (Dall'Orto, *'Adora più presto'*, p. 48). Ludovico was the son of Luigi (Alvise): the Calini were one of the most prominent families in Brescia, and this Luigi Calini could be the well-known friend of, among others, Pietro Carnesecchi; probably he is the same as the one mentioned in Contarini's letters to Querini and Giustinian. Giovanni Paolo Boldrino was a collaborator of Giovan Francesco Gambara. Both Luigi Calini and Giovan Francesco Gambara should be identified as two of the interlocutors in a dialogue by Giovanni Andrea Ugoni, the *Ragionamento nel quale si ragiona di tutti gli stati dell'humana vita*, which dealt with the reformation of society. Ugoni's polemical target was the idleness of nobility and the practice of forcing the scions of noble family into monasteries and convents. Ugoni published his work in 1562 but he probably composed it in 1549, one year before Calcagno's trial. Ugoni was himself twice put on trial by the Inquisition, in 1554 and in 1567. See Anne Jacobson Schutte, *By Force and Fear: Taking and Breaking Monastic Vows in Early Modern Europe* (Ithaca, NY: Cornell University Press, 2011), pp. 28–30; Marco Faini, 'A proposito di Giovanni Andrea Ugoni: Temi e spunti dalle *Rime* e dai *Trattati*', in *Riformatori bresciani del '500: Indagini*, ed. by Roberto A. Lorenzi (Brescia: Grafo, 2006), pp. 79–103 and 265–77; and Marco Faini, '"Mentre il lungo error piango e sospiro": Le "Rime" di Giovanni Andrea Ugoni', *Giornale storico della letteratura italiana*, 126 (2009), 51–83.

168. 'Parole così neffande e turpissime [...] che mai né turco né hebreo [e] neancho i demoni non solamente non le hanno mai dite, [ma] neancho imaginate.' Dall'Orto, *'Adora più presto'*, p. 53.

CONCLUSION

Toward a New Season

In reconstructing how Renaissance Italian society took delight in reading, watching, and telling stories of doubt and doubters, this book documents how doubt turned into a recognizable cultural object. Doubt seems to have shaped peculiar forms of sociability, moving outside the university classroom as well as out of the clutches of philosophers and theologians, so to speak. A cross-cutting phenomenon, doubt can manifest in all fields of human activity. However, once those authors who make up the canon of early modern scepticism are left behind, the problem arises of where to turn for sources, since a recognizable corpus, a canon of authors clearly thematicizing doubt, is not to be found. This poses a fascinating methodological challenge, one that has forced me to broaden the spectrum of my sources and include unconventional approaches to doubt. This has allowed for an understanding of doubt as a broad and shared cultural and social phenomenon, something that has been missing in existing scholarship. Poems and *novelle*, emblems and dictionaries, trials and religious pamphlets, manuals for confessors and parlour games, paintings and letters, *artes moriendi* and hagiographies all document the rising interest in doubt in early sixteenth century. By taking these sources into account, we can better understand the explosion of the sceptical crisis in the second half of the century and the pervasive role of uncertainty on so many levels in late Renaissance European culture.

This book lies in a grey area, keeping its distance between the Scylla of an intellectual history of early modern scepticism and the Charybdis of an emotional history of doubt, or of doubt as a purely individual condition. On the one hand, it was important to move away from the peaks of high culture and turn to sources more representative of larger segments of the Italian populace. If we want to determine if and how doubt was part of the mental landscape of early modern Italians, the works of Aristotle, Cicero, Augustine, Thomas Aquinas, Machiavelli can hardly suffice; besides, other scholars have covered this territory better than I ever could.[1] One must then follow the rivers that depart from those peaks, and be ready to sail waters other than those of philosophical speculation. To early modern Italians, doubt was much more than an intellectual tool that could be used to dissect official narratives: doubt was an experience at the same time uncanny and exhilarating, tempting and distressing, a social fact as well as an isolating experience. Most of all, doubt involved the entirety of one's being — mind, body, and soul.

It is to overcome the limits of an entirely intellectual approach and remain consistent with my intention to leave the 'peaks' in the background that I have avoided discussing the role of doubt in the evolution of Renaissance learning. Within each discipline doubt can be seen as playing a double role. First, the subjects studied by each discipline were doubtful: jurisprudence, medicine, textual criticism, and history often dealt with doubtful cases, open to multiple explanations and lacking the necessary amount of evidence. Scholars found themselves in a doubtful position, having to make uncertain and often entirely conjectural choices; doubt thus became part of the methodology itself. The philologist who, in the absence of other clues, resorted to *divinatio* or intuition to make emendations to a corrupt text might be compared to a person who had to make a choice while in a state of doubt, as we have seen in Chapter 1.[2] As the curators of a recent volume on textual criticism and scepticism ask: 'But what did the textual critic do when faced with the equivalent strength of contrasting arguments, that is, of contrasting manuscript readings?'[3] In 'the equivalent strength of contrasting arguments' we find a crisp formulation of the essence of doubt as we have learned to understand it. This leads to the second point of the relationship between doubt and scholarly disciplines: it is precisely because of this frequent lack of evidence, because of the role of conjecture, that disciplines could come under attack from a sceptical perspective. Already in 1548, for example, in his *De historica facultate disputatio* (A discourse on the historical discipline), the humanist Francesco Robortello addressed Sextus Empiricus's sceptical criticism of history.[4] Since then, historians have striven to conceive an *ars historica* based on a series of rules or a methodology that would grant reliability.[5] The reconstruction of how and when given forms of knowledge had to face sceptical attacks and the ways in which a theoretical reflection on their epistemological status came about lies beyond the boundaries of this work.

In the same way, although individual emotions and feelings play a part in this book, more than documenting individual anxieties, I have aimed to reconstruct how such anxieties gave birth to a broad range of discourses. What my sources have in common is the attempt to use doubt as a tool to act on reality in a variety of contexts (hence the allusions to a 'culture of doubt'). Therefore, I chose not to include each instance of individuals voicing their doubts or, more generally, declaring their doubtful condition. Surely writing a history of doubt as an existential condition in the sixteenth century would be a captivating task. A systematic survey of letters, diaries, conversion narratives, and ego-documents in general would yield fascinating results. Unfortunately, for the period under consideration — a time of highly codified literary genres, including letter-writing — these documents tend to be quite scarce. This is not to deny that letters and (auto)biographical accounts from the early sixteenth century open windows into their authors' interiority. However, ego-documents appear to increase in number in the second half of the century and into the seventeenth century; they also seem to devote more space to the expression of inner anxiety, making it easier for us to ascertain their authors' state of mind and emotions.[6] In the same way, because of the tightened grip of the Roman Church's institutions in the post-Tridentine period, tales of conversion as well as ego-documents produced at the behest of confessors and inquisitors, especially by charismatic women, dramatically increase.[7] To what extent we can trust these documents and whether they actually allow us to map the emotions and doubts of commoners is debatable. Judicial sources, of course, give us back the voices of ordinary folk, but in these stories doubt has usually overstepped the line that separates an existential condition from deviance.[8] Ego-documents produced by members of minorities are fascinating sources, but as Serena Di Nepi has recently highlighted, their survival often depends on material conditions such as the existence of circles interested in such survival, or the availability of space and apt conditions for the creation of an archive (which explains, for example, the relative paucity of materials coming from otherwise highly literate groups such as Jews).[9] This in turn suggests that these documents refer to individuals of particular significance more than to ordinary people. Conversion narratives, especially in the form of declarations to the Inquisition Tribunal, are problematic sources that have prompted discussions among historians about the issue of sincerity.[10] Also frequent was the case of individuals changing their faith more than once for reasons of convenience, thus calling into question the deeper meaning of 'conversion'.[11] Finally, in the case of ego-documents produced by women, we should point out that, as Adriano Prosperi has shown, literary patterns played a crucial role, often overlapping with lived experience, again suggesting caution.[12] Retrieving the emotions, feelings, and doubts of the humblest people, the illiterate, the city labourers as well as the peasants remains, in other words, a difficult and at times perhaps unattainable task, and the subject for future research that is focused on a different set of sources and a different time frame than that employed here.

What I hope this book shows is the emergence of doubt as an object of reflection, as the centre and fulcrum of a field of discourses exploring, describing, and circumscribing the very act of doubting. The construction of an iconography of doubt seems to go precisely in this direction. Making doubt recognizable through visualization allows for its isolation from a plethora of concurring categories and an understanding of its functions, its consequences, and therefore its uses. Documenting the richness of ways in which early modern Italians turned doubt from a moment of impasse into a useful tool to act upon their reality has been another goal of this book. Doubt could serve a number of purposes that go well beyond those we label as scepticism. We can see this richness of approaches to doubt as part of the historical process leading to the 'sceptical crisis' of the second half of the sixteenth century and the first decades of the seventeenth. Although it will be outside Italy that philosophical doubt produces its momentous consequences, some of the seeds of this revolution were planted in Italy. Italian culture did not produce a Montaigne or a Descartes; however, over several decades it produced a culture of doubt of astonishing vitality and richness.

This long-lasting culture of doubt probably contributed to shaping the encounter with non-European peoples, which in itself proved crucial to the history of doubt, not only because it prompted a relativistic reflection on the part of Europeans (best exemplified by Montaigne's essay on cannibals) but also because it played a large part in the rejuvenation of moral theology and in the rise of probabilism, as recently explored by Stefania Tutino.[13] The Jesuits' accounts of their mission show how Christian religion caused doubts in non-European populations. The ability to turn these doubts into an instrument of proselytization and conversion certainly testifies to the Jesuits' theological and rhetorical skills as well as to the flexibility of doubt as an intellectual tool. Nonetheless, it also shows their keen perception that doubt could be key to gaining the favour of prospective converts. Engaging in disputes, acknowledging doubts, and providing rational explanations were crucial to the conversion process as Jesuits presented it. For example, Francis Xavier's letters sent from Japan in the early 1550s (he had arrived in Japan in 1549) offer fascinating descriptions of the many doubts of Japanese people and of how they engaged the Jesuits in complex discussions in which rational persuasion was key to opening the way to religious belief.[14] Japanese converts, in Xavier's words, would tell *bonzes* (Buddhist monks) that 'the law of God was more reasonable than theirs', and this 'because they saw that we answered to their doubts'.[15] In fact, the Japanese were, in Xavier's definition, 'more obedient to reason than all the other infidel people whom I met, and they are so curious and insistent in asking, and so yearning for learning that they never stop asking'.[16] The people from Yamaguchi, for example, had 'a mighty doubt [...] against God's goodness', and this doubt concerned God's lack of compassion in not having revealed himself to the Japanese before the Jesuits came. That so many people could be thrust into hell because God inexplicably had never made himself known to them was one of 'their grave doubts'.[17] Another doubt of the Japanese had to do with the existence of another principle, opposite to God, for they could not fathom the existence of demons, given that God was supposed to be good. This was a powerful doubt, for it called into question God's very essence: if he was good, he would not have created humankind so weak and so inclined to evil, nor would he leave demons free to tempt humans. Things were in fact more complex and the conversion of Japanese people less straightforward and triumphant than the Jesuits would have us think, entailing a great deal of hybridization.[18] In the process, Jesuits could also fall into the abyss of self-doubt, as beautifully shown in Martin Scorsese's movie *Silence* (2016, inspired by the 1966 eponymous novel by Shūsaku Endō).[19]

Doubts were not only experienced by non-European peoples, though. Missionaries had to face all sorts of doubts concerning the sacraments, the ways they were administered, their validity, the possibility of adapting them to new contexts. Missionaries turned to Roman institutions to be enlightened, and the dossiers containing their doubts and questions are known as *dubia circa sacramenta*. These documents are crucial in reconstructing an institutional history of the Roman Church as well as in showing how 'missionary spaces are the reign of exception, of deviation from norms, of particular cases' — or in other words, of doubt.[20]

A story of 'global' doubt, exploring the emotional and intellectual responses of non-European peoples to their encounter with European beliefs, should be part of the larger story of doubt in the post-Tridentine world that still waits to be written. Such a story, constructed from trials, letters, diaries, and ego-documents could be a fascinating and diverse fresco of the voices not only of converts, women, members of religious minorities, and non-European peoples, but also of commoners (such as those studied by Federico Barbierato in his seminal book on unbelief in seventeenth- and eighteenth-century Venice).[21] As such, it would certainly give us a more nuanced picture of how, beyond the peaks of high culture (from Shakespeare to Donne and Montaigne, from Galileo to Pascal, Descartes, and Bayle), ordinary people experienced and voiced their anxiety, uncertainty, and doubt in a time of rigid control. Again, this story lies beyond the scope of the present book, but it certainly forms the central theme for a future companion volume.

Some of the questions that underlie this book — why doubt became a social phenomenon, why understanding the nature of doubt was more urgent than addressing specific doubts, who had access to doubt and why — may resonate with our own present-day anxieties. In sixteenth-century Italy doubt appeared to have been a flexible and effective tool with which one could intervene on a complex and rapidly evolving reality. Can early modern doubt still teach us lessons?

Compared to our early modern ancestors, we are more advanced in the political use of doubt. Raising doubts about intellectual authority, political opponents, and science has become part of the new populist politics. In the last decades we have witnessed the systematic use of doubt to delegitimize teachers, researchers, and intellectuals, and prepare the coming to power of certain political groups. Casting suspicion on 'official' narratives and replacing them with alternative explanations is a recognizable feature of our contemporary society. In a 2017 *New York Times* article titled '"Kompromat" and the Danger of Doubt and Confusion in a Democracy', Amanda Taub wrote:

> By eroding the very idea of a shared reality, and by spreading apathy and confusion among a public that learns to distrust leaders and institutions alike, kompromat undermines a society's ability to hold the powerful to account and ensure the proper functioning of government.[22]

'Kompromat', the uncontrolled spread of compromising information, fosters doubt, and doubt erodes the spaces of democracy. In contrast to this advanced deployment of doubt, we tend to respond by opposing 'facts' and 'certainties' to manipulated knowledge, a patently ineffective strategy. Acquiescence to facts (or to their non-existence) is probably the major risk of contemporary society; opposing 'facts' to 'doubts' is simplistic, if not dangerous, for the nature of 'facts' is often weak. Doubt can be the sign of a problem but also the means to engage with the problem. In the face of a radical mistrust of authority, opposing a destructive form of doubt with a constructive one could prove more expedient. Doubt, more than facts, requires being active, being creative, and making experiments in critical thinking. If there is something that our early modern ancestors can teach us it is that doubt, and not certainty, is an instrument of self-defense and a means to build bridges. Like our early modern ancestors, we might rebuild a form of sociability based on critical, self-conscious doubt. After all, if disinformation is a 'fog', as Taub puts it, early moderns teach us that doubt is a young man who walks in the night holding a lantern. It is not for me to say where this lantern can lead us and how: I am certain, however, that early modern doubt has much to teach us about our current condition.

Notes to the Conclusion

1. Among the volumes that adopt this approach, see at least *Scepticism in the Modern Age: Building on the Work of Richard Popkin*, ed. by José R. Maia Neto, Gianni Paganini, and John Christian Laursen (Leiden: Brill, 2009); *La centralità del dubbio: Un progetto di Antonio Rotondò*, ed. by Camilla Hermanin and Luisa Simonutti (Florence: Olschki, 2011); Gianni Paganini, *Il dubbio dei moderni: Una storia dello scetticismo* (Rome: Carocci, 2022); see also the works by Don Cameron Allen, Richard Popkin, and Marco Sgattoni, quoted passim.

2. Anthony Grafton, 'Divination: Toward the History of a Philological Term', in *The Marriage of Philology and Scepticism: Uncertainty and Conjecture in Early Modern Scholarship and Thought*, ed. by Gian Mario Cao, Anthony Grafton, and Jill Kraye (London: University of London Press, 2019), pp. 47–69.

3. Gian Mario Cao, Anthony Grafton, and Jill Kraye, foreword to *The Marriage of Philology and Scepticism*, pp. ix–x (p. ix).

4. See Marco Sgarbi, *Francesco Robortello (1516–1567): Architectural Genius of the Humanities* (New York: Routledge, 2020), Chap. 6; Carlo Ginzburg, *Threads and Traces: True False Fictive*, trans. by Ann C. Tedeschi and John Tedeschi (Berkeley: University of California Press, 2012), pp. 13–16.

5. Among the vast bibliography, see at least Anthony Grafton, *What Was History?* (Cambridge: Cambridge University Press, 2007); Cherchi, *Ignoranza ed erudizione*, pp. 186–213.

6. On women's letters see *Per lettera*, ed. by Zarri.

7. Anne Jacobson Schutte, *Aspiring Saints: Pretense of Holiness, Inquisition, and Gender in the Republic of Venice, 1618–1750* (Baltimore: Johns Hopkins University Press, 2001); Adelisa Malena, 'Madri in spirito: Note di lettura su direzione spirituale e discorso autobiografico negli scritti di Paola Maria di Gesù Centurione (1586–1646) e Francesca Toccafondi (1638–1685)', in *Donne tra saperi e poteri: Nella storia delle religioni*, ed. by Sofia Boesch Gajano and Enzo Pace (Brescia: Morcelliana, 2007), pp. 317–39; Adelisa Malena, 'Ego-documents or "Plural Compositions"? Reflections on Women's Obedient Scriptures in the Early Modern Catholic World', *Journal of Early Modern Studies*, 1 (2012), 97–113.

8. Thomas V. Cohen and Elizabeth S. Cohen, Introduction to *Words and Deeds in Renaissance Rome: Trials before the Papal Magistrates* (Toronto: University of Toronto Press, 1993), pp. 3–33.

9. Serena Di Nepi, 'Fede e scrittura: Libri e testimonianze personali nei processi di autodefinizione religiosa (XVI–XVII secolo)', *Società e storia*, 160 (2018), 241–48; Serena Di Nepi, 'Autobiografie di minoranza: Prospettive individuali tra scritture personali e racconti di vita di ebrei e musulmani a Roma in età moderna', *Società e storia*, 160 (2018), 289–313.

10. See also, for further references, E. Nathalie Rothman, 'Becoming Venetian: Conversion and Transformation in the Seventeenth-Century Mediterranean', *Mediterranean Historical Review*, 21 (2006), 39–75. See also some of the essays quoted below.

11. Among the many publications on the topic, see Adelisa Malena, 'Introduzione: Racconti di conversione e relazioni di genere in età moderna e contemporanea', *Genesis*, 6 (2007), 5–12; Irene Fosi, 'Conversion and Autobiography: Telling Tales before the Roman Inquisition', *Journal of Early Modern History*, 17 (2013), 437–56; Moshe Sluhovski, 'Recidivist Converts in Early Modern Europe', in *Dissimulation and Deceit in Early Modern Europe*, ed. by Miriam Eliav-Feldon and Tamar Herzig (Basingstoke: Palgrave-Macmillan, 2015), pp. 94–109; Chiara Petrolini, 'Il giornale di conversione di Toby Matthews', *Società e storia*, 160 (2018), 269–87; Irene Fosi, *Inquisition, Conversion, and Foreigners in Baroque Rome* (Leiden: Brill, 2020).

12. Adriano Prosperi, 'Diari femminili e discernimento degli spiriti: Le mistiche della prima età moderna in Italia', *Dimensioni e problemi della ricerca storica*, 2 (1994), 77–103.

13. Tutino, *Uncertainty in Post-Reformation Catholicism*.

14. Shagan, *The Birth of Modern Belief*, pp. 195–206.

15. 'Loro pareva che la lege di Dio fusse più raggionevole che le sue e ancora perciochè vedevano che noi rispondevamo alli loro dubij.' *Diversi avisi particolari dall'Indie di Portogallo ricevuti dall'anno 1551 fino al 1558 dalli reverendi padri della compagnia di Gesù* [...] (Venice: Michele Tramezzino, 1565), fol. 125ᵛ.

16. 'I Giaponesi sono più obedienti alla ragione che gente infidele che già mai habbia visto e tanto

curiosi e importuni in dimandare, tanto desiderosi del sapere, che mai finiscono d'interrogare.' Ibid., fol. 126^v.

17. 'Quelli d'Amangucci tenevano uno gran dubbio, prima che si battezzassero, contra la somma bontà di Dio. Essi dicevano ch'el non era misericordioso poi che non si era a loro manifestato innanzi che noi là andassimo [...]. Questa fu una delle gravi loro dubitationi che per non adorare Dio tenevano.' Ibid., fol. 127^r.

18. Ikuo Higashibaba, *Christianity in Early Modern Japan: Kirishitan Belief and Practice* (Leiden: Brill, 2001).

19. On doubt and conversion in modern Japanese culture see Mark Williams, 'Bridging the Divide: Writing Christian Faith (and Doubt) in Modern Japan', in *Handbook of Christianity in Japan*, ed. by Mark R. Mullin (Leiden: Brill, 2003), pp. 295–320.

20. 'En ce sens les espaces missionnaires sont le règne de l'exception, de la déviation de la norme, des cas particuliers.' Broggio, Castelnau-L'estoile, and Pizzorusso, 'Le temps des doutes', p. 19.

21. Barbierato, *The Inquisitor in the Hat Shop.*

22. Taub's article discusses the leaked dossier concerning the alleged ties between former US president Donald Trump and Russia. *New York Times*, 15 January 2017 <https://www.nytimes.com/2017/01/15/world/europe/kompromat-donald-trump-russia-democracy.html> [accessed 28 May 2022].

BIBLIOGRAPHY

AARON, PIETRO, *Compendiolo di molti dubbi, segreti, et sentenze intorno al canto fermo et figurato* [...] (Milan: Io. Antonio da Castelliono, *c.* 1550)

Acta Patris Ignatii scripta a P. Lud. Gonzalez de Camara, in *Fontes narrativi de S. Ignatio de Loyola et de Societatis Iesu initiis*, I: *Narrationes scriptae ante annum 1557*, ed. by Dionysius Fernandez Zapico S. I. and Candidus de Dalmases S. I. (Rome: Monumenta Historica Societatis Iesu, 1943), pp. 323–507.

ADDANTE, LUCA, 'Dal radicalismo religioso del Cinquecento al deismo (e oltre): Vecchie e nuove prospettive di ricerca', *Rivista storica italiana*, 127 (2015), pp. 770–807.

——*Eretici e libertini nel Cinquecento italiano* (Rome: Laterza, 2010).

——'Hérésie radicale et libertinage: Le valdésien Giulio Basalù et Domenico Scandella dit Menocchio', in *Dissidence et dissimulation*, ed. by Antony Molho and Jean-Pierre Cavaillé (= *Les dossiers du Grihl*, 3–2 (2009)), <https://journals.openedition.org/dossiersgrihl/3779> [accessed 7 June 2021].

——'"Parlare liberamente": I libertini del Cinquecento tra tradizioni storiografiche e prospettive di ricerca', *Rivista storica italiana*, 123 (2011), 927–1001.

——'Radicalisme politique et religieux: Les libertins italiens au XVIe siècle', in *Libertin! Usage d'une invective au XVIe et XVIIe siècle*, ed. by Thomas Berns, Anne Staquet, and Monique Weis (Paris: Garnier, 2013), pp. 29–50.

——'Renato, Camillo (Paolo Ricci, Lisia Fileno)', *Dizionario biografico degli Italiani*, LXXXVI (Rome: Istituto dell'Enciclopedia italiana, 2016) <https://www.treccani.it/enciclopedia/camillo-renato_%28Dizionario-Biografico%29/> [accessed 15 November 2022].

ADORNI BRACCESI, SIMONETTA, 'L'"Agrippa Arrigo" e Ortensio Lando: Fra eresia, cabbala e utopismo: Ipotesi di lettura', *Historia philosophica: An International Journal*, 2 (2004), 97–113.

ALBERIGO, GIUSEPPE, 'Aragona, Giovanna d'', in *Dizionario biografico degli Italiani*, III (Rome: Istituto dell'Enciclopedia italiana, 1961) <https://www.treccani.it/enciclopedia/giovanna-d-aragona_(Dizionario-Biografico)/> [accessed 26 September 2020].

——'Aragona, Maria d'', in *Dizionario biografico degli Italiani*, III (Rome: Istituto dell'Enciclopedia italiana, 1961) <https://www.treccani.it/enciclopedia/maria-d-aragona_(Dizionario-Biografico)/> [accessed 26 September 2020].

ALBERTI, MARCELLO, *Istoria delle donne scientiate*, I (Naples: Felice Mosca, 1740).

ALCIATO, ANDREA, *Emblemata cum commentarijs amplissimis* (Padua: apud Petrum Paulum Tozzium, 1621).

——*Emblematum liber* (Augsburg: Heinrich Steyner, 1531).

ALFANI, GUIDO, *Calamities and the Economy in Renaissance Italy: The Grand Tour of the Horsemen of the Apocalypse*, trans. by Christine Calvert (Basingstoke: PalgraveMacMillan, 2013).

ALIGHIERI, DANTE, *Paradiso*, ed. by Anna Maria Chiavacci Leonardi (Milan: Mondadori, 1994).

——*Paradiso*, transl. by Robert Hollander and Jean Hollander (New York: Anchor Books, 2007).

AL-KALAK, MATTEO, *L'eresia dei fratelli: Una comunità eterodossa nella Modena del Cinquecento* (Rome: Edizioni di Storia e Letteratura, 2011).

Allen, Don Cameron, *Doubt's Boundless Sea: Skepticism and Faith in the Renaissance* (Baltimore: Johns Hopkins Press, 1964).

Alunno, Francesco, *Della fabbrica del mondo* [...] (Venice: appresso Gio. Battista Uscio, 1588).

—— *Della fabbrica del mundo libri dieci ne quali si contengono le voci di Dante, del Petrarca, del Boccaccio, del Bembo e d'altri buoni autori, mediante le quali scrivendo si possono esprimere con facilità e eloquenza tutti i concetti dell'huomo e di qualunque cosa creata* [...] (Venice: N. de Bascarini, 1546; repr. 1548).

Ambrosini, Federica, *L'eresia di Isabella: Vita di Isabella da Passano, signora della Frattina 1542–1601* (Milan: Angeli, 2005).

—— *Una gentildonna davanti al Sant'Uffizio: Il processo per eresia di Isabella della Frattina, 1568–1570* (Geneva: Droz, 2014).

Amidei, Beatrice Barbiellini, *Alla luna: Saggio sulla poesia del Cariteo* (Florence: La Nuova Italia, 1999).

Anderson, Wendy Love, *The Discernment of Spirits: Assessing Visions and Visionaries in the Late Middle Ages* (Tübingen: Mohr Siebeck, 2011).

Angelo da Pizzighettone, *Fior angelico di musica* [...] *nel qual si contengono alcune bellissime dispute contra quelli che dicono, la musica non esser scienza. Con altre molte questioni, & solutioni di varii dubii* (Venice: Agostino Bindoni, 1547).

'The Arabic Gospel of the Infancy of the Savior', in *The Ante-Nicene Fathers*, VIII: *Fathers of the Third and Fourth Century*, ed. by Rev. Alexander Roberts, Sir James Donaldson, and Arthur Cleveland Coxe (New York: Cosimo, 2007 (1886)), pp. 405–15.

Aragona, Tullia d', *Dialogue on the Infinity of Love*, ed. and trans. by Rinaldina Russell and Bruce Merry (Chicago: University of Chicago Press, 1997).

Aretino, Pietro, *Vita di Maria Vergine*, in *Opere religiose*, II: *Vita di Maria Vergine; Vita di santa Caterina; Vita di san Tommaso*, ed. by Paolo Marini (Rome: Salerno Editrice, 2011), pp. 91–302.

—— *Vita di santa Caterina*, in *Opere religiose*, II: *Vita di Maria Vergine; Vita di santa Caterina; Vita di san Tommaso*, ed. by Paolo Marini (Rome: Salerno Editrice, 2011), pp. 303–456.

Arnigio, Bartolomeo, *Lettera, rime, et oratione* [...] *in lode della bellissima et gentilissima signora Ottavia Baiarda* (Brescia: Ludovico Britannico il vecchio, 1558).

Arnold, John, *Belief and Unbelief in Medieval Europe* (London: Bloomsbury, 2011 (2005)).

Assaf, Sharon, 'The Ambivalence of the Sense of Touch in Early Modern Prints', *Renaissance and Reformation*, 29 (2005), 75–98.

Avila, Luis Lobera de, *Fabrica del'huomo* [...]. *Aggiuntovi alcune dotte, e curiose dubitationi* [...] (Alessandria: Ercole Quinciano, 1597).

Azpilcueta, Martín de, *Manuale de' confessori, et penitenti* [...] (Venice: Gabriel Giolito de' Ferrari, 1569).

Bacchiddu, Rita, 'Pagani, Marco (in religione Antonio)', in *Dizionario biografico degli Italiani*, LXXX (Rome: Istituto dell'Enciclopedia italiana, 2014) <https://www.treccani.it/enciclopedia/marco-pagani_%28Dizionario-Biografico%29/≥ [accessed 16 October 2020].

Bacci, Giacomo Pietro, *Vita di S. Filippo Neri* [...] (Bologna: Eredi di Domenico Maria Barbieri, 1666).

Baernstein, P. Renée, *A Convent Tale: A Century of Sisterhood in Spanish Milan* (New York: Routledge, 2002).

Baltrušaitis, Jurgis, *Anamorfosi o Thaumaturgus opticus* (Milan: Adelphi, 1990).

B. Antonini Archiepiscopi Florentini [...] *Summa Sacrae Theologiae* [...] *pars prima* [...] (Venice: apud Bernardum Iuntam & socios, 1571).

Barbaro, Daniele, *Della eloquenza*, in *Trattati di poetica e retorica del Cinquecento*, ed. by Bernard Weinberg, II (Bari: Laterza, 1970), pp. 335–451.

——— *La pratica della perspettiva* [...] (Venice: Camillo et Rutilio Borgominieri, 1569).

[BARBARO, DANIELE], *Predica de i sogni composta per lo reverendo padre d. Hypneo da Schio* (Venice: Francesco Marcolini, 1542).

BARBIERATO, FEDERICO, *The Inquisitor in the Hat Shop: Inquisition, Forbidden Books, and Unbelief in Early Modern Venice* (Farnham: Ashgate, 2012).

BARGAGLI, GIROLAMO, *Dialogo de' giuochi che nelle vegghie sanesi si usano di fare*, ed. by Patrizia D'Incalci Ermini, intro. by Riccardo Bruscagli (Siena: Accademia Senese degli Intronati, 1982).

Beati Alberti Magni [...] Summa de creaturis divisa in duas partes quarum prima est de quatuor coaevis, secunda de homine [...]. Operum tomus decimus-nonus (Lyon: sumptibus Claudii Prost., Petri et Claudii Rigaud, Hieronymi Delagarde, Ioan. Ant. Huguetam, 1651).

BENAY, ERIN E., 'Touching Is Believing: Caravaggio's *Doubting Thomas* in Counter-Reformatory Rome', in *Caravaggio: Reflections and Refractions*, ed. by Lorenzo Pericolo and David M. Stone (Farnham: Ashgate, 2014), pp. 59–82.

BENAY ERIN E., and LISA M. RAFANELLI, *Faith, Gender, and the Senses in Italian Renaissance and Baroque Art: Interpreting the Noli me tangere and Doubting Thomas* (Farnham: Ashgate, 2015).

BENEDETTO DA MANTOVA, *Il beneficio di Cristo: Con le versioni del secolo XVI documenti e testimonianze*, ed. by Salvatore Caponetto (Florence: Sansoni; Dekalb: Northern Illinois University Press; Chicago: Newberry Library, 1972).

BENIGNO, FRANCESCO, *Words in Time: A Plea for Historical Re-Thinking* (London: Routledge, 2017).

BERRETTINI, SERENA, 'Le "Sorti" come macchina ludica: regole e procedure', in *Studi per le 'Sorti': Gioco, immagini, poesia oracolare a Venezia nel Cinquecento*, ed. by Paolo Procaccioli (Treviso and Rome: Fondazione Benetton-Viella, 2007), pp. 21–38.

BERTI, DOMENICO, 'Di Giovanni Valdes e di taluni suoi discepoli secondo nuovi documenti tolti dall'Archivio Veneto', *Atti della R. Accademia dei Lincei*, 275 (1887/88), 61–81.

BERTINI, GIUSEPPE, 'Una proposta di identificazione dell'*Antea* del Parmigianino: Ottavia Baiardi Beccaria', *Aurea Parma*, 86 (2002), 361–68.

BETT, RICHARD, 'Pyrrho', in *The Stanford Encyclopedia of Philosophy* (Winter 2014), ed. by Edward N. Zalta <http://plato.stanford.edu/archives/win2014/entries/pyrrho/> [accessed 28 October 2016].

BIANCHI, LUCA, '"Aristotele fu un uomo e poté errare": Sulle origini medievali della critica al "principio di autorità"', in *Studi sull'aristotelismo del Rinascimento* (Padua: Il Poligrafo, 2003), pp. 101–24.

BIASIORI, LUCIO, '"Empietà e bestemmie anche alle orecchie dei saraceni infedeli": La condanna di Zanino da Solza tra rafforzamento ecclesiastico e progetti di crociata (1459)', in *Prima di Lutero: Nonconformismi religiosi nel Quattrocento italiano*, ed. by Daniele Conti and Lucio Biasiori (= *Rivista storica italiana*, 129 (2017)), pp. 862–86.

Biblia vulgare istoriata (Venice: Giovanni Ragazo a instantia di Luchantonio Giunta, 1490).

BIETENHOLZ, PETER G., *Encounters with a Radical Erasmus: Erasmus' Work as a Source for Radical Thought in Early Modern Europe* (Toronto: University of Toronto Press, 2008).

BLAIR, ANN, 'The *Problemata* as a Natural Philosophical Genre', in *Natural Particulars: Nature and the Disciplines in Renaissance Europe*, ed. by Anthony Grafton and Nancy Siraisi (Cambridge, MA: MIT Press, 1999), pp. 171–204.

BONORA, ELENA, *I conflitti della Controriforma: Santità e obbedienza nell'esperienza religiosa dei primi barnabiti* (Florence: Le Lettere, 1998).

——— 'Nei labirinti della censura libraria cinquecentesca: Antonio Pagani (1526–1589) e le "Rime spirituali"', in *Per Marino Berengo: Studi dagli allievi*, ed. by Livio Antonelli, Carlo Capra, and Mario Infelise (Milan: Franco Angeli, 2000), pp. 114–36.

BOTTONI, CESARE, *Osservationi sopra i giubilei* [...]. *Opera utile et necessaria, non solo a semplici, ma anco a persone ecclesiastice per saper rispondere alli dubbij che vengono mossi sopra gli giubilei* (Piacenza: Giovanni Bazachi, 1587).

BOUWSMA, WILLIAM J., 'Anxiety and the Formation of Early Modern Culture', in *A Usable Past: Essays in European Cultural History* (Berkeley: University of California Press, 1990), pp. 157–89.

BOWD, STEPHEN, *Reform before the Reformation: Vincenzo Querini and the Religious Renaissance in Italy* (Leiden: Brill, 2002).

BRASAVOLA, ANTONIO MUSA, *La vita di Iesu Cristo*, ed. by Adriano and Anna Prosperi (Turin: Nino Aragno, 2020).

BROGGIO, PAOLO, CHARLOTTE DE CASTELNAU-L'ESTOILE, and GIOVANNI PIZZORUSSO, 'Le temps des doutes: Les sacrements et l'Église romaine aux dimensions du monde', in *Administrer les sacrements en Europe et au Nouveau Monde: La curie romaine et les dubia circa sacramenta*, ed. by Paolo Broggio, Charlotte de Castelnau-L'estoile, and Giovanni Pizzorusso (= *Mélanges de l'École française de Rome: Italie et Méditerranée*, 121 (2009)), pp. 5–22.

BROGL, THOMAS, '"Ÿegliches näch sín vermugen": Johannes Nider's Idea of Conscience', in *Between Creativity and Norm-Making: Tensions in the Early Modern Era*, ed. by Sigrid Müller and Cornelia Schweiger (Leiden: Brill, 2013), pp. 61–76.

BROWN, ALISON, 'Lucretius and the Epicureans in the Social and Political Context of Renaissance Florence', *I Tatti Studies in the Italian Renaissance*, 9 (2001), 11–62.

——*The Return of Lucretius to Renaissance Florence* (Cambridge, MA: Harvard University Press, 2010).

BRUNDIN, ABIGAIL, 'Vittoria Colonna in Manuscript', in *A Companion to Vittoria Colonna*, ed. by Abigail Brundin, Tatiana Crivelli, and Maria Serena Sapegno (Leiden: Brill, 2016), pp. 39–68.

BRUNI, ROBERTO L., and DIEGO ZANCANI, 'Antonio Cornazzano: Le opere a stampa', *La Bibliofilia*, 86 (1984), 1–61 (p. 9).

BULBECK, R., 'The Doubt of St. Joseph', *Catholic Biblical Quarterly*, 10 (1948), 296–309.

BUONARROTI, MICHELANGELO, *Rime e lettere*, ed. by Antonio Corsaro and Giorgio Masi (Milan: Bompiani, 2016).

BURANELLO, ROBERT, 'The Hidden Ways and Means of Antonio Vignali's *La Cazzaria*', *Quaderni d'italianistica*, 26 (2005), 59–76.

——'The *Zoppino* Dialogue: Malice, Misogyny, and Meretricious Misrepresentation', *Rivista di studi italiani*, 23 (2005), 45–62.

BURKE, PETER, *Tradition and Innovation in Renaissance Italy: A Sociological Approach* (London: Fontana-Collins, 1974).

BYRNE, EDMUND F., *Probability and Opinion: A Study in the Medieval Presuppositions of Post-Medieval Theories of Probability* (The Hague: Martinus Nijhoff, 1968).

CACIOLA, NANCY, *Discerning Spirits: Divine and Demonic Possession in the Middle Ages* (Ithaca, NY: Cornell University Press, 2006).

CAHILL, PATRICIA A., 'Take Five: Renaissance Literature and the Study of the Senses', *Literature Compass*, 6 (2009), 1014–30.

CALEPIO, AMBROGIO DA, *F. Ambrosii Calepini Bergomatis* [...] *Dictionarium* [...] (Paris: Josse Bade, 1510).

CAMPEGGIANI, IDA, *Le varianti della poesia di Michelangelo* (Lucca: Pacini Fazzi, 2012).

CANTELMO, MARIA CHIARA, 'La paura del turco in Europa tra la caduta di Costantinopoli e la battaglia di Lepanto (1453–1571)', in *Per un lessico della paura in Europa: Spunti per una riflessione*, ed. by Fabiana Ambrosi, Carolina Antonucci, Ida Xoxa (Rome: Sapienza Università Editrice, 2018), pp. 47–55.

CANTIMORI, DELIO, *Eretici italiani del Cinquecento e altri scritti*, ed. by Adriano Prosperi (Turin: Einaudi, 1992).

CAO, GIAN MARIO, 'L'eredità pichiana: Gianfrancesco Pico tra Sesto Empirico e Savonarola', in *Pico, Poliziano e l'Umanesimo di fine Quattrocento*, ed. by Paolo Viti (Florence: Olschki, 1994), pp. 231–45.

CAPRANICA, DOMENICO, *Arte del ben morire, cioè in gratia di Dio* (Florence: Bartolommeo di Libri?, 150–).

CARGNONI COSTANZO et al., *Storia della spiritualità italiana*, ed. by Pietro Zovatto (Rome: Città Nuova, 2002).

CARRAI, STEFANO, *Ad somnum: L'invocazione al sonno nella lirica italiana* (Padua: Antenore, 1990).

CARRÉ, ANTÒNIA, and LLUÍS CIFUENTES, 'Girolamo Manfredi's *Il Perché*: I. The *Problemata* and Its Medieval Tradition'; 'Girolamo Manfredi's *Il Perché*: II. The *Secretum secretorum* and the Book's Publishing Success', *Medicina & storia*, 10 (2010), 13–38, 39–58.

CASALI, ELIDE, 'Libri di ventura e divinazione nel Cinquecento', in *Un giardino per le arti: 'Francesco Marcolino da Forlì': La vita, l'opera, il catalogo*, ed. by Paolo Procaccioli, Paolo Temeroli, and Vanni Tesei (Bologna: Editrice Compositori, 2009), pp. 315–35.

CASIO DE' MEDICI, GIROLAMO, *Libro de fasti giorni sacri* [...] (Bologna: Benedetto de Hettor Libraro, 1528).

CAVAZZA, SILVANO, 'Una vicenda europea: Vergerio e il caso Spiera, 1548–49', in *La fede degli Italiani: Per Adriano Prosperi*, ed. by Guido Dall'Olio, Adelisa Malena, and Pierroberto Scaramella (Pisa: Edizioni della Normale, 2011), I, pp. 41–51.

La centralità del dubbio: Un progetto di Antonio Rotondò, ed. by Camilla Hermanin and Luisa Simonutti (Florence: Olschki, 2011).

CERRETA, FLORINDO, *Alessandro Piccolomini: Letterato e filosofo senese del Cinquecento* (Siena: Accademia Senese degli Intronati, 1960).

CERRETANI, BARTOLOMEO, *Dialogo della mutatione di Firenze*, ed. by Giuliana Berti (Florence: Olschki, 1993).

CERUTI BURGIO, ANNA, *Studi sul Quattrocento parmense* (Pisa: Giardini, 1988).

CHERCHI, PAOLO, 'La *Cazzaria* di Vignali e *Il libro del perché* di Manfredi', *Annali Online di Ferrara — Lettere*, I (2007), 106–16.

—— *Ignoranza ed erudizione: L'Italia dei dogmi di fronte all'Europa scettica e critica (1500–1750)* (Padua: Libreria universitaria, 2020).

—— *Polimatia di riuso: Mezzo secolo di plagio (1539–1589)* (Rome: Bulzoni, 1998).

—— 'Il quotidiano, i *Problemata* e la meraviglia: Ministoria di un microgenere', in *Ministorie di microgeneri*, ed. by Chiara Fabbian, Alessandro Rebonato, and Emanuela Zanotti Carney (Ravenna: Longo, 2003), pp. 11–48.

CHIVASSO, ANGELO DA, *Della somma angelica* [...] *nuovamente di Latino in lingua italiana tradotta dal reverendo frate Girolamo Menghi* [...] *parte prima* [...] (Venice: alla Libraria della Speranza, 1594).

CLARK, STUART, *Vanities of the Eye: Vision in Early Modern European Culture* (Oxford: Oxford University Press, 2007).

CODRO, ANTONIO URCEO, *Sermones (I–IV): Filologia e maschera nel Quattrocento*, ed. by Loredana Chines and Andrea Severi (Rome: Carocci, 2013).

—— *Sermones (V–VIII): Filologia e maschera nel Quattrocento*, ed. by Andrea Severi and Giacomo Ventura (Rome: Carocci, 2018).

COHEN, THOMAS V., and ELIZABETH S. COHEN, *Words and Deeds in Renaissance Rome: Trials before the Papal Magistrates* (Toronto: University of Toronto Press, 1993).

COLAFRANCESCHI, STEFANIA, *San Giuseppe nelle sacre rappresentazioni italiane (sec. XIII–XV)* <https://movimentogiuseppino.files.wordpress.com/2011/01/s-giuseppe-nelle-sacre-rappresentazioni-italiane-sec-xiii-xv.pdf> [accessed 12 December 2017].

COLE, ROSALIE, *Paradoxia Epidemica: The Renaissance Tradition of Paradox* (Princeton: Princeton University Press, 1966).

Collected Works of Erasmus, XXXI: *Adages I i 1 to I v 100*, trans. by Margaret Mann Phillips, annotated by R. A. B. Mynors (Toronto: University of Toronto Press, 1982).

COLLENUCCIO, PANDOLFO, *Operette morali: Poesie latine e volgari*, ed. by Alfredo Saviotti (Bari: Laterza, 1929).

COLONNA, VITTORIA, *La raccolta di rime per Michelangelo*, ed. by Veronica Copello (Florence: Società Editrice Fiorentina, 2020).

—— *Rime*, ed. by Alan Bullock (Rome: Laterza, 1982).

—— *Sonnets for Michelangelo: A Bilingual Edition*, ed. and transl. by Abigail Brundin (Chicago: University of Chicago Press, 2005)

The Complete Essays by Montaigne, trans. by Donald M. Frame (Stanford: Stanford University Press, 1965).

CONGREGA DEI ROZZI DI SIENA, *Quistioni e chasi di più sorte*, ed. by Claudia Chierichini (Siena: Accademia dei Rozzi, 2019).

CONTI, DANIELE, '"Initium abolendae fidei": Dagli accademici romani a Machiavelli: Una nuova fonte per la storia dell'anticristianesimo quattrocentesco', in *Prima di Lutero: Nonconformismi religiosi nel Quattrocento italiano*, ed. by Lucio Biasiori and Daniele Conti (= *Rivista storica italiana*, 129 (2017)), pp. 984–1021.

COPELLO, VERONICA, 'Lettere a un "singularissimo amico": Le epistole di Vittoria Colonna a Michelangelo', in *Michelangelo e Vittoria Colonna: Amicizia, arte, poesia, spiritualità dall'assedio di Firenze all'apertura del Concilio di Trento*, ed. by Veronica Copello and Andrea Donati (Todi: D'Arte, 2022) pp. 135–44.

CORNAZZANO, ANTONIO, *Vita della gloriosa vergine Maria* (Venice: per Nicolo d'Aristotile detto Zoppino, 1531).

CORSARO, ANTONIO, 'L'artista, l'opera, l'anima: Sul dialogo poetico fra Michelangelo e Vittoria Colonna', in *Michelangelo e Vittoria Colonna: Amicizia, arte, poesia, spiritualità dall'assedio di Firenze all'apertura del Concilio di Trento*, ed. by Veronica Copello and Andrea Donati (Todi: D'Arte, 2022), pp. 121–33.

—— 'Parodia del sacro dal Medioevo al Rinascimento', in *Gli irregolari nella letteratura: Eterodossi, parodisti, funamboli della parola* (Rome: Salerno, 2007), pp. 63–92.

COTUGNO, ALESSIO, *La scienza della parola: Retorica e linguistica in Sperone Speroni* (Bologna: il Mulino, 2019).

CREMONINI, STEFANO, 'Il linguaggio biblico nelle *Laude* di Feo Belcari', in *Sotto il cielo delle scritture: Bibbia, retorica e letteratura religiosa (secc. XIII–XVI)*, ed. by Carlo Delcorno and Giovanni Baffetti (Florence: Olschki, 2009), pp. 171–92.

—— 'Sui sonetti di Feo Belcari: Intertestualità di una 'poetica theologia', *Studi e problemi di critica testuale*, 68 (2004), 5–36.

CRIMI, GIUSEPPE, 'Per l'edizione dei *Dubbi amorosi* attribuiti ad Aretino: Nuove acquisizioni e qualche indizio di paternità', *Filologia e critica*, 40 (2015), 3–46.

CRIVELLATI, CESARE, *Trattato de bagni di Viterbo* [...]. *Nel quale si trattano le qualità, & il valore di essi. Il modo di usarli, la regola del vivere, & alcuni dubbij, curiosi intorno a tal materia* (Viterbo: Agostino Colaldi, 1596).

—— *Trattato de i bagni di Viterbo* [...]. *Si mostra il modo di usarli, e si adducono molti dubbij intorno a tal materia* (Viterbo: Girolamo Discepolo, 1604).

CRIVELLI, TATIANA, 'Godere di cattiva stampa: Spunti per una rilettura della tradizione editoriale delle rime di Vittoria Colonna', in *Al crocevia della storia: Poesia, religione e politica in Vittoria Colonna*, ed. by Maria Serena Sapegno (Rome: Viella, 2016), pp. 137–57.

CRIVELLI, TATIANA, 'The Print Tradition of Vittoria Colonna's *Rime*', in *A Companion to Vittoria Colonna*, ed. by Abigail Brundin, Tatiana Crivelli, and Maria Serena Sapegno (Leiden: Brill, 2016), pp. 69–139.

DAENENS, FRANCINE, 'Donne valorose, eretiche, finte sante: Note sull'antologia giolitina del 1548', in *Per lettera: Scrittura epistolare femminile tra archivio e tipografia — secoli XV–XVII*, ed. by Gabriella Zarri (Rome: Viella, 1999), pp. 181–207.

D'ALESSANDRO, PAOLO, 'Perotti, Niccolò', in *Dizionario biografico degli Italiani*, LXXXII (Rome: Istituto dell'Enciclopedia italiana, 2015) <http://www.treccani.it/enciclopedia/niccolo-perotti_(Dizionario-Biografico)/> [accessed 21 May 2020].

DALL'OLIO, GUIDO, *Eretici e inquisitori nella Bologna del Cinquecento* (Bologna: Istituto per la storia di Bologna, 1999).

——'Gonzaga, Giulia', in *Dizionario biografico degli Italiani*, LVII (Rome: Istituto dell'Enciclopedia italiana, 2001) <https://www.treccani.it/enciclopedia/giulia-gonzaga_(Dizionario-Biografico)> [accessed 15 November 2022].

DALL'ORTO, GIOVANNI, *'Adora più presto un bel putto, che Domenedio*: Il processo a un libertino omosessuale: Francesco Calcagno (1550)', *Sodoma*, 6 (1993), 43–55.

Daniele Barbaro (1514–1570): Letteratura, scienza e arti nella Venezia del Rinascimento, ed. by Susy Marcon and Laura Moretti (Crocetta del Montello: Antiga Edizioni, 2015).

DASTON, LORRAINE J., and KATHARINE PARK, *Wonders and the Order of Nature, 1150–1750* (New York: Zone Books, 1998).

DAVI, MARIA ROSA, 'Filosofia e retorica nell'opera di Sperone Speroni', in *Sperone Speroni*, ed. by Antonio Daniele (Padua: Programma, 1989), pp. 89–112.

DAVIDSON, NICHOLAS, 'Unbelief and Atheism in Italy, 1500–1700', in *Atheism from the Reformation to the Enlightenment*, ed. by Michael C. W. Hunter and David Wootton (Oxford: Oxford University Press, 1992), pp. 63–93.

DECOCK, WIM, 'Martín de Azpilcueta (Dr Navarrus)', in *Great Christian Jurists in Spanish History*, ed. by Rafael Domingo and Javier Martínez Torrón (Cambridge: Cambridge University Press, 2018), pp. 115–32.

DEFERRARI, ROY J., M. INVIOLATA BARRY, and IGNATIUS McGUINESS, *A Lexicon of St. Thomas Aquinas Based on the 'Summa theologica' and Selected Passages of His Other Works* (Baltimore: Catholic University of America Press, 1948).

DE GREGORIO, MARIO, 'Un *long-seller* agiografico: La Vita di San Filippo Neri di Giacomo Pietro Bacci', in *Le fusa del gatto: Libri, librai e molto altro* (Torrita di Siena: Società Bibliografica Toscana, 2015), pp. 115–30.

DEL POPOLO, CONCETTO, 'Anastasia levatrice di Maria', *Lettere italiane*, 57 (2005), 261–71.

Delle lettere di diversi autori raccolte per Venturino Ruffinelli [...] (Mantua: [Venturino Ruffinelli], 1547).

DELUMEAU, JEAN, *Sin and Fear: The Emergence of a Western Guilt Culture, 13th–18th Centuries*, trans. by Eric Nicholson (New York: St Martin's Press, 1990).

DEMAN, THOMAS, 'Probabilis', *Revue des sciences philosophiques et théologiques*, 22 (1933), 260–90.

DESCARTES, RENÉ, *Meditations on First Philosophy: With Selections from the Objections and Replies*, ed. by Michael Moriarty (Oxford: Oxford University Press, 2008).

DE VIVO, FILIPPO, *Information and Communication in Venice: Rethinking Early Modern Politics* (Oxford: Oxford University Press, 2007).

——*Patrizi, informatori, barbieri: Politica e comunicazione a Venezia* (Milan: Feltrinelli, 2012).

Dieci paradosse degli academici intronati (Milan: Gio. Antonio degli Antonij, 1564).

DI MONTE, MICHELE, 'Vedere, credere, dubitare: Lorenzo Lotto e l'ambiguità', *Venezia Cinquecento*, 25 (2015), 75–113.

DI NEPI, SERENA, 'Autobiografie di minoranza: Prospettive individuali tra scritture personali e racconti di vita di ebrei e musulmani a Roma in età moderna', *Società e storia*, 160 (2018), 289–313.

——'Fede e scrittura: Libri e testimonianze personali nei processi di autodefinizione religiosa (XVI–XVII secolo)', *Società e storia*, 160 (2018), 241–48.

Diversi avisi particolari dall'Indie di Portogallo ricevuti dall'anno 1551 fino al 1558 dalli reverendi padri della compagnia di Gesù [...] (Venice: Michele Tramezzino, 1565).

DOLCE, LODOVICO, *Terzetti per le 'Sorti': Poesia oracolare nell'officina di Francesco Marcolini*, ed. by Paolo Procaccioli (Treviso: Fondazione Benetton-Viella, 2006).

DONI, ANTON FRANCESCO, *I marmi*, ed. by Carlo Alberto Girotto and Giovanna Rizzarelli (Florence: Olschki, 2017).

——*Le novelle*, II/I: *La zucca*, ed. by Elena Pierazzo (Rome: Salerno, 2003).

DOOLEY, BRENDAN, *The Social History of Skepticism: Experience and Doubt in Early Modern Culture* (Baltimore: Johns Hopkins University Press, 1999).

ELLI, ANGELO, *Specchio spirituale del principio, e fine della vita humana; diviso e distinto in quindici ragionamenti et in cento cinquanta dubbi principali fatti tra 'l maestro e il suo discepolo in dialogo* (Brescia: Policreto Turlini, 1598).

EQUICOLA, MARIO, *Libro de natura de amore*, ed. by Enrico Musacchio (Rome: Aracne, 2018).

Espositione letterale del testo di Mattheo Evangelista, di m. Bernardino Tomitano (Venice: Gio. del Griffo, 1547).

ERNST, GERMANA, 'Aspetti celesti e profezia politica: Sul "Prognosticon" di Arquato', *Bruniana & Campanelliana*, 11 (2005), 635–46.

FABRINI, SEBASTIANO, *Dichiaratione del giubileo dell'Anno santo. Nel quale si tratta ancora il modo di conseguirlo, & di fare il peregrinaggio di Roma; con la risolutione di molti dubij bellissimi sopra questa materia* (Venice: Fioravante Prati, 1599).

FAINI, MARCO, 'A proposito di Giovanni Andrea Ugoni: Temi e spunti dalle *Rime* e dai *Trattati*', in *Riformatori bresciani del '500: Indagini*, ed. by Roberto A. Lorenzi (Brescia: Grafo, 2006), pp. 79–103 and 265–77.

——'Fortunato Martinengo e Ortensio Lando: Dubbi e dubbiosi alla metà del Cinquecento', in *Fortunato Martinengo: Un gentiluomo del Rinascimento fra arti, lettere e musica*, ed. by Marco Bizzarini and Elisabetta Selmi (Brescia: Morcelliana, 2018), pp. 74–97.

——'Fortunato Martinengo, Girolamo Ruscelli e l'Accademia dei Dubbiosi tra Brescia e Venezia', in *Girolamo Ruscelli: Dall'accademia alla corte alla tipografia: Itinerari e scenari per un letterato del Cinquecento*, ed. by Paolo Procaccioli and Paolo Marini (Manziana: Vecchiarelli, 2011), II, 455–519.

——'"Mentre il lungo error piango e sospiro": Le "Rime" di Giovanni Andrea Ugoni', *Giornale storico della letteratura italiana*, 126 (2009), 51–83.

——'Reading, Devotion and Religious Print in Early *Cinquecento* Naples: The Case of Francesco Sovaro's *Christiade*', *Italian Studies*, 72 (2017), 238–55.

FANTI, SIGISMONDO, *Triompho di fortuna* (Venice: Agostin da Portese ad instantia di Iacomo Giunta, 1527).

FAVARO, MAIKO, *Ambiguità del petrarchismo: Un percorso fra trattati d'amore, lettere e templi di rime* (Milan: Franco Angeli, 2021).

——'Duttilità di una metafora: Note sui "Templi" letterari profani del Cinquecento', in *Le carte e i discepoli: Studi in onore di Claudio Griggio*, ed. by Fabiana di Brazzà et al. (Udine: Forum, 2016), pp. 201–09.

FECI, SIMONA, 'Mazzolini, Silvestro', in *Dizionario biografico degli Italiani*, LXXII (Rome: Istituto dell'Enciclopedia italiana, 2008) <https://www.treccani.it/enciclopedia/silvestro-mazzolini_%28Dizionario-Biografico%29/> [accessed 14 November 2022].

Felici, Lucia, 'Ateismo e sodomia nella Repubblica di Venezia. Ancora sul caso di Francesco Calcagno (1528-1550)', *Riforma e movimenti religiosi*, 8 (2020), 59–80.

——'A Sixteenth-Century Libertine Priest. Francesco Calcagno', in *Cursed Blessings. Sex and Religious Radical Dissent in Early Modern Europe*, ed. by Umberto Grassi (London-New York: Routledge, 2024), pp. 21–39.

FEYLES, GABRIELE, *Serafino da Fermo canonico regolare lateranense (1496–1540)* (Turin: SEI, 1942).

FIOGHI, FABIANO, *Dialogo fra il cathecumino e il padre cathechizante composto per Fabiano Fioghi [...] lettore della lingua hebrea nel collegio de neophiti. Nel qual si risolvono molti dubij, li quali soglioni far li hebrei, contro la verità della santa fede christiana* (Rome: heredi d'Antonio Blado, 1582).

FIRPO, MASSIMO, *Juan de Valdés and the Italian Reformation* (London: Routledge, 2016).

—— *Nel labirinto del mondo: Lorenzo Davidico tra santi, eretici, inquisitori* (Florence: Olschki, 1997).

—— 'Paola Antonia Negri, monaca Angelica (1508–1555)', in *Rinascimento al femminile*, ed. by Ottavia Niccoli (Rome: Laterza, 2008 (1991)), pp. 35–82.

—— *Riforma protestante ed eresie nell'Italia del Cinquecento* (Rome: Laterza, 1993).

FLANIGAN, TOM, 'Everyman or Saint? Doubting Joseph in the Corpus Christi Cycle', *Medieval and Renaissance Drama in England*, 8 (1996), 19–48.

FLORIDI, LUCIANO, 'Scepticism and Animal Rationality: The Fortune of Chrysippus' Dog in the History of Western Thought', *Archiv für Geschichte der Philosophie*, 79 (1997), pp. 27–57.

Fortunato Martinengo: Un gentiluomo del Rinascimento fra arti, lettere e musica, ed. by Marco Bizzarini and Elisabetta Selmi (Brescia: Morcelliana, 2018).

FOSI, IRENE, 'Conversion and Autobiography: Telling Tales before the Roman Inquisition', *Journal of Early Modern History*, 17 (2013), 437–56.

—— *Inquisition, Conversion, and Foreigners in Baroque Rome* (Leiden: Brill, 2020).

FRAGNITO, GIGLIOLA, '"Per lungo e dubbioso sentero": L'itinerario spirituale di Vittoria Colonna', in *Al crocevia della storia: Poesia, religione e politica in Vittoria Colonna*, ed. by Maria Serena Sapegno (Rome: Viella, 2016), pp. 177–213.

FRANCESI, MATTIO, 'Capitolo sopra le nuove', in *Il secondo libro dell'opere burlesche di M. Francesco Berni, del Molza [...] et di diversi autori [...]* (Florence: Heredi di Bernardo Giunti, 1555), fols 58^r–59^v.

FRUGONI, CHIARA, *La voce delle immagini: Pillole iconografiche dal Medioevo* (Turin: Einaudi, 2010).

FUREY, CONSTANCE, 'The Communication of Friendship: Gasparo Contarini's Letters to Hermits in Camaldoli', *American Society of Church History*, 72 (2003), 71–101.

—— *Erasmus, Contarini, and the Religious Republic of Letters* (Cambridge: Cambridge University Press, 2006).

GAMBERINI, DILETTA, 'Rappresentare le lacerazioni dell'animo: Archetipi letterari dell'*amphibolía* di Pomponio Gaurico', *I Tatti Studies in the Italian Renaissance*, 23 (2020), 213–40.

GARDEIL, AMBROISE, 'La "certitude probable"', *Revue des sciences philosophiques et théologiques*, 5 (1911), 237–66 and 441–85.

GARETH, BENEDETTO, *Le rime di Benedetto Gareth detto il Chariteo [...]*, ed. by Erasmo Pèrcopo (Naples: Tipografia dell'Accademia delle Scienze, 1892).

GARIMBERTO, GIROLAMO, *Concetti divinissimi [...] per iscrivere, e ragionar familiarmente* (Venice: Comin da Trino, 1562).

—— *Problemi naturali, e morali* (Venice: Vicenzo Valgrisi, 1550).

GENTILI, AUGUSTO, 'Marcolini, Doni e le immagini della "maniera" veneziana', in *Un giardino per le arti: 'Francesco Marcolino da Forlì': La vita, l'opera, il catalogo*, ed. by Paolo Procaccioli, Paolo Temeroli, and Vanni Tesei (Bologna: Editrice Compositori, 2009), pp. 339–52.

—— 'Il problema delle immagini nell'attività di Francesco Marcolini', *Giornale storico della letteratura italiana*, 157 (1980), 117–25.

GINZBURG, CARLO, *I costituti di don Pietro Manelfi* (Florence: Sansoni; Chicago: Newberry Library, 1970).

—— 'Diventare Machiavelli: Per una nuova lettura dei "Ghiribizzi al Soderini"', in *Nondimanco: Machiavelli, Pascal* (Milan: Adelphi, 2018), pp. 43–65.

—— 'Un letterato e una strega al principio del '500: Panfilo Sasso e Anastasia la Frappona', in *Studi in memoria di Carlo Ascheri* (Urbino: Argalìa, 1970), pp. 129–37.

—— *Nondimanco: Machiavelli, Pascal* (Milan: Adelphi, 2018).

——'Stregoneria e pietà popolare: Note a proposito di un processo modenese del 1519', *Annali della Scuola Normale Superiore di Pisa: Lettere, storia e filosofia*, 30 (1961), 269–87.

——*Threads and Traces: True False Fictive*, trans. by Ann C. Tedeschi and John Tedeschi (Berkeley: University of California Press, 2012).

Gioanni Gerson de gli remedij contra la pusillanimità, scrupolosità et deceptorie consolationi et suttile tentationi del'inimico (Venice: Simon de Luere, 1510).

GIRARDI, MARIA TERESA, and LUCIA SIGNORI, 'Daniele Barbaro letterato e il *Della eloquenza*', *Aevum*, 71 (1997), 651–89.

GIZZIO, FRANCESCO, *L'echo armoniosa delle sfere celesti* (Naples: per il De Bonis Stampatore Arcivescovile, 1693).

GNOCCHI, ALESSANDRO, 'Tommaso Giustiniani, Ludovico Ariosto e la Compagnia degli Amici', *Studi di filologia italiana*, 67 (1999), 277–93.

GORNI, GUGLIELMO, 'Le ottave dei giganti', in *Michelangelo poeta e artista*, ed. by Paolo Grossi and Matteo Residori (Paris: Istituto Italiano di Cultura, 2005), pp. 41–52.

GRAFTON, ANTHONY, 'Divination: Toward the History of a Philological Term', in *The Marriage of Philology and Scepticism: Uncertainty and Conjecture in Early Modern Scholarship and Thought*, ed. by Gian Mario Cao, Anthony Grafton, and Jill Kraye (London: University of London Press, 2019), pp. 47–69.

——*What Was History?* (Cambridge: Cambridge University Press, 2007).

GRAFTON, ANTHONY, with APRIL SHELFORD and NANCY SIRAISI, *New Worlds, Ancient Texts: The Power of Tradition and the Shock of Discovery* (Cambridge, MA: Belknap Press of Harvard University Press, 1992).

GREENBLATT, STEPHEN, *The Swerve: How the World Became Modern* (New York: W. W. Norton & Company, 2012).

GRENDLER, PAUL, *Critics of the Italian World (1530–1560): Anton Francesco Doni, Nicolò Franco and Ortensio Lando* (Madison: University of Wisconsin Press, 1969).

GRILLENZONI, RAFFAELE, *Affanni dell'anima timorata, co' suoi conforti e rimedii. Aggiuntovi il metodo per risanare un'anima inferma di scrupoli* (Venice: Francesco Salerni, 1676).

GROBLER, ANTON, ANGELO NICOLAIDES, and CLIFTON SINGH, 'The Doubting Apostle "Dydimus" — Saint Thomas: Theological, Psychological and Historical Perspectives', *Pharos Journal of Theology*, 96 (2015), 1–17.

GUERRINI, PAOLO, *I Conti di Martinengo: Una celebre famiglia lombarda: Studi e ricerche genealogiche* (Brescia: Geroldi, 1930).

——'La prima "legenda volgare" de la beata Stefana Quinzani d'Orzinuovi secondo il codice vaticano-urbinate latino 1755', in *Memorie storiche della diocesi di Brescia* (Brescia: Scuola Tip. Istituto Figli di Maria, 1930), pp. 65–186.

GUIDI, REMO L., *L'inquietudine del Quattrocento* (Rome: Tielle Media, 2007).

HAIRSTON, JULIA, 'Tullia d'Aragona', in *Dizionario biografico degli Italiani*, XCVII (Rome: Istituto dell'Enciclopedia italiana, 2020) <http://www.treccani.it/enciclopedia/tullia-d-aragona_%28Dizionario-Biografico%29/> [accessed 13 May 2020].

HARVEY, ELIZABETH D., 'Introduction: The "Sense of All Senses"', in *Sensible Flesh: On Touch in Early Modern Culture*, ed. by Elizabeth D. Harvey (Philadelphia: University of Pennsylvania Press, 2003), pp. 1–21.

HAWK, BRANDON W., *The Gospel of the Pseudo-Matthew and the Nativity of Mary* (Cambridge: Lutterworth Press, James Clarke & Co., 2019).

HENRY, CHRISCINDA, 'Leonardo da Vinci, Parody, and Pictorial Magic', in *Playthings in Early Modernity: Party Games, Word Games, Mind Games*, ed. by Allison Levy (Kalamazoo: Western Michigan University, 2017), pp. 73–96.

HIGASHIBABA, IKUO, *Christianity in Early Modern Japan: Kirishitan Belief and Practice* (Leiden: Brill, 2001).

A Historical Approach to Casuistry: Norms and Exceptions in a Comparative Perspective, ed. by Carlo Ginzburg with Lucio Biasiori (London: Bloomsbury, 2018).

HOFFMANN, VIKTORIA VON, 'Epistemology of Touch in Early Modern Autopsies', *Renaissance Quarterly*, 75 (2022), 542–82.

HUDON, WILLIAM V., '"In the End, God Helped Me Defeat Myself": Autobiographical Writings by Camilla Battista da Varano', *Religions*, 9 (2018) <https://www.mdpi.com/2077–1444/9/3/65≥ [accessed 2 February 2021].

HUIZINGA, JOHAN, *The Autumn of the Middle Ages*, trans. by Rodney J. Payton and Ulrich Mammitzsch (Chicago: University of Chicago Press, 1996 (1921)).

Iconologie ou la science des emblemes, devises, etc. [...] par J.[ean] B.[audoin], 1 (Amsterdam: Adrian Baakman, 1698).

INFELISE, MARIO, *Prima dei giornali: Alle origini della pubblica informazione (secoli XVI e XVII)* (Rome: Laterza, 2005).

ISIDORE OF SEVILLE, *The Etymologies of Isidore of Seville*, trans. with introduction and notes by Stephen A. Barney et al. (Cambridge: Cambridge University Press, 2006).

ISIDORO DI SIVIGLIA, *Etimologie o origini*, ed. by Angelo Valastro Canale (Turin: Utet, 2004).

The Italian Academies 1525–1700: Networks of Culture, Innovation and Dissent, ed. by Jane E. Everson, Denis V. Reidy, and Lisa M. Sampson (Oxford: Legenda, 2016).

JEDIN, HUBERT, 'Contarini und Camaldoli', *Archivio italiano per la storia della pietà*, 2 (1959), 51–117.

JOSSA, STEFANO, 'Verso il barocco: Sperone Speroni e Carlo Borromeo (tra retorica e mistica)', *Aprosiana*, 11–12 (2004), 11–34.

KATINIS, TEODORO, *Sperone Speroni and the Debate over Sophistry in the Italian Renaissance* (Leiden: Brill, 2018).

KELLY, JESSEN, 'Predictive Play: Wheels of Fortune in the Early Modern Lottery Book', in *Playthings in Early Modernity: Party Games, Word Games, Mind Games*, ed. by Allison Levy (Kalamazoo: Medieval Institute Publications, Western Michigan University, 2017), pp. 145–66.

LANDI, SERGIO, *Naissance de l'opinion publique dans l'Italie moderne: Sagesse du people et savoir de gouvernement de Machiavel aux Lumières* (Rennes: Presses universitaires de Rennes, 2006).

LANDO, ORTENSIO, *Dialogo [...] nel quale si ragiona della consolatione, & utilità, che si gusta leggendo la Sacra Scrittura* (Venice: Al Segno del Pozzo [Andrea Arrivabene], 1552).

——*Lettere di molte valorose donne* (Venice: Giolito, 1548; rev. edn 1549).

[LANDO, ORTENSIO], *Quattro libri de dubbi con le solutioni a ciascun dubbio accommodate [...]* (Venice: Gabriel Giolito de Ferrari, 1556).

LANDO, ORTENSIO, *Sette libri de cathaloghi a varie cose appartenenti [...]* (Venice: Gabriel Giolito de' Ferrari, 1552).

Il laudario dei Battuti di Modena, ed. by Mahmoud Salem Elsheikh (Bologna: Commissione per i testi di lingua, 2001).

Laude fatte e composte per più persone spirituali [...]. Et tutte le infrascripte laude ha raccholto & insieme ridotto Iacopo di maestro Luigi de Marsi Cittadino fiorentino [...] (Florence: Francesco Bonaccorsi, 1485).

LAVENIA, VINCENZO, *L'infamia e il perdono: Tributi, pene e confessione nella teologia morale della prima età moderna* (Bologna: il Mulino, 2004).

LEVI, GIUSEPPE, *L'eredità immateriale: Carriera di un esorcista nel Piemonte del Seicento* (Milan: Il Saggiatore, 2020 (1985)).

LIENHARD, THOMAS, 'Athéisme, scepticisme et doute religieux au Moyen Âge: Notes de lecture à propos de trois publications récentes', *Revue de l'Institut français d'histoire en Allemagne*, 3 (2011) <https://journals.openedition.org/ifha/194> [accessed 23 July 2021].

Lirici toscani del Quattrocento, ed. by Antonio Lanza (Rome: Bulzoni, 1973).

LODONE, MICHELE, 'Direzione spirituale e autorità eremitica: Paolo Giustiniani e le seguaci fiorentine di Gabriele Biondo', *Aevum*, 90 (2016), pp. 523–45.

——'L'eredità dei francescani spirituali fra Quattro e Cinquecento: Una ricerca in corso su Gabriele Biondo', *Oliviana*, 4 (2012) <https://journals.openedition.org/oliviana/487?lang=en> [accessed 13 May 2019].

——*Invisibile come Dio: La vita e l'opera di Gabriele Biondo* (Pisa: Edizioni della Normale, 2020).

——'L'opera poetica volgare di Gabriele Biondo', *Interpres*, 35 (2017), 39–97.

——*I segni della fine: Storia di un predicatore nell'Italia del Rinascimento* (Rome: Viella, 2021).

——'Un teologo, un medico e un libro (Padova, 1502)', *Riforma e movimenti religiosi*, 6 (2019), 141–84.

LORENZI, ROBERTO ANDREA, 'Per un profilo di Massimiliano Celso Martinengo, riformatore (1515–1557)', *Bollettino della società di studi valdesi*, 122 (2005), 23–68.

LORENZINI, SILVIA, 'Stefana Quinzani', in *Le stanze segrete: Le donne bresciane si rivelano*, ed. by Elisabetta Selmi (Brescia: Fondazione Civiltà Bresciana, 2008), pp. 11–35.

LOVATO, GUERRINO, *La levatrice incredula nella leggenda della Natività* (Venice: Lupi & Sirene, 2014).

MACHIAVELLI, NICCOLÒ, *Lettere a Francesco Vettori e a Francesco Guicciardini*, ed. by Giorgio Inglese (Milan: Rizzoli, 1989).

MALENA, ADELISA, 'Ego-documents or "Plural Compositions"? Reflections on Women's Obedient Scriptures in the Early Modern Catholic World', *Journal of Early Modern Studies*, 1 (2012), 97–113.

——'Introduzione: Racconti di conversione e relazioni di genere in età moderna e contemporanea', *Genesis*, 6 (2007), 5–12.

——'Madri in spirito: Note di lettura su direzione spirituale e discorso autobiografico negli scritti di Paola Maria di Gesù Centurione (1586–1646) e Francesca Toccafondi (1638–1685)', in *Donne tra saperi e poteri: Nella storia delle religioni*, ed. by Sofia Boesch Gajano and Enzo Pace (Brescia: Morcelliana, 2007), pp. 317–39.

MALINVERNI, MASSIMO, '*Lectiones faciliores* e varianti redazionali nella tradizione delle rime di Panfilo Sasso', *Studi di filologia italiana*, 56 (1998), 203–28.

——'Sasso, Panfilo', in *Dizionario biografico degli Italiani*, XC (Rome: Istituto dell'Enciclopedia italiana, 2017) <https://www.treccani.it/enciclopedia/panfilo-sasso_(Dizionario-Biografico)/> [accessed 16 October 2020].

——'Sulla tradizione del sonetto "Hor te fa terra, corpo" di Panfilo Sasso', *Studi di filologia italiana*, 49 (1991), 123–65.

MALNIPOTE, NICCOLÒ, *Il tesoro celeste dell'indulgenza per li vivi, et per li morti. [...] Con le resolutioni de molti dubbii* (Naples: Horatio Salviani, 1580).

MAMPIERI, MARTINA, ' "The Jews and Their Doubts": Anti-Jewish Polemics in the *Fascicolo della vanità giudaiche* (1583) by Antonino Stabili', *Yearbook of the Maimonides Centre for Advanced Studies*, 1 (2016), 59–75.

MANSELLI, RAOUL, 'Aceti de' Porti, Serafino', in *Dizionario biografico degli Italiani*, I (Rome: Istituto dell'Enciclopedia italiana, 1960) <https://www.treccani.it/enciclopedia/aceti-de-porti-serafino_%28Dizionario-Biografico%29/> [accessed 15 November 2022].

MANUZIO, ALDO, *Eleganze insieme con la copia della lingua toscana e latina* (Venice: Paolo Manuzio, 1556).

MARCOLINI, FRANCESCO, *Le sorti di Francesco Marcolino da Forlì intitolate giardino di pensieri [...]* (Venice: Francesco Marcolino, 1540).

MARCONDES, DANILO, 'The Anthropological Argument: The Rediscovery of Ancient Skepticism in Modern Thought', in *Skepticism in the Modern Age: Building on the Work of Richard Popkin*, ed. by José R. Maia Nieto, Gianni Paganini, John Christian Laursen (Leiden: Brill, 2009), pp. 37–53.

MARINI, PAOLO, 'Un libro di sorti nella Romagna post-tridentina: Il manoscritto I 66 della Biblioteca Comunale "Aurelio Saffi" di Forlì', *Rara volumina*, 20 (2013), 23–50.

The Marriage of Philology and Scepticism, ed. by Gian Mario Cao, Anthony Grafton, and Jill Kraye (London: University of London Press, 2019).

MARTIN, JOHN JEFFRIES, *Myths of Renaissance Individualism* (Basingstoke: Palgrave Macmillan, 2004).

—— *Venice's Hidden Enemies: Italian Heretics in a Renaissance City* (Baltimore: Johns Hopkins University Press, 2004).

MARYKS, ROBERT A., *Saint Cicero and the Jesuits: The Influence of the Liberal Arts on the Adoption of Moral Probabilism* (London: Routledge, 2016).

MASSA, EUGENIO, *L'eremo, la Bibbia e il Medioevo in umanisti veneti del primo Cinquecento* (Naples: Liguori, 1992).

MAYLENDER, MICHELE, *Storia delle accademie d'Italia,* II (Bologna: Cappelli, 1927).

MAZZOLINI, SILVESTRO, *Sylvestrinae Summae, quae Summa Summarum merito nuncupatur pars prima* [...] (Lyon: apud Ioannem Frellonium, 1554).

—— *Sylvestrinae summae* [...] *pars secunda* [...] (Lyon: apud Ioannem Frellonium, 1554).

MAZZONCINI, CARLOTTA, 'L'occhio nel calcagno: Fioritura e fortuna di un'immagine delle "ottave dei giganti" di Michelangelo', *L'ellisse,* 10 (2015), 111–32.

McGUIRE, BRIAN P., 'When Jesus Did the Dishes: The Transformation of Late Medieval Spirituality', in *The Making of Christian Communities in Late Antiquity and the Middle Ages,* ed. by Mark Williams (London: Anthem Press, 2005), pp. 131–52.

McMANAMON, JOHN M., S.J., *The Text and Context of Ignatius of Loyola's 'Autobiography'* (New York: Fordham University Press, 2013).

MEGALE, TERESA, 'Gizzio, Francesco', in *Dizionario biografico degli Italiani,* LVII (Rome: Istituto dell'Enciclopedia italiana, 2001) <http://www.treccani.it/enciclopedia/francesco-gizzio_(Dizionario-Biografico)/> [accessed 23 August 2020].

MELFI, EDUARDO, 'Collenuccio, Pandolfo', in *Dizionario biografico degli Italiani,* XXVII (Rome: Istituto dell'Enciclopedia italiana, 1982) <https://www.treccani.it/enciclopedia/pandolfo-collenuccio_%28Dizionario-Biografico%29/> [accessed 27 May 2021].

MERCATI, ANGELO, *Il sommario del processo a Giordano Bruno: Con appendice di documenti sull'eresia e l'Inquisizione a Modena nel secolo XVI* (Vatican City: Biblioteca Apostolica Vaticana, 1973).

MINNICH, NELSON H., and ELISABETH G. GLEASON, 'Vocational Choices: An Unknown Letter of Pietro Querini to Gasparo Contarini and Niccolò Tiepolo (April, 1512)', *Catholic Historical Review,* 75 (1989), 1–20.

MINUTELLI, MARZIA, *'La miracolosa aqua': Lettura delle 'Porretane novelle'* (Florence: Olschki, 1990).

MITTARELLI, JOHANNES BENEDICTUS, and ANSELMUS COSTADONI, *Annales Camaldulenses ordinis sancti Benedicti,* t. IX (Venice: aere monasterii sancti Michaelis de Muriano, 1773).

Un mondo perduto? Religione e cultura popolare, ed. by Lucia Felici and Pierroberto Scaramella (Rome: Aracne, 2020).

MONTALCINO, AGOSTINO DA, *Lucerna dell'anima. Somma de' casi di conscientia* [...] (Venice: Damian Zenaro, 1590).

MORELLI, GIOVANNI DI PAGOLO, 'Ricordi', in *Mercanti scrittori: Ricordi nella Firenze tra Medioevo e Rinascimento,* ed. by Vittore Branca (Florence: Le Monnier, 1986), pp. 101–339.

MOST, GLENN W., *Doubting Thomas* (Cambridge, MA: Harvard University Press, 2005).

MOULTON, IAN F., 'The Greatest Tangle of Pricks There Ever Was: Knowledge, Sex, and Power in Renaissance Italy', introduction to ANTONIO VIGNALI, *La Cazzaria — The Book of the Prick,* ed. and trans. by Ian Frederick Moulton (London: Routledge, 2003), pp. 1–70.

MUIR, EDWARD, *The Culture Wars of the Late Renaissance: Skeptics, Libertines, and Opera* (Cambridge, MA: Harvard University Press, 2007).

MURALTO, FRANCESCO, *Annalia,* ed. by Pierluigi Donini (Milan: cura et impensis Aloisii Daelli, 1861).

MURRAY, ALEXANDER, 'Piety and Impiety in Thirteenth-Century Italy', *Studies in Church History*, 8 (1972), 83–106.

——'The Epicureans', in *Intellectuals and Writers in Fourteenth-Century Europe*, ed. by Piero Boitani and Anna Torti (Tübingen: Gunter Narr-Brewer, 1986), pp. 138–63.

MUZZARELLI, MARIA GIUSEPPINA, 'Beatrice de Luna, vedova Mendes, alias donna Gracia Nasi: Un'ebrea influente (1510–1569 ca.)', in *Rinascimento al femminile*, ed. by Ottavia Niccoli (Rome: Laterza, 1991), pp. 83–116.

NADIN, LUCIA, *Carte da gioco e letteratura tra Quattrocento e Ottocento* (Lucca: Pacini Fazzi, 1997).

NANI MIRABELLI, DOMENICO, *Polyanthea. Opus suavissimis floribus exornatum* [...] (Savona: Francesco Selva, 1503).

NELSON, JENNIFER, *Disharmony of the Spheres: The Europe of Holbein's 'Ambassadors'* (University Park: Pennsylvania State University Press, 2019).

NICCOLI, OTTAVIA, 'Cultura popolare: Un relitto abbandonato?', *Studi storici*, 56 (2015), 997–1010.

——*Prophecy and People in Renaissance Italy*, trans. by Lydia G. Cochrane (Princeton: Princeton University Press, 1990).

Opera nuovamente composta in la solutione di tre grandissimi dubbi sopra de gli asini, cani, gatti e topi (Florence: Domenico Celamaio, 1571/72).

Opera omnia Desiderii Erasmi Roterodami, II/I: *Adagiorum Chilias prima*, ed. by M. L. van Poll-van de Lisdonk, M. Mann Phillips, and Chr. Robinson (Amsterdam: North Holland, 1992).

Opera volgare intitolata Specchio de la santa madre Chiesa, ne la quale si dechiarano molte bellissime espositioni e dubii circa la fede nostra (Venice: Guglielmo da Fontaneto, 1523).

Oral Culture in Early Modern Italy: Performance, Language, Religion, ed. by Stefano Dall'Aglio, Luca Degl'Innocenti, Brian Richardson, Massimo Rospocher, and Chiara Sbordoni (= *The Italianist*, 34 (2014)).

ORVIETO, PAOLO, *Pulci medievale: Studio sulla poesia volgare Fiorentina del Quattrocento* (Rome: Salerno, 1978).

——'Uno "scandalo" del '400: Luigi Pulci ed i sonetti di parodia religiosa', *Annali d'italianistica*, 1 (1983), 19–33.

PACCAGNELLA, IVANO, 'La grammatica nei primi vocabolari: Le *Regolette particolari della volgar lingua* di Francesco Alunno', in *La nascita del vocabolario*, ed. by Antonio Daniele, Ivano Paccagnella, and Riccardo Drusi (Padua: Esedra, 2014), pp. 11–31.

PAGANI, ANTONIO, *Ragionamenti di diverse notabili materie ne i quali si contengono le risolutioni di vari dubbi, intorno a cose molto giovevoli per l'ammaestramento, & per l'essercitio pratico di persone spirituali, così ecclesiastiche e religiose, come secolari* [...] (Venice: apresso Domenico Farri, 1587).

PAGANINI, GIANNI, *Il dubbio dei moderni: Una storia dello scetticismo* (Rome: Carocci, 2022).

PALMER, ADA, *Reading Lucretius in the Renaissance* (Cambridge, MA: Harvard University Press, 2014).

PALMIERI, MATTEO, *Vita civile*, ed. by Gino Belloni (Florence: Sansoni, 1982).

PALUMBO, MARGHERITA, 'Conscientia, casus conscientiae', in *Coscienza nella filosofia della prima modernità*, ed. by Roberto Palaia (Florence: Olschki, 2013), pp. 203–33.

Pamphili Saxi [...] *Epigrammatum libri quattuor* [...] (Brescia: Angeli Britannici civis Brix. sumptu Bernardinus Misinta impressit, 1499).

PANIZZA, LETIZIA, 'The Semantic Field of Paradox in 16th and 17th Century Italy: From Truth in Appearance False to Falsehood in Appearance True: A Preliminary Investigation', in *Il vocabolario della République des Lettres: Terminologia filosofica e storia della filosofia — Problemi di metodo*, ed. by Marta Fattori (Florence: Olschki, 1997), pp. 197–220.

PANOFSKY, ERWIN, *Ercole al bivio e altri materiali iconografici dell'Antichità tornati in vita nell'età moderna*, ed. by Monica Ferrando (Macerata: Quodlibet, 2010; 1st edn: *Hercules am Scheidewege und anderen antike Bildstoffe in der neueren Kunst* (Leipzig: B. G. Teubner, 1930).

PAPI, ANGELO, 'Le perigliose sorti del duca Ercole: Considerazioni a margine di una dedica', in *Studi per le 'Sorti': Gioco, immagini, poesia oracolare a Venezia nel Cinquecento*, ed. by Paolo Procaccioli (Treviso and Rome: Fondazione Benetton-Viella, 2007), pp. 157–71.

PARLATO, ENRICO, 'Abecedario iconografico marcoliniano', in *Un giardino per le arti: 'Francesco Marcolino da Forlì': La vita, l'opera, il catalogo*, ed. by Paolo Procaccioli, Paolo Temeroli, and Vanni Tesei (Bologna: Editrice Compositori, 2009), pp. 249–68.

—— 'Le allegorie nel giardino delle "Sorti"', in *Studi per le 'Sorti': Gioco, immagini, poesia oracolare a Venezia nel Cinquecento*, ed. by Paolo Procaccioli (Treviso and Rome: Fondazione Benetton-Viella, 2007), pp. 113–37.

—— 'L'editoria veneziana e Marcolini', in *Francesco Salviati 'spirito veramente pellegrino ed eletto'*, ed. by Antonio Geremicca (Rome: Campisano, 2015), pp. 75–85.

—— 'Sogno e conoscenza nella Venezia del Cinquecento: Daniele Barbaro, alias Hypneo da Schio, e Francesco Marcolini', in *Forme e storia: Scritti di arte medievale e moderna per Francesco Gandolfo*, ed. by Walter Angelelli and Francesca Pomarici (Rome: Artemide, 2011), pp. 505–14.

—— 'Le *Sorti* nell'*Iconologia*, l'*Iconologia* nelle *Sorti*: Un percorso tra immagini e parole all'ombra di Anton Francesco Doni', in *Cesare Ripa e gli spazi dell'allegoria*, ed. by Sonia Maffei (Naples: La Stanza delle Scritture, 2010), pp. 39–60.

PARMEGGIANI, RICCARDO, ' "Ad extirpandos sortilegiorum, divinatorum ad malleficorum iniquas operationes": Riflessi teorico-pratici della repressione nello specchio di un registro quattrocentesco dell'inquisizione bolognese', in *Prima di Lutero: Nonconformismi religiosi nel Quattrocento italiano*, ed. by Daniele Conti and Lucio Biasiori (= *Rivista storica italiana*, 129 (2017)), pp. 842–62.

PASCHETTI, BARTOLOMEO, *Dubbi morali et naturali* [...] (Genua: [Antonio Roccatagliata], 1581).

PASINI, ENRICO, 'Dubbio e scetticismo in Erasmo da Rotterdam', in *Erasmo da Rotterdam e la cultura europea/Erasmus of Rotterdam and European Culture*, ed. by Enrico Pasini and Pietro B. Rossi (Florence: Sismel-Edizioni del Galluzzo, 2008), pp. 199–250.

PASQUINI, EMILIO, 'Il mito della casa del sonno', in *Le botteghe della poesia: Studi sul Tre-Quattrocento italiano* (Bologna: il Mulino, 1991), pp. 115–98.

La Passione di Revello: Sacra rappresentazione quattrocentesca di ignoto autore, ed. by Anna Cornagliotti (Turin: Stamperia artistica nazionale, 1976).

PASTORE, STEFANIA, *Un'eresia spagnola: Spiritualità conversa, alumbradismo e Inquisizione (1449–1559)* (Florence: Olschki, 2004).

Per lettera: La scrittura epistolare femminile tra archivio e tipografia — secoli XVI–XVII, ed. by Gabriella Zarri (Rome: Viella, 1999).

PÈRCOPO, ERASMO, 'Una tenzone su amore e fortuna fra Lorenzo de' Medici, P. Collenuccio, il Poliziano e G. Benivieni', *Rassegna critica della letteratura italiana*, 1 (1896), 9–14 and 42–46.

PEROTTI, NICOLÒ, *Cornucopiae sive commentarii linguae latinae* [...] (Milan: Giovanni Maria De Ferrariis, 1506).

PETRARCA, FRANCESCO, *Canzoniere*, ed. by Marco Santagata (Milan: Mondadori, 2004).

—— *Le senili: Libri I–VI*, ed. by Ugo Dotti and Felicita Audisio (Turin: Nino Aragno, 2004).

—— *Letters of Old Age: Rerum Senilium libri I–XVIII, vol. I: Books I–IX*, trans. by Aldo S. Bernardo, Saul Levin, and Reta A. Bernardo (Baltimore: Johns Hopkins University Press, 1992).

Petrarch: The Canzoniere, or Rerum vulgarium fragmenta, trans. by Mark Musa (Bloomington: Indiana University Press, 1999).

PETROCCHI, MASSIMO, *Storia della spiritualità italiana*, II: *Il Cinquecento e il Seicento* (Rome: Edizioni di Storia e Letteratura, 1978).

PETROLINI, CHIARA, 'Il giornale di conversione di Toby Matthews', *Società e storia*, 160 (2018), 269–87.

PEZZINI, SERENA, 'Dissimulazione e paradosso nelle "Lettere di molte valorose donne" (1548) a cura di Ortensio Lando', *Italianistica: Rivista di letteratura italiana*, 31 (2002), 67–83.

PICCAT, MARCO, 'San Michele in Piemonte: La "Passione di Revello" (1481)', in *L'arcangelo Michele: Dalla storia alla leggenda*, ed. by Giampietro Casiraghi (Stresa: Edizioni Rosminiane, 2012), pp. 155–88.

PICCOLOMINI, ALESSANDRO, *La seconda parte de la filosofia naturale* [...] (Venice: Vincenzo Valgrisi, 1554).

PIERGUIDI, STEFANO, 'Un anonimo repertorio di personificazioni della fine del Cinquecento', *Studi romani*, 53 (2005), pp. 51–93.

——'Verità e menzogna: I motti e le marche tipografiche di Aretino, Marcolini e Doni', *Venezia Cinquecento*, 33 (2007), 5–21.

PIETRO DA LUCCA, *Dottrina del ben morire composta per el reverendo padre Petro da Lucha* [...] *con molte utile resolutione de alcuni belli dubii theologici* (Venetia: per Comino de Luere, 1529).

PIRRI, PIERRE, 'Elli (Ange)', in *Dictionnaire de spiritualité ascétique et mystique*, IV/1 (Paris: Beauchesne, 1960), cols. 599–600.

PISCINI, ANGELA, 'Del Bailo, Francesco', in *Dizionario biografico degli Italiani*, XXXVI (Rome: Istituto dell'Enciclopedia italiana, 1988) <http://www.treccani.it/enciclopedia/francesco-del-bailo_(Dizionario-Biografico)/> [accessed 27 April 2020].

The Poetry of Michelangelo: An Annotated Translation, ed. and trans. by James M. Saslow (New Haven, CT: Yale University Press, 1991).

POLCRI, ALESSANDRO, *Luigi Pulci e la Chimera: Studi sull'allegoria nel Morgante* (Florence: Società Editrice Fiorentina, 2010).

POMMIER, ÉDOUARD, 'L'itinéraire religieux d'un moine vagabond italien au XVIᵉ siècle', *Mélanges d'archéologie et d'histoire*, 66 (1954), 293–322.

POPKIN, RICHARD H., *The History of Scepticism: From Savonarola to Bayle* (Oxford: Oxford University Press, 2003).

POPPI, ANTONINO, 'Il prevalere della "vita activa" nella paideia del Cinquecento', in *Rapporti tra le università di Padova e Bologna: Ricerche di filosofia, medicina e scienza*, ed. by Lucia Rossetti (Trieste: Lint, 1988), pp. 97–125.

PROCACCIOLI, PAOLO, 'Un cultore del dubbio dell'Italia del Rinascimento: Ortensio Lando', in *Le doute dans l'Europe moderne*, ed. by Élise Boillet and Marco Faini (Turnhout: Brepols, 2022), pp. 189–206.

——'Marcolini autore "ingegnoso"', in *Studi per le 'Sorti': Gioco, immagini, poesia oracolare a Venezia nel Cinquecento*, ed. by Paolo Procaccioli (Treviso and Rome: Fondazione Benetton-Viella, 2007), pp. 3–18.

PROCACCIOLI, PAOLO, and SILVIA URBINI, 'Fortuna donna di palazzo: Libri di sorte da Lorenzo Spirito a Giuseppe Maria Mitelli', in *Dea Fortuna: Iconografia di un mito*, ed. by Manuela Kahn-Rossi (Carpi: Edizioni del Comune di Carpi, 2010), pp. 28–37.

PROSPERI, ADRIANO, 'America e Apocalisse: Note sulla "conquista spirituale" del Nuovo Mondo', in *America e Apocalisse e altri saggi* (Rome: Istituti Editoriali e Poligrafici, 1999), pp. 15–63.

——'Antonio Musa Brasavola e la sua *Vita di Cristo*: Introduzione', in ANTONIO MUSA BRASAVOLA, *La vita di Iesu Cristo*, ed. by Adriano and Anna Prosperi (Turin: Nino Aragno, 2020), pp. ix–lxxx.

——'Casistica', in *Dizionario storico dell'Inquisizione*, ed. by Adriano Prosperi, Vincenzo Lavenia, and John Tedeschi (Pisa: Edizioni della Normale, 2010), I, 291–92.

——'Diari femminili e discernimento degli spiriti: Le mistiche della prima età moderna in Italia', *Dimensioni e problemi della ricerca storica*, 2 (1994), 77–103.

——*Infanticide, Secular Justice, and Religious Debate in Early Modern Europe* (Turnhout: Brepols, 2016).

PULCI, LUIGI, *Opere minori*, ed. by Paolo Orvieto (Milan: Mursia, 1986).

QUAQUARELLI, LEONARDO, 'Pandolfi, Girolamo', in *Dizionario biografico degli Italiani*, LXXX (Rome: Istituto dell'Enciclopedia italiana, 2014) <https://www.treccani.it/enciclopedia/girolamo-pandolfi_(Dizionario-Biografico)> [accessed 23 August 2022].

QUERINI, VINCENZO, 'Relazione di Borgogna [...]', in *Relazioni degli ambasciatori veneti al Senato*, ed. by Eugenio Alberi, serie I, I (Florence: Tipografia all'insegna di Clio, 1839).

QUONDAM, AMEDEO, 'Nel giardino del Marcolini: Un editore veneziano tra Aretino e Doni', *Giornale storico della letteratura italiana*, 157 (1980), 75–116.

—— 'Strumenti dell'officina classicistica: *Polyanthea* & Co.', *Modern Philology*, 101 (2003), 316–35.

RABB, THEODORE K., *The Struggle for Stability in Early Modern Europe* (New York: Oxford University Press, 1975).

RAFANELLI, LISA M., 'Michelangelo's *Noli me tangere* for Vittoria Colonna, and the Changing Status of Women in Renaissance Italy', in *Mary Magdalene: Iconographic Studies from the Middle Ages to the Baroque*, ed. by Michelle M. Erhardt and Amy M. Morris (Leiden: Brill, 2012), pp. 223–48.

—— 'Sense and Sensibilities: A Feminist Reading of Titian's *Noli me tangere* (1509–1515)', *Critica d'arte*, 70 (2008), 28–47.

—— 'To Touch or Not to Touch: The "Noli me tangere" and "Incredulity of Thomas" in Word and Image from Early Christianity to the Ottonian Period', in *To Touch or Not to Touch? Interdisciplinary Perspectives*, ed. by Reimund Bieringer, Karlijn Demasure, and Barbara Baert (Leuven: Peeters, 2013), pp. 135–73.

RAIMONDI, EZIO, *Codro e l'umanesimo a Bologna* (Bologna: il Mulino, 1987 (1950)).

RAJNA, PIO, 'L'episodio delle questioni d'amore nel *Filocolo* di Boccaccio', *Romania*, 31 (1902), 28–81.

RAMBALDI, SUSANNA PEYRONEL, *Una gentildonna irrequieta: Giulia Gonzaga fra reti familiari e relazioni eterodosse* (Rome: Viella, 2012).

RAY, MEREDITH K., 'Textual Collaboration and Spiritual Partnership in Sixteenth-Century Italy: The Case of Ortensio Lando and Lucrezia Gonzaga', *Renaissance Quarterly*, 62 (2009), 694–747.

—— *Writing Gender in Women's Letter Collections of the Italian Renaissance* (Toronto: University of Toronto Press, 2009).

REFINI, EUGENIO, 'Struggling with Power: Alessandro Piccolomini between *vita activa* and *vita contemplativa*', in *Penser et agir à la Renaissance/Thought and Action in the Renaissance*, ed. by Philippe Desan and Véronique Ferrer (Geneva: Droz, 2020), pp. 265–82.

Regula del sanctissimo Benedetto patre nostro: Tradutta in quelle parte che conuengono a noi monache; con le declarationi sopra quella, fatte per satisfactione della conscientia delle religiose che viuano sotto la regula del sancto Benedetto della osseruanza regulare composta per commissione & authoritade del nostro reuerendissimo monsignor episcopo circa le dubitationi che possino occorrere in obseruatione de ditta regula (Venice: a Santo Moyse nelle case noue Iustiniane, appresso il Bastione, per Francesco di Alessandro Bindoni & Mapheo Pasini compagni, 1529).

Renaissance Rewritings, ed. by Helmut Pfeiffer, Irene Fantappiè, and Tobias Roth (Berlin: De Gruyter, 2017).

RENATO, CAMILLO, *Opere: Documenti e testimonianze*, ed. by Antonio Rotondò (Florence: Sansoni; Chicago: Newberry Library, 1968).

RENDA, UMBERTO, *Il processo di Panfilo Sasso* (Modena: Ferraguti, 1911).

RESCHER, NICHOLAS, 'Choice without Preference: A Study of the History and of the Logic of the Problem of "Buridan's Ass"', *Kant-Studien*, 51 (1960), 142–75.

Revelationes Sanctae Birgittae, Revelaciones lib. V: Liber questionum, ed. by Birger Bergh (Uppsala: Almqvist & Wiksells Boktrickery, 1971).

The Revelations of St. Birgitta of Sweden, II: *Liber caelestis, Books IV–V*, trans. by Denis Searby, introduction and notes by Bridget Morris (Oxford: Oxford University Press, 2008).

REYNOLDS, SUSAN, 'Social Mentalities and the Cases of Medieval Scepticism', *Transactions of the Royal Historical Society*, 1 (1991), 21–41.

RICCI, LUCIA BATTAGLIA, *Palazzo Vecchio e dintorni: Studio su Franco Sacchetti e le fabbriche di Firenze* (Rome: Salerno, 1990).

RICCI, MARIA TERESA, 'Antonio Vignali e *La Cazzaria*', in *Extravagances amoureuses: L'amour au-delà de la norme à la Renaissance/Stravaganze amorose: L'amore oltre la norma nel Rinascimento*, ed. by Élise Boillet and Chiara Lastraioli (Paris: Honoré Champion, 2010), pp. 181–90.

RIPA, CESARE, *Iconologia*, ed. by Sonia Maffei and Paolo Procaccioli (Turin: Einaudi, 2012).

—— *Iconologia* [...] *notabilmente accresciuta d'immagini, di annotazioni, e di fatti dall'abate Cesare Orlandi* [...], II (Perugia: Piergiovanni Costantini, 1765).

—— *Nova iconologia* (Padua: Tozzi, 1618).

RIVOLETTI, CHRISTIAN, 'L'uno e il molteplice: Il sistema dei destini incrociati tra Ariosto, Marcolini e Calvino', in *Studi per le 'Sorti': Gioco, immagini, poesia oracolare a Venezia nel Cinquecento*, ed. by Paolo Procaccioli (Treviso and Rome: Fondazione Benetton-Viella, 2007), pp. 99–110.

ROBERT, AURÉLIEN, *Épicure aux enfers: Hérésie, athéisme et hédonisme au Moyen Âge* (Paris: Fayard, 2021).

ROBIN, DIANA, *Publishing Women: Salons, the Presses, and the Counter-Reformation in Sixteenth-Century Italy* (Chicago: University of Chicago Press, 2007).

ROGGERO, MARINA, *Le vie dei libri: Letture, lingua e pubblico nell'Italia moderna* (Bologna: il Mulino, 2021).

ROMEI, ANNIBALE, *Discorsi* [...]. *Con le risposte a tutti i dubbii che in simili materie proponer si sogliono* (Venice: Ziletti, 1585).

ROSE, COLIN, 'Plague and Violence in Early Modern Italy', *Renaissance Quarterly*, 71 (2018), 1000–35.

ROTHMAN, E. NATHALIE, 'Becoming Venetian: Conversion and Transformation in the Seventeenth-Century Mediterranean', *Mediterranean Historical Review*, 21 (2006), 39–75.

ROTONDÒ, ANTONIO, 'Per la storia dell'eresia a Bologna nel secolo XVI', *Rinascimento*, 13 (1962), 107–54.

RUSCELLI, GIROLAMO, ed., *Del tempio alla divina signora Giovanna d'Aragona* [...] (Venice: Plinio Pietrasanta, 1554).

—— *Lettura* [...] *sopra un sonetto dell'illustriss. signor marchese della Terza alla divina signora marchesa del Vasto. Ove con nuove et chiare ragioni si pruova la somma perfettione delle donne; et si discorrono molte cose intorno alla scala platonica dell'ascendimento per le cose create alla contemplatione di Dio* [...] (Venice: Giovan Griffio, 1552).

RUSCONI, RUGGERO, *L'ordine dei peccati: La confessione tra Medioevo ed età moderna* (Bologna: il Mulino, 2002).

RUSSINO, GUGLIELMO, 'Un medioevo incredulo: A proposito di scetticismo e imposture', *Mediaeval Sophia: Studi e ricerche sui saperi medievali*, 3 (2008), 162–68.

RYAN, DENISE, 'Playing the Midwife's Part in the English Nativity Plays', *Review of English Studies*, 54 (2003), 435–48.

RYRIE, ALEC, *Unbelievers: An Emotional History of Doubt* (Cambridge, MA: Harvard University Press, 2019).

SABADINO DEGLI ARIENTI, GIOVANNI, *Le Porretane*, ed. by Bruno Basile (Rome: Salerno, 1981).

SACCHETTI, FRANCO, *Il libro delle rime*, ed. by Alberto Chiari (Bari: Laterza, 1936).

—— *Il trecentonovelle*, ed. by Valerio Marucci (Rome: Salerno, 1996).

SANESI, IRENEO, *Il Cinquecentista Ortensio Lando* (Pistoia: Fratelli Bracali, 1893).

SASSO, PANFILO, *Opera del preclarissimo poeta Miser Pamphilo Sasso modenese* [...] (Venice: Guilielmum de Fontaneto de Monferrato, 1519).

SAVONAROLA, GIROLAMO, *Predica dell'arte del ben morire* (Florence: Bartolommeo de Libri, after 2 November 1496).

—— *Rime*, ed. by Giona Tuccini (Genoa: il melangolo, 2015).

SAVONAROLA, MICHELE, *Libreto* [...] *de tute le cose che se manzano comunamente e piu che comune, e di quelle se bevono per Italia, e de sei cose non naturale, et le regule per conservare la sanita delli corpi humani con dubij notabilissimi* (Venice: Simone de Luere, 1508).

SCARSELLA, MARCO, *Giardino di sommisti* [...] *parte prima* [...] (Venice: Giacomo Antonio Somasco, 1600).

Scepticism in the Modern Age: Building on the Work of Richard Popkin, ed. by José R. Maia Neto, Gianni Paganini, and John Christian Laursen (Leiden: Brill, 2009).

SCHMIDT, SUZANNE KARR, *Interactive and Sculptural Printmaking in the Renaissance* (Leiden: Brill, 2017).

SCHMITT, CHARLES B., *Cicero Scepticus: A Study of the Influence of the 'Academica' in the Renaissance* (The Hague: Martinus Nijhoff, 1972).

SCHUESSLER, RUDOLF, *The Debate on Probable Opinions in the Scholastic Tradition* (Leiden: Brill, 2019).

—— 'Equi-Probability prior to 1650', *Early Science and Medicine*, 21 (2016), 54–74.

—— 'Jean Gerson, Moral Certainty, and the Renaissance of Ancient Scepticism', *Renaissance Studies*, 23 (2009), 445–62.

SCHÜSSLER, RUDOLF, *Moral im Zweifel*, I: *Die Scholastische Theorie des Entscheidens unter moralischer Unsicherheit* (Paderborn: Mentis, 2003).

SCHUTTE, ANNE JACOBSON, *Aspiring Saints: Pretense of Holiness, Inquisition, and Gender in the Republic of Venice, 1618–1750* (Baltimore: Johns Hopkins University Press, 2001).

—— *By Force and Fear: Taking and Breaking Monastic Vows in Early Modern Europe* (Ithaca, NY: Cornell University Press, 2011).

SCHWARTZ, DANIEL, 'Probabilism Reconsidered: Deference to Experts, Types of Uncertainty, and Medicines', *Journal of the History of Ideas*, 75 (2014), pp. 373–93.

SEIDEL MENCHI, SILVANA, 'Chi fu Ortensio Lando?' *Rivista storica italiana*, 106 (1994), 501–64.

—— *Erasmo in Italia (1520–1580)* (Turin: Bollati Boringhieri, 1987).

—— 'Spiritualismo radicale nelle opere di Ortensio Lando attorno al 1550', *Archiv für Reformationsgeschichte*, 65 (1974), 210–77.

—— 'Sulla fortuna di Erasmo in Italia: Ortensio Lando e altri eterodossi della prima metà del Cinquecento', *Schweizerische Zeitschrift für Geschichte*, 24 (1974), 537–634.

SELMI, ELISABETTA, 'Tendenze erasmiane e calviniste tra i Martinengo nel '500', in *Fortunato Martinengo: Un gentiluomo del Rinascimento fra arti, lettere e musica*, ed. by Marco Bizzarini and Elisabetta Selmi (Brescia: Morcelliana, 2018), pp. 273–94.

SERAFINO DA FERMO, *Alcuni dubi circa l'oratione, per modo de problemi, numero cento, non meno utili che succinti*, in *Opere del R. P. Serafino da Fermo* [...] (Venice: Comin da Trino di Monferrato, 1569), fols 56^v–94^v.

—— *Breve dichiaratione sopra l'Apocalisse* (Milan, 1538).

—— *Operetta del discernimento de i spiriti*, in *Opere del R. P. Serafino da Fermo* [...] (Venice: Comin da Trino di Monferrato, 1569), fols 392^r–427^r.

—— *Vita di due beatissime donne, Margarita e Gentile*, in *Opere del R. P. Serafino da Fermo* [...], (Venice: Comin da Trino di Monferrato, 1569), fols 365^r–391^r.

SEXTUS EMPIRICUS, *Outlines of Pyrrhonism*, ed. by R. G. Bury (Cambridge, MA: Harvard University Press, 1933).

SGARBI, MARCO, *Francesco Robortello (1516–1567): Architectural Genius of the Humanities* (New York: Routledge, 2020).

—— *The Italian Mind: Vernacular Logic in Renaissance Logic (1540–1551)* (Leiden: Brill, 2014).

—— *Profumo di immortalità: Controversie sull'anima nella filosofia volgare del Rinascimento* (Rome: Carocci, 2016).

SGATTONI, MARCO, *La rinascita dello scetticismo tra eresia e riforma* (Urbino: Quattroventi, 2018).

SHAGAN, ETHAN, *The Birth of Modern Belief: Faith and Judgment from the Middle Ages to the Enlightenment* (Princeton: Princeton University Press, 2018).

SHEMEK, DEANNA, ' "Mi mostrano a dito tutti quanti": Disease, Deixis, and Disfiguration in the *Lamento di una cortigiana ferrarese*', in *Medusa's Gaze: Essays on Gender, Literature, and Aesthetics in the Italian Renaissance in Honor of Robert J. Rodini*, ed. by Paul A. Ferrara, Eugenio Giusti, and Jane Tylus (Lafayette, IN: Bodighera, 2004), pp. 49–64.

SIMONETTA, ELISABETTA, 'Il dissidente segretario delle valorose donne: Ortensio Lando tra *camouflage* epistolare e retorica del paradosso', *Bruniana & Campanelliana*, 22 (2016), 553–63.

SLUHOVSKI, MOSHE, 'Recidivist Converts in Early Modern Europe', in *Dissimulation and Deceit in Early Modern Europe*, ed. by Miriam Eliav-Feldon and Tamar Herzig (Basingstoke: Palgrave-Macmillan, 2015), pp. 94–109.

SPERA, LUCINDA, 'Gigli, Girolamo', in *Dizionario biografico degli Italiani*, LIV (Rome: Istituto dell'Enciclopedia italiana, 2000) <https://www.treccani.it/enciclopedia/girolamo-gigli_ (Dizionario-Biografico)> [accessed 1 October 2020].

SPERONI, SPERONE, *Dialogo della retorica*, in *Trattatisti del Cinquecento*, I, ed. by Mario Pozzi (Milan and Naples: Ricciardi, 1978), pp. 637–82.

——*Dialogo della vita attiva e contemplativa*, in *Opere* [...] *tratte da' mss. originali*, II (Venice: Domenico Occhi, 1740), pp. 1–43.

SPIRITO, LORENZO, *Libro de la ventura* (Venice: per Mattio Pagan, 1557).

STELLA, ALDO, *Anabattismo e antitrinitarismo in Italia nel XVI secolo: Nuove ricerche storiche* (Padua: Liviana, 1969).

STONE, M. W. F., 'The Origins of Probabilism in Late Scholastic Moral Thought: A Prolegomenon to Further Study', *Recherches de théologie et philosophie médiévales*, 67 (2000), pp. 114–57.

SWANN, ALAYA, ' "By Expresse Experiment": The Doubting Midwife Salome in Late Medieval England', *Bulletin for the History of Medicine*, 89 (2015), 1–24.

TALLINI, GENNARO, '*La piccola Athene*: Giulia Gonzaga e il circolo di Fondi tra letteratura ed eterodossia (1526–1566)', in *La donna nel Rinascimento: Amore, famiglia, cultura, potere*, ed. by Luisa Secchi Tarugi (Florence: Cesati, 2019), pp. 303–19.

TASSO, BERNARDO, *Rime*, ed. by Domenico Chiodo (Turin: RES, 1995).

TAUB, AMANDA, ' "Kompromat" and the Danger of Doubt and Confusion in a Democracy', *New York Times*, 15 January 2017 <https://www.nytimes.com/2017/01/15/world/europe/kompromat-donald-trump-russia-democracy.html> [accessed 28 May 2022].

TENENTI, ALBERTO, *Il senso della morte e l'amore della vita nel Rinascimento (Francia e Italia)* (Turin: Einaudi, 1989).

Tesoro di varii secreti naturali. Tratta da diversi auttori famosissimi, & più volte spremmentati in molte persone, opera molto giovevole alla sanità de' corpi humani, con la dichiaratione di molti dubij. Et il modo di far e conservar il vino (Venice: Gio. Battista Bonfadino, 1600).

TOFFOLO, ATTILIO, ' "Servire a Dio in l'habito mio seculare": Ludovica Torelli e l'esperienza religiosa dei primi Barnabiti', *Barnabiti studi*, 30 (2013), 21–78.

TOMASI, FRANCO, 'L'Accademia degli Intronati e Alessandro Piccolomini: Strategie culturali e itinerari biografici', in *Alessandro Piccolomini (1508–1579): Un siennois à la croisée des genres et des savoirs*, ed by Marie-Françoise Piéjus, Michel Plaisance, and Matteo Residori (Paris: Cirri, 2011), pp. 23–38.

——'Le "Rime" di Marco Antonio Pagani', *Bollettino della Società di Studi Valdesi*, 218 (2016), 71–102.

TOMITANO, BERNARDINO, *Oratione* [...] *alli Signori de la Santissima Inquisitione di Vinetia* (Padua: Gratioso Perchacino, 1556).

TRAVERSA, PAOLA MARIA, *Il 'Fidele' di Giovanni Filoteo Achillini: Poesia, sapienza e 'divina' conoscenza* (Modena: Mucchi, 1992).

TROMBETTA, ANTONIO, *Antonij Trombette* [...] *opus in Metaphysicam Arist.* [...] (Venice: [Giacomo Penzio], 1504).

TURRINI, MIRIAM, *La coscienza e le leggi: Morale e diritto nei testi per la confessione della prima età moderna* (Bologna: il Mulino, 1991).

TUTINO, STEFANIA, *Shadows of Doubt: Language and Truth in Post-Reformation Catholic Culture* (Oxford: Oxford University Press, 2014).

——*Uncertainty in Post-Reformation Catholicism: A History of Probabilism* (Oxford: Oxford University Press, 2018).

UGOLINI, PAOLA, *The Court and Its Critics: Anti-Court Sentiments in Early Modern Italy* (Toronto: University of Toronto Press, 2020).

——'The Satirist's Purgatory: *Il Purgatorio delle cortegiane* and the Writer's Discontent', *Italian Studies*, 64 (2009), 1–19.

UGUCCIONE DA PISA, *Derivationes*, ed. by Enzo Cecchini et al. (Florence: Sismel-Edizioni del Galluzzo, 2004).

VALDÉS, JUAN DE, *Alfabeto cristiano*, ed. by Adriano Prosperi (Rome: Istituto Storico Italiano per l'età moderna e contemporanea, 1988).

——*Le cento e dieci divine considerazioni*, ed. by Teodoro Fanlo y Cortés (Genoa: Marietti, 2004).

——'Christian Alphabet', in *Spiritual and Anabaptist Writers*, ed. by George H. Williams and Angel M. Mergal (Philadelphia: Westminster Press, 1957), pp. 351–90.

VALENTE, MICAELA, '*Fuggire la burrasca*: Inquietudini e paure nell'Europa della prima età moderna', in *Per un lessico della paura in Europa: Spunti per una riflessione*, ed. by Fabiana Ambrosi, Carolina Antonucci, and Ida Xoxa (Rome: Sapienza Università Editrice, 2018), pp. 11–21.

VAN HASSELT, MARIE-CÉCILE, 'Être/paraître, de fausses perceptions sous l'enseigne de la vérité', in *Studi per le 'Sorti': Gioco, immagini, poesia oracolare a Venezia nel Cinquecento*, ed. by Paolo Procaccioli (Treviso and Rome: Fondazione Benetton-Viella, 2007), pp. 85–97.

VARANO, CAMILLA BATTISTA DA, 'La vita spirituale', in *Le opere spirituali*, ed. by Giacomo Boccanera (Jesi: Scuola Tipografica Francescana, 1958), pp. 5–67.

VARESE, CLAUDIO, *Pandolfo Collenuccio umanista* (Pesaro: Ente Olivieri editore, 1957).

VENTURA, IOLANDA, '*Per modum quaestionis compilatum*: The Collections of Natural Questions and Their Development from the 13th to the 16th Century', in *Allgemeinwissen und Gesellschaft*, ed. by Paul Michel, Madeleine Herren, and Martin Rüesch (Düren: Shaker, 2007), pp. 275–317.

VIANELLO, VALERIO, *Il letterato, l'accademia, il libro: Contributi sulla cultura veneta del Cinquecento* (Padua: Antenore, 1988).

——'*Res* e *verba* nel "Dialogo della retorica" di Sperone Speroni', *Atti dell'Istituto Veneto di scienze, lettere ed arti*, 138 (1979–80), 231–53.

VIGNALI, ANTONIO (Arsiccio Intronato), *La Cazzaria*, ed. by Pasquale Stoppelli, intro. by Nino Borsellino (Rome: Edizioni dell'elefante, 1984).

——*La Cazzaria — The Book of the Prick*, ed. and trans. by Ian Frederick Moulton (London: Routledge, 2003).

VORAGINE, JACOBUS DE, *The Golden Legend: Readings on the Saints*, trans. by William Granger Ryan, intro. by Eamon Duffy (Princeton: Princeton University Press, 2012).

VUONG, LILY C., *The Protevangelium of James* (Eugene, OR: Cascade Books, 2018).

WILLIAMS, ANNE L., 'Satirizing the Sacred: Humor in Saint Joseph's Veneration and Early Modern Art', *Journal of Historians of Netherlandish Art*, 10 (2018) <https://jhna.org/articles/satirizing-sacred-humor-saint-josephs-veneration-early-modern-art/#citation> [accessed 16 July 2021].

WILLIAMS, GEORGE H., *The Radical Reformation*, 3rd edn (Kirksville, MO: Sixteenth Century Journal Publishers, 1992).

WILLIAMS, MARK, 'Bridging the Divide: Writing Christian Faith (and Doubt) in Modern Japan', in *Handbook of Christianity in Japan*, ed. by Mark R. Mullin (Leiden: Brill, 2003), pp. 295–320.

WILSON, CAROLYN C., 'The Cult of St. Joseph in Early Cinquecento Venice and the Testimony of Marino Sanudo's *Diaries*', *Studi veneziani*, 47 (2004), 287–312.

——'Francesco Vecellio's *Presepio* for San Giuseppe, Belluno: Aspects and Overview of the Cult and Iconography of St. Joseph in Pre-Tridentine Art', *Venezia Cinquecento*, 6 (1996), 39–74.

——'Some Further Evidence of St. Joseph's Cult in Renaissance Italy and Related St. Joseph Altarpieces', in *Die Bedeutung des hl. Josef in der Heilsgeschichte*, ed. by Joannes Hattler and Germán Rovira (Kisslegg: Fe–Medienverlag, 2006), pp. 903–33.

——'St Joseph and the Process of Decoding Vincenzo Catena's *Warrior Adoring the Infant Christ and the Virgin*', *Artibus et historiae*, 67 (2013), 117–36.

——*St. Joseph in Italian Renaissance Society and Art: New Directions and Interpretations* (Philadelphia: Saint Joseph's University Press, 2001).

WOOD, KELLI, 'Chancing It: Print, Play, and Gambling Games at the End of the Sixteenth Century', *Art History*, 42 (2019), 450–81.

ZAGORIN, PEREZ, *Ways of Lying: Dissimulation, Persecution, and Conformity in Early Modern Europe* (Cambridge, MA: Harvard University Press, 1990).

ZANOTTI CARNEY, EMANUELA, 'I *Dubbi* di Ortensio Lando e il *Perché* di Girolamo Manfredi', *Giornale storico della letteratura italiana*, 185 (2008), 64–78.

ZARRI, GABRIELLA, 'L'autobiografia religiosa negli scritti autobiografici di Camilla Battista da Varano: La 'Vita spirituale' (1491) e le 'Istruzioni al discepolo' (1501)', in *'In quella parte del libro de la mia memoria': Verità e finzioni dell''io' autobiografico*, ed. by Francesco Bruni (Venice: Marsilio, 2003), pp. 133–58.

——*Libri di spirito: Editoria religiosa in volgare nei secoli XV–XVII* (Turin: Rosenberg & Sellier, 2009).

——'La Maddalena nel Cinquecento bolognese: Immagini e contesti', in *Tra archivio e storia: Scritti dedicati ad Alessandra Contini Bonacossi*, ed. by Elisabetta Insabato, Rosalia Manno, Ernestina Pellegrini, Anna Scattigno (Florence: Florence University Press, 2018), pp. 333–54.

——'Note su diffusione e circolazione di testi devoti (1520–1550)', in *Libri di spirito: Editoria religiosa in volgare nei secoli XV–XVII* (Turin: Rosenberg & Sellier, 2009), 103–46.

——*Le sante vive: Cultura e religiosità femminile nella prima età moderna* (Turin: Rosenberg & Sellier, 1990).

INDEX

www.ingramcontent.com/pod-product-compliance
Lightning Source LLC
Chambersburg PA
CBHW080014040726

47501CB00017B/2455